ORKNEY AND
SHETLAND ISLANDS

0 Km   50

0 miles   50

THE HIGHLANDS
AND ISLANDS

CENTRAL
SCOTLAND

GLASGOW   EDINBURGH

SOUTHERN
SCOTLAND

Glasgow
Pages 98–113

Edinburgh
See pp56–83

EYEWITNESS TRAVEL

SCOTLAND

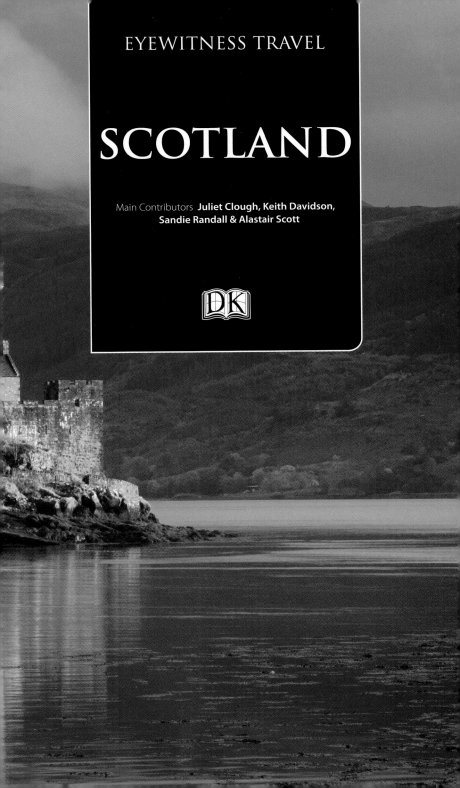

EYEWITNESS TRAVEL

SCOTLAND

Main Contributors **Juliet Clough, Keith Davidson, Sandie Randall & Alastair Scott**

DK

DK

LONDON, NEW YORK,
MELBOURNE, MUNICH AND DELHI
www.dk.com

Project Editor Rosalyn Thiro
Art Editor Marisa Renzullo
Editors Felicity Crowe, Emily Green
Designer Paul Jackson
Managing Editors Fay Franklin, Louise Bostock Lang
Managing Art Editor Annette Jacobs
Senior Editor Helen Townsend
Editorial Director Vivien Crump
Art Director Gillian Allan
Publisher Douglas Amrine
Picture Research Brigitte Arora
DTP Designers Maite Lantaron, Lee Redmond
Contributors Juliet Clough, Keith Davidson, Alan Freeman, Sandie Randall,
Alastair Scott, Roger Smith
Maps Ben Bowles, Rob Clynes (Colourmap Scanning, London)
Photographers Joe Cornish, Paul Harris, Stephen Whitehorn
Illustrators Richard Bonson, Gary Cross, Jared Gilby, Paul Guest, Kevin Jones Associates, Claire
Littlejohn, Chris Orr & Associates, Ann Winterbotham

Printed and bound in Malaysia by Vivar Printing Sdn Bhd.

First American Edition, 1999

14 15 10 9 8 7 6 5 4 3 2 1

Published in the United States by DK Publishing,
345 Hudson Street, New York, New York 10014

**Reprinted with revisions 2000, 2001, 2002, 2004, 2004, 2006,
2008, 2010, 2012, 2014**

Throughout this book, floors are referred to in accordance with European usage ie the
"first floor" is one floor above ground level

MIX
Paper from
responsible sources
FSC™ C018179
www.fsc.org

The information in this DK Eyewitness Travel Guide is checked regularly.
Every effort has been made to ensure that this book is as up-to-date as possible at
the time of going to press. Some details, however, such as telephone numbers,
opening hours, prices, gallery hanging arrangements and travel information, are
liable to change. The publishers cannot accept responsibility for any consequences
arising from the use of this book, nor for any material on third party websites, and
cannot guarantee that any website address in this book will be a suitable source of
travel information. We value the views and suggestions of our readers highly. Please
write to: Publisher, DK Eyewitness Travel Guides, Dorling Kindersley, 80 Strand,
London WC2R 0RL, Great Britain, or email: travelguides@dk.com.

Front cover main image: Quiraing at sunrise, Isle of Skye

◀ The castle of Eilean Donan, Loch Duich in Glen Shiel

The dramatic, sunlit ruins of Tantallon
Castle, on the southeast coast

Contents

Introducing
Scotland

Detail of the decorated vaulting in Rosslyn
Chapel, in the Pentland Hills

Travellers' Needs

Survival Guide

Kestrel in the Highlands

Scotland Region By Region

Mary, Queen of Scots (1542–87) of the House of Stuart

Royal Scots Greys Memorial to the Scottish soldiers of the Boer War

Walkers enjoying a glorious summer's day in Glen Etive

Edinburgh Castle on its volcanic rock above the city centre

INTRODUCING
SCOTLAND

DISCOVERING SCOTLAND

The following tours have been designed to take in as many of Scotland's highlights as possible, while keeping long-distance travel to a minimum. First come two two-day tours of Scotland's great rival "capitals", Edinburgh and Glasgow. Then there is a three-day tour of the Lowlands, the varied region south of the Highlands. These tours can be followed individually or combined to form a week-long tour. Next comes a ten-day tour of the Highlands and Islands on a route of outstanding beauty, which includes magnificent castles, mysterious Loch Ness, tiny islands off the coast of Mull, the best of mountain and glen, and unlimited whisky-tasting opportunities. Combine and follow your favourite tours, or dip in and out picking those experiences that most inspire.

Dryburgh Abbey
One of the most evocative monastic abbeys in the Borders, Dryburgh is the final resting place of novelist Sir Walter Scott. Visit nearby Scott's View to enjoy wonderful panoramas over the surrounding countryside.

Three Days in the Lowlands

- Stand among the astonishing masonic symbols of **Rosslyn Chapel**, immortalized in *The Da Vinci Code*.

- Follow the twisting roads through the romantic land and villages that inspired Scotland's greatest writers, **Robert Burns** and **Sir Walter Scott**.

- Explore the great **Border abbeys** – Dryburgh, Melrose, Jedburgh, Kelso – all of which are utterly majestic, especially in ruin.

- Admire the mighty walls of **Caerlaverock Castle** as it rises defiantly above its moat.

- Don't miss **Culzean Castle** on the Ayrshire coast, a magnificent showcase of opulence in Robert Adam's Neo-Classical style.

- Be blown away by **New Lanark**, an 18th-century industrial village built by a philanthropist who was ahead of the times.

- Be lifted skywards in a barge on the unique engineering marvel of the **Falkirk Wheel**.

◀ Princes Street and Princes Street Gardens, Edinburgh

Crail Harbour
Explore the picturesque medieval villages of East Neuk, full of lovely cottages, winding streets and restaurants serving fresh seafood.

Ten Days in the Highlands & Islands

- Behold the sumptuous royal apartments in **Stirling Castle**, home to 500 years' worth of Scottish monarchs.

- Stroll among exotic plants from as far afield as Tibet and Tasmania in the beguiling **Crarae Gardens**.

- Take a ferry to **Iona**, the Cradle of Christianity, or to the Isle of Staffa for the basalt columns of **Fingal's Cave** and plenty of puffins.

- Drive through the mountain splendour of **Glencoe** and discover the darker side of its history.

- Cruise on awesome **Loch Ness** and look for its secretive monster – or see photos on exhibit in Drumnadrochit.

- Sample **whisky** or simply enjoy the fascinating process of its production – on the **Speyside Malt Whisky Trail**.

- Visit beautiful **St Andrews**, the home of golf, and follow the trail of charming villages on the **East Neuk** coast.

Findhorn
Cawdor Castle
Inverness
ch Ness
Speyside Malt Whisky Trail
Balmoral Castle
Royal Deeside
Dundee
Scone Palace
Perth
St Andrews
ossachs
Falkland Castle
The East Neuk
erfoyle
Stirling
Curloss
Dunfermline Abbey
Falkirk Wheel
Forth Bridge
Roslynn Chapel
Edinburgh
New Lanark
Scott's View
Melrose
Dryburgh
Moffat
Dumfries
Caerlaverock Castle
Kirkcudbright

Key
— Ten Days in the Highlands & Islands
— Three Days in the Lowlands

Urquhart Castle, Loch Ness
Enjoy the breathtaking scenery of Loch Ness and the surrounding Great Glen with a cruise on the lakes and a drive through the hills.

The Military Tattoo, performed in the shadow of Edinburgh Castle

Two Days in Edinburgh

Beautiful, stately and full of history and parks, the nation's capital is truly "the festival city" with constant cultural events throughout summer.

- **Arriving** Edinburgh Airport is 12 km (7 miles) west of the city. Buses and taxis take 25 minutes outside rush hour.

- **Moving on** Trains run every 15 mins to Glasgow (50-minute journey).

- **Booking ahead** Edinburgh Castle (to beat the queues)

Day 1
Morning Edinburgh Castle *(pp64–5)* is the city's crowning glory – the official free tour is well worth it. Don't try to escape in less than 2.5 hours and don't miss the Honours of Scotland and Mons Meg, a medieval supercannon. Then stroll down the **Royal Mile** *(pp60–63)*, a delightful mayhem of entertainers during The Festival *(pp82–3)*, and pop into **St Giles Cathedral** to see the bagpiping angel.
Afternoon Pause for lunch as you descend this historic street. At the bottom let the dazzling exhibition **Our Dynamic Earth** *(p71)* (closed Mon & Tue Nov–Mar) literally shake the ground under your feet or, if you're still thirsting for more history, visit **Holyrood Palace** *(p70)*. Take a look at the adjacent love-it-or-hate-it **Scottish**

Parliament building *(p71)*, a controversial piece of architecture costing over £400 million to build. If you're fit, hike up **Arthur's Seat** (1 hr) *(p71)* for great views. Later, take in some evening theatre, a concert or a ghost tour.

Day 2
Morning Start at the **National Museum of Scotland's** *(p66)* bright and modern presentation of everything from whales to the famous Lewis chessmen. Be sure to enjoy a coffee on the roof. Pass the emotive statue of **Greyfriars Bobby** *(p66)* on your way to the shopping haven of **Princes Street** *(pp68–9)*, or find peace in the adjacent gardens, which boast a floral clock.
Afternoon Explore the Georgian architecture of the **New Town** *(pp68–9)* but leave a couple of hours free for the **National Gallery** *(p67)* – don't miss Raeburn's iconic painting commonly dubbed *The Skating Minister*. Everything on this day's tour is close together so you might have energy left to walk up **Carlton Hill** (25 minutes) *(p70)* for fine city perspectives, or pick an alternative evening entertainment from Day 1. As the "festival city" Edinburgh is never short of shows or performances.

Two Days in Glasgow

Glasgow has everything Edinburgh has but perhaps with more wit, friendliness and a determination to be different.

- **Arriving** Glasgow airport is 12 km (7 miles) west of the city centre. Taxis and shuttle buses take 25 minutes outside rush hour.

- **Moving on** Trains run every 15 mins to Edinburgh (50-minute journey) or hire a car to explore elsewhere.

Day 1
Morning Start with a quick visit to 13th-century **Glasgow Cathedral** *(p103)*, a rarity in Scotland having escaped destruction during the Reformation. Walk from here past the imposing **City Chambers** in **George Square** *(p102)*, but save at least an hour for the **Gallery of Modern Art** *(p102)* to see outrageously brilliant and challenging exhibits. Shop and lunch in **Sauchiehall Street**, the city's vibrant retail centre. The street is also a highlight for fans of Art Nouveau designer **Charles Rennie Macintosh** *(p105)* whose works can be seen at the **Willow Tea Room** *(p104)* or **Glasgow School of Art** *(p104)*.
Afternoon Travel further out to see **Kelvingrove Art Gallery and Museum** *(p106)* and marvel at Dali's *Christ of St John of the Cross*. Afterwards take a relaxing

Gallery of Modern Art, Glasgow

walk under Scottish palm trees in the nearby **Botanic Gardens** *(p107)*. In the evening, sample the city's pub life or take in a concert, perhaps of hybrid Scottish music.

Day 2

Morning Start the day at the world-renowned **Burrell Collection** *(pp108–9)* – a spacious and masterful display of treasures collected by a 19th-century shipping magnate. Many visitors fall for the tapestries and the stained glass – keep an eye out for the scenes of everyday life, such as a man warming his feet before a fire.
Afternoon Lunch here or at the **Glasgow Science Centre** *(p106)*, a striking, titanium structure at the edge of the River Clyde. Wonderful and whacky, this place will keep children busy for hours and expand their minds in the process. Adults too will find themselves enthralled as they "walk" on the moon or watch their faces rejuvenate. It's easy to use up what's left of the afternoon here, so end the day with a well-deserved pint and some live music at a pub.

Art installation hanging over the grand stairway at Kelvingrove Art Gallery, Glasgow

Three Days in the Lowlands

- **Arriving** Either Glasgow or Edinburgh airport. Do the tour in either direction.
- **Transport** A car is essential.

Day 1: Chapel and Abbeys

Start at 15th-century **Rosslyn Chapel** *(p91)*, just outside of Edinburgh and star of *The Da Vinci Code*, to see its treasure of cryptic stone sculptures, especially the Apprentice Pillar. Drive to Melrose and devote most of the day to the ruins of the **Border abbeys** *(p89)*: Melrose, Kelso, Jedburgh and Dryburgh. If time is tight, or if four abbeys is just too many, set your sights on **Dryburgh** *(p89)* – it's particularly evocative and nestled in a bend of the River Tweed. Lunch here or have a picnic at nearby **Scott's View** *(p89)*, a

beautiful vista over the Tweed to the Eildon Hills. In the afternoon drive through woods and sheep-covered hills via Moffat to Dumfries for the night. Check out its lively performance venues.

Day 2: Explore Castles

First stop just south of Dumfries is **Caerlaverock Castle** *(p94)*, one of the few castles to have retained its moat. With its immense towers, the castle is an impressive sight. If you'd prefer, head straight from Dumfries to tranquil **Loch Trool** for a walk in **Galloway Forest Park** *(p94)*. Either way, stop for lunch or a break in **Kirkcudbright** *(p94)*, a charming seaside town. This part of Scotland displays a love of crafts and sculpture and feels like a welcome step

Moat around Caerlaverock Castle, one of the finest castles in Scotland

back in time. Don't linger too long as the day's highlight awaits – the exquisite interiors of the stately mansion **Culzean Castle** *(pp96–7)*. Its Oval Staircase is nothing short of perfection. Spend the night in Ayr or the golfing town of Troon.

Day 3: New Lanark and Falkirk

From Ayr, which is the heartland of **Robert Burns** country *(p93)* with charming lanes and hedgerows, you can either follow a trail dedicated to the national poet (via Alloway and Mauchline) or enjoy similar scenery on the way to **New Lanark** *(p92)*. Allow two hours to explore the village, located by the falls on the River Clyde, and head to the Visitor Centre for an insight into the Victorian mills and the philanthropic industrialist who ran them. Lunch here and continue to the **Falkirk Wheel** *(p129)*. Board a barge and be hoisted 35 m (115 ft) from one section of canal to another, a unique and exhilarating experience with fabulous views. Spend the night in Glasgow.

> **To extend your trip...**
> Head to Stirling and follow the ten-day tour of the Highlands & Islands.

Snow-capped pinnacle at the entrance of Glencoe

Ten Days in the Highlands & Islands

- **Arriving** Glasgow or Edinburgh airport.
- **Transport** A car is essential.
- **Booking ahead** Loch Katrine cruise; Oban–Mull Ferry (return); Fingal's Cave boat trip; Mallaig–Armadale ferry (one-way); Golf at St Andrew's (book months ahead); all Highland Games events.

Day 1: Stirling and The Trossachs

Start early and climb by foot or car to crag-top **Stirling Castle** (pp124–25) to see far-reaching views. Admire the best Renaissance architecture in Scotland, particularly the Palace and Great Hall. You'll need two or three hours to do it justice. Drive to Callendar for lunch and then continue on to the beauty of **The Trossachs** national park (pp120–21). Take a trip aboard a genuine Victorian steamship on **Loch Katrine** (Apr–Oct) to best appreciate the wildlife and rugged mountains. Spend the night at Aberfoyle.

Day 2: The Trossachs to Oban

This is a day of lochs, both freshwater and sea. From Aberfoyle drive up the western shore of **Loch Lomond** (p120), taking in the pretty village of Luss on the way, then over the mountains to **Loch Fyne**, famous for its seafood. Catch a glimpse of **Inveraray Castle** (p134) as you head for the superb **Crarae Gardens** (p134). Here you can wander among exotic flora from around the world –always delightful but at its best in spring. In the afternoon you can afford to enjoy time-out in the town of Lochgilphead and to make the most of the scenery on the sinuous road to **Oban** (p136). Spend two nights in this bustling harbour town.

Day 3: Fingal's Cave and Iona

Pack a picnic, board the Oban–Mull car ferry, and then drive to

Boats moored in the bright blue waters off the shore of Iona

Bunessan for a boat trip (Apr–Oct) to **Fingal's Cave** (p137) – a wonder of volcanic rock formations on the Isle of Staffa. Weather permitting, the boat will motor into the cave and let you land. You may even spot a puffin. If the boat is cancelled due to bad weather (or you have time afterwards), drive on to Fionnphort to visit **Iona** (p137), a gem of The Hebrides. The ferry is reliable and you don't need to book for the narrow crossing. The abbey, once with broad influence across Europe, is hugely popular with visitors. The isle has dazzling beaches too. Return to Oban for the night.

Day 4: Oban to Skye

A route of stunning scenery starts with **Loch Awe** (p136) which lives up to its name but is completely over-shadowed by the massive rent in the mountains that comes later at **Glencoe** (p138). Call in at the Visitor Centre and learn about the tragic massacre in 1692. Have lunch here or below Ben Nevis. At Fort William you'll join the scenic **Road to the Isles Tour** (pp140–41). **Glenfinnan** has a moving memorial to **Bonnie Prince Charlie** (p157) and is the location of the 21-arch viaduct featured in the Harry Potter movies. Overnight in the fishing port of **Mallaig** (p141).

Day 5: Skye to Inverness

Cross over the sea to **Skye** (Easter–mid-Oct; fewer ferries in winter) *(pp156–7)* and use it as a stepping stone back to the main land by means of the bridge near the quaint village of Kyleakin. Soon you'll pass **Eilean Donan Castle** *(p155)*, one of the most picturesque in the land. Take a slightly longer route via Lochs Garry and Oich to charming **Fort Augustus** and the **Caledonian Canal** to reach the day's highlight – **Loch Ness** *(pp152–3)*, mysterious and inspiring whether you believe in monsters or not. Judge the evidence for yourself at exhibitions in **Drumnadrochit**, where you'll also find the ruins of **Urquhart Castle**. Sleep in **Inverness** *(pp150–51)*.

Day 6: Around Inverness

Take a picnic and spend the morning on a **Jacobite Cruise** (Mar–Sep) *(p151)* on Loch Ness, ideally one that includes the **Caledonian Canal** rather than just the loch. Alternatively hunt for dolphins in the **Moray Firth** or, depending on your interests, plan to spend part of the morning at **Culloden** *(p150)* or **Fort George** *(p150)*. To really understand Highlanders and their history, see the moving exhibition on the Battle of Culloden which ended the old clan culture. A walk around Fort George, among the best examples of military fortification in Europe, is equally impressive. Stay a second night in Inverness or move on to Nairn.

Day 7: Macbeth and Whisky

Shakespeare probably invented Macbeth's association with **Cawdor Castle** (May–Oct) *(p150)*, but visit this wonderful building anyway. It is small and manageable and everything about it is bewitching. Lunch by the sandy lagoon of Findhorn and then drive to Dufftown, the capital of **Speyside whiskies** *(pp148–9)*. Even if you don't like the taste of the "water of life", a distillery tour is fascinating. Sleep wherever the whisky trail takes you! Dufftown is a good option.

Day 8: Deeside to the "Antarctic"

From Dufftown a roller-coaster road leads past ski slopes into Queen Victoria's favourite landscape, **Royal Deeside** *(p148)*. Go to Ballater and take the route south which gives the option of visiting **Balmoral Castle** (limited opening) or **Scone Palace** (Apr–Oct) *(p126)*, or shopping in the fair city of **Perth** *(p126)* if the other sights are closed. Leave enough time to spend at least one-and-a-half hours in the Antarctic, brilliantly recreated at **Discovery Point** in Dundee *(p127)*. Spend the night in this friendly wee city.

Day 9: St Andrews and the East Neuk

The famous golf course is always fully booked months ahead, but visit **St Andrews** *(p127)* for its golfing museum,

Gardens at Cawdor Castle, still the stately home of the Thanes of Cawdor

cathedral and its carefree student atmosphere. Then find a place for lunch on the drive around the **East Neuk** coastline *(p128)*, which shows, without question, Scotland's most picturesque harbour villages. Nowadays there are more artists than fishermen here. Tear yourself away in time for a visit to **Falkland Palace** (summer only) *(p128)*, a stunning Renaissance hunting lodge designed for the Stuart kings, and a favourite haunt of Mary, Queen of Scots. Return to your favourite East Neuk spot for the night.

Day 10: East Neuk back to the start

The distances from the East Neuk to where you started this whole tour are short so the final day's route possibilities are many. **Dunfermline Abbey** (mid-Mar–mid-Oct) *(pp128–9)* is the last of the imposing landmarks well worth a visit, or head to the beautifully preserved 16th-century village of **Culross** *(p129)*. Walk a section of the **Fife Coastal Trail** *(p211)* or, if you missed them, take in either the magnificent **Stirling Castle** *(pp124–5)* or the impressive **Falkirk Wheel** *(p129)*. If you return to Edinburgh you'll see the amazing **Forth Rail Bridge** *(p73)* on the way and might have time to follow in the Queen's footsteps on board the **Royal Yacht Britannia** *(p72)*.

The Caledonian Canal at Fort Augustus, along the scenic route to Loch Ness

Putting Scotland on the Map

Separated from Continental Europe by the North Sea,
Scotland forms the northern part of Great Britain.
It is a mountainous, sparsely populated land.
The highest peak is Ben Nevis, at 1,344 m (4,406
ft). The coastline is also ringed by hundreds
of islands; at the farthest extreme Shetland
lies just six degrees south of the Arctic
Circle. Edinburgh is the historic capital,
and Glasgow is the largest city with a
population of 578,000. The country
has good road, rail and ferry
connections.

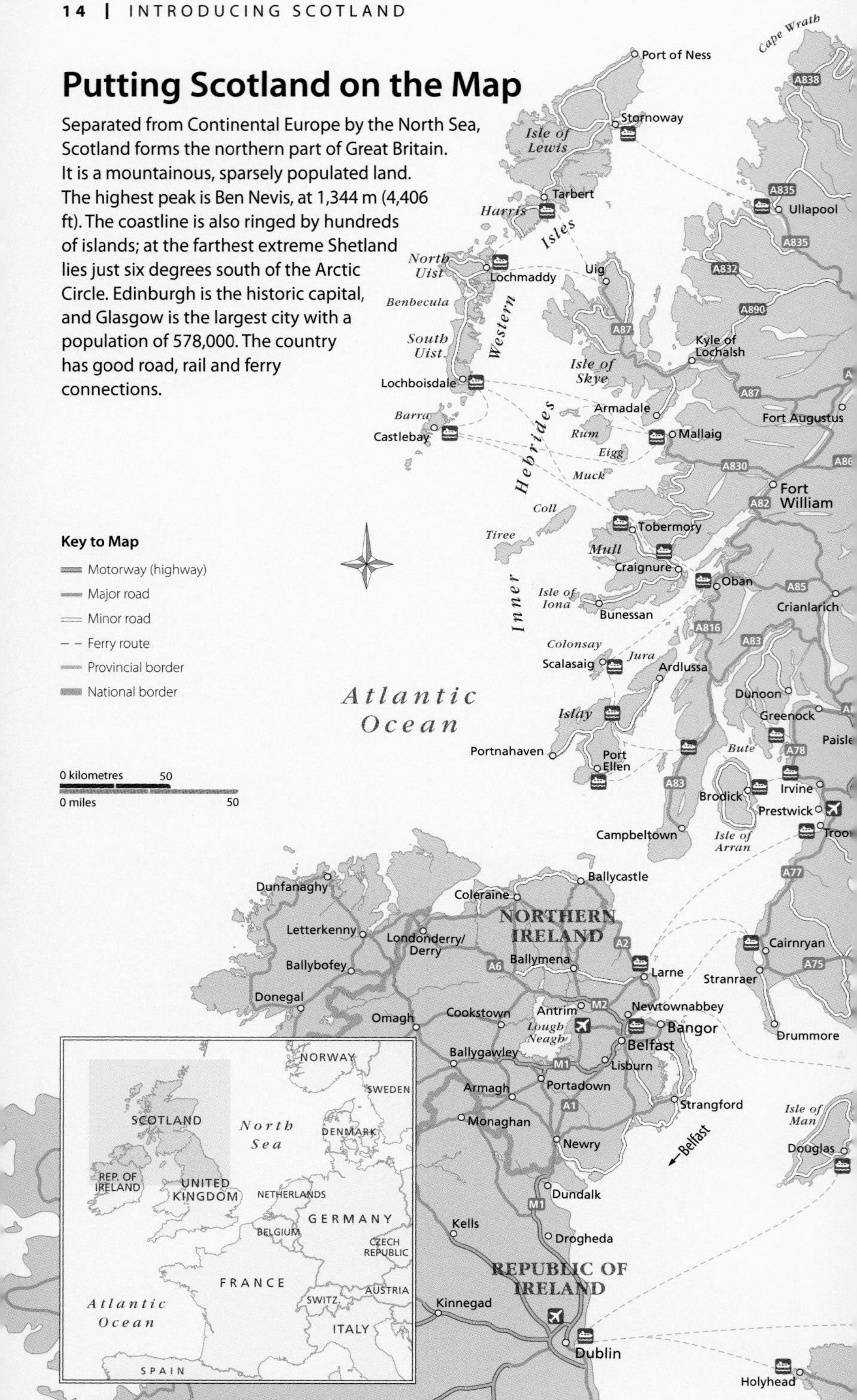

Key to Map

- Motorway (highway)
- Major road
- Minor road
- Ferry route
- Provincial border
- National border

0 kilometres   50
0 miles   50

Port of Ness
Cape Wrath
A838
Isle of Lewis
Stornoway
A835
Ullapool
Tarbert
A835
Harris
Isles
A832
North Uist
Lochmaddy   Uig
Benbecula
A890
South Uist
Western
Isle of Skye
Kyle of Lochalsh
A87
Lochboisdale
A87
Hebrides
Armadale   Fort Augustus
Barra
Rum
Mallaig
A86
Castlebay
Eigg
A830
Muck
Fort William
Coll
A82
Tiree
Tobermory
Mull
Craignure
Oban   A85
Inner
Isle of Iona
Bunessan
A816   Crianlarich
Colonsay
A83
Scalasaig
Jura   Ardlussa
Dunoon
Greenock
Paisle
Atlantic
Ocean
Islay
Bute
A78
Portnahaven
Port Ellen
Irvine
Brodick   Prestwick
Troo
Campbeltown
Isle of Arran
A77
Ballycastle
Coleraine
NORTHERN
IRELAND   A2
Cairnryan
A75
Dunfanaghy
Letterkenny
Londonderry/Derry
A6   Ballymena
Larne
Stranraer
Ballybofey
Antrim   M2   Newtownabbey
Drummore
Donegal
Omagh   Cookstown
Lough Neagh
Belfast   Bangor
Ballygawley
M1   Lisburn
Armagh   Portadown
Strangford
Monaghan   A1
Newry
Isle of Man
Belfast
Douglas
M1   Dundalk
Kells
Drogheda
REPUBLIC OF
IRELAND
Kinnegad
Dublin
Holyhead

NORWAY
SWEDEN
SCOTLAND
North Sea
DENMARK
REP. OF IRELAND
UNITED KINGDOM
NETHERLANDS
BELGIUM   GERMANY
CZECH REPUBLIC
FRANCE
SWITZ.   AUSTRIA
ITALY
Atlantic Ocean
SPAIN

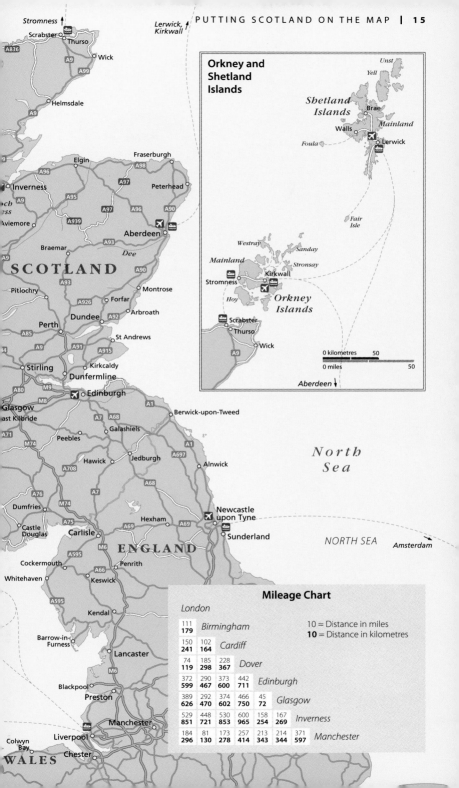

Orkney and Shetland Islands

Shetland Islands

Unst

Yell

Brae

Mainland

Walls

Lerwick

Foula

Fair Isle

Westray

Sanday

Mainland

Stronsay

Stromness

Kirkwall

Hoy

Orkney Islands

Scrabster

Thurso

Wick

A9

0 kilometres   50

0 miles   50

Aberdeen

Stromness

Scrabster

Thurso

Wick

A836

A9

A99

Helmsdale

A9

Inverness

A96

Elgin

Fraserburgh

A98

A97

Peterhead

A95

A97

A96

A90

Aviemore

A939

A9

Aberdeen

A93

Braemar

Dee

SCOTLAND

A90

Pitlochry

A93

Montrose

A926

Forfar

Perth

Dundee

A92

Arbroath

A85

A9

A91

St Andrews

A915

Stirling

Kirkcaldy

A80

M9

Dunfermline

M8

Edinburgh

Glasgow

A1

East Kilbride

A7

A68

Berwick-upon-Tweed

A71

M74

Peebles

Galashiels

A708

Hawick

Jedburgh

A697

Alnwick

A7

A68

Dumfries

M74

Hexham

North Sea

A76

A75

Newcastle upon Tyne

Castle Douglas

Carlisle

A69

A69

Sunderland

Cockermouth

M6

ENGLAND

Penrith

NORTH SEA

A595

A66

Amsterdam

Whitehaven

Keswick

A595

Kendal

Barrow-in-Furness

Lancaster

M6

Blackpool

Preston

Manchester

Liverpool

Colwyn Bay

Chester

WALES

Mileage Chart

London

111 / 179	*Birmingham*						10 = Distance in miles
150 / 241	102 / 164	*Cardiff*					**10** = Distance in kilometres
74 / 119	185 / 298	228 / 367	*Dover*				
372 / 599	290 / 467	373 / 600	442 / 711	*Edinburgh*			
389 / 626	292 / 470	374 / 602	466 / 750	45 / 72	*Glasgow*		
529 / 851	448 / 721	530 / 853	600 / 965	158 / 254	167 / 269	*Inverness*	
184 / 296	81 / 130	173 / 278	257 / 414	213 / 343	214 / 344	371 / 597	*Manchester*

A PORTRAIT OF SCOTLAND

With such a distinctive national dress, drink, bagpipe music, landscape and folklore, Scotland has shaped an identity recognizable the world over. It is a land of contrasts and often possesses a magical quality, whether seen shrouded in mist or rising majestically above the mirror of a loch.

In a straight line from the far south to the far north, the Scottish mainland reaches about 440 km (275 miles), yet its coastline stretches nearly 10,000 km (6,200 miles). There are 787 major islands, almost all lying off the northern or western coasts. The topography is generally extremely mountainous with wild heather moorlands in the north and west, pine forests mixed with quality pasture in the middle, fertile farmland in the east and, in the south, the rounded, grass-covered hills of the Lowlands. Picturesque lochs and rivers are scattered throughout. Most of Scotland's five million people live in the

country's Central Belt. The Scots cherish the differences that set them apart from the English, and cling tenaciously to the distinctions that differentiate them region by region – their customs, dialects and the Gaelic language. It is perhaps more by their differences than similarities that the Scots can be defined but, for all that, they are immensely proud of their nation and its separate institutions, such as education and law. The Scots can be dour but equally they can flash with inspiration. They delight in self-deprecating humour and continue to honour a long tradition of hospitality.

A view from Edinburgh Castle with Calton Hill and the Firth of Forth in the distance

◀ Pipers in full regalia at the Braemar Gathering in Royal Deeside

An event at the Braemar Gathering

Politics and the Economy

Ever since the Treaty of Union in 1707, which combined the parliaments of Scotland and England into one governing body convening in Westminster (London), Scotland has often felt estranged from the mechanisms of government, and short-changed by the small allocation of time given to Scottish affairs. The 2011 election gave the SNP a majority, which means there is currently enough support to hold a referendum on Scottish independence. In 1997 the Scots voted for the re-establishment of a Scottish parliament, which began in 1999. This parliament has a wide-ranging administrative role, though major financial controls and decisions of national interest are retained by Westminster.

Scotland's economy has fluctuated in the last 100 years. It has had to fight back from the demise of its heavy industries: shipbuilding, coal mining and steel production. Today, the major contributors to the economy are North Sea oil, tourism and services, aided by a range of light industries. Chief among these is the manufacture of electronic components and microchips, giving rise to the notion of a "Silicon Glen", but this industry, has become shaky in response to the global market. Whisky production is a leading source of revenue, although it employs few people. Agriculture retains its importance but has been beleaguered by disastrous markets. Fishing remains an important industry, though there is increasing competition for dwindling stocks. Scotland's level of unemployment is on a par with the UK, though in some areas, such as the Western Isles, it reaches 15 per cent.

Society

The Scots are a gregarious people and enjoy company, whether this be in a small group at a Highland ceilidh (literally, a "visit"), a bar, or as part of the Saturday armies of football (soccer) fans. Sometimes they have to travel far to find company; the Highland region has a population density of eight people per square kilometre (20 per sq mile), and the lack of public transport means a car is vital.

Edinburgh bagpiper

Church attendance is in decline in all but the Gaelic-speaking areas, where Sundays are observed as days of rest. In most towns, and all cities, a full range of leisure activities and entertainment runs into the wee hours, but in rural areas opening hours are shorter, and restaurants may stop serving early.

Scotland is renowned as the home of golf, but football is the national passion. Other popular sports include hill-walking, skiing, rugby, shinty and curling. There are also annual Highland Games – great gatherings of whisky, music, craft stalls and tests of stamina and strength (see p35).

The Viking fire festival, *Up Helly Aa* in Shetland

Small-scale farming in the Western Isles

Despite their love of sports, the Scots are statistically speaking an unhealthy race. Their appetite for red meat and greasy food contributes to a high incidence of heart problems, and they have the highest consumption of alcohol in the UK. Tobacco sales, however, are in decline after smoking was banned in public places in 2006.

Culture and the Arts

Scotland offers an excellent programme of performing arts, subsidized by the Scottish Arts Council. The Edinburgh

Edinburgh's Festival Fringe Office detail

Festival and Fringe *(see pp82–3)* is the largest celebration of its kind in the world, and there are many smaller festivals that take place throughout the year. The Scottish film industry is small but creative and lively. The music scene is also enjoying a time of vibrancy, ranging from opera, Gaelic song and *pibroch* (the classical music of the bagpipes) to such varied international acts as Franz Ferdinand and Snow Patrol, not to mention a strong electronic music scene. Traditional music has experienced a renaissance using rhythms and instruments from around the world. Bands like Salsa Celtica combine Scottish folk and jazz with Latin American sounds. With an estimated four Scots living abroad for every one in the homeland, outside influences are not surprising. In dance, there are the varied delights of Scottish country, Highland and *ceilidh* dancing and step dancing, as well as the Scottish ballet. Although only about 50,000 people speak Gaelic, the language has been boosted by increased funding for Gaelic radio and TV shows. Literature also has a strong following, with no shortage of Scottish authors and poets *(see pp30–31)*.

The blue waters of Loch Achray in the heart of the Trossachs, north of Glasgow

The Geology of Scotland

Scotland is a geologist's playground, with rocks displaying three billion years of geological time. Starting with the hard granitic gneiss in the Western Isles, which was formed before life developed on earth, the rocks tell a story of lava flows, eras of mountainbuilding, numerous ice ages and even a time when the land was separated from England by the ancient Iapetus Ocean. Four major fault and thrust lines, running across Scotland from northeast to southwest, define the main geological zones.

Fault and Thrust Lines

– – Moine Thrust

– – Great Glen Fault *(see pp152–3)*

– – Highland Boundary Fault

– – Southern Uplands Fault

The gabbro *(dark rock)* of the Cuillin Hills on Skye was created by subterranean magma in the Tertiary period, a time when the dinosaurs had died out and mammals were flourishing.

Changing Earth

☐ Ancient landmass

About 500 million years ago
Scotland was part of a landmass that included North America, while England was part of Gondwana. After 75 million years of continental breakup and drift, the two countries "collided", not far from the modern political boundary.

☐ Glaciation in the last Ice Age

• • • Present-day national boundaries

The last Ice Age, which ended 10,000 years ago, was the most recent chapter in Scotland's geological history when, like Scandinavia, it became glaciated.

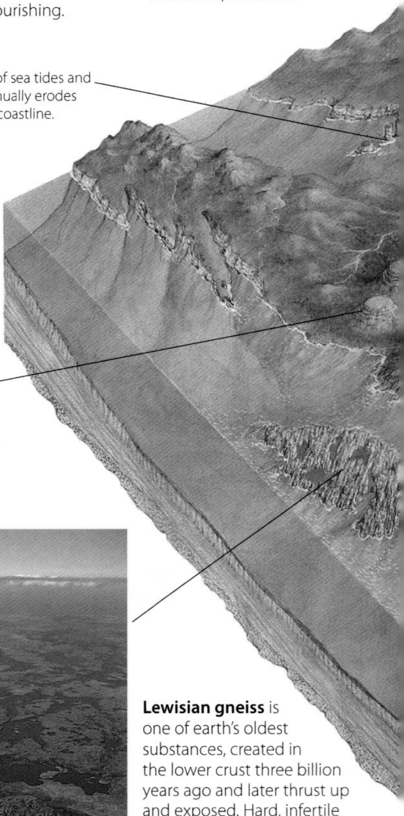

The action of sea tides and waves continually erodes the existing coastline.

Plateau-topped hills on the island are the exposed remains of a basalt lava flow.

Lewisian gneiss is one of earth's oldest substances, created in the lower crust three billion years ago and later thrust up and exposed. Hard, infertile and grey, it forms low plateaus filled with thousands of small lochs in the Western Isles.

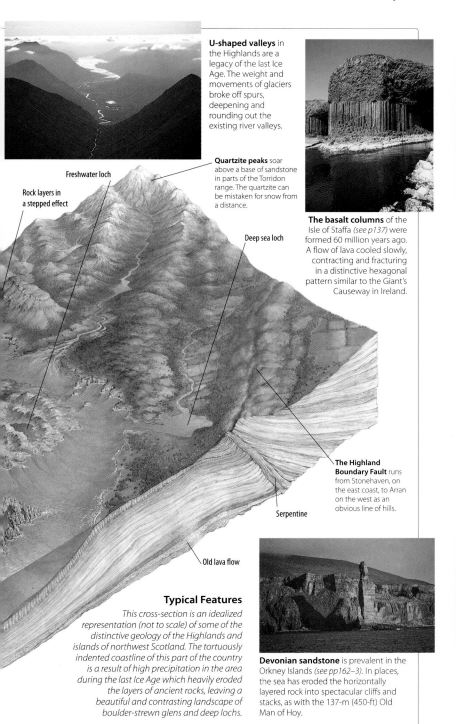

U-shaped valleys in the Highlands are a legacy of the last Ice Age. The weight and movements of glaciers broke off spurs, deepening and rounding out the existing river valleys.

Freshwater loch

Rock layers in a stepped effect

Quartzite peaks soar above a base of sandstone in parts of the Torridon range. The quartzite can be mistaken for snow from a distance.

Deep sea loch

The basalt columns of the Isle of Staffa *(see p137)* were formed 60 million years ago. A flow of lava cooled slowly, contracting and fracturing in a distinctive hexagonal pattern similar to the Giant's Causeway in Ireland.

The Highland Boundary Fault runs from Stonehaven, on the east coast, to Arran on the west as an obvious line of hills.

Serpentine

Old lava flow

Typical Features

This cross-section is an idealized representation (not to scale) of some of the distinctive geology of the Highlands and islands of northwest Scotland. The tortuously indented coastline of this part of the country is a result of high precipitation in the area during the last Ice Age which heavily eroded the layers of ancient rocks, leaving a beautiful and contrasting landscape of boulder-strewn glens and deep lochs.

Devonian sandstone is prevalent in the Orkney Islands *(see pp162–3)*. In places, the sea has eroded the horizontally layered rock into spectacular cliffs and stacks, as with the 137-m (450-ft) Old Man of Hoy.

The Landscape and Wildlife of Scotland

Scotland is a land of contrasts, from the austere majesty of the mountains to the subtle undulations of the Lowland valleys, and from dramatic coastal cliffs to dense forests. It is in the wilds of the Highlands and islands that you are most likely to encounter Scotland's wealth of wildlife. Many once-prolific species are under threat; preserving them and their habitats is now paramount.

Native Animals

There are no large or dangerous wild animals in Scotland, but there are a few which are rarely found living wild elsewhere in the British Isles. Shetland ponies and Highland cattle, by their names alone, are instantly associated with Scotland, and you are unlikely to see a golden eagle outside of the Scottish Highlands.

Coastal

The immense, windswept coastline of Scotland provides some of the best chances to view the country's wildlife. Islands such as Skye *(see pp156–7)*, pictured above, sustain myriad nesting seabirds, including puffins, guillemots and kittiwakes, while the Bass Rock, off the east coast near North Berwick, has a breeding colony of gannets. The Scottish coast is also home to seals, whales and dolphins.

Puffin

Grey seals have long inhabited the rocky Scottish coasts, such as in Shetland or in North Rona, and are easily spotted.

Kittiwakes, with their white and grey plumage, are widespread along the Scottish cliffs, from St Abb's Head on the east coast to Handa Island off the northwest coast *(see p161)*.

Lochs and Rivers

Dragonfly

Scotland has an abundance of sea lochs, fresh water lochs and rivers, enabling a wide range of animal and insect life to flourish. Sea lochs, such as those shown above on the western isle of North Uist, may contain wild salmon and otters, although the latter are more likely to be spotted at a manmade sanctuary, such as the one at Kylerhea on Skye. Many Scottish rivers, the Tay being just one example, provide a wonderful opportunity for fishermen to catch salmon and trout.

Wild otters breed along many parts of Scotland's coast and in its sea lochs. Unlike their Asian cousins, they have webbed feet with which they catch and eat their prey.

Salmon swim into Scotland's lochs and rivers every year to breed. They travel miles upstream and up steep waterfalls in order to spawn.

Shetland ponies are indigenous to the windswept, northerly isles of the same name, but can also be found on the mainland. The ponies are small, with thick, wiry coats.

Highland cattle, bred in Scotland since the 1500s, are recognizable by their long horns and shaggy coats.

The golden eagle is one of Scotland's most enduring emblems. Found at high altitudes, this majestic bird takes its prey in one silent swoop.

Mountain and Moorland

The hills and mountains of Scotland are a refuge for rare arctic and alpine plants, while heather and grasses flourish on the moorlands and Lowlands. This contrast of landscapes can be seen right across the Scottish Highlands and islands, as shown here on Mull. Birds of prey, such as eagles and kestrels, favour this terrain; red deer graze on the bleak moorland.

Kestrel

Woodland and Forest

Pine marten

Some of Scotland's forests form part of a protected Forest Park. Woodland refuges, such as the one in the Borders shown above, are home to red squirrels and goldcrests, while pine martens and wildcats favour the rockier terrain of the Highland forests. Birch and oak woods are dotted around the country.

Sheep roam freely on the moorland and hills of Scotland, but they are usually marked so they can be identified by the farmer.

Wildcats can still be found in forest areas, but their numbers are dwindling. A stocky body, thick fur and short, blunt tail distinguish them from a domestic cat.

Red deer are the most common deer in Europe and can often be sighted in the Highlands of Scotland. Their signature coats are at their most vibrant in summer. The stags shed their antlers in spring.

Red squirrels are far rarer than their grey counterparts, but they share the same bushy tail for agility and communication, and sharp, hooked claws for a sure grip on trees.

Evolution of the Scottish Castle

Few sights can match the romance of a Scottish castle set upon a small island in the middle of a quiet loch. These formidable retreats, often in remote settings, were built all over the Highlands, where incursions and strife between the clans were common. From the earliest Pictish *brochs* (Iron Age stone towers) and Norman-influenced motte and bailey castles, the distinctively Scottish stone tower-house evolved, first appearing in the 14th century. By the mid-17th century fashion had become more important than defence, and there followed a period in which numerous huge Scottish palaces were built.

Detail of the Baroque façade, Drumlanrig

Motte and Bailey

These castles first appeared in the 12th century. They stood atop two adjacent mounds enclosed by a wall, or palisade, and defensive ditches. The higher mound, or motte, was the most strongly defended as it held the keep and chief's house. The lower bailey was where the ordinary people lived.

The keep contained the chief's house, lookout and main defence.

Duffus Castle, Morayshire

Duffus Castle (c.1150) was atypically made of stone rather than wood. Its fine defensive position dominates the surrounding flatlands north of Elgin.

The Bailey enclosed dwellings and storehouses.

The Motte of earth or rock was sometimes partially man-made.

Early Tower-house

Designed to deter local attacks rather than a major assault, the first tower-houses appeared in the 13th century, and their design lived on for 400 years. They were built initially on a rectangular plan, with a single tower divided into three or four floors. The walls were unadorned, with few windows. Defensive structures were on top, and extra space was made by building adjoining towers. Extensions were vertical, to minimize the area open to attack.

Crenellated parapet for sentries

Claypotts Castle (c.1570), with uniquely projecting garrets above its towers

Braemar Castle (c.1630), a conglomeration of extended towers

Neidpath Castle, standing upon a steep rocky crag above the River Tweed, is an L-shaped tower-house dating from the late 14th century. Once a stronghold for Charles II, its walls still bear damage from a siege conducted by Oliver Cromwell.

Featureless, straight walls contain arrow slits for windows.

Later Tower-house

Though the requirements of defence were being replaced by those of comfort, the style of the early tower-house remained popular. By the 17th century wings for accommodation were being added around the original tower (often creating a courtyard). The battlements and turrets were kept more for decorative than defensive reasons.

Drum Castle, near Aberdeen, a 13th-century keep with a mansion house extension from 1619

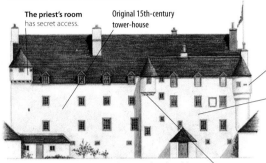

The priest's room has secret access.

Original 15th-century tower-house

This round angle tower contains a stairway.

Sixteenth-century horizontal extension

Decorative, corbelled turret

Traquair House *(see p91)*, by the Tweed, is the oldest continuously inhabited house in Scotland. The largely unadorned, roughcast exterior dates from the 16th century, when a series of extensions were built around the original 15th-century tower-house.

Blair Castle *(see p143)*, incorporating a medieval tower

Classical Palace

By the 18th century the defensive imperative had passed and castles were built in the manner of country houses; the vertical tower-house was rejected in favour of a horizontal plan (though the building of imitation fortified buildings continued into the 19th century with the mock-Baronial trend). Outside influences came from all over Europe, including Renaissance and Gothic revivals, with echoes of French châteaux.

Dunrobin Castle (c.1840), Sutherland

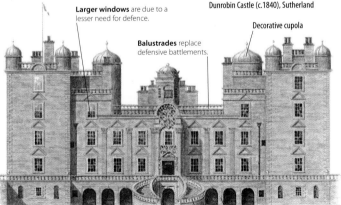

Larger windows are due to a lesser need for defence.

Balustrades replace defensive battlements.

Decorative cupola

Drumlanrig Castle *(see p92)* was built in the 17th century and has traditional Scots aspects as well as Renaissance features, such as the decorated stairway and façade.

Renaissance-style colonnade

Baroque horseshoe stairway

Scottish Gardens

Scotland has a great number of diverse and beautiful gardens. Some are renowned for their layout, such as Pitmedden, or for particular plants. Rhododendrons flourish in Scotland's acidic, peaty soil, and the Royal Botanic Garden in Edinburgh is famous for its spectacular, colourful display. Some gardens have a striking backdrop of lakes or mountains, while others form the grounds of a stately home. Gulf Stream gardens like Inverewe offer visitors a rare chance to view exotic, subtropical flora at a northern latitude. The gardens shown here are some of Scotland's finest.

Inverewe Garden *(see p160)* is renowned for its lush, exotic, subtropical flora. Ferns, lilies, giant forget-me-nots and rare palms are just some of the 2,500 species that thrive in the mild climate.

Crarae Gardens *(see p134)* are sited on a slope overlooking Loch Fyne, surrounded by mature woodland. There are many walks, all designed to cross a picturesque burn at the centre. The gardens are riotous with spectacular rhododendrons in spring and ablaze with golden and russet leaves during the autumn.

The Botanic Gardens, Glasgow *(see p107)*, have a wonderful collection of orchids, begonias and cacti. Kibble Palace, a domed, iron conservatory designed by engineer John Kibble, houses tropical tree ferns from around the world.

Inverewe Garden

Kyle of Lochalsh

Inverne

Mallaig

Fort William

Angus' Garden

Arduaine Garden

Crarae Gardens

Younger Botanic Garden

Glasg Botar Garde

Achamore Gardens

Glasgow

Ayr

Stranraer

Logan Botanic Garden *(see p95)* is an outpost of the Royal Botanic Garden in Edinburgh. The garden is divided into two main areas – a walled garden with cabbage palms, and a woodland area. The Gulf Stream enables subtropical plants to grow here.

Logan Bota Garden

The Rhododendron

These examples illustrate three of the 900 rhododendron varieties. The first is tropical, grown under glass in Scotland; the second is evergreen; the third is an azalea, which used to be considered a separate species. Rhododendrons also fall into scalyleaved and non-scaly groups.

Macgregoriae

Augustini

Medway

Drummond Castle Gardens are laid out as a large boxwood parterre in the shape of a St Andrew's Cross. Yellow and red roses and antirrhinums provide the colour, and a sundial forms the centrepiece.

The Gulf Stream

The west coast of Scotland is the surprising location for a number of gardens where tropical and subtropical plants bloom. Although on the same latitude as Siberia, this area of Scotland lies in the path of a warm water current from the Atlantic. Inverewe is the most famous of the Gulf Stream gardens, with plants from South America, South Africa and the South Pacific. Other gardens include Achamore on the Isle of Gigha and Logan Botanic Garden near Stranraer.

Tree ferns warmed by the Gulf Stream, Logan Botanic Garden

Pitmedden Garden was created in 1675 and later restored to its full glory as a formal garden by the National Trust for Scotland. Split into two levels, it has four parterres, two gazebos, box hedges and a splendid fountain at its centre.

Crathes Gardens' topiary and scented borders are centred around the beautiful tower house, Crathes Castle (see p149). There are eight different themed gardens, such as the Golden Garden designed in the style of Gertrude Jekyll.

Dawyck Botanic Garden is another branch of Edinburgh's Royal Botanic Garden, and specializes in rare trees, such as the Dawyck Beech, flowering shrubs and blankets of narcissi.

Elgin

Pitmedden Garden

Aberdeen

Crathes Gardens

Perth

Drummond Castle Gardens

Edinburgh Royal Botanic Garden

dinburgh

Kailzie Gardens

Dawyck Botanic Garden

Priorwood Gardens

Dumfries

| 0 kilometres | 50 |
| 0 miles | 50 |

The Royal Botanic Garden, Edinburgh (see p72), is internationally renowned as a base for scientific research. With almost 17,000 species, the garden has a marvellous range of plants. Exotic plants are found in the many glasshouses, and the grounds are enhanced by beautifully maintained lawns.

Great Scottish Inventions

Despite its relatively small size and population, Scotland has produced a remarkable number of inventors over the centuries. The late 1700s and 1800s were years of such intense creativity that the period became known as the Scottish Enlightenment. Many technological, medicinal and mechanical breakthroughs were made at this time, including the invention of the steam engine, antiseptic and the telephone. Out of the country's factories, universities and laboratories came a breed of men who were intrepid and forward-thinking. Their revolutionary ideas and experiments produced inventions that have shaped our modern, progressive society.

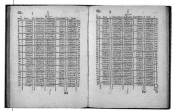

Logarithm tables (1594) were devised by John Napier as a practical way of multiplying and dividing large numbers. Though easy to use, the tables took 20 years to create.

Continous electric light (1834) was invented by James Bowman Lindsay using galvanic cells in a revolutionary design.

Parallel motion operated all the valves in time.

A flywheel stored energy so that the engine ran smoothly.

The pneumatic tyre/tire (John Dunlop, 1887), was originally patented by RW Thomson and then developed by Dunlop for use on bicycles and, later, cars.

Piston rod

Golf clubs were originally wooden and hand-crafted by carpenters such as Old Tom Morris. By 1890, aluminium-headed clubs had been introduced.

The rotative steam engine (James Watt, 1782) was a refinement of the existing steam engine. This new model soon became the driving force behind the Industrial Revolution in Britain, powering all manner of machinery. Watt's success led to his name being given to the modern unit of power.

The bicycle (Kirkpatrick Macmillan, 1839) was originally known as a velocipede. Macmillan's version was an important stage in the development of cycling.

Colour photography (1861) was developed by the Scottish physicist, James C Maxwell. The first to experiment with three-colour photography, he photographed this tartan ribbon using coloured water as a filter.

Spray nozzle

Steam generator

Antiseptic (Joseph Lister, 1865) in the form of carbolic acid was a most important breakthrough in surgery. Lister discovered that, applied to wounds and sprayed around the theatre, the acid helped to prevent germs and infection.

Carbolic acid reservoir

The thermos flask (Sir James Dewar, 1892) was first designed as a vacuum for storing low-temperature gases. The flask was later mass produced as the thermos, for maintaining the temperature of hot and cold drinks.

The telephone (Alexander Graham Bell, 1876) was the scientific breakthrough that revolutionized the way the world communicated, introducing the transmission of sound by electricity.

Penicillin (Alexander Fleming, 1928) is a discovery that has changed the face of medicine. Fleming's brainchild was the first antibiotic drug to treat diseases, and by 1940 it was being used to save the lives of wounded soldiers.

The radar receiver (Robert Watson-Watt, 1935) was in use long before World War II, since Watson-Watt's team had built the first working radar defence system by 1935. Radar is an acronym for "radio detection and ranging".

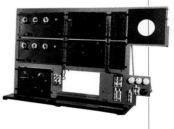

The first television (John Logie Baird, 1926), or "televisor", was black and white, and unable to produce sound and pictures together, but it was nevertheless hailed as a monumental invention. In 1928, Baird demonstrated the possibilities of creating colour images.

Dolly the cloned sheep was created in 1996 by a team of scientists at Edinburgh's Roslin Institute. Dolly, the first successful clone of an adult animal in the world, gave birth in 1998.

Writers and Intellectuals

From medieval poets through Robert Burns to Irvine Welsh, writers in the three literary languages of Scotland – Scots, English and Gaelic – have created a body of literature expressing both their place in the European mainstream and the diversity within Scotland. In 1999, a new parliament was established in Scotland, three centuries after the dissolution of the last one. Political devolution followed three decades of ferment in which literature reached new heights of success.

Robert Burns encircled by images of his literary creations

The Golden Age Before Enlightenment

Often regarded as the golden age of Scottish literature, the century leading up to the Reformation of 1560 was characterized by strong links with the Continent and a rich tradition of poetry, culminating in the achievements of William Dunbar and Robert Henryson. John Barbour established the mythic heroism of the national hero in *The Bruce* (c.1375). Other early works were James I's *Kingis Quair* (c.1424) and Blind Harry's *Wallace* (c.1478).

Dunbar rose to pre-eminence for his polished art, from *Lament for the Makars* (1508), an elegy to poets, to his insult poetry known as "flyting". Henryson's work is rich in insight, as in *The Testament of Cresseid* (c.1480), which tells the legend from the woman's point of view. Gavin Douglas translated Virgil's *Aeneid* into Scots in 1513. The golden age ended with Sir David Lindsay's much-revived play, *A Satire of the Three Estates*, in 1540.

Enlightenment and Romanticism

The intellectual triumphs of the Enlightenment in Scotland were fuelled by the expanding educational system. Among the great thinkers of the time were Adam Smith (1723–90), who theorized on political economy, and Adam Ferguson (1723–1816), who founded modern sociology. Other prominent figures were William Robertson (1721– 93) and David Hume (1711–76), both of whom helped to define modern history.

Philosopher David Hume

Hume's greatest legacy was in philosophy – his rigorous empiricism offended Christian orthodoxy and foretold crises of faith versus scientific knowledge. James Macpherson published the *Ossian Chronicles* in 1760, supposedly the documentation of his discovery of an old Celtic tradition in the Hebrides. This fictional work tapped a nostalgia for ancient civilizations and, allied to fears about progress, Romanticism was born. Allan Ramsay wrote poems in Scots, as did the tragic Robert Fergusson, who died in poverty aged 25.

The country's most fêted literary figure, Robert Burns (1759– 96), was a man of his time. His popular "heaven-taught ploughman" image belied a sound education. His works ranged from love lyrics to savage satire *(Holy Willie's Prayer)*, nationalism to radical ideals *(A Man's a Man for a' That)*.

The 19th Century

Despite the importance of Edinburgh in British culture, it was the pattern of leaving Scotland to achieve fame in London, initiated in the mid-18th century by James Boswell and Tobias Smollett, that would predominate in the Victorian period.

The poetry of Walter Scott (1771–1832) enjoyed phen-omenal success. His novels, especially *Waverley* (1814), rose to greater glory. Francis Jeffrey's Whig-orientated *Edinburgh Review* led opinion, challenged by *Blackwood's* Tory alternative. James Hogg was published by the latter before writing his startling, gothic *Private Memoirs and Confessions*

Map of Robert Louis Stevenson's Treasure Island, based on an island in the Firth of Forth

of a Justified Sinner (1824). Following Susan Ferrier and John Galt, standards were modest, despite the prodigious career of Margaret Oliphant. Thomas Carlyle noted the provinciality of Edinburgh in the 1830s.

A later response to anxieties of the age came from Robert Louis Stevenson (1850–94) in Dr Jekyll and Mr Hyde. This contrasted with the sentimentality of home-spun or so-called kailyard (literally "cabbage patch") fiction, led by JM Barrie and SR Crockett. Barrie's dramas often catered for bourgeois tastes, as did the Sherlock Holmes stories of Arthur Conan Doyle (1859– 1930), which endure today.

Arthur Conan Doyle's sleuth, Sherlock Holmes, in The Graphic (1901)

Poster for the film Rob Roy (1995), based on Walter Scott's 1817 novel

Early 20th-century Renaissance

George Douglas Brown's fierce anti-kailyard novel, The House with the Green Shutters (1901), opened the century and serious art was reborn. Hugh MacDiarmid's poetry in the 1920s carried literature into the stream of modernism. A Drunk Man Looks at the Thistle (1926) combines disparate Scottish dialects with political and social commentary in one of the century's great symbolist works. Edwin Muir also won international acclaim. Successors included Sidney Goodsir Smith and

William Soutar. Fiction reached epic and innovative proportions with Neil Gunn (Butcher's Broom, 1933) and Lewis Grassic Gibbon (A Scots Quair, 1932–4). Others included Willa Muir, Nan Shepherd and Fionn MacColla. John Buchan attempted serious work and popular thrillers. Nationalist impetus was dissipated by the rise of fascism, and new directions were sought after World War II.

Post-1945

Sorley Maclean wrote in his native Gaelic of the ancient Highland culture's plight. Norman MacCaig began a career characterized by metaphysical whimsy, and George Bruce and Robert Garioch evoked the strictures of nature and social class.

Edwin Morgan has celebrated art and modernity (Sonnets from Scotland, 1984), Liz Lochhead continues to produce fresh drama and poetry, and Jackie Kay explores the experience of being a black Scottish citizen. While James Bridie, Bill Bryden and John Byrne made an impact in the theatre, Muriel Spark rose to international acclaim for her

blackly comic novels (The Prime of Miss Jean Brodie, 1961). Urban realism developed quietly before William MacIlvanney's breakthrough with The Big Man (1985).

Following Alasdair Gray's bizarre Lanark (1981), a powerful wave propelled fiction into the highly productive present, in which Iain Banks remains a bestseller (The Crow Road, 1992). Tom Leonard's poems initiated a tradition using urban demotic speech. James Kelman elevated this to new levels, winning the Booker Prize for How Late It Was, How Late (1994).

Irvine Welsh's portrayal of drug culture is now world famous, though the energy of Trainspotting (1993) is absent from its successors. The private dramas articulated in AL Kennedy's stories are poignant and mysterious (So I Am Glad, 1995), while Ian Rankin's thrillers receive international acclaim, as do JK Rowling's hugely successful Harry Potter books.

"Trainspotting is the best British film of the decade" ★★★★★ EMPIRE

Poster for the film version of Irvine Welsh's novel

Clans and Tartans

The clan system, by which Highland society was divided into tribal groups led by autocratic chiefs, can be traced to the 12th century, when clans were already known to wear the chequered wool cloth later called tartan. All members of the clan bore the name of their chief, but not all were related by blood. Though they had noble codes of hospitality, the clansmen had to be warriors to protect their herds, as can be seen from their mottoes. After the Battle of Culloden *(see p150)*, all the clan lands were forfeited to the Crown, and the wearing of tartan was banned for nearly 100 years.

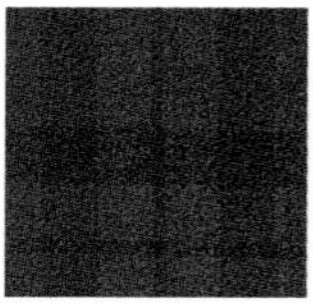

The Mackays, also known as the Clan Morgan, won lasting renown during the Thirty Years War.

The MacLeods are of Norse heritage. The clan chief still lives in Dunvegan Castle, Skye.

The MacDonalds were the most powerful of all the clans, holding the title of Lords of the Isles.

The Mackenzies received much of the lands of Kintail *(see p155)* from David II in 1362.

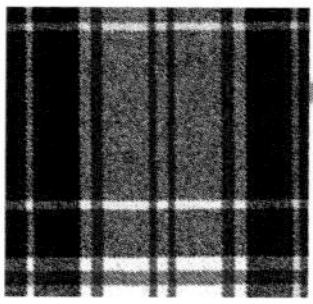

Clan Chief

The chief was the clan's patriarch, judge and leader in war, commanding absolute loyalty from his clansmen who gave military service in return for his protection. The chief summoned his clan to do battle by sending a runner across his land bearing a burning cross.

Bonnet with eagle feathers, clan crest and plant badge.

Dirk

Sporran, or pouch, made of badger's skin.

Feileadh-mor, or "great plaid" (the early kilt), wrapped around waist and shoulder.

Basket-hilted sword

The Campbells were a widely feared clan who fought the Jacobites in 1746 *(see p134)*.

The Black Watch, raised in 1729 to keep peace in the Highlands, was one of the Highland regiments in which the wearing of tartan survived. After 1746, civilians were punished by exile for up to seven years for wearing tartan.

The Sinclairs came from France in the 11th century and became Earls of Caithness in 1455.

The Frasers came over to Britain from France with William the Conqueror and his followers in 1066.

George IV, dressed as a Highlander, visited Edinburgh in 1822, the year of the tartan revival. Many tartan "setts" (patterns) date from this time, as the original ones were lost.

The Gordons were famously good soldiers; the clan motto was "by courage, not by craft".

The Stuarts were Scotland's royal dynasty. Their motto was "no one harms me with impunity".

Clan Territories

The territories of 10 major clans are marked here with their clan crests and tartan. The patterns shown are modern versions of original tartan designs.

The Douglas clan was prominent in Scottish history, though its origin is unknown.

Plant Badges

Each clan had a plant associated with its territory. It was worn on the bonnet, especially on the day of battle.

Scots pine was worn by the MacGregors of Argyll.

Rowan berries were worn by the Clan Malcolm.

Ivy was worn by the Clan Gordon of Aberdeenshire.

Spear thistle, now a national symbol, was a Stuart badge.

Cotton grass was worn by the Clan Henderson.

Highland Clans Today

Once the daily dress of the clansmen, the kilt continues to be a symbol of national pride. The one-piece *feileadh-mor* has been replaced by the *feileadh-beag*, or "small plaid", made from approximately 7 m (23 ft) of material with a double apron fastened at the front with a silver pin. Though they exist now only in name, the clans are still a strong source of pride for Scots, and many still live in areas traditionally belonging to their clans. Many visitors to Britain can trace their Scots ancestry back to the Highlands.

Modern Highland formal dress

Highland Music and Games

The Highlands and Islands of Scotland have been the focus of Gaelic culture for hundreds of years. Although the language itself is little spoken today, the legacy of the Gaelic lifestyle lives on in the music and activities of the people. The bagpipes, a traditional Highland instrument, are an important part of Scotland's identity around the world, and the Highland Games are an amalgamation of the Gaelic customs of music, dancing and contests of strength.

Pibroch is the classical music of the piping world. Played by solo pipers, these slow, melancholy tunes produce a haunting sound that is easier on the ear than the almost discordant sound a group of bagpipers makes.

The blow-pipe is used to inflate the bag by blowing air, as continuously as possible, into the pipe's mouthpiece.

A piper's hat is made traditionally from ostrich feathers.

The chanter pipe has eight finger-holes, used to play the melody.

The drones or "borduns", are the three pipes that give the pitch. They are pitched on a fixed note, one bass and the other two higher, each at intervals of a fifth.

The bag, made from animal hide, is inflated by air from the blow-pipe; the air is then expelled under pressure applied by the piper's elbow.

The Bagpipes

Bagpipes have been the traditional sound of the Highlands for many centuries and are thought to have been introduced to Britain by the Romans. After the Battle of Culloden in 1746 they were banned for 11 years, along with Highland dress, for inspiring the Highlanders to rebel against English rule. The pipes have now become one of the most recognized emblems of Scotland.

Traditional Gaelic Music

Music has always featured strongly in the Highlands' Gaelic communities. Solo instruments include the harp and accordion, and *ceilidh* bands are still common.

Accordions have accompanied ceilidhs ever since the dances began in the crofting communities of the Scottish Highlands and islands.

Ceilidh bands are an alternative to the solo accordion as accompaniment for the modern ceilidh (a Gaelic word for "visit"). The band's instruments usually include fiddles, accordions and penny whistles.

The harp is Irish in origin but was introduced to Scotland in the 1800s. The "clarsach", as it is known, has enjoyed a revival in recent years.

Re-enacting Highland battles is popular with modern-day clansmen to commemorate their forefathers' fight for freedom. The above occasion was the 250th anniversary of the Battle of Culloden, where over 2,000 Highland warriors died.

Highland Games and Activities

As well as music, the Highlands of Scotland are famous for their Games. The first Games took place many hundreds of years ago, and may have served a military purpose by allowing clan chiefs to choose the strongest men from those competing in contests of strength. Highland Games are held annually at Braemar (see p42), as well as at Oban and Dunoon, among others. Another activity in the Highlands is the re-enactment of past battles and rebellions.

The Highland Games (or Gatherings) as they are played today date from the 1820s. The most common contests and events are tossing the caber, weight shifting, piping, singing, dancing and throwing the hammer. The result is a cacophony of sound and activity, which can be overwhelming to a first-time spectator.

Tossing the caber is one of the most famous Highland sports, and requires strength and skill. The athlete must run with the tree trunk and toss it so that it flips over 180° and lands vertically, straight ahead.

Throwing the hammer involves revolving on the spot to gather speed, while swinging the hammer (a weight on the end of a long pole) around the head, before launching it across the field. The winner is the contestant whose hammer reaches the furthest distance.

Highland dancing is an important part of the Games, and the dances often have symbolic meanings – for instance the circle in a reel represents the circle of life. In the sword dance, the feet skip nimbly over the swords without touching them.

Weight shifting is a severe test of strength and stamina. Here, the man stands with his back to a bar, over which he must throw the huge weight. The bar is raised after each successful attempt, until only one person is left in the competition.

Scotch Whisky

Whisky is to the Scots what Champagne is to the French, and a visit to Scotland would not be complete without sampling this fiery, heart-warming spirit. All malt whiskies are produced using much the same process, but the environment, maturity and storage of the whisky have such a strong bearing on its character that every one is a different experience. There is no "best" malt whisky – some are suited to drinking at bedtime, others as an aperitif. All the distilleries named below produce highly rated Single Malt Scotch Whiskies, a title that is revered by true whisky connoisseurs.

A 1920s steam wagon transporting The Glenlivet to the nearby railways

Talisker is a highly distinctive malt with an extremely hot, peppery, powerful flavour that is guaranteed to warm the toes.

Glenmorangie is the biggest selling single malt in Scotland, with a light, flowery taste and strong perfume.

Lochnagar is reputed to have been a favourite with Queen Victoria, who visited this distillery located near Balmoral. This is a sweet whisky with overtones of sherry.

Lagavulin is a classic Islay whisky with a dry, smoky palate. Islay is thought to be the best of the whisky-producing islands.

Edradour is the smallest distillery in Scotland but it succeeds in producing a deliciously minty, creamy whisky.

Speyside Whiskies

The region of Speyside (see p148), where barley is widely grown, is the setting for over half of Scotland's malt whisky distilleries.

Map labels:
- Pulteney
- Glenmorangie
- Highland Park
- Glen Ord
- See inset
- SPEYSIDE
- Lochnagar
- Dalwhinnie
- Blair Athol
- Edradour
- Fettercairn
- Glencadam
- Tobermory
- Aberfeldy
- Oban
- Tullibardine
- Auchentoshan
- Edinburgh
- Glasgow
- Glenkinchie
- Lagavulin
- CAMPBEL-TOWN
- Glen Scotia
- Springbank
- LOWLANDS
- Bladnoch
- Talisker
- NORTHERN HIGHLANDS
- ISLANDS
- WESTERN HIGHLANDS
- CENTRAL HIGHLANDS
- EASTERN HIGHLANDS
- ISLAY

Speyside inset labels:
- Glen Moray
- Linkwood
- Glenlossie
- Glen Elgin
- Dallas Dhu
- Speyburn
- Glen Rothes
- Macallan
- Glendfiddich
- Glenfarclas
- Mortlach
- Cragganmore
- The Glenlivet
- Balmenach
- Tamnavulin

The Macallan is widely acknowledged as being the "Rolls Royce of Single Malts". Aged in sherry casks, it has a full flavour.

The Glenlivet is the most famous of the Speyside malts, distilled since 1880.

Malt Regions

Single malts vary according to regional differences in the peat and stream water used. This map illustrates the divisions of the traditional whisky distilling regions in Scotland. Each whisky has subtle but recognizable regional flavour characteristics.

Key

- Single malt distilleries

How Whisky is Made

Traditionally made from just barley, yeast and stream water, Scottish whisky (from the Gaelic usquebaugh, *or the "water of life") takes a little over three weeks to produce, though it must be given at least three years to mature. Maturation usually takes place in oak casks, often in barrels previously used for sherry. The art of blending was pioneered in Edinburgh in the 1860s.*

Barley grass

1 Malting is the first stage. Barley grain is soaked in water and spread on the malting floor. With regular turning the grain germinates, producing a "green malt". Germination stimulates the production of enzymes which turn the starches into fermentable sugars.

2 Drying of the barley halts germination after 12 days of malting. This is done over a peat fire in a pagoda-shaped malt-kiln. The peat-smoke gives flavour to the malt and eventually to the mature whisky. The malt is gleaned of germinated roots and then milled.

3 Mashing of the ground malt, or "grist", occurs in a large vat or "mash tun", which holds a vast quantity of hot water. The malt is soaked and begins to dissolve, producing a sugary solution called "wort", which is then extracted for fermentation.

4 Fermentation occurs when yeast is added to the cooled wort in wooden vats, or "washbacks". The mixture is stirred for hours as the yeast turns the sugar into alcohol, producing a clear liquid called "wash".

5 Distillation involves boiling the wash twice so that the alcohol vaporizes and condenses. In copper "pot stills", the wash is distilled – first in the "wash still", then in the "spirit still". Now purified, with an alcohol content of 57 per cent, the result is young whisky.

6 Maturation is the final process. The whisky mellows in oak casks for a legal minimum of three years. Premium brands give the whisky a 10- to 15-year maturation, though some are given up to 50 years.

Traditional drinking vessels, or *quaichs*, made of silver

Blended whiskies are made from a mixture of up to 50 different single malts.

Single malts are made in one distillery, from pure barley malt that is never blended.

Touring Scotland by Car

The ten routes marked on this map are excellent examples of the options open to motorists touring Scotland. Some routes are circular, using a major city as a base; some can be combined into longer itineraries. Main roads are few and far between in the Highlands, but driving conditions are generally good, and traffic is light outside the peak July and August holiday period. The driving times given in the key assume normal conditions without lengthy stops. Further information about road travel is on pages 222–3.

The far northwest can be visited in a circular tour starting at Braemore Junction, near Ullapool, heading west on a series of single-track roads past tiny crofting settlements and some of the oldest rocks in Britain. The route rejoins the two-lane road near Unapool.

From Kyle of Lochalsh, this route along the west coast encompasses the magnificent mountains and coastline of Wester Ross, taking in Loch Carron, Torridon, Loch Maree, Gairloch and Inverewe Gardens.

Key to Touring Routes

- The Border Abbeys & Scott's View *195 km (120 miles), 3–4 hours*
- Walter Scott's Country *185 km (115 miles), 3–4 hours*
- Fife Fishing Villages & St Andrews *195 km (120 miles), 3–4 hours*
- Eastern Grampians & Royal Deeside *180 km (110 miles), 4 hours*
- High Mountains of Breadalbane *180 km (110 miles), 4 hours*
- Loch Lomond & the Trossachs *225 km (140 miles), 5 hours*
- Inveraray & the Mountains of Lorne *225 km (140 miles), 4 hours*
- Glencoe & the Road to the Isles *160 km (100 miles), 3 hours*
- Sea Lochs of the West Coast *195 km (120 miles), 4 hours*
- The Far Northwest *160 km (100 miles), 3–4 hours*

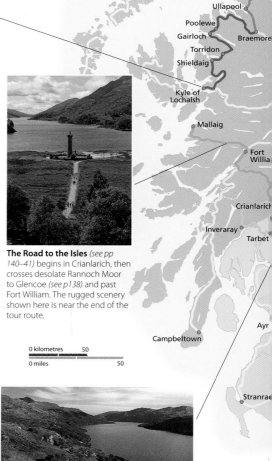

The Road to the Isles *(see pp 140–41)* begins in Crianlarich, then crosses desolate Rannoch Moor to Glencoe *(see p138)* and past Fort William. The rugged scenery shown here is near the end of the tour route.

Loch Lomond is the first point of interest on a tour of Inveraray and the Mountains of Lorne. After Tarbet is a pass known as "The Rest and Be Thankful", then a drive to the 18th-century town of Inveraray *(see p134)*, and on past Kilchurn Castle.

0 kilometres 50
0 miles 50

Unapool
Lochinver
Ullapool
Poolewe
Gairloch
Braemore
Torridon
Shieldaig
Kyle of Lochalsh
Mallaig
Fort William
Crianlarich
Inveraray
Tarbet
Ayr
Campbeltown
Stranraer

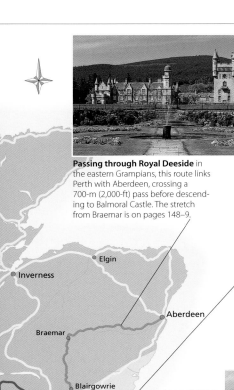

Passing through Royal Deeside in the eastern Grampians, this route links Perth with Aberdeen, crossing a 700-m (2,000-ft) pass before descending to Balmoral Castle. The stretch from Braemar is on pages 148–9.

Tips for Drivers

Hazards Watch out for sharp bends and animals on the roads in the Highlands. The sudden noise of jets above the glens can also startle drivers. Minor roads are often single track. Snowfall may result in road closures.
Fuel Fill up your car with fuel in towns, as there are few filling stations in rural areas.

St Andrews *(see p127)* and the historic fishing villages of East Fife can be reached from Edinburgh over the Forth Bridge, and back via the hunting palace of the Stuart kings at Falkland *(see p128)*.

A tour of Walter Scott's Country takes in the River Tweed Valley, with its attractive hills, market towns and an arboretum at Dawyck.

Melrose Abbey is one of the highlights of a tour taking in attractive Border towns, the famous Border Abbeys and Scott's View – one of the finest viewpoints in southern Scotland. More details of part of this tour are on page 89.

From Glasgow, this route includes Loch Lomond, Lochearnhead and Balquhidder. Just north of Callander, it turns west into the Trossachs. Heading back via Drymen, there is access to Loch Lomond.

Stirling, with its castle, is the base from which to explore the high mountains of Breadalbane. The route passes through Callander, past Rob Roy's grave and Loch Earn. It then climbs over a mountain pass down to Glen Lyon, one of the most beautiful glens, and on through Crieff.

SCOTLAND THROUGH THE YEAR

Most visitors come to Scotland between May and August, when they enjoy the best weather, long hours of daylight and the chance to sample world-class events such as the Edinburgh International Festival or the Glasgow International Jazz Festival. The countryside lures tourists and Scots alike, and at the height of summer, it gets very busy in areas such as Loch Ness (monster spotting) or Royal Deeside (site of Balmoral Castle, the British Royal Family's Scottish residence). Out of season, a good winter snowfall in the Highlands provides an opportunity for snowboarding or skiing. Edinburgh's organized celebration at New Year – known locally as Hogmanay – has seen a rise in visitor numbers. During most weeks of the year, but especially in the summer, a festival is held somewhere across the country.

Full colours of gorse in springtime

Spring

The snow clears off the mountains after April, the salmon swim upstream and the country prepares for visitors. There are some excellent festivals and a series of important sporting events. British Summer Time, when the clocks go forward one hour, starts at the end of March.

March

Inverness Music Festival *(early Mar)*. Over 1000 entrants battle it out in a week-long Gaelic music festival.
MV Festival *(third weekend)*, Aviemore. Daytime events at the Cairngorm ski area and evening street parades in Aviemore.

Glasgow International Comedy Festival *(mid- to late Mar)*. Comedy acts from around the world.

April

Puppet and Animation Festival *(first two weeks)*. Workshops and displays at 70 venues nationwide.
International Science Festival *(two weeks, early Apr)*, Edinburgh. The world's largest science festival.
Scottish Grand National *(mid-Apr)*, Ayr Racecourse. Scotland's top steeplechase event.
The Melrose Sevens *(mid-Apr or early May)*, Melrose, Borders. International seven-a-side rugby union event.

Glasgow Art Fair *(late Apr)*. Commercial art show in various galleries.
Beltane *(30 Apr)*, Calton Hill, Edinburgh. Pagan celebration to welcome start of summer.
Scottish Rugby Union Cup Final *(late Apr)*, Murrayfield Stadium, Edinburgh. Scotland's showpiece club rugby event.

May

Shetland Folk Festival *(first week)*. Traditional Scottish music in an island setting.
Scottish Cup Final *(mid-May)*, Hampden Park, Glasgow. Scottish football's showpiece club event.
Imaginate *(fourth week)*, Edinburgh. Performing arts event for children and young people.
Knockengorroch World Ceilidh *(late May)*, Galloway. World and folk music festival on remote farmland, with fire spectaculars, workshops and stalls.

An inter-Scotland rugby match at Murrayfield Stadium, Edinburgh

Average Daily Hours of Sunshine

Hours

Jan	Feb	Mar	Apr	May	Jun	Jul	Aug	Sep	Oct	Nov	Dec

Sunshine Chart
Although Scotland is not in any way synonymous with sunshine, its summers are marked by very long hours of daylight, due to the country's northerly latitude. In the winter, days are very short, so there's little time for the sun to poke through the clouds.

Summer

This is the busiest time of year. Many towns and villages stage their own version of the Highland Games, at varying scales. Days are long – in Shetland there is no proper night at midsummer, while even the south sees sunrise around 4:30am, sunset around 10pm.

The traditional event of tossing the caber at the Highland Games

June
Gardening Scotland (late May/early Jun), Edinburgh. Large gardening show.
Rockness Music Festival (early Jun), Inverness. Huge multi-day rock and techno festival in a wonderful setting beside Loch Ness.
Edinburgh International Film Festival (mid-Jun), Edinburgh. The world's oldest film festival.
Royal Highland Show (mid-Jun), Ingliston, Edinburgh. Agricultural and food fair.
Glasgow International Jazz Festival (late Jun). Various venues across the city.

St Magnus Festival (third week), Orkney. Arts event.
Traditional Boats Festival (last weekend), Portsoy harbour, Banffshire. Displaying Scotland's fisheries heritage.

July
Game Conservancy Scottish Fair (first weekend), Scone Palace, Perth. Major shooting and fishing event.
T in the Park (second weekend), Balado, Fife. Scotland's biggest rock festival.
Aberdeen Asset Management Scottish Open (mid-Jul), Aberdeen. Fixture on European golf tour.
Highland Feast (mid-Jul), the Highland's largest food festival with events throughout the region.

August
Traquair Fair (late Jul/early Aug), Innerleithen, Borders. Folk music, theatre and food stalls.
Piping Live (mid-Aug), Glasgow. Week-long celebration, immediately followed by the World Pipe Band Championships.

Grouse shooting on the "Glorious Twelfth" of August

Edinburgh Festival (various dates in Aug). "The Festival" comprises an international arts festival, an extensive fringe festival and other events dedicated to television, comedy, books, jazz and blues music (see pp82–3).
Edinburgh Military Tattoo (throughout Aug). Martial music and displays on Edinburgh Castle Esplanade.
Glorious Twelfth (12 Aug). Grouse shooting season opens.
Connect Festival (late Aug), Inveraray. A grown-up alternative to T in the Park.

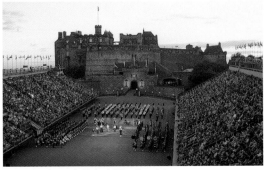

Drums and marching at the Edinburgh Military Tattoo in August

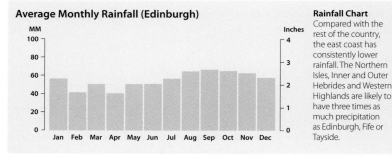

Average Monthly Rainfall (Edinburgh)

Rainfall Chart
Compared with the rest of the country, the east coast has consistently lower rainfall. The Northern Isles, Inner and Outer Hebrides and Western Highlands are likely to have three times as much precipitation as Edinburgh, Fife or Tayside.

The soft colours of autumn in Tayside

Autumn

Catch a fine day in the countryside and the autumn colours can be spectacular. Scotland may be beginnning to wind down after the summer, but there are still some attractions to be found for the attentive visitor. Schools have a week's holiday in October, which was traditionally a break to allow the children to work on the potato harvest.

September

Ben Nevis Hill Race
(first Sat), Fort William. Annual race up and down the highest mountain in Britain.
Braemar Gathering
(first weekend), Braemar, Aberdeenshire. One of the country's leading Highland Games *(see p35)* with

Shot-putting at Braemar

members of the Royal Family usually in attendance.
Pedal for Scotland *(early Sep)*. Huge cycling event with rides to suit all, including the 47-mile Glasgow–Edinburgh route.
Leuchars Air Show *(several dates in Sep)*, RAF Leuchars, Fife. Airshow with flying displays and other attractions.
Ayr Gold Cup *(mid-Sep)*, Ayr Racecourse. Prestigious flat-race for horses.
Open Doors Day *(last Sat)*, different cities across Scotland. A number of the city's finest private buildings are opened to the public (0141 221 1466 or www.doorsopendays.org.uk).
Wigtown Book Festival *(late Sep)*, Wigtown, Dumfries and Galloway. Scotland's National Book Town welcomes book lovers and collectors.

October
Glasgay *(early Oct–early Nov)*. A longstanding month-long celebration of gay culture in several central Glasgow venues, involving film, theatre, music and club nights.
Royal National Mod *(second week)*, venue changes yearly. Performing arts competition promoting Gaelic language and Gaelic culture in general.
Great Scottish Run *(early Oct)*, Glasgow. A half-marathon for all to enter.

November
St Andrew's Week *(last week)*. Various venues in St Andrews host ceilidh evenings and festivals of Scottish food and drink.
St Andrew's Night *(30 Nov)*. National day of Scotland's patron saint. Many private and society dinners.

Public Holidays

These public holidays are observed throughout Scotland. Some local authorities declare extra holidays.

New Year *(1–2 Jan)*. Two days in Scotland, compared with just the one day in England.
Good Friday *(late Mar or early Apr)*. Easter Monday is not an official holiday in Scotland.
May Day *(first Monday in May)*.
Spring Bank Holiday *(last Monday in May)*.
Summer Bank Holiday *(first Monday in Aug)*.
Christmas Day *(25 Dec)*.
Boxing Day *(26 Dec)*.

Average Monthly Temperature (Edinburgh)

Temperature Chart
This bar chart illustrates the average minimum and maximum monthly temperatures recorded in Edinburgh. The west of Scotland tends to be warmer than the east, while the Highlands can be arctic-like, with heavy snowfalls during the winter.

Winter

This is a season of short days and cold weather, but Christmas and New Year celebrations provide a welcome antidote. Haggis sales peak in late January with Burns Night parties. This quiet period is probably the best time of year to visit Scotland's museums and galleries.

December

Edinburgh's Hogmanay (*late Dec into early Jan*). World's biggest New Year celebration. Several days of events, including processions and street theatre, in the capital. The centrepiece is a vast street party on 31 December.

Stonehaven Fireball Festival (*31 Dec*). Century-old Hogmanay festival that involves throwing

Edinburgh's Royal Mile overflowing with Hogmanay revellers

fireballs around the streets, then heaving them into the harbour. As mad as it sounds and great fun to watch.

January

The Ba' Game (*1 Jan*), Kirkwall, Orkney Isles. Young men play a ball game on the town's streets to welcome the New Year. A centuries-old tradition.

Celtic Connections (*second half of month*), Glasgow. Two weeks of *ceilidhs* and Celtic-themed music.

Burns Night (*25 Jan*). Scotland celebrates the birth of its national poet with readings and "Burns Suppers". Haggis, potatoes, turnips and whisky are on the menu.

Up Helly Aa (*last Tue*), Lerwick, Shetland Isles. Midwinter, Viking-themed fire festival.

February

Glasgow Film Festival (*mid-Feb*), Glasgow. Show-cases a range of blockbusters and independent films.

Walker surveying the winter landscape in the Mamores in the Scottish Highlands

THE HISTORY OF SCOTLAND

Scotland has been torn apart by religion and internal politics, coveted by a richer and more powerful neighbour and wooed and punished for 400 years as the vital partner in the power struggles between England, France and Spain. She has risen and fallen through the ages, acquiring romance from tragedy, producing genius out of poverty and demonstrating an irrepressible spirit.

"They spend all their time in wars, and when there is no war, they fight one another" is a description of the Scots written in about 1500. For the visitor, the chief delight in this turbulent history is that so much is still tangible and visible.

The earliest settlers in the country are believed to have been Celtic-Iberians, who worked their way north along the coast from the Mediterranean, and arrived in Scotland about 8,000 years ago. Around 2000 BC their descendants erected majestic standing stones, which are found all over the country. The layout of those at Callanish in the Western Isles shows an advanced knowledge of astronomy. These people also built underground round-houses and an abundance of forts, indicating that they were no strangers to invasion and warfare.

In AD 82 the Romans penetrated deep into "Caledonia", as they called the country, and Tacitus recorded victories against the Picts (the "painted people") and other tribes. Yet the Romans never conquered Caledonia because their resources were stretched too thin. Instead, they built Hadrian's Wall from Wallsend on the east coast to Bowness-on-Solway in the west, and later the Antonine Wall, a shorter wall further north, thereby endeavouring to shut out the Caledonians. Despite the country's relative isolation from the rest of Britain, however, it is believed that the original form of the Scottish kilt derived from the Roman tunic, or toga.

By AD 400 the Romans had abandoned their northern outposts, and Scotland was divided between four races, each with its own king. These were the predominant Picts, the Britons and Angles in the south, and the smallest group – the Scots – who originally came from Ireland and occupied the southwest of the country.

In the late 4th century AD a Scot, St Ninian, travelled to Rome and, upon his return, built a church at Whithorn, thereby introducing Christianity to "Dalriada", the Kingdom of the Scots.

4000 BC	2500 BC	1000 BC	AD 500

Skara Brae

300 BC Iron Age begins; weapons are improved

AD 82–4 Romans invade but do not conquer "Caledonia"

AD 121 Hadrian's Wall built

3100 BC Skara Brae settlement on Orkney buried by a storm

2900–2600 BC Callanish standing stones and others erected, showing advanced astronomical knowledge

Roman coin

AD 400 Romans abandon Caledonian outposts. Picts, Scots, Britons and Angles have separate kingdoms

◀ *Return of Mary, Queen of Scots to Edinburgh* in 1561, by James Drummond (1816–77)

Christianity and Unification

Christianity remained in an isolated pocket centred around Whithorn on the Solway Coast, until the great warrior-missionary, St Columba, arrived from Ireland and established his monastery on the small Hebridean island of Iona in 563. Fired by his zeal, the new religion spread rapidly. By 800, Iona had achieved widespread influence, and Columban missionaries worked all over Europe. The Celtic Church developed along monastic lines and remained predominantly reclusive by nature, dedicating itself to worship and scholarship. Among its surviving works of art is the famous *Book of Kells*. This lavish, illuminated 8th- to 9th-century manuscript is thought to have been started on Iona, and later moved to Ireland for safe-keeping.

An illustrated page from the ornate *Book of Kells*, now kept in Trinity College, Dublin

The consolidation of a common religion helped to ease the merging of tribes. In 843 the Picts and Scots united under Kenneth MacAlpin. Curiously, the once-mighty Picts were the ones to lose their identity. They remain a mystery, except for their exquisite stone carvings depicting interwoven patterns, warriors and a wondrous mythology.

A long era of terrible Viking raids began in 890, resulting in the Norse occupation of the Western Isles for 370 years, and Shetland and Orkney for almost 600 years. The Norse threat possibly encouraged the Britons to join "Scotia", and in 1018 the Angles were defeated. Scotland became one united kingdom for the first time.

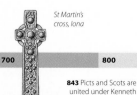

Viking axe

Feudalism and the Clans

Under the powerful influence of Margaret, the English wife of Malcolm III (1057–93), a radical shift occurred during the king's reign away from the Gaelic-speaking culture of most of Scotland to the English-speaking culture of the south. This divide was widened under "good king" David I (1124– 53). Under his reign Royal Burghs were created – towns built on the king's land and given special trading privileges in exchange for annual payments to him. He also introduced a national system of justice and weights and measures and, in the Lowlands, a feudal system based on Anglo-Norman lines.

Power devolved through an introduced aristocracy, largely French-speaking, and a structure bonded through land tenure.

David I tried to impose this system in the north, but the region remained out of his control and, indeed, had its own "kings" – the Lords of the Isles. In the Highlands a different social structure based on kinship – that of families, or clans – had evolved. The chief was a patriarch who held land, not privately, but on behalf of his people. It was an inheritable position, but the chief remained accountable to the clan and could be removed by common consent, unlike the feudal landlords whose power was vested through legal title to the land. This subtle difference was mirrored on a national level – in England, the monarch was the King of England; in Scotland, he was known as the King of Scots.

The lion of Scotland, dating from 1222

The Wars of Independence and the Battle of Bannockburn

In 1222 the lion of Scotland's coat of arms first appeared on the great seal of Alexander II. This was during a relatively peaceful interlude among frequent periods of turmoil when it seemed that Scotland was in danger of breaking apart.

When Alexander III's infant daughter died in 1290, there was no heir to the throne. Edward I of England installed a puppet king and, in 1296, led a devastating invasion that carried off the Stone of Destiny – the Scots' coronation throne – and earned him the title "Hammer of the Scots". Scotland was crushed and, but for one

man, lost. William Wallace rose and led a revolt that rekindled hope until his capture and execution six years later. His cause was taken up by Robert the Bruce who, against all odds, won support and raised an army that changed the course of history by winning a decisive victory over the English at the Battle of Bannockburn, near Stirling, on 23 June 1314.

Confronted by the largest English army to cross the border, the Scots were outnumbered three to one, and their arms were inferior. Yet Bruce had chosen his ground and his strategy carefully and, despite the enemy's skilful bowmen and heavy cavalry, the Scots gained the victory they so badly needed. Scotland had won back its independence, but it was not until 1329 that its sovereign status was recognized and secured by a Papal bull (six days after Bruce had died). Even so, the wars with England would continue for another 300 years.

Robert the Bruce in combat at the Battle of Bannockburn (1314)

1124–53 David I imposes Norman feudal system. A clan system prevails in Highlands

1296 Edward I takes Stone of Destiny from Scone Abbey to Westminster

1320 Declaration of Arbroath sent to the Pope – an eloquent appeal for recognition of Scottish independence and sovereignty

1100   **1200**   **1300**   **1400**

1154 Loss of "southern counties" to England

Edward I (1239–1307)

1263 Western Isles won back from Norse

1314 Robert the Bruce defeats the English at Bannockburn

1328–9 Independence and sovereignty affirmed by Treaty with England and Papal bull

1326 Meeting of first Scottish Parliament

The Stuarts

In 1371 began the long dynasty of the House of Stuart, a family distinguished by intelligence and flair but prone to tragedy. James I introduced wide legal reforms and approved the first university. James III won Orkney and Shetland from King Christian of Denmark and Norway through marriage to his daughter. James IV ended his illustrious reign with uncharacteristic misjudgement at the Battle of Flodden, in which 10,000 Scots died. But the most famous of the Stuarts was Mary, Queen of Scots (1542–87) who acceded to the throne as an infant.

Raised in France, Mary was beautiful, clever, gentle and spirited, but her reign was destined to be difficult. She was a Catholic in a country changing to Protestantism, and a threat to her cousin, Elizabeth I, whose claim to the English throne was precarious. Had Mary married wisely she might have ruled successfully, but her husbands alienated her potential supporters.

Mary returned to Scotland aged 18, already a widow and Dowager Queen of France, and spent just six turbulent years as Scotland's queen. She married again and following the public scandal of her secretary's murder by her second husband and his subsequent murder, she married for a third time. However, her choice was unacceptable to both the public and the church. She was deposed and held captive, making a daring escape from an island castle to England, only to be imprisoned there for 18 years and then finally executed on the orders of her cousin, Elizabeth.

Woodcut of Protestant martyr George Wishart being burned at the stake in 1546

The Reformation

Until Mary's reign, Scotland's national religion, like the rest of Europe, was the Church of Rome. It had become extremely rich and powerful and, in many ways, self-serving and divorced from the people. When Martin Luther sparked the Reformation in Germany in 1517, the ripples of Protestantism spread. In Scotland the most vociferous leader was the firebrand preacher John Knox (see p62), who fearlessly denounced Mary.

There followed a long period of religious tension and strife. At first the main contentions were between Roman Catholics and Protestants. As Catholicism was purged, albeit with revivals and impregnable strongholds in the Highlands and islands, the conflicts shifted to Presbyterians versus Episcopalians. The differences lay in the structures of the churches and in their forms of worship. The feuds blazed and spluttered for 150 years.

Mary, Queen of Scots, of the House of Stuart

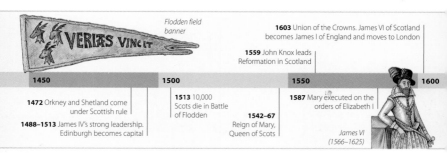

VERITAS VINCIT

Flodden field banner

1603 Union of the Crowns. James VI of Scotland becomes James I of England and moves to London

1559 John Knox leads Reformation in Scotland

1450	1500	1550	1600

1472 Orkney and Shetland come under Scottish rule

1488–1513 James IV's strong leadership. Edinburgh becomes capital

1513 10,000 Scots die in Battle of Flodden

1542–67 Reign of Mary, Queen of Scots

1587 Mary executed on the orders of Elizabeth I

James VI (1566–1625)

Union with England

Mary's son, James VI, had reigned for 36 years when he became heir to the English throne. In 1603 he moved his court to London (taking his golf clubs), thus removing the monarchy from a permanent presence in Scotland for good. Scotland still retained its own parliament but found it increasingly difficult to trade in the face of restrictive English laws. In 1698 it tried to break the English monopoly on foreign trade by starting its own colony in Panama, a scheme that failed and brought financial ruin.

Articles of Union between England and Scotland, signed 22 July 1706 and accepted in 1707

Protestant preacher John Knox

The first proposal to unite the two parliaments received a hostile reception from the public. Yet influential Scots saw union as a means of securing equal trading rights. The English saw it as a means of securing the Protestant line of succession to the throne, for by now the deposed Stuarts were threatening to reinstate the Catholic line. James VII was deposed in 1689 and fled to France. In 1707 the Act of Union was passed and the Scottish Parliament was dissolved.

Bonnie Prince Charlie and the Jacobites

In 1745 James VII's grandson, Prince Charles Edward Stuart, secretly entered Scotland, landing on the west Highland coast with seven men and a promise of French military support, which never materialized.

His call to arms to overthrow the Hanoverian usurper, George II, drew a poor response and only a few Highland chiefs offered support. From this dismal start his campaign achieved remarkable success, but indecisive leadership weakened the side.

The rebel army came within 200 km (125 miles) of London, throwing the city into panic, before losing heart and retreating. At Culloden, near Inverness, the Hanoverian army (which included many Scots, for this was not an issue of nationalism) defeated the Jacobites on a snowy 16 April 1746. The cause was lost. Bonnie Prince Charlie became a fugitive hotly pursued for six months, but despite a £30,000 reward on his head he was never betrayed.

Feather-capped Scottish Jacobites being attacked by Royalists at Glen Shiel in the Highlands, 1719

MacDonald shield

1642 Civil war in England

1692 Massacre of Glencoe – a Campbell-led force murders its hosts, the MacDonalds, as an official punitive example

1745–6 Jacobite rising. Bonnie Prince Charlie tries to recover throne, but loses the Battle of Culloden and flees

1650

1700

1750

1689 James VII loses throne as he tries to restore Catholicism

1698 First Darien (Panama) Expedition to found a trading colony. Bank of Scotland established

1706–7 Union of Parliaments. Scottish Parliament dissolved

1726 Roadbuilding under General Wade

1746 Abolition of Feudal Jurisdictions

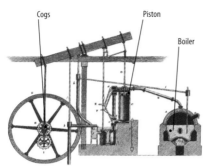

James Watt's steam engine, which shifted the source of industrial power from water to steam

The Aftermath of Culloden and the Clearances

Culloden was the turning point in Highland history, such was the severity of the oppressive measures following the battle. An Act was passed banning the wearing of tartan, the playing of pipes and the carrying of arms. The ties of kinship between chief and people were severed, and a way of life was extinguished. From then on chiefs assumed the roles of feudal landlords, and the land, once held for the people, became their private property. When sheep were found to thrive profitably on the land, the people became a hindrance and, as a result, were removed.

The evictions, or so-called Clearances, began in the 1760s. Some were achieved quite peacefully through financial incentives, but increasingly they were enforced through violence and burning, the most notorious taking place on the Duke of Sutherland's estate in 1814. In the 1860s, by which time Queen Victoria had made the Highlands

popular and sporting estates all the rage for hunting deer, the inland glens were as empty as they are today.

Industrialization and the Scottish Enlightenment

While the Highlands were emptying, parts of southern Scotland were booming. For a large part of the 18th century Glasgow's tobacco lords operated a lucrative stranglehold on the European market, and linen, cotton and coal in their turn became important national industries.

The Industrial Revolution, made possible by Scotsman James Watt's revolutionary contribution to the steam engine, brought wealth to the nation (yet at the expense of health and social conditions) and turned Glasgow into the "Workshop of the Empire"– a reputation it retained until the demise of its famous shipbuilding industry in the 20th century.

A flowering of original thinkers also emerged in Scotland in the 18th century (*see pp30–31*), most notably the philosopher David Hume, economist Adam

Shipbuilding factory in Clydeside, now closed

1786 Robert Burns publishes *Poems, Chiefly in the Scots Dialect*

1814 "The Year of Burning" of the Sutherland Clearances

1832 Sir Walter Scott buried at Dryburgh Abbey

Early telephone

1886 Crofters Act provides secure tenure and fair rents

| 1775 | 1800 | 1825 | 1850 | 1875 | 1900 |

1769 James Watt patents his steam engine

1840 Glasgow's population reaches 200,000 as its shipbuilding and cotton industries flourish

1848 Queen Victoria uses Balmoral as a retreat, and Scottish culture becomes fashionable with the English

1876 Alexander Graham Bell patents the first working telephone

1888 Scottish Labour Party founded by James Keir Hardie

Smith and the "Bard of Humanity", Robert Burns.

In the 19th century, Scotland's architecture led the way in Europe, as epitomized by the development of Edinburgh's New Town *(see pp68–9)*. This bold plan to create a residential centre away from the congested Old Town was begun in 1770, and the design was greatly expanded in 1822 to produce a model of elegance that is outstanding to this day. Among the more famous of those who have occupied these classic Georgian houses was Sir Walter Scott, one of the world's earliest best-selling novelists.

A North Sea oil rig, providing prosperity in the late 20th century

In this same period, known as the Scottish Enlightenment, Thomas Telford excelled in engineering and, ever increasingly, Scots were finding fame and fortune abroad by exploring and developing foreign lands.

The Process of Devolution

For a long time, following the Act of Union, it was clear that England and Scotland were never intended to be equal. The political centre moved to Westminster and accordingly forced any Scot with a talent or aptitude for politics to leave Scotland. This, and an imbalance in the system weighted in favour of English affairs, caused a general feeling of apathy and impotence to take root in the Scottish psyche. Various reforms adjusted the imbalance, but the sense of political estrangement continued to fester.

The Scottish National Party (SNP), founded in 1934, was at first seen by many as too extremist, but they have had continuous representation at Westminster since 1967. The exploration of North Sea oil started in the late 1960s, boosting Scotland's economy and its ability to self govern. In 1997 the Labour government held a referendum in which, by a large majority, the Scots voted for the re-establishment of a Scottish Parliament in 1999. Although its tax-raising powers are restrained, the Scottish Parliament has devolved authority over health, education and local government. In 2007, the SNP's Alex Salmond became the leader of a minority government, and then achieved an outright majority in 2011. The party will be holding a referendum on Scottish independence in September 2014.

SNP demonstrations in 1997, encouraging voters to say "Yes" to Scottish devolution

1914–18 74,000 Scots die in World War I

1931 Economic slump – 65 per cent unemployment in Clyde shipyards

1967 North Sea oil exploration begins

1996 Stone of Destiny *(see p64)* returns to Scotland

1999 Scottish Parliament re-established

2011 SNP win land-slide majority vote and begin a second term in government

1925	1950	1975	2000	2025

1920s Hugh MacDiarmid reinstates Scots as literary language

1945 Alexander Fleming wins Nobel Prize

1934 Scottish National Party founded

Stone of Destiny

2004 Opening of new Scottish Parliament building

2014 Scots vote on Scottish independence

SCOTLAND REGION BY REGION

Scotland at a Glance

Stretching from the rich farmlands of the Borders to a chain of isles only a few degrees south of the Arctic Circle, the Scottish landscape has a diversity without parallel in Britain. The vibrant cities of Glasgow and Edinburgh offer numerous attractions. The northeast is an area rich in wildlife, and as you travel northwest, the land becomes more mountainous and its archaeological treasures more numerous. In the far northwest, in the Western Isles, Scotland's earliest relics stand upon some of the oldest rock on earth.

The Isle of Skye *(see pp156–7)*, renowned for its dramatic scenery, has one of Scotland's most striking coastlines. On the east coast, a stream plunges over Kilt Rock, a cliff of hexagonal basalt columns named after its likeness to the Scottish national dress.

Stornoway

Ullapool

HIGHLAND

Kyle of Lochalsh

Mallaig

Fort William

Oban

ARGYLL AND BUTE

GLASGO (See pp98–1

AYRSH
Ayr

Campbeltown

DUMFRI
AND
GALLOW

Stranraer

The Trossachs *(see pp120–21)* are a beautiful range of hills straddling the border between the Highlands and the Lowlands. At their heart, the forested slopes of Ben Venue rise above the still waters of Loch Achray.

The Burrell Collection *(see pp108–9)*, on the southern outskirts of Glasgow, is a museum of some of the city's greatest art treasures. It is housed in a spacious, glass building opened in 1983.

Culzean Castle *(see pp96–7)* stands on a cliff's edge on the Firth of Clyde, amid an extensive country park. One of the jewels of southern Scotland, Culzean is a magnificent showcase for the work of the Scottish-born architect, Robert Adam (1728–92).

◀ Low cloud in the Tummel Valley, near Pitlochry in the central Highlands

The Cairngorms *(see pp144–5)* cover an area prized for its beauty and diversity of wildlife, though there are also many historical relics to be found, such as this early 18th-century arch at Carrbridge.

SHETLAND ISLANDS

Lerwick

ORKNEY ISLANDS

Kirkwall

Dornoch

Fraserburgh

Elgin

nverness *MORAY*

ABERDEEN-SHIRE

Aberdeen

THE HIGHLANDS AND ISLANDS
(See pp130–67)

ANGUS

Royal Deeside *(see pp148–9)* in the Grampians has been associated with British royalty since Queen Victoria bought Balmoral Castle in 1852.

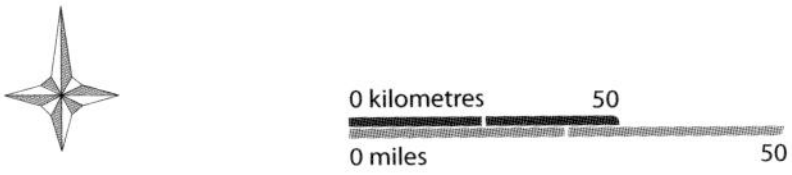

ERTH AND KINROSS

Perth

Dundee

FIFE

ENTRAL SCOTLAND
(See pp114–29)

TIRLING

EDINBURGH
(See pp56–83)

Dunbar

Motherwell

Galashiels

SOUTHERN SCOTLAND
(See pp84–97)

SCOTTISH BORDERS

Dumfries

| 0 kilometres | 50 |
| 0 miles | 50 |

Edinburgh *(see pp56–83)* is the capital of Scotland. Between its medieval castle and The Palace of Holyroodhouse stretches the Royal Mile. Here, the historic sights range from the old Scottish Parliament buildings to the house of John Knox. By contrast, Georgian terraces predominate in the New Town.

EDINBURGH

The historic status of Edinburgh, the capital of Scotland, is beyond question, with ancient buildings scattered across the city, and the seat of Scotland's parliament lying close to the royal residence of The Palace of Holyroodhouse. The range of historical and artistic attractions draws visitors from all over the world.

Castle Rock in Edinburgh has been occupied since around 1,000 BC in the Bronze Age, which is no surprise given its strategic views over the Firth of Forth. The Castle itself houses the city's oldest building, St Margaret's Chapel, dating from the 11th century. A few years after it was built, Margaret's son, King David I, founded Holyrood Abbey a mile to the east. The town that grew along the route between these buildings, the "Royal Mile", became a popular residence of kings, although not until the reign of James IV (1488–1513) did Edinburgh gain the status of Scotland's capital. James built The Palace of Holyroodhouse as a royal residence in 1498 and made the city an administrative centre.

Overcrowding made the Old Town a dirty and difficult place to live, and threw rich and poor together. The construction of a Georgian New Town to the north in the late 1700s gave the wealthy an escape route, but even today Edinburgh has a reputation for social extremes. It has major law courts, is second only to London as a financial centre in the British Isles and houses the Scottish parliament. Bankers and lawyers form the city's establishment, and the most ambitious architectural developments have been for financial sector companies. Yet outlying housing estates, built after World War II, still have echoes of the Old Town poverty.

Edinburgh is best known today as a major tourist centre. There are wonderful museums and galleries to visit, and the city enjoys a widely renowned nightlife. At the height of the International Festival, in August, it is estimated that the population doubles from 400,000 to 800,000.

A juggler performing at the annual arts extravaganza, the Edinburgh Festival

◀ Dugald Stewart Monument and the view over Edinburgh's city centre from Calton Hill

Exploring Edinburgh

The centre of Edinburgh is divided neatly in half by Princes Street, the principal shopping area. To the south lies the Old Town, site of the ancient city, which grew along the route of the Royal Mile, from the Castle Rock in the west to the Palace of Holyroodhouse in the east. At the end of the 18th century, building for the New Town started to the north of Princes Street. The area is still viewed today as a world-class example of Georgian urban architecture, with its elegant façades and broad streets. Princes Street has lots to offer, including shopoing, art galleries, the towering Scott Monument and the landmark Balmoral Hotel clock tower, as well as the city's main train station, Waverley.

North Bridge, opened in 1772 – the main route connecting the Old and New Towns

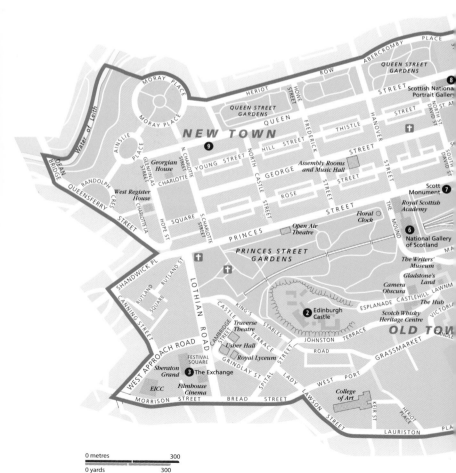

Getting Around

Central Edinburgh is compact, so walking is an excellent way to explore the centre. Other options include a comprehensive bus service and a multitude of black taxis. Avoid exploring the centre by car, because the streets tend to be congested with traffic, and parking may be difficult; car use is discouraged by the local authority. On main routes special lanes are provided for buses, taxis and bicycles, and in the suburbs there is also a good network of bicycle paths. A tram network is under construction and should open in 2014 or 2015.

Sights at a Glance

Historic Areas, Streets and Buildings

1. *The Royal Mile pp60–63*
2. *Edinburgh Castle pp64–5*
3. The Exchange
4. Greyfriars Kirk
9. *New Town pp68–9*
11. Palace of Holyroodhouse
13. Scottish Parliament

Monuments

7. Scott Monument

Landmarks

10. Calton Hill
14. Holyrood Park and Arthur's Seat

Museums, Galleries and Exhibitions

5. National Museum of Scotland
6. Scottish National Gallery
8. Scottish National Portrait Gallery
12. Our Dynamic Earth

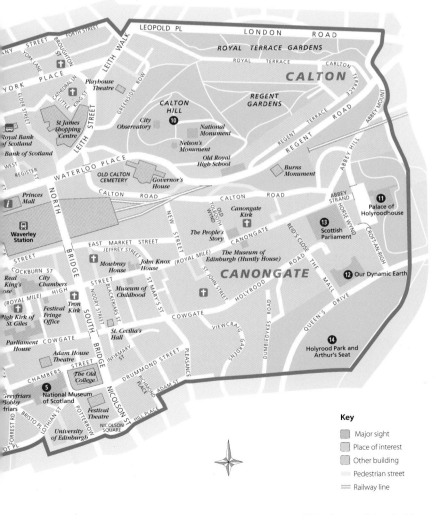

Key

Major sight

Place of interest

Other building

Pedestrian street

Railway line

For additional map symbols *see back flap*

❶ The Royal Mile

The Royal Mile is a stretch of four ancient streets (from Castlehill to Canongate) which formed the main thoroughfare of medieval Edinburgh, linking the castle to the Palace of Holyroodhouse. Confined by the city wall, the "Old Town" grew upwards, with some tenements climbing to 20 floors. It is still possible, among the 66 alleys and closes off the main street, to imagine Edinburgh's medieval past.

Locator Map

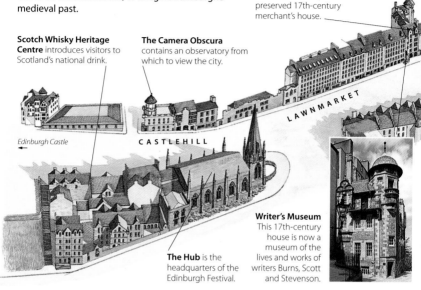

Scotch Whisky Heritage Centre introduces visitors to Scotland's national drink.

The Camera Obscura contains an observatory from which to view the city.

Gladstone's Land is a preserved 17th-century merchant's house.

Edinburgh Castle

CASTLEHILL

LAWNMARKET

The Hub is the headquarters of the Edinburgh Festival.

Writer's Museum This 17th-century house is now a museum of the lives and works of writers Burns, Scott and Stevenson.

🎦 Camera Obscura

Tel (0131) 226 3709. **Open** daily. Apr–Oct: 9:30am–6pm (to 8pm Jul & Aug); Nov–Mar: 10am–6pm. 🅰 🅲

The lower floors of this building date from the early 17th century and were once the home of the Laird of Cockpen. In 1852, Maria Short added

The bedroom of Gladstone's Land

the upper floor, the viewing terrace and the Camera Obscura – a large pinhole camera that pictures life in the city centre as it happens. A marvel at the time, it remains one of Edinburgh's most popular attractions.

🏠 Gladstone's Land (NTS)

477B Lawnmarket. **Tel** (0844) 493 2120. **Open** Apr–Oct: 10am–5pm daily (to 6:30pm Jul & Aug). 🅰 🅱

This restored 17th-century merchant's house provides a window on life in a typical Old Town house before over-crowding drove the rich inhabitants northwest to the Georgian New Town. "Lands", as they were then known, were tall, narrow buildings erected on small plots of land. The six-floor Gladstone's Land was named

after Thomas Gledstanes, the merchant who built it in 1617. The house still has the original arcade booths on the street façade as well as a painted ceiling.

Although the house is extravagantly furnished, it also contains items, such as wooden overshoes that had to be worn in the dirty streets, which serve as a reminder of the less salubrious features that were part of the old city.

A chest in the beautiful Painted Chamber is said to have been given by a Dutch sea captain to a Scottish merchant who saved him from a shipwreck. A similar house, named Morocco's Land (see p63), can be found further to the east, on Canongate.

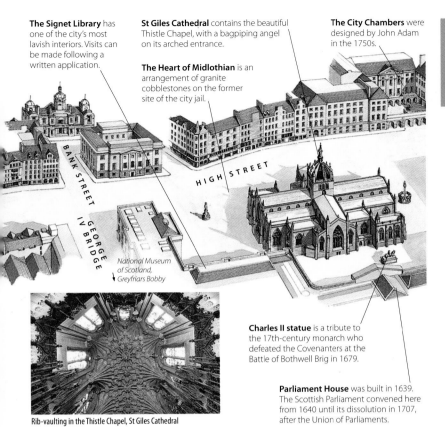

The Signet Library has one of the city's most lavish interiors. Visits can be made following a written application.

St Giles Cathedral contains the beautiful Thistle Chapel, with a bagpiping angel on its arched entrance.

The City Chambers were designed by John Adam in the 1750s.

The Heart of Midlothian is an arrangement of granite cobblestones on the former site of the city jail.

BANK STREET

HIGH STREET

GEORGE IV BRIDGE

National Museum of Scotland,
↓ Greyfriars Bobby

Charles II statue is a tribute to the 17th-century monarch who defeated the Covenanters at the Battle of Bothwell Brig in 1679.

Parliament House was built in 1639. The Scottish Parliament convened here from 1640 until its dissolution in 1707, after the Union of Parliaments.

Rib-vaulting in the Thistle Chapel, St Giles Cathedral

🏛 Writers' Museum

Lady Stair's Close. **Tel** (0131) 529 4901. **Open** 10am–5pm Mon–Sat (Aug: noon–5pm Sun).

This fine Old Town mansion was built in 1622. In the 1720s it was acquired by Elizabeth, Dowager Countess of Stair, and has since been called Lady Stair's House. Its official title reflects its role as a museum of memorabilia from Robert Burns, Sir Walter Scott and Robert Louis Stevenson.

🏛 Parliament House

Parliament Sq, High St. **Tel** (0131) 225 2595. **Open** 9am–4:30pm Mon–Fri. ♿ limited.

This majestic, Italianate building was constructed in the 1630s for the Scottish Parliament. It has been home to the Court of Session and the High Court since the Union of Parliaments (see p49) in 1707. It is well worth seeing, as

much for the spectacle of its many gowned and wigged advocates as for the beautiful stained-glass window in the Great Hall, commemorating the inauguration of the Court of Session by King James V in 1532.

🏛 St Giles Cathedral

Royal Mile. **Tel** (0131) 225 9442. **Open** May–Sep: 9am–7pm Mon–Fri, 9am–5pm Sat, 1–5pm Sun. Oct–Apr: 9am–5pm Mon–Sat, 1–5pm Sun. 📷

Properly known as the High Kirk (church) of Edinburgh, St Giles is popularly known as a cathedral. Though it was twice the seat of a bishop in the 17th century, it was from here that John Knox directed the Scottish Reformation, with its emphasis on

individual worship freed from the authority of bishops. A tablet marks the place where Jenny Geddes, a local market stallholder, scored a victory for the Covenanters in 1637 by hurling her stool at a preacher as he read from an English prayer book.

St Giles's Gothic exterior has a 15th-century tower, the only part to escape heavy renovation in the 1800s. Inside, the Thistle Chapel, with its rib-vaulted ceiling and carved heraldic canopies, honours the knights of the Most Ancient and Most Noble Order of the Thistle. The carved royal pew in the Preston Aisle is used by Queen Elizabeth II when staying in Edinburgh.

Bagpiping angel from the entrance of the cathedral

Exploring Further Down the Royal Mile

The section of the Royal Mile from High Street to Canongate passes two monuments to the Reformation: John Knox's house and the Tron Kirk. The Canongate was once an independent district, owned by the canons of the Abbey of Holyrood, and sections of its south side have been restored. Beyond Morocco's Land, the road stretches for the final half-mile (800 m) to the Palace of Holyroodhouse.

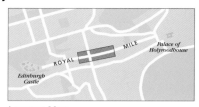

Locator Map

HIGH STREET

SOUTH BRIDGE STREET

The Mercat Cross marks the city centre. It was here that Bonnie Prince Charlie *(see p157)* proclaimed his father king in 1745.

The Tron Kirk was built in 1630 for the Presbyterians who left St Giles Cathedral when it came under the control of the Bishop of Edinburgh.

🎙 John Knox House
45 High St. **Tel** (0131) 556 9579. **Open** 10am–6pm Mon–Sat, noon–6pm Sun (Jul–Aug only). 🚻 limited. 📷 📹 by appointment.

As a leader of the Protestant Reformation and minister at St Giles, John Knox (1513–72) was one of the most important figures in 16th-century Scotland. Ordained as a priest in 1536, Knox later became convinced of the need for religious change. He took part in the Protestant occupation of St Andrews Castle in 1547 and served two years as a galley slave in the French navy as punishment. On release, Knox went to London and Geneva to espouse the Protestant cause, returning to Edinburgh in 1559. This townhouse on the Royal Mile dates from 1450, and it was here that he spent the last few months of his life. Displays tell the story of Knox's life in the context of the political and religious upheavals of his time. The building also incorporates the Scottish Storytelling Centre.

🏛 Museum of Childhood
42 High St. **Tel** (0131) 529 4142. **Open** 10am–5:45pm daily. 🚻 limited.

This museum is not merely a toy collection but an insight into childhood, with all its joys and trials. Founded in 1955 by a city councillor, Patrick Murray (who claimed to eat children for breakfast), it was the world's first museum of childhood. The collection includes medicines, school books, clothing and uniforms, old-fashioned toys and a growing collection of computer games. With its nickelodeon and antique slot machines, this has been called the world's noisiest museum.

🏛 Canongate Tolbooth: The People's Story Museum
163 Canongate. **Tel** (0131) 529 4057. **Open** 10am–5pm Mon–Sat (Sun during Edinburgh Festival).

Edinburgh's social history museum is housed in the Canongate Tolbooth, dating

An 1880 automaton of the Man on the Moon, Museum of Childhood

John Knox House
Dating from 1450, the oldest house in the city was the home of the preacher John Knox during the 1560s. He is said to have died in an upstairs room. It contains relics of his life.

Morocco's Land is a reproduction of a 17th-century tenement house. It takes its name from the statue of a Moor which adorns the entrance.

*Museum of Edinburgh
Canongate Tolbooth*

CANONGATE

Moubray House was to be the signing place of the Act of Union in 1707, until a mob forced the authorities to retreat to another venue.

Museum of Childhood
Though created as a museum for adults by a city councillor who was known to dislike children, this lively musem now attracts flocks of young visitors.

from 1591. With its distinctive clock tower, this was the focal point for life in the Burgh of Canongate. Until the mid-19th century it contained law courts, a jail and the meeting place for the burgh council. It has been a museum since 1954.

Focusing on the lives of ordinary citizens from the late 18th century to the present, it covers subjects such as public health, recreation, trade unions and work. The riots, disease and poverty of the 19th century are also covered, and with subjects as diverse as wartime, football and punk rock, this collection gives a valuable insight into life in Edinburgh.

A prison cell in the Canongate Tolbooth: The People's Story Museum

Life Below the Old Town

Until the 18th century most residents of Edinburgh lived along and beneath the Royal Mile and Cowgate. The old abandoned cellars and basements, which lacked any proper water supply, daylight or ventilation, were once centres of domestic life and industry. Under these conditions, cholera, typhus and smallpox were common. Mary King's Close, under the City Chambers, is one of the most famous of these areas – its inhabitants were all killed by the plague around 1645.

In 2003 many of these closes were opened up for the first time and guided visits are now possible through The Real Mary King's Close: (0845) 070 6244, www.realmarykingsclose.com.

🏛 The Museum of Edinburgh
142–146 Canongate. **Tel** (0131) 529 4143. **Open** 10am–5pm Mon–Sat (noon–5pm Sun during Aug).

Huntly House was built in the early 16th century and damaged in the English raid on Edinburgh in 1544. First used as a family townhouse, it was later divided into apartments but by the 19th century it was little more than a slum. In 1924 the local authority bought the property and opened the museum in 1932. The collection includes exhibits such as Neolithic axe heads, Roman coins, military artifacts and glassware. A section is also dedicated to Field Marshal Earl Haig, Commander-in-Chief of the British Army during World War I.

❷ Edinburgh Castle

Standing upon the basalt core of an extinct volcano, Edinburgh Castle is an assemblage of buildings dating from the 12th to the 20th century, reflecting its changing role as fortress, royal palace, military garrison and state prison. Though there is evidence of Bronze Age occupation of the site, the original fortress was built by the 6th-century Northumbrian king, Edwin, from whom the city takes its name. The castle was a favourite royal residence until the Union of the Crowns *(see p49)* in 1603, after which the king resided in England. After the Union of Parliaments in 1707, the Scottish regalia were walled up in the Palace for over a hundred years. The Palace is now the zealous possessor of the so-called Stone of Destiny, a relic of ancient Scottish kings which was seized by the English and not returned to Scotland until 1996.

The Honours of Scotland
The Crown was restyled by James V of Scotland in 1540.

Governor's House
Complete with Flemish-style crow-stepped gables, this building was constructed for the governor in 1742 and now serves as the Officers' Mess for the castle garrison.

Vaults
This French graffiti, dating from 1780, recalls the many prisoners who were held in the vaults during the wars with France in the 18th and 19th centuries.

KEY

① **Military Prison**

② **The Half Moon Battery** was built in the 1570s as a platform for the artillery defending the eastern wing of the castle.

③ **The Esplanade** is the location of the Military Tattoo *(see p83)*.

Mons Meg

Positioned outside St Margaret's Chapel, this siege gun (or *bombard*) was made in Belgium in 1449 for the Duke of Burgundy, who gave it to his nephew, James II of Scotland. It was used by James against the Douglas family in their stronghold of Threave Castle *(see p93)* on the Dee in 1455, and later by James IV against Norham Castle in England. After exploding during a salute to the Duke of York in 1682, it was kept in the Tower of London until it was returned to Edinburgh in 1829, at Sir Walter Scott's request.

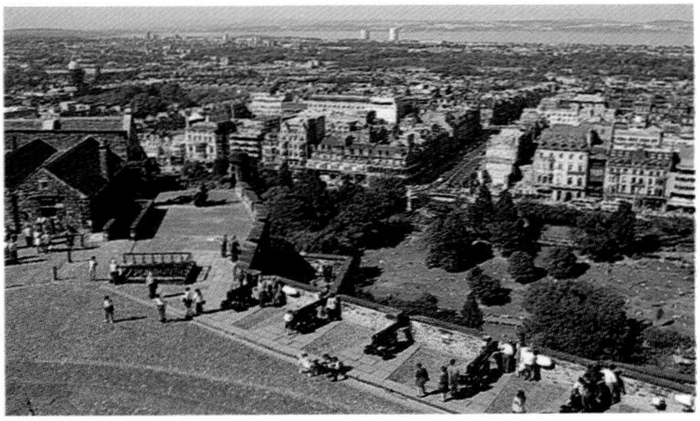

Argyle Battery
These battlements offer a panoramic view north over Princes Street to the city's New Town, the Firth of Forth and Fife.

VISITORS' CHECKLIST

Practical Information
Castle Hill.
Tel (0131) 225 9846.
Open Apr–Sep: 9:30am–6pm daily; Oct–Mar: 9:30am–5pm daily (last admission: 45 mins before closing).
edinburghcastle.gov.uk

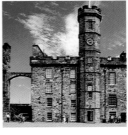

★ Palace
Mary, Queen of Scots, gave birth to James VI in this 15th-century palace, where the Stone of Destiny and Crown Jewels are displayed.

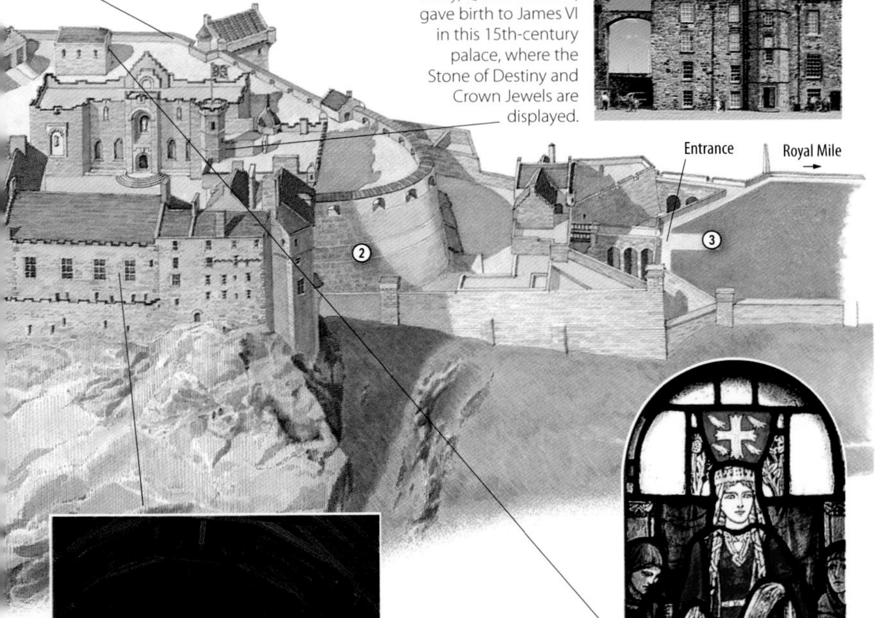

Entrance
Royal Mile
2
3

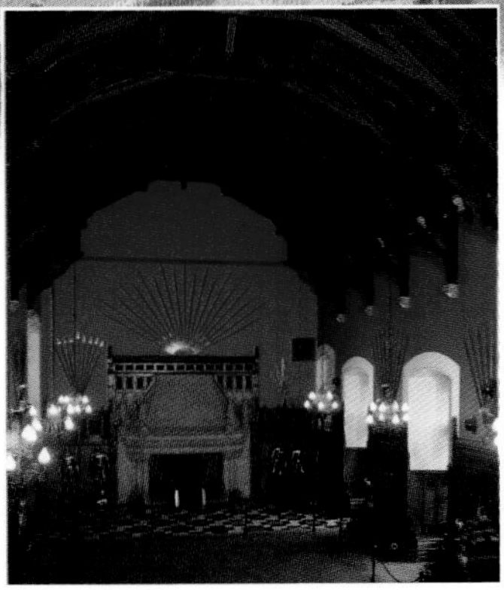

★ Great Hall
With its restored open-timber roof, the hall dates from the 15th century and was the meeting place of the Scottish Parliament until 1639.

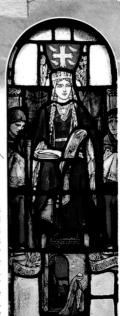

St Margaret's Chapel
This stained glass window depicts Malcolm III's saintly queen, to whom the chapel is dedicated. Probably built by her son, David I, in the early 12th century, the chapel is the castle's oldest existing building.

The Standard Life Building, at the heart of the city's financial centre

❸ The Exchange

Lothian Rd, West Approach Rd and Morrison St.

The Exchange, once an unsightly area, was rejuvenated when Festival Square and the Sheraton Grand Hotel were built in 1985. Three years later the local authority published a plan to promote the area as a financial centre. In 1991 investment management firm Baillie Gifford opened Rutland Court on West Approach Road.

The ambitious **Edinburgh International Conference Centre**, on Morrison Street, was designed by Terry Farrell and opened in 1995. Standard Life opened a headquarters on Lothian Road in 1997, and in 1998, Scottish Widows opened a bold building.

The Exchange has grown into a trendy area, with restaurants, shops and the famous Filmhouse Cinema on Lothian Road (Tel: 0131 228 2688).

🛈 **Edinburgh International Conference Centre**
Tel (0131) 300 3000. ♿
🌐 eicc.co.uk

❹ Greyfriars Kirk

Greyfriars Place. **Tel** (0131) 226 5429.
Open Apr–Oct: 10:30am–4:30pm Mon–Fri, 11am–2pm Sat; Nov–Mar: 1:30–3:30pm Thu. ♿ 📷

Greyfriars Kirk occupies a key role in the history of Scotland, as this is where the National

Covenant was signed in 1638, marking the Protestant stand against the imposition of an episcopal church by King Charles I. Greyfriars was then a relatively new structure, having been completed in 1620 on the site of a Franciscan friary.

Throughout the 17th century, during years of bloodshed and religious persecution, the kirkyard was used as a mass grave for executed Covenanters. The kirk also served as a prison for Covenanter forces captured after the 1679 Battle of Bothwell Brig. The Martyrs' Monument is a sobering reminder of those times. The original kirk building was severely damaged by fire in 1845 and substantially rebuilt. Greyfriars is best known for its association with a dog, Bobby, who kept a vigil by his master's grave from 1858 to 1872. Bobby's statue stands outside Greyfriars Kirk.

A tribute to Greyfriars Bobby

❺ National Museum of Scotland

Chambers St. **Tel** (0300) 123 6789.
Open 10am–5pm Mon–Sun. ♿ 📷
📷 🌐 nms.ac.uk

The National Museum of Scotland comprises two radically different buildings, which stand side by side on Chambers Street. The older of the two is a great Victorian palace of self improvement. Designed by Captain Francis Fowke of the Royal Engineers, the building was completed in 1888, and was substantially restored and expanded in 2011. It includes an eclectic assortment of exhibits, which range from stuffed animals to ethnographic and

technological items, displayed in rooms leading off the large and impressive central hall. There are also absorbing exhibits on world cultures, science and technology, art and design and the natural world.

As far back as the 1950s, recommendations were made that a new facility be built to house Scotland's own historical treasures. Work on a site next door to the Victorian building on Chambers Street started in 1993, and took five years to complete. The result is a contemporary flourish of confident design by architects Gordon Benson and Alan Forsyth, which opened to the public in December 1998.

Described as one of the most important buildings erected in Scotland in the second half of the 20th century, the National Museum of Scotland tells the story of the country, starting with its geology and natural history. It then moves through to the early peoples of Scotland, the centuries when Scotland was a kingdom in its own right, and then on to later industrial developments. Some stunning items are on show, including St Fillan's Crozier, which was said to have been carried at the head of the Scottish army at Bannockburn in 1314, and the famous Lewis Chessman, carved from walrus ivory in the twelfth century. The Monymusk

The 9th-century Monymusk Reliquary on display at Edinburgh's National Museum of Scotland

Reliquary is also on display. Dated to around AD 800, it was a receptacle for the remains of the Christian missionary, St Columba *(see p46)*.

A museum highlight of a different kind is The Tower (www.tower-restaurant.com), a glamorous rooftop restaurant at the highest point of the new building, which appropriately enough uses seasonal Scottish ingredients.

❻ Scottish National Gallery

The Mound. **Tel** (0131) 624 6200.
Open 10am–5pm daily (to 7pm Thu).
📷 ✏ 🖼 🏛
🌐 nationalgalleries.org

One of Scotland's finest art galleries, the Scottish National Gallery is worth visiting for its 15th- to 19th-century British and European paintings alone, though plenty more can be found to delight art-lovers.

Some of the highlights among the Scottish works exhibited are the society portraits by Allan Ramsay and Sir Henry Raeburn, including the latter's *Reverend Robert Walker Skating on Duddingston Loch*, thought to date from the beginning of the 19th century.

The collection of early German pieces contains Gerard David's almost comic-strip treatment of the *Three Legends of St Nicholas*, from around the beginning of the 16th century. Works by Raphael, Titian and Tintoretto accompany other southern European paintings, including Velazquez's *An Old Woman Cooking Eggs*, from 1620.

There is an entire room devoted to *The Seven Sacraments* by Nicholas Poussin, dating from around 1640. Flemish painters represented include Rembrandt, Van Dyck and Rubens, while among the British offerings are important works by Ramsay, Reynolds and Gainsborough.

Rev Robert Walker Skating on Duddingston Loch

❼ Scott Monument

Princes Street Gardens East.
Open Apr–Sep: 10am–7pm Mon–Sat, 10am–6pm Sun; Oct–Mar: 9am–4pm Mon–Sat, 10am–6pm Sun). 📷

Sir Walter Scott (1771–1832) is one of the most important figures in Scottish literature *(see p90)*. Born in Edinburgh, Scott initially pursued a legal career but he soon turned to writing full time as his ballads and historical novels began to bring him success. His works looked back to a time of adventure, honour and chivalry, and did much to promote this image of Scotland abroad.

In addition to being a celebrated novelist, Sir Walter was also a major public figure – he organized the visit of King George IV to Edinburgh in 1822. After Scott's death in 1832, the Monument was constructed on the south side of Princes Street as a tribute to his life and work. This Gothic tower was designed by George Meikle Kemp and reaches a height of 61 m (200 ft). It was completed in 1840, and includes a statue of Sir Walter at its base, sculpted by Sir John Steell. Inside the huge structure, 287 steps give access to the topmost platform. The rewards for those who climb up are great views around the city centre and across the Forth to Fife.

The imposing Gothic heights of the Scott Monument on Princes Street

❽ Scottish National Portrait Gallery

1 Queen St. **Tel** (0131) 556 8921.
Open 10am–5pm daily (to 7pm Thu).
📷 🖼 🌐 nationalgalleries.org

An exhibition on the 12 generations of the Royal House of Stuart, from the time of Robert the Bruce to Queen Anne, is a highlight here. Memorabilia include Mary, Queen of Scots' jewellery and a silver travelling canteen left by Bonnie Prince Charlie *(see p157)* at the Battle of Culloden. The upper gallery has a number of portraits of famous Scots, including a picture of Robert Burns.

The museum was completely refurbished in 2011, in order to display more of the collection.

Van Dyck's *Princess Elizabeth and Princess Anne*, National Portrait Gallery

❾ Street-by-Street: New Town

The first phase of Edinburgh's "New Town" was built in the 18th century, to relieve the congested and unsanitary conditions of the medieval old town. Charlotte Square at the western end formed the climax of this initial phase, and its new architectural concepts were to influence all subsequent phases. Of these, the most magnificent is the Moray Estate, where a linked series of very large houses forms a crescent, an oval and a twelve-sided circus. The walk shown here explores this area of monumental Georgian town planning.

Moray Place
The crowning glory of the Moray Estate, this circus consists of a series of immense houses and apartments, many still inhabited.

Dean Bridge
This was built in 1829 to the design of Thomas Telford. It gives views down to the Water of Leith and upstream to the weirs and old mill buildings of Dean Village.

The Water of Leith is a small river running through a delightful gorge below Dean Bridge. There is a riverside walkway to Stockbridge.

Ainslie Place, an oval pattern of town houses, forms the core of the Moray Estate, linking Randolph Crescent and Moray Place.

| 0 metres | 100 |
| 0 yards | 100 |

Key
— Suggested route

New Town Architects

The driving force behind the creation of the New Town was George Drummond (1687–1766), the city's Provost, or Mayor. James Craig (1744–95) won the overall design competition in 1766. Robert Adam (1728–92) introduced Classical ornamentation to Charlotte Square. Robert Reid (1774–1856) designed Heriot Row and Great King Street, and William Playfair (1790–1857) designed Royal Circus. The monumental development of the Moray Estate was the work of James Gillespie Graham (1776–1855).

Robert Adam

No. 14 was the residence of judge and diarist Lord Cockburn from 1813 to 1843.

★ The Georgian House
No. 7 is owned by the National Trust for Scotland and is open to the public. It has been repainted in its original colours and furnished with appropriate antiques, and is a testament to the lifestyle of the upper sector of 18th-century Edinburgh society.

Locator Map
See Edinburgh Map pp58–9

Bute House is the official residence of the First Minister of the Scottish Parliament.

★ Charlotte Square
The square was built between 1792 and 1811 to provide a series of lavish town houses for the most successful city merchants. Most of the buildings are now used as offices.

No. 39 Castle Street was the home of the writer Sir Walter Scott *(see p90)*.

York Place →

Princes Street Gardens
Princes Street was part of the initial building phase of the New Town. The north side is lined with shops; the gardens to the south lie below the castle.

No. 9 was the home of surgeon Joseph Lister *(see p29)* from 1870 to 1877. He developed methods of preventing infection both during and after surgery.

West Register House was originally St George's Church, designed by Robert Adam.

A view from Edinburgh Castle across the towers and spires of the city to Calton Hill in the distance

⑩ Calton Hill

City centre east, via Waterloo Pl.

Calton Hill, at the east end of Princes Street, has one of Edinburgh's most memorable and baffling landmarks – a half-finished Parthenon. Conceived as the National Monument to the dead of the Napoleonic Wars, building began in 1822 but funds ran out and it was never finished. Public shame over its condition has given way to affection, as attitudes have softened over the last 170 years or so.

Fortunately, the nearby tower commemorating the British victory at Trafalgar was completed, in 1816. Named the **Nelson Monument**, the tower is designed to resemble a telescope standing on its end. It provides a fine vantage point from which to admire the views of Edinburgh and the surrounding area.

The Classical theme continues on top of Calton Hill with the old **City Observatory**, designed by William Playfair in 1818 and based on Athens' Tower of the Winds. At present it is closed to the public, but it's still worth a trip to see the impressive exterior.

Another Classical building, the **Royal High School**, was created during the 1820s on the Regent Road side of Calton Hill. It was designed by Thomas Hamilton, with the Temple of Theseus at Athens in mind. Often cited as a possible home for a Scottish parliament, the building was the focus for the Vigil for Scottish Democracy, which campaigned from 1992 to 1997 for self government. A discreet cairn marking this effort stands a little way east of the National Monument on Calton Hill. The cairn contains several "gift" stones, including one from Auschwitz in memory

of a Scottish missionary who died there.

The final resting place of Thomas Hamilton is the **Old Calton Cemetery**, south of Waterloo Place, which he shares with philosopher David Hume and other celebrated Edinburgh residents.

 Nelson Monument
Tel (0131) 556 2716. **Open** Apr–Sep: 10am–7pm Mon–Sat, noon–5pm Sun; Oct–Mar: 10am–3pm Mon–Sat ♿

⑪ Palace of Holyroodhouse

East end of the Royal Mile. Palace & Queen's Gallery: **Tel** (0131) 556 5100. **Open** Nov–Mar: 9:30am–4:30pm daily; Apr–Oct: 9:30am–6pm daily. ♿ 📷 🅿 🅦 royalcollection.org.uk

Known today as Queen Elizabeth II's official Scottish residence, the Palace of Holyroodhouse was built by James IV in the grounds of an abbey in 1498. It was later the home of James V and his wife, Mary of Guise, and was remodelled in the 1670s for Charles II. The Royal Apartments (including the Throne Room and Royal Dining Room) are used for investitures and for banquets whenever the Queen visits the palace. A chamber in the so-called James V tower is famously associated with the unhappy reign of Mary, Queen of Scots *(see p48)*. It was probably in this room, in 1566, that Mary saw

City Observatory, based on Classical Greek architecture

the murder of her trusted Italian secretary, David Rizzio, authorized by her jealous husband, Lord Darnley. She was six months pregnant when she witnessed the murder, during which Rizzio's body was pierced "with fifty-six wounds".

In the early stages of the Jacobite uprising of 1745 (see p49), the last of the pretenders to the British throne, Charles Edward Stuart (Bonnie Prince Charlie) held court at Holyroodhouse, dazzling Edinburgh society with his magnificent parties.

Tours of the State and Historic apartments are given throughout the day from April to October or take an audio tour; both are included in the price of your ticket. The **Queen's Gallery** displays changing exhibitions from the Royal Collection.

⑫ Our Dynamic Earth

Holyrood Road. **Tel** (0131) 550 7800.
Open Apr–Oct: 10am–5:30pm daily;
Nov–Mar: Wed–Sun. 🅿 🛇 ♿ 🅿
w dynamicearth.co.uk

Our dynamic earth is a permanent exhibition about the planet. Visitors are taken on a journey from the earth's volcanic beginnings to the first appearance of life. Further displays concentrate on the world's climatic zones and dramatic natural phenomena such as tidal waves and earthquakes. State-of-the-art lighting and interactive techniques produce the special effects for 90 minutes of learning and entertainment.

The exhibition building is fronted by a 1,000-seat stone amphitheatre designed by Sir Michael Hopkins, and it incorporates a translucent tented roof. Situated beneath Salisbury Crags, the modern lines of Our Dynamic Earth contrast sharply with the natural landscape.

⑬ Scottish Parliament

Holyrood. **Tel** 0131 348 5200.
Open 10am–5:30pm Mon, Fri & Sat (to 4pm Oct–Mar), 9am–6:30pm Tue–Thu.
🅿 ♿ 🅿 **w** scottish.parliament.uk

Following decades of Scottish calls for more political self-determination, a 1997 referendum on the issue of whether or not to have a Scottish parliament, with some powers devolved from the UK parliament in London, resulted in a majority "yes" vote (see p51). Designed by the late Enric Miralles, known for his work on buildings at the 1992 Barcelona Olympics, the parliament building was opened

James V's arms, Holyroodhouse

in October 2004 by Queen Elizabeth II. It's well worth taking one of the regular tours of this architecturally exciting public building.

⑭ Holyrood Park and Arthur's Seat

Main access via Holyrood Park Rd, Holyrood Rd and Meadowbank Terrace.

Holyrood Park, adjacent to the Palace of Holyroodhouse, covers over 260 hectares (640 acres) of varying terrain, topped by a rugged 250-m (820-ft) hill. Known as Arthur's Seat, the hill is actually a volcano that has

been extinct for 350 million years. The area has been a royal hunting ground since at least the time of King David I, who died in 1153, and a royal park since the 16th century.

The name Holyrood, which means "holy cross", comes from an episode in the life of David I when, in 1128, he was knocked from his horse by a stag while out hunting. Legend has it that a cross appeared miraculously in his hands to ward off the animal and, in thanksgiving, the king founded the Abbey of the Holy Cross, Holyrood Abbey. The name Arthur's Seat is probably a corruption of Archer's Seat, a more prosaic explanation for the name than any link with the legendary King Arthur.

The park has three small lochs. St Margaret's near the Palace is the most romantic, with its resident swans and position under the ruins of St Anthony's Chapel. Dunsapie Loch is the highest, sitting 112 m (367 ft) above sea level under Arthur's Seat. Duddingston Loch, on the south side of the park, is home to a large number of wildfowl.

The **Salisbury Crags** are among the park's most striking features. Their dramatic profile, along with that of Arthur's Seat, can be seen from many kilometres away. The Crags form a parabola of red cliffs that sweep round and up from Holyrood Palace, above a steep supporting hillside. A rough track, called the Radical Road, follows their base.

Arthur's Seat and the Salisbury Crags, looming above the city

Further Afield

Although inextricably linked to the rest of Edinburgh, the inhabitants of Leith insist that they do not live in the city itself. More than just a docks area, Leith has plenty of attractions for the visitor. Close by is the magnificent Royal Botanic Garden. Dean Village offers riverside walks, galleries and antique shops. To the west of the city are the historic Hopetoun House and Linlithgow Palace, to the east is Haddington and a dramatic coastline.

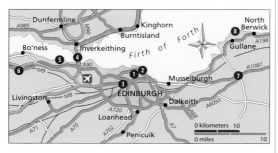

KEY

- ▦ Urban area
- ✈ Airport
- — Intercity train line
- ▬ Motorway (highway)
- ▬ Major road
- ═ Minor road

Sights at a Glance

- ❶ Royal Botanic Garden
- ❷ Leith
- ❸ Dean Village
- ❹ Forth Bridges
- ❺ Hopetoun House
- ❻ Linlithgow Palace
- ❼ Haddington
- ❽ East Lothian Coast

A specimen from the Palm House in the city's Royal Botanic Garden

❶ Royal Botanic Garden

Inverleith Row. **Tel** (0131) 552 7171.
▦ **Open** Feb & Oct: 10am–5pm daily; Mar–Sep: 10am–6pm daily; Nov–Jan: 10am–4pm daily. ♿ 📷 🖥 📷
🌐 **rbge.org.uk**

This magnificent garden lies a short way to the north of the New Town, across the Water of Leith (a river that runs from the Pentland Hills down through Edinburgh and into the Firth of Forth at Leith). The garden is a descendant of a Physic Garden near Holyroodhouse that was created by two doctors in 1670. It was moved to its present location in 1820, and since then has been progressively enlarged and developed. Public access is from the east (well served by buses) and from the west (offering better car parking). The garden benefits from a hill site, giving southerly views across the city.

There is a rock garden in the southeast corner and an indoor exhibition and interpretation display in the northeast corner. There are also extensive greenhouses in traditional and modern architectural styles, offering fascinating hideaways on rainy days. Be sure not to miss the alpine display to the northwest of the greenhouses, or the beautiful and fragrant rhododendron walk.

❷ Leith

Northeast of the city centre, linked by Leith Walk.

Leith is a historic port that has traded for centuries with Scandinavia, the Baltic and Holland, and has always been the port for Edinburgh. It was incorporated into the city in 1920, and now forms a northeastern suburb.

The medieval core of narrow streets and quays includes a number of historic warehouses and merchants' houses dating from the 13th and 14th centuries. There was a great expansion of the docks in the 19th century, and many port buildings date from this period.

Shipbuilding and port activities have diminished, but there has been a renaissance in recent years in the form of conversions of warehouse buildings to offices, residences and, most notably, restaurants and bars. The Shore and Dock Place now has Edinburgh's most dense concentration of seafood bistros and varied restaurants (see pp182–3).

The tourist attractions have been further boosted by the presence of the former British **Royal Yacht Britannia**, which is on display in Leith's Ocean Terminal.

🚢 **Royal Yacht Britannia**
Ocean Terminal, Leith Docks. **Tel** (0131) 555 5566. **Open** daily. 📷 ♿
📷 🌐 **royalyachtbritannia.co.uk**

The British Royal Yacht Britannia, berthed at Leith's Ocean Terminal

❹ Forth Bridges

Lothian. 🚆 🚌 Dalmeny, Inverkeithing.

The small town of South Queensferry is dominated by the two great bridges that span 1.5 km (1 mile) across the River Forth to the town of Inverkeithing. The spectacular rail bridge, the first major steel-built bridge in the world, was opened in 1890 and remains one of the greatest engineering achievements of the late Victorian era. Its massive cantilevered sections are held together by more than eight million rivets, and the painted area adds up to some 55 ha (135 acres). The saying "it's like painting the Forth Bridge" has become a byword for nonstop, repetitive endeavour.

The neighbouring road bridge was the largest suspension bridge outside the US when it was opened in 1964 by Her Majesty Queen Elizabeth II. The two bridges make an impressive contrast, best seen from the promenade at South Queensferry. The town got its name from Queen Margaret (see p65), who reigned with her husband, King Malcolm III, in the 11th century. She used the ferry here on her frequent journeys between Edinburgh and the royal palace at Dunfermline in Fife (see p128). From Queensferry you can take a boat trip down the River Forth to visit the island of Inchcolm with its exceptionally well-preserved 12th-century abbey. A new Forth road-bridge is due for completion in 2016.

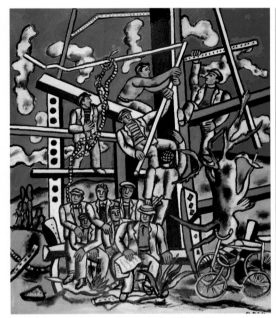

Leger's *The Team at Rest* (1950), Scottish National Gallery of Modern Art

❸ Dean Village

Northwest of the city centre.

This interesting, tranquil area lies in the valley of the Water of Leith, just a few minutes' walk northwest from Charlotte Square (see map p58). A series of water mills along the river have been replaced by attractive buildings of all periods.

Access to Dean Village can be gained by walking down Bell's Brae from Randolph Crescent. A riverside walk threads its way between the historic buildings, crossing the river on a series of footbridges. Upstream from Dean Village the riverside walk leads in a few minutes to a footbridge and a flight of steps giving access to the **Scottish National Gallery of Modern Art** and its sculpture garden. The main access for vehicles, and less energetic pedestrians, is on Belford Road.

Downstream from Dean Village, the riverside walkway passes under the magnificent high level bridge designed by Thomas Telford. It then passes St Bernard's Well before arriving in the urban village of Stockbridge.

Antiques, curios, vintage clothes and jewellery can be found in the shops on the south side of the river in St Stephen Street. The riverside walk continues northeast, close to the Royal Botanic Garden. The city centre is just a short walk away, via Royal Circus and Howe Street.

17th-century stone houses on the historic Bell's Brae

🏛 **Scottish National Gallery of Modern Art**
75 Belford Rd. **Tel** (0131) 624 6200. **Open** daily. 🎨 special exhibitions only. ♿ 🖥 w **nationalgalleries.org**

The huge, cantilevered Forth Rail Bridge, seen from South Queensferry

❺ Hopetoun House

West Lothian. **Tel** (0131) 331 2451.
🚆 Dalmeny then taxi. **Open** Apr– Sep:
10am–5:30pm daily. 🅿️ ♿ 🎁 📷
🌐 **hopetoun.co.uk**

An extensive parkland by the
Firth of Forth, designed in the
style of Versailles, is the setting
for one of Scotland's finest stately
homes. The original house was
completed in 1707 and later
absorbed into William Adam's
grand extension. The dignified,
horseshoe-shaped plan and
lavish interior represent Neo-
Classical 18th-century architecture at its best. The red and
yellow state drawing rooms,
with their Rococo plasterwork
and ornate mantelpieces, are
particularly impressive. A
highlight of a visit here is the
afternoon tea available in the
stables tearoom, with the
option of a champagne tea.

A wooden panel above the main stairs
depicting Hopetoun House

❻ Linlithgow Palace

Kirk Gate, Linlithgow, West Lothian.
Tel (01506) 842896. 🚆 🚌 **Open** Apr–
Sep: 9:30am–5:30pm daily; Oct–Mar:
9:30am–4:30pm daily. 🅿️ ♿ limited.

Standing on the edge of
Linlithgow Loch, the former
royal palace of Linlithgow is one
of the country's most-visited
ruins. It dates back largely to the
building commissioned by
James I in 1425, though some
sections date from the 14th
century. The vast scale of the
building is best seen in the
28-m- (94-ft-) long Great Hall,

Ornate fountain in the ruins of Linlithgow Palace

with its huge fireplace and
windows. The restored fountain
in the courtyard was a wedding
present in 1538 from James V
to his wife, Mary of Guise. His
daughter, Mary, Queen of Scots
(*see p48*), was born at Linlithgow
in 1542.

The adjacent Church of St
Michael is Scotland's largest
pre-Reformation church and
a fine example of the Scottish
Decorated style. Consecrated
in the 13th century, the
church was damaged by the
fire of 1424.

❼ Haddington

East Lothian. ℹ️ Edinburgh & Lothians
(0845) 225 5121.

This attractive county town
is situated about 24 km (15
miles) east of Edinburgh. It
was destroyed on various
occasions during the Wars of
Independence in the 13th–14th
centuries, and again in the 16th
century. The agricultural revolution brought great prosperity,

giving Hadding-
ton many historic
houses, churches,
and other public
buildings. A
programme of
restoration has
helped the town
to retain its char-
acter. The River
Tyne encloses the
town, and there
are attractive
riverside walks
and parkland.
("A walk around
Haddington"
guide is available from
newsagents.) The parish church
of St Mary's, southeast of the
centre, dates from 1462 and is
one of the largest in the area.
Parts of the church have been
rebuilt in later years, having
been destroyed in the siege of
1548. A short way south of the
town lies **Lennoxlove House**,
with its ancient tower house.

🏛️ **Lennoxlove House**
Tel (01620) 828619. **Open** Apr–Oct:
1:30–3:30pm Wed–Thu & Sun. 🅿️ 🎁

❽ East Lothian Coast

ℹ️ Edinburgh Lothians (0845) 225
5121. 🌐 **visitscotland.com**

Stretching east from Musselburgh for some 65 km (40
miles), the coast of East Lothian
offers many opportunities for
beach activities, windsurfing,
golf, viewing seabirds and
coastal walks. The coastline is a
pleasant mixture of beaches,
low cliffs, woodland, golf

The historic and tranquil town of Haddington on the River Tyne

courses and some farmland. Although the A198 and A1 are adjacent to the coast for only short distances, they give easy access to a series of public car parks (a small charge is made in summer) close to the shore. Among these visitor points is Gullane, perhaps the best beach for seaside activities. Yellowcraig, near Dirleton, is another lovely bay, lying about 400 m (440 yds) from the car park. Limetree Walk, near Tyninghame, has the long, east-facing beach of Ravensheugh Sands (a ten-minute walk along a woodland track). Belhaven Bay, just west of Dunbar, is a large beach providing walks along the estuary of the River Tyne. Barns Ness, east of Dunbar, offers a geological nature trail

Tantallon Castle, looking out to the North Sea

and an impressive lighthouse. Skateraw Harbour is an attractive small bay, despite the presence of Torness nuclear power station to the east. Finally, there is another delightful beach to be found at Seacliff, reached by a private toll road that leaves the A198 about 3 km (2 miles) east of North Berwick. This sheltered bay has

spectacular views of the Bass Rock, home to one of the largest gannet (a type of marine bird) colonies in Britain. The rock itself can be seen at close quarters by taking the boat trip from North Berwick harbour (summer only). At the town's **Scottish Seabird Centre** it is possible to control cameras on the rock and on the Island of Fidra, for live coverage of the birdlife without disturbing it. Also of interest along this coastline are the medieval strongholds of **Dirleton Castle** and **Tantallon Castle**, both badly damaged during Cromwell's sieges of 1650. There is a small industrial museum at Prestonpans. North Berwick and Dunbar are towns worthy of a visit.

Scottish Seabird Centre
Tel (01620) 890202. **Open** daily.
seabird.org

Dirleton Castle
Tel (01620) 850330. **Open** daily.

Tantallon Castle
Tel (01620) 892727. **Open** daily.

East Lothian Coastal Walk

For a very attractive longer coast walk, there is easy public access along the footpath from Gullane Bay to North Berwick. The path follows the coastline, crossing grassy heathland between the alternating sandy bays and low rocky headlands, with views of the coast of Fife to the north. There are small islands along the way. The last part of the walk into North Berwick has wonderful views east to the white slopes of the Bass Rock.

Tips for Walkers

Starting point: Gullane Bay.
Finishing point: North Berwick.
Length: 10 km (6 miles); 3 hours.
Getting there: by car; a bus service between Edinburgh and North Berwick gives access to both ends.
Level: easy (one steep section).

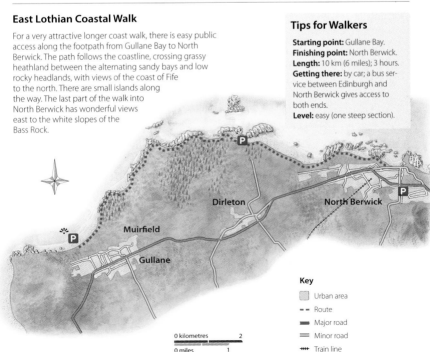

Dirleton

North Berwick

Muirfield

Gullane

Key

Urban area
- - Route
Major road
Minor road
++++ Train line

0 kilometres   2
0 miles   1

For additional map symbols see back flap

SHOPPING IN EDINBURGH

Despite the growth of new out-of-town malls, Princes Street remains one of the top 12 retail centres in the British Isles. With the ancient Castle rising above the gardens along the street's south side, it is a unique and picturesque place to shop. Although many familiar chain stores can be found here, the capital also boasts its very own department store, Jenners, a marvellous institution that has been in business for over 150 years. But there are shopping attractions away from Princes Street, too, including Scotland's best delicatessen (Valvona & Crolla), several excellent wine merchants, a selection of Highland clothing outfitters and an appealing collection of specialist stores.

Department Stores

Princes Street has several good department stores, with **House of Fraser** at the west end being one of the best. Located opposite the Scott Monument, is **Jenners**. Founded on a different site in the late 1830s, it has gained a reputation as Edinburgh's top store. During the Christmas season it is famed for its central atrium housing a Christmas tree. **John Lewis**, belonging to a nationwide chain of stores, is in a contemporary building on Leith Street. The famous **Harvey Nichols** is on St Andrew Square.

Traditional Highland dress and accessories, for sale on the Royal Mile

Clothing

Designer labels for men and women can be found in both Jenners and House of Fraser *(see Department Stores)*. **Corniche** on Jeffrey Street offers more interesting and exciting women's fashion by designers such as Jean-Paul Gaultier and Vivienne Westwood, while **Jane Davidson** is home to a more traditional, chic look. George Street contains a number of women's stores, including **Phase Eight** and **Whistles**. **Cruise** has a dedicated menswear shop. Men can also go to **Thomas Pink**, and **Austin Reed** for smart suits and shirts. The **Schuh** chain has fashionable footwear for men and women. Several shops on the Royal Mile, including **Ragamuffin**, sell interesting knitwear. The Royal Mile also boasts Highland outfitters offering made-to-measure kilts; **Hector Russell** is one of the best. **Kinloch Anderson** in Leith is also a leading example, and the shop has a small display on the history of tartan. Outdoor equipment and waterproof clothing can be found at leading supplier **Graham Tiso**.

Food and Drink

Edinburgh has a reputation as Scotland's top city for eating out, and it matches this status on the shopping front, with some very good food stores. **Valvona & Crolla**, a family-run delicatessen trading since the 1930s, is acknowledged as one of the best of its kind in the UK, let alone Scotland, and stocks good breads and an award-winning Italian wine selection. The **Peckham's** chain is present here, while **Glass & Thompson** is a good deli serving the New Town. For the perfect selection of after-dinner chocolates, try local chocolatier **Coco**. Celebrated cheese-monger **Iain Mellis** started his business in Edinburgh, **MacSweens** are master haggis makers, and **Real Foods** is one of Scotland's longest-established whole-food stores.

Specialist wine merchants include **Peter Green** and **Villeneuve Wines**, as well as chains such as **Oddbins**, while **Cadenheads** supplies rare whiskies. **Justerini &**

Princes Street from the top of Calton Hill

Brooks is the most distinguished wine and spirit merchant in the city centre, and **Henderson Wines** has an extensive selection of wines, beers and malts.

Books and Newspapers

The high-street **Waterstone's** chain has two stores in Princes Street (the west end branch has a fine coffee shop) and a third branch on George Street nearby. There are still some small, friendly independent bookshops, such as the design-focused **Analogue Books**. **The International Newsagents** offers a good selection of foreign newspapers and magazines.

Art, Design and Antiques

Original artworks are on sale at a variety of galleries in the city. **The Scottish Gallery** in the New Town has everything from jewellery for under £100, to pieces by well-known Scottish artists sold at £10,000 or more. The prices at the **Printmakers Workshop** are more affordable, with an innovative range of limited-edition prints for sale, and the **Collective Gallery** offers experimental works. **Inhouse** has some remarkable designer furniture. Browsers looking for antiques should try Victoria Street, St Stephen's Street, the Grassmarket and Causewayside. For large-scale fixtures and fittings, the **Edinburgh**

Architectural Salvage Yard sells everything from Victorian baths to staircases and doors.

Intricately patterned Edinburgh Crystal, a popular souvenir

DIRECTORY

Department Stores

Harvey Nichols
30–34 St Andrew's Sq,
EH2 2AD.
Tel (0131) 524 8388.

House of Fraser
145 Princes St, EH2 4YZ.
Tel (0844) 800 3724.

Jenners
48 Princes St, EH2 2YJ.
Tel (0844) 800 3725.

John Lewis
69 St James Centre, EH1
3SP. **Tel** (0871) 432 1335.

Clothing

Austin Reed
39 George St, EH2 2HN.
Tel (0131) 225 6703.

Corniche
2 Jeffrey St, EH1 1DT.
Tel (0131) 556 3707.

Cruise
94 George St, EH2 3DF.
Tel (0131) 226 3524.

Graham Tiso
41 Commercial St, EH6
6JD. **Tel** (0131) 554 0804.
123–125 Rose St, EH2
3DT. **Tel** (0131) 225 9486.

Hector Russell
137–141 High St, EH1
1SG. **Tel** (0131) 558 1254.

Jane Davidson
52 Thistle St, EH2 1EN.
Tel (0131) 225 3280.

Kinloch Anderson
Commercial St,
EH6 6EY.
Tel (0131) 555 1390.

Phase Eight
47b George St, EH2 2HT.
Tel (0131) 226 4009.

Ragamuffin
278 Canongate, EH8 8AA.
Tel (0131) 557 6007.

Schuh
6/6a Frederick St,
EH2 2HB.
Tel (0131)2200290.

Thomas Pink
32a Castle St, EH2 3HT.
Tel (0131) 225 4264.

Whistles
97 George St, EH2 3ES.
Tel (0131) 226 4398.

Food and Drink

Cadenheads
172 Canongate,
EH8 8BN.
Tel (0131) 556 5864.

Coco Chocolate
174 Bruntsfield Place,
EH10 4ER.
Tel (0131) 228 4526.

Glass & Thompson
2 Dundas St,
EH3 6HZ.
Tel (0131) 557 0909.

Henderson Wines
109 Comiston Rd,
EH10 6AQ.
Tel (0131) 447 8580.

Iain Mellis
30a Victoria St,
EH1 2JW.
Tel (0131) 226 6215.

Justerini & Brooks
14 Alva Street, EH2 4QG.
Tel (0131) 226 4202.

MacSweens
Dryden Rd, Bilston Glen,
Loanhead, EH20 9LZ.
Tel (0131) 440 2555.

Oddbins
Elm Row,
94–96 Brunswick St,
EH7 5HN.
Tel (0131) 556 4075.

Peckham's
49 South Clerk St, EH8
9NZ. **Tel** (0131) 668 3737.

Peter Green
37 Warrender Park Rd,
EH9 1HJ.
Tel (0131) 229 5925.

Real Foods
37 Broughton St, EH1 3JU.
Tel (0131) 557 1911.

Valvona & Crolla
19 Elm Row, EH7 4AA.
Tel (0131) 556 6066.

Villeneuve Wines
49a Broughton St, EH1
3RJ. **Tel** (0131) 558 8441.

Books and Newspapers

Analogue Books
39 Candlemaker Row,
EH1 2BQ.
Tel (0131) 220 0601.

The International Newsagents
351 High St, EH1 1PW.
Tel (0131) 225 4827.

Waterstone's
128 Princes St, EH2 4AD.
Tel (0843) 290 8313.

Art, Design and Antiques

Collective Gallery
28 Cockburn St, EH1 1NY.
Tel (0131) 220 1260.

Edinburgh Architectural Salvage Yard
31 West Bowling Green St,
EH6 5NX.
Tel (0131) 554 7077.

Inhouse
28 Howe St, EH3 6TG.
Tel (0131) 225 2888.

Printmakers Workshop
23 Union St, EH1 3LR.
Tel (0131) 557 2479.

The Scottish Gallery
16 Dundas St, EH3 6HZ.
Tel (0131) 558 1200.

What to Buy

Scotland offers a wide range of goods and souvenirs to tempt its visitors. Most food and drink items can be found in Edinburgh's food stores and off-licences (liquor stores that also stock tobacco). A number of specialist shops in the city sell more unusual Scottish crafts and products, from handcrafted jewellery to clothing, such as tartan kilts and knitwear. Certain areas of Scotland specialize in particular crafts – Orkney is famed for its jewellery, Caithness and Edinburgh for their beautifully engraved glassware.

Edinburgh glass goblet

Amethyst brooch

Celtic brooch

Celtic earrings

Caithness glass paperweight

Scottish glass is beautifully decorated. The Caithness glass factories in Oban, Perth and Wick offer tours to show how delicate patterns are engraved.

Scottish jewellery reflects either the area in which it was made, a culture (such as Celtic) or an artistic movement such as Art Nouveau. The unbroken, intricate patterns and knotwork in the jewellery pictured above symbolize the wish for eternal life.

Dagger ("sgian dubh")

Sporran

Classic Scottish kilt

Tartan tie and scarf

Stag horn is carved into all manner of objects, both functional, as with this ashtray, and decorative.

Scottish tartan originally existed in the form of a *feileadh-mor* (meaning "great plaid" or "great kilt"), an untailored garment draped over the shoulder and around the waist. It was worn by Highlanders in the 15th and 16th centuries. Today, "tartan" refers to the distinctive patterns woven into cloth. Some are based on the designs of centuries past.

Scottish textiles vary greatly, but the most distinctive include chunky woollens from the islands; smart tweeds, such as Harris tweed with its fine-toothed check; softest cashmere, used to make sweaters, cardigans and scarves; and fluffy sheepskin rugs.

Cable-knit sweater

Tweed jacket

Packaged Foods

Food is a popular and accessible form of souvenir or gift to purchase during a visit to Scotland. Teatime is a favourite meal with the Scottish, offering such treats as Dundee cake, butter shortbread, Abernethy biscuits, Scotch pancakes and parlies (ginger cookies). Oatcakes are the traditional accompaniment to cheese in Scotland, although they also complement pâté and sweet toppings such as jam or honey. They are also delicious toasted and served with plenty of butter.

Vegetarian haggis    Original haggis

Haggis, the most famous of Scottish foods, traditionally consists of sheep's offal and oatmeal. It is now also available in vegetarian, venison and whisky-laced varieties.

Traditional pure butter shortbread

Oatcakes

Scotch Abernethy biscuits

Fudge is an extremely sweet confectionary made almost entirely of sugar and condensed milk. There are many different flavours, from vanilla to rum and raisin, walnut, chocolate and whisky.

Dairy vanilla fudge   LochRanza whisky fudge

Bottled Drinks

Home to a large number of distilleries and breweries, Scotland is perhaps associated most with its alcoholic beverages. There is certainly a good range on sale, including locally brewed beers and ales, many varieties of Scotch whisky (see pp36–7) and an assortment of spirits and liqueurs, such as Drambuie and Glayva. But Scotland is also famed for its mountain spring water, which is sold still, fizzy (carbonated) or flavoured with fruits such as peach or melon.

Historic Scottish ales

Beers and ales figure prominently in the drink produced in Scotland. Traditionally served by the pint in pubs, they can also be purchased in bottles. Alternative choices include fruit ales and heather ales, brewed using ancient Highland recipes.

Highland spring water

Whisky is undoubtedly the most famous of all Scottish spirits. There are a huge number of whiskies from which to choose, each with a unique taste (see pp36–7). Drambuie is a variation on a theme, being a whisky-based, herb flavoured liqueur.

Drambuie   Glenfiddich   LochRanza   Glen Ord   Bell's

ENTERTAINMENT IN EDINBURGH

Although the majority of people associate entertainment in Edinburgh with the festivals that take place in August, the city also benefits from its status as the Scottish capital by acting as a centre for drama, dance and music. The Filmhouse is an important venue on the arthouse cinema circuit and some argue that Edinburgh's nightclubs are as good as those in Glasgow these days. Many bars offer an excellent range of Scotch whiskies and cask ales, while the expansion of the café-bar scene in the last few years means it is now possible to find a decent cup of coffee later on in the evening. Edinburgh is home to Scotland's national rugby union stadium, Murrayfield, host to international matches.

Entertainment Guides

The twice-monthly arts and entertainments magazine, *The List* (www.list.co.uk), covers events in both Edinburgh and Glasgow. A similar publication, *The Skinny* (www.theskinny. co.uk), is available free from restaurants and clubs.

Theatre and Dance

Edinburgh's **The King's Theatre** hosts pantomimes and perfor-mances by touring companies. Run by the same organization that manages Edinburgh Festival Theatre *(see Classical Music and Opera)*, it focuses on contemporary dance and ballet, but there are children's shows and music hall-style perform-ances too. **Edinburgh Playhouse** often hosts internationally successful musicals, such as "Mamma Mia!" and "Chicago", while **The Traverse** is home to more experimental work and has helped launch the careers

Edinburgh Festival Theatre, venue for dance, classical music and opera

of young Scottish playwrights. **The Royal Lyceum** opts for a repertory of well-known plays and adaptations, but showcases some new work too. Edinburgh University's theatre company stages shows at **Bedlam.**

Classical Music and Opera

Visits from the Glasgow-based Scottish Opera and the Royal Scottish National Orchestra are hosted at the glass-fronted **Edinburgh Festival Theatre,** which opened in 1994. Edinburgh is home to the world-renowned Scottish Chamber Orchestra, which performs at the **Queen's Hall. Usher Hall** is another key venue for classical music, with regular appearances by the Scottish Symphony Orchestra. Smaller venues host recitals, such as Edinburgh University's **Reid Concert Hall** and **St Cecilia's Hall. St Giles Cathedral** hosts classical concerts by small groups.

Rock, Jazz and World Music

For major rock concerts, Murrayfield Stadium *(see Sports)* is sometimes called into use. Edinburgh Playhouse *(see Theatre and Dance)* has also played host to major pop stars, as have **Cabaret Voltaire** and **The Liquid Room**. The city has an eclectic nightclub scene, and intimate sessions – including jazz and world music – often take place at clubs *(see Café-bars, Bars and Clubs)*. The Queen's Hall *(see Classical Music and Opera)* also hosts smaller shows. Folk and jazz musicians appear at the **The Tron** and **Henry's Cellar Bar**, respectively.

Some pubs have resident folk musicians and jazz bands; check *The List* magazine for details. **The Assembly Rooms** hosts *ceilidhs* (traditional Highland dance evenings).

Cinema

Edinburgh, like other cities, has seen a move to multiplex cinemas. However, **Cineworld** and **Odeon Multiplex** are quite far from the centre; the **Odeon Edinburgh** is the most central. A few minutes from Princes Street is the **OMNI** leisure centre, with a 12-screen cinema village. **The Dominion** is an old-fashioned affair, while **The Cameo** shows offbeat modern classics. **The Filmhouse** is the arthouse movie theatre, and centre for the International Film Festival.

EDINBURGH INTERNATIONAL FILM FESTIVAL

Logo for the annual Film Festival

The ornate, colourful interior of The King's Theatre, opened in 1906

Opening ceremony of a Five Nations rugby union match at Murrayfield

Sports

The impressive **Murrayfield Stadium** is the national centre for Scottish rugby and international matches are played from late January to March. There are two association football (soccer) sides, **Heart of Midlothian** in the west and **Hibernian** in Leith. **Meadowbank Stadium and Sports Centre** hosts league basketball and a range of athletics events throughout the summer.

Café-bars, Bars and Clubs

For good cask ales and an extensive selection of single-malt Scotch whiskies, try **The Café Royal**, **Bennet's**, **The Cumberland** or **The Bow Bar**.
   The George Street area is the obvious centre for café-bars. Some serve good food but are predominantly night-time spots, such as **Indigo Yard**, the **Voodoo Rooms**, **Tigerlily** and the **Opal Lounge**. The latter two are considered particularly stylish choices. Other's, including **Lola Lo**, are late-night clubs dedicated to drinking and dancing, but most Edinburgh clubs are based on or around the Cowgate, such as the perennially popular multi-level **Espionage** club.

DIRECTORY

Theatre and Dance

Bedlam
11b Bristow Place, EH1 1E2. **Tel** (0131) 225 9893.

Edinburgh Playhouse
18–22 Greenside Place, EH1 3AA.
Tel (844) 871 3014.

The King's Theatre
2 Leven St, EH3 9LQ.
Tel (0131) 529 6000.

The Royal Lyceum
30b Grindlay St, EH3 9AX.
Tel (0131) 248 4848.

The Traverse
10 Cambridge St, EH1 2ED. **Tel** (0131) 228 3223.

Classical Music and Opera

Edinburgh Festival Theatre
13–29 Nicolson St, EH8 9FT.
Tel (0131) 529 6000.

The Queen's Hall
85–89 Clerk St, EH8 9JG.
Tel (0131) 668 2019.

Reid Concert Hall
Bristo Sq, EH8 9AG.
Tel (0131) 651 3212.

St Cecilia's Hall
Niddry St, EH1 1LG.
Tel (0131) 668 2019.

St Giles Cathedral
High St, EH1 1RE.
Tel (0131) 225 9442.

Usher Hall
Lothian Road, EH1 2EA.
Tel (0131) 228 8616.

Rock, Jazz and World Music

Assembly Rooms
54 George St, EH2 2LR.
Tel (0131) 220 4348.

Cabaret Voltaire
36 Blair St, EH1 1QR.
Tel (0131) 247 4704.

Henry's Cellar Bar
8–16a Morrison St, EH3 8BJ. **Tel** (0131) 629 4101.

The Liquid Room
9c Victoria St, EH1 2HE.
Tel (0131) 225 2564.

The Tron
9 Hunter Sq, EH1 1QW.
Tel (0131) 225 3784.

Cinema

The Cameo
38 Home St, EH3 9LZ.
Tel (0871) 902 5723.

Cineworld
130 Dundee Street, EH1 1AF. **Tel** (0871) 200 2000.

The Dominion
18 Newbattle Terrace, EH10 4RT.
Tel (0131) 447 4771.

Edinburgh Odeon
118 Lothian Road, EH3 3BG.
Tel (0871) 224 4007.

The Filmhouse
88 Lothian Rd, EH3 9BZ.
Tel (0131) 228 2688.

Odeon Multiplex
120 Wester Hailes Rd, EH14 1SW.
Tel (0871) 224 4007.

OMNI Edinburgh
Greenside Place, EH1 3BN.
Tel (0871) 224 0240.

Sports

Heart of Midlothian
Tynecastle Stadium, Gorgie Rd, EH11 2NL.
Tel (0871) 663 1874.

Hibernian Football Club Ltd
12 Albion Place, EH7 5QG.
Tel (0131) 661 2159.

Meadowbank Stadium and Sports Centre
139 London Rd, EH7 6AE.
Tel (0131) 661 5351.

Murrayfield Stadium
Murrayfield, EH12 5PJ.
Tel (0131) 346 5000.

Café-bars, Bars and Clubs

Bennet's
8 Leven St, EH3 9LG.
Tel (0131) 229 5143.

The Bow Bar
80 West Bow, EH1 2HH.
Tel (0131) 226 7667.

The Café Royal
19 W Register St, EH2 2AA.
Tel (0131) 556 1884.

The Cumberland
1–3 Cumberland St, EH3 6RT. **Tel** (0131) 558 3134.

Espionage
4 India Buildings, Victoria St, EH1 2EX.
Tel (0131) 477 7007.

Indigo Yard
7 Charlotte Lane, EH2 4QZ.
Tel (0131) 220 5603.

Lola Lo
43b Frederick St, EH2 1EP.
Tel (0131) 226 2224.

Opal Lounge
51a George Street, EH2 2HT.
Tel (0131) 226 2275.

Tigerlily
125 George St, EH2 4JN.
Tel (0131) 225 5005.

Voodoo Rooms
19a West Register St, EH2 2AA.
Tel (0131) 556 7060.

The Edinburgh Festival

August in Edinburgh means "the Festival", one of the world's premier arts jamborees, covering drama, dance, opera, music and ballet. The more eclectic "Fringe" developed in parallel with the official event, but has now exceeded it in terms of size. Both have been going strong for over 60 years, as has the Edinburgh International Film Festival, which is held in June and has become a renowned festival in its own right. The British Army contributes with the Military Tattoo, and the Edinburgh Book Festival and Jazz & Blues Festival are also staged in August. A total of half a million people visit these events.

Entrance to the Fringe information office, located on the Royal Mile

Edinburgh International Festival

As a cultural antidote to the austerity of post-war Europe, where many cities were devastated and food rationing was common even in the victorious countries, Edinburgh held its first arts festival in 1947. Over the years it grew in scope and prestige, and it is now one of the top events in the world calendar of performing arts.

It boasts a strong programme of classical music, traditional ballet, contemporary dance, opera and drama, and is held in major venues across the city (see Directory p81).

The grand finale of the International Festival is a breathtaking spectacle, with some 250,000 crowding into the city centre to see a magnificent fireworks display based at the Castle. The lucky few with tickets for the Ross Bandstand in Princes Street Gardens also experience the fireworks concert by the Scottish Chamber Orchestra.

The Fringe

The Fringe started with a few performances providing an alternative to the official events of the International Festival, in the first year it was staged. A decade later, coming to Edinburgh to appear "on the Fringe" was an established pastime for amateurs, student drama companies or anyone else. All that was needed was a space to perform in the city in August. This haphazard approach has long since given way to a more formal one, with an administrative body running the Fringe and, in recent years, a core of professionally-run venues attracting the bulk of the Fringe audiences. The Assembly Rooms in George Street (see Directory p81) and the Pleasance Theatre in The Pleasance host shows by television celebrities whose stand-up comedy or cabaret fails to fit the International Festival format.

The original vibrancy of the Fringe still exists, and in church halls and other odd venues across Edinburgh, including the city's streets, Fringe-goers can find everything from musicals performed by school children to experimental adaptations of Kafka's works.

Enjoying the August sun and street entertainment on the Royal Mile

Edinburgh International Film Festival

Dating from 1947, the Edinburgh International Film Festival was one of the world's first international film festivals, and is held in June. Although it started with a focus on documentary cinema, it soon began to widen and include arthouse and popular movies.

The Festival invented "the retrospective" as a means of studying a film-maker's work. It has seen premieres by such noted directors as Woody Allen and Steven Spielberg. Since its 1995 relaunch, the Festival has been broken down into four

Crowds throng around the colourful Fringe street performers

The Military Tattoo at Edinburgh Castle, with an audience of thousands

main sections. There is a showcase for young British talent, a world premieres section, a film study category, and a major retrospective.

Although the showings are screened primarily at The Filmhouse on Lothian Road, every city centre cinema now takes part in the festival to some extent *(see Directory p81 for details of all the cinemas).*

Edinburgh Military Tattoo

The enduring popularity of the Military Tattoo never fails to surprise some people, or to charm others. It has been running since 1950, when the British Army decided to contribute to Edinburgh's August events with displays of martial prowess and music on the picturesque Castle Esplanade.

Temporary stands are built on the Esplanade each summer in preparation for the 200,000 visitors who watch the Tattoo over its three-week run. This enormous spectacle heralds the approach of the other, assorted August arts festivals. Marching bands and musicians from the

A painted street performer showing his skill at staying as still as a statue

armed forces of other countries are invited every year to enhance the show. For many, the highlight of the Tattoo is a solo piper playing a haunting pibroch lament *(see p34)* from the Castle battlements.

A temporary marquee selling books at the Edinburgh Book Festival

Edinburgh Book Festival

Every August, a mini-village of marquees is erected in the beautiful Georgian surroundings of Charlotte Square Gardens in the city centre. This temporary village plays host to two weeks of book-related events and talks by a variety of writers, from novelists and poets to those who specialize in cook books or children's fiction. Scottish authors are always well represented.

Originally held every other year, the Book Festival became so popular that since 1998 it has been an annual event coinciding with the other festivals.

Edinburgh Jazz & Blues Festival

For around ten days in early August a selection of international jazz performers comes to Edinburgh to give concerts, accompanied by Scotland's principal jazz musicians.

Most venues are dotted around Edinburgh's University district including the main venue Queen's Hall *(see p81).* Only the Hub *(see below)* sells tickets to all events. There is also a free, open-air Mardi Gras day in the Grassmarket, in the Old Town, on the opening Saturday. The Blues element is also very successful, attracting many UK and American performers.

DIRECTORY

Edinburgh International Festival
The Hub, Edinburgh's Festival Centre, Castlehill, Royal Mile, EH1 2NE.
Tel (0131) 473 2099 (info).
Tel (0131) 473 2000 (booking).
W eif.co.uk

Edinburgh International Film Festival
88 Lothian Rd, EH3 9BZ.
Tel (0131) 228 2688.
W edfilmfest.org.uk

Edinburgh International Book Festival
5a Charlotte Sq, EH2 4DR.
Tel (0845) 373 5888.
W edbookfest.co.uk

Edinburgh Jazz and Blues Festival
Assembly Direct, 89 Giles St, EH6 6BZ.
Tel (0131) 467 5200.
Tel Box office: (0131) 473 2000.
W edinburghjazzfestival.com

The Fringe
The Fringe Office, 180 High St, EH1 1QS.
Tel (0131) 226 0026.
W edfringe.com

Military Tattoo
Edinburgh Tattoo, 32 Market St, EH1 1QB.
Tel (0131) 225 1188.
W edintattoo.co.uk

SOUTHERN SCOTLAND

Southern Scotland is a blend of attractive landscapes and historic houses, castles and abbeys. Sadly, many of these ancient buildings exist only in fortified or ruined form due to the frontier wars that dated from the late 13th century. The rounded hills of the Scottish Borders and the more rugged peaks of Dumfries & Galloway bore the brunt of this fierce conflict between Scotland and England.

In 1296 Scotland committed itself to the Wars of Independence against the English, and it was Southern Scotland that suffered the most. The strife caused by the many battles lasted for three centuries, as first Scottish self-determination, and then alliances with France, led to strained relations between Scotland and its southern neighbour, England. Dryburgh, one of the area's magnificent 12th-century abbeys, was burned twice, first by the English in 1322 and then again in 1544.

The virtual independence of the Borders district brought further conflict. Powerful families had operated under local laws set in place since the mid-12th century, and when Scottish kings were not fighting the English, they led raids into the Border country to try and bring it back under central control. Over the years, some of the great dramas of Scottish history have been played out in the South. Robert the Bruce's guerrilla army defeated an English force at Glen Trool in 1307, but Flodden, near Coldstream, was the scene of the country's worst military reverse in 1513, when King James IV of Scotland and thousands of his men fell in battle. Today, the quiet countryside around the Borders market towns, and the beautiful mountain scenery in Dumfries & Galloway, seem to belie such violent history. The area is now known for its manufacturing of textiles and for promoting its literary associations, as Sir Walter Scott lived at Abbotsford, near St Boswells. But it is the ruins of the great Border abbeys, castles and battlegrounds that serve as a reminder of Southern Scotland's turbulent past.

Fishing in the tranquil waters of the River Tweed, which weaves its way through the Border country

◀ Ruins of 12th-century Jedburgh Abbey, one of many abbeys destroyed during conflicts with England

Exploring Southern Scotland

Southern Scotland has a variety of landscapes and small towns of great character, but the region is often overlooked by visitors keen to reach Edinburgh, Glasgow or the Highlands. The hills around Glen Trool in Dumfries and Galloway are beautiful and dramatic while, further east, the Border hills are less rugged but offer some classic panoramas such as Scott's View, near Melrose. The Ayrshire coast has a string of holiday resorts; the Solway Firth coast is fine touring country, quiet and picturesque; and St Abb's Head in the east is one of Scotland's most important wildlife reserves.

The Gothic abbey church at Melrose, once one of the richest abbeys in Scotland

Getting Around

Travelling east to west and vice versa can be problematic as all the main routes run north–south from Edinburgh and Glasgow to England. There are rural bus services but these tend to be infrequent and slow. Rail links down the east coast from Edinburgh, and from Glasgow to Ayrshire, are good, and there is also a train service from Glasgow to Stranraer, the ferry port for Northern Ireland. Exploring scenic areas away from the coasts is best done by car.

Key

═══ Motorway (highway)
─── Major road
─── Minor road
═══ Other road
─── Scenic route
─●─ Main line railway
─── Minor railway
△ Summit

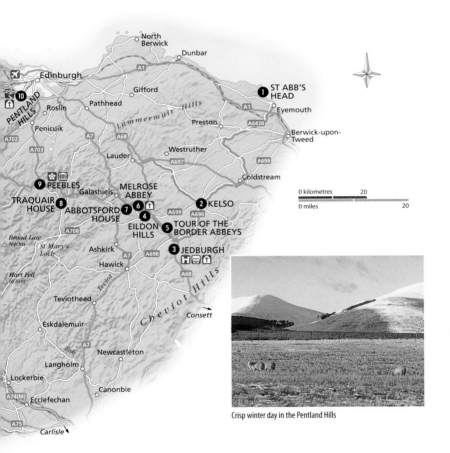

Crisp winter day in the Pentland Hills

Sights at a Glance

1. St Abb's Head
2. Kelso
3. Jedburgh
4. Eildon Hills
5. Melrose Abbey
6. Abbotsford House
7. Traquair House
8. Peebles
9. Pentland Hills

11. New Lanark
12. Dumfries House
13. Drumlanrig Castle
14. Threave Castle
15. Burns Heritage Trail
16. Caerlaverock Castle
17. Kirkcudbright
18. Whithorn
19. Galloway Forest Park

20. The Rhinns of Galloway
21. *Culzean Castle pp96–7*

Tour

5. Tour of the Border Abbeys

For additional map symbols *see back flap*

The shattered crags and cliffs of St Abb's Head

❶ St Abb's Head

The Scottish Borders. 🚂 Berwick-upon-Tweed. 🚌 from Edinburgh. **Tel** (01890) 771672. **Open** Easter–Oct: 10am–5pm daily.

The jagged cliffs of St Abb's Head, rising 91 m (300 ft) from the North Sea, offer a spectacular view of thousands of seabirds wheeling and diving below. During the May to June breeding season, this nature reserve becomes an important site for more than 50,000 cliff-nesting sea birds, including fulmars, guillemots, kittiwakes and puffins.

St Abb's village has one of the few unspoiled working harbours on Scotland's east coast. A clifftop trail begins at the visitors' centre, where displays include identification boards and a touch table where young visitors can get to grips with wings and feathers.

❷ Kelso

The Scottish Borders. 🏔 6,500. 🚌 **i** The Square, (01573) 228 055; open Apr–Oct. 🌐 **visitscottishborders.com**

Kelso has a charming centre, with a cobbled square surrounded by Georgian and Victorian buildings. Nearby **Kelso Race Course** holds regular horse races. The focus of the town, however, is the ruin of the 12th-century **abbey**. This was the oldest and wealthiest of the four Border Abbeys founded by David I, but it suffered from wars with England and was severely

damaged in 1545. **Floors Castle** on the northern edge of Kelso was designed by William Adam in the 1720s, and reworked by William Playfair after 1837.

i **Kelso Race Course**
Tel (01668) 280800. ♿ ♿

🏰 **Floors Castle**
Tel (01573) 223333. **Open** Mar–Oct: daily. ♿ ♿ 📷

❸ Jedburgh

The Scottish Borders. 🏔 4,100. 🚌 **i** Murray's Green (01835) 863170. 🌐 **visitscottishborders.com**

The town is home to the mock-medieval **Jedburgh Castle, Jail and Museum**. Built in the 1820s and once the local jail, it now serves as a museum with some good displays on the area's history and life in a 19th-century prison.

Built around 1500, **Mary, Queen of Scots' House** is so-called due to a visit by the queen in 1566. The house was converted into a general

Jedburgh's medieval Abbey church at the centre of the attractive town

museum in the 1930s, and in 1987 (on the 400th anniversary of Mary's execution) it became a centre dedicated to telling her life story. Exhibits include a copy of her death mask.

Jedburgh Abbey is one of the great quartet of 12th-century Border Abbeys, along with Dryburgh, Kelso and Melrose. The Abbey church has some interesting features including a rose window.

🏰 **Jedburgh Castle, Jail and Museum**
Tel (01835) 863254. **Open** Easter–Oct: daily (Sun: pm). 📷

🏛 **Mary, Queen of Scots' House**
Tel (01835) 863331. **Open** Mar–Nov: daily. 📷

🏰 **Jedburgh Abbey**
Tel (01835) 863925. **Open** daily. 📷

A picturesque view of the Eildon Hills in late summer sunshine

❹ Eildon Hills

The Scottish Borders. 🚌 **i** Melrose (01896) 822 283.

The three peaks of the Eildon Hills dominate the central Borders landscape. Mid Hill is the tallest at 422 m (1,385 ft), while North Hill once had a Bronze Age hill fort dating from before 500 BC, and later a Roman fort. In this part of the country the most celebrated name is Sir Walter Scott (see p90), who had a particular affection for these hills. A panorama of the Eildons called **Scott's View** lies just east of Melrose, near Dryburgh Abbey, and this is the best location to see the hills' position as they rise above the Tweed Valley.

❺ Tour of the Border Abbeys

The Scottish Borders are scattered with the ruins of ancient buildings destroyed in conflicts between England and Scotland. Most poignant of all are the Border Abbeys, whose magnificent architecture bears witness to their former spiritual and political power. Founded during the 12th-century reign of David I, the abbeys were destroyed by Henry VIII in 1545. This tour takes in the abbeys and some other sights.

② **Kelso Abbey** The largest of the four Border Abbeys, Kelso was founded in 1128 and took 84 years to complete.

⑥ **Melrose Abbey**
Once one of the richest abbeys in Scotland, it is here that Robert the Bruce's heart is buried (see p90).

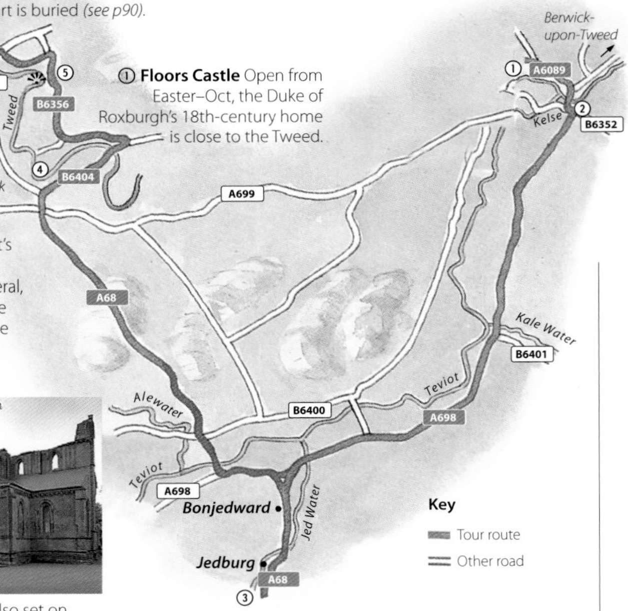

① **Floors Castle** Open from Easter–Oct, the Duke of Roxburgh's 18th-century home is close to the Tweed.

⑤ **Scott's View**
This was Sir Walter Scott's favourite view of the Borders. During his funeral, the hearse stopped here briefly as Scott had done so often in life.

④ **Dryburgh Abbey** Also set on the bank of the Tweed, Dryburgh is considered the most evocative monastic ruin in Scotland. Sir Walter Scott is buried here.

Key

■■ Tour route
═══ Other road

0 kilometres   5
0 miles   3

Tips for Drivers

Length: 50 km (32 miles).
Stopping-off points: Leave the car at Dryburgh Abbey and take a walk northwards to the foot bridge over the River Tweed.

③ **Jedburgh Abbey** The abbey was established in 1138, though fragments of 9th-century Celtic stonework survive from an earlier structure. The visitors' centre illustrates the lives of Augustinian monks.

For additional map symbols see back flap

The ruins of Melrose Abbey, viewed from the southwest

❻ Melrose Abbey

Melrose, The Scottish Borders.
Tel (01896) 822562. **Open** Apr–Sep:
9:30am–5:30pm daily; Oct–Mar:
9:30am–4:30pm daily. 🅿️ ♿ limited.
Ⓦ **historic-scotland.gov.uk**

The rose-pink ruins of this beautiful Border abbey bear testimony to the devastation of successive English invasions. Built by David I in 1136 for Cistercian monks, and also to replace a 7th-century monastery, Melrose was repeatedly ransacked by English armies, most notably in 1322 and 1385. The final blow, from which none of the abbeys recovered, came in 1545, when Henry VIII of England implemented his destructive Scottish policy

known as the "Rough Wooing". This resulted from the failure of the Scots to ratify a marriage treaty between Henry VIII's son and the infant Mary, Queen of Scots. What remains of the abbey are the outlines of cloisters, the kitchen, monastic buildings and the shell of the abbey church, with its soaring east window and profusion of medieval carvings. The decorations of the south exterior wall include a gargoyle shaped like a pig playing the bagpipes and several animated figures, including a cook with his ladle.

An embalmed heart, found here in 1920, is probably that of Robert the Bruce, the abbey's chief benefactor, who had decreed that his heart be

taken on a crusade to the Holy Land. It was returned to Melrose Abbey after its bearer, Sir James Douglas, was killed in Spain.

❼ Abbotsford House

Galashiels, The Scottish Borders.
Tel (01896) 752043. 🚌 from Galashiels.
Open Jul–Sep: 10am–5pm daily; Oct–late Dec: 10am–4pm daily. 🅿️ 🎒 📷 📶
♿ limited. Ⓦ **scottsabbotsford. co.uk**

Few houses bear the stamp of their creator so intimately as Abbotsford House, the home of Sir Walter Scott for the final 20 years of his life. He bought a farm here in 1811, known as Clarteyhole ("dirty hole" in Borders Scots), though he soon renamed it Abbotsford, in memory of the monks of Melrose Abbey who used to cross the River Tweed nearby. He later demolished the house to make way for the turreted building we see today, its construction funded by the sales of his popular novels.

Scott's library contains over 9,000 rare books and his collections of historic relics reflect his passion for the heroic past. The walls display an extensive collection of arms and armour, including Rob Roy's broadsword *(see p121)*. Stuart mementoes include one of many crucifixes belonging to Mary, Queen of Scots and a lock of Bonnie Prince Charlie's hair. The study in which Scott wrote his *Waverley* novels, is open to the public, as is the room where he died in 1832.

Sir Walter Scott

Sir Walter Scott (1771–1832) was born in Edinburgh and trained as a lawyer. He is best remembered as a major literary figure and champion of Scotland, whose poems and novels (most famously his *Waverley* series) created enduring images of a heroic wilderness filled with the romance of the clans. His orchestration, in 1822, of the state visit of George IV to Edinburgh was an extravaganza of Highland culture that helped establish tartan as the national dress of Scotland. He served as Clerk of the Court in Edinburgh's Parliament House and for 30 years was Sheriff of Selkirk. He loved Central and Southern Scotland, putting the Trossachs *(see pp120–21)* firmly on the map with the publication of the *Lady of the Lake* (1810). His final years were spent writing to pay off a £114,000 debt following the failure of his publisher in 1827. He died with his debts paid, and was buried at Dryburgh Abbey in 1832.

The Great Hall at Abbotsford, adorned with arms and armour

❽ Traquair House

Peebles, The Scottish Borders.
Tel (01896) 830323. 🚌 from Peebles.
Open Apr–Sep: 11am–5pm daily; Oct:
11am–4pm daily; Nov: 11am–3pm Sat
& Sun. 🅿 ⬛ ♿ limited.
🌐 **traquair.co.uk**

Scotland's oldest continuously
inhabited house has deep roots
in Scottish religious and political
history stretching back over
900 years. Evolving from
a fortified tower to a
17th-century
mansion *(see p25)*,
the house was a
Catholic Stuart
stronghold for 500
years. Mary, Queen of
Scots was among the
many monarchs to
have stayed here.
Her crucifix is kept in
the house and her
bed is covered by
a counterpane
that she made.
Family letters and
engraved Jacobite
drinking glasses are among
the relics recalling the period
of the Highland rebellions.
Following a vow made by
the fifth Earl, Traquair's Bear
Gates (the "Steekit Yetts"),
which closed after Bonnie
Prince Charlie's visit in 1745,
will not reopen until a Stuart
reascends the throne. A secret

*Mary's crucifix,
Traquair House*

stairway leads to the Priest's
Room, which, with its clerical
vestments that could be
disguised as bedspreads, attests
to the problems faced by Catholic
families until Catholicism was
legalized in 1829.

❾ Peebles

The Scottish Borders. 🎟 8,000.
🚌 from Edinburgh. 🛈 23 High St
(01721) 723159.

This charming Borders town
has some fascinating
sights, including the
**Tweeddale Museum and
Gallery** which houses fullscale
plaster casts of part of the
Parthenon Frieze, and casts of a
frieze depicting the entry of
Alexander the Great into Babylon.
The walled **Kailzie Gardens**
attract day-trippers from
Edinburgh. **Glentress Forest**,
which begins on the fringes
of town, is very popular with
hikers and mountain bikers
from the city as well.

🏛 **Tweeddale Museum
and Gallery**
Tel (01721) 724820. **Open** Mon–Sat.

🌳 **Kailzie Gardens**
Tel (01721) 720007. **Open** daily. 🅿 🅶

🌲 **Glentress Forest**
Tel (0845) 367 3787. **Open** daily. 🅿
🌐 **forestry.gov.uk/glentress**

❿ Pentland Hills

The Lothians. 🚆 Edinburgh, then bus.
🛈 Regional Park Headquarters,
Edinburgh (0131) 529 2401.

The wilds of the Pentland Hills
stretch for 26 km (16 miles)
southwest of Edinburgh, and
offer some of the best hill-walking
country in Southern Scotland.
Walkers can saunter along the
many signposted footpaths,
while the more adventurous
can take the chairlift at the
Hillend dry ski slope to reach the
higher ground leading to the
493 m (1,617 ft) hill of Allermuir.
Even more ambitious is the classic
scenic route along the ridge from
Caerketton to West Kip.
To the east of the A703, in the
lee of the Pentlands, stands the
exquisite and ornate 15th-century
Rosslyn Chapel, which features
in *The Da Vinci Code*. It was
originally intended as a church,
but after the death of its
founder, William Sinclair, it was
used as a burial ground for his
descendants. The delicately
wreathed Apprentice Pillar
recalls the legend of the
apprentice carver who was
killed by the master stone-
mason in a fit of jealousy at his
pupil's superior skill.

🏠 **Rosslyn Chapel**
Tel (0131) 440 2159. **Open** daily. 🅿
🅶 🌐 **rosslynchapel.org.uk**

Details of the highly ornate, decorative carved-stone vaulting in Rosslyn Chapel

The Classical 18th-century tenements of New Lanark on the banks of the Clyde

⓫ New Lanark

Clyde Valley. 🗺 185. 🚌 🚆 Lanark.
ℹ Horsemarket, Ladyacre Rd, Lanark
(01555) 661661. **w** **newlanark.org**

Situated by the beautiful falls
of the River Clyde, with three
separate waterfalls, the village
of New Lanark was founded in
1785 by the industrial entre-
preneur David Dale. Ideally
located alongside the river for

David Livingstone

Scotland's great missionary
doctor and explorer was born
in Blantyre where he began
working life as a mill boy at
the age of ten. Livingstone
(1813–73) made three epic
journeys across Africa, from
1840, promoting "commerce
and Christianity". He became
the first European to see
Victoria Falls, and died in
1873 while searching for the
source of the Nile. His body is
buried in Westminster Abbey
in London.

the working of its water-driven
mills, the village had become
the largest producer of cotton
in Britain by 1800. Dale and his
successor, and son-in-law, Robert
Owen, were philanthropists
whose reforms demonstrated
that commercial success need
not undermine the wellbeing of
the workforce. The manu-
facturing of cotton continued
here until the late 1960s.

The **New Lanark Visitor
Centre** has exhibits illustrating
the World Heritage Site's signifi-
cance as a window on to working life in the early 19th century.
Head to the centre to purchase
a passport giving access to the
town's historical buildings.

Environs
24 km (15 miles) north, the town
of Blantyre has a memorial to the
Clyde Valley's most famous son,
the explorer David Livingstone.

🏛 **New Lanark Visitor Centre**
Tel (01555) 661345. **Open** daily. ♿
♿ 🖥 by appointment.

⓬ Dumfries House

Cumnock, Ayrshire. **Tel** (01290) 425959.
Open Mar: 12:15pm–1:45pm Sun–Fri;
Apr–Oct: 11am–3:30pm Sun–Fri; Nov–
Feb: 12:15pm–1:45pm Sat & Sun. ♿
🖥 **w** **dumfries-house.org.uk**

This wonderful Palladian villa is
off the beaten track, but worth a
detour. Sitting in sweeping
parkland, the grand symmetrical

villa was built for the fifth Earl of
Dumfries, William Crichton
Dalrymple. Designed to lure a
prospective wife, it was decorated
in fashionable Rococo style
between 1756 and 1760.
Amongst the treasures is a priceless collection of Chippendale
furniture, some of it purpose
built and incorporating Scottish
saltires. The house and contents
were saved in 2007 by a trust
established by Prince Charles.

⓭ Drumlanrig Castle

Thornhill, Dumfries & Galloway.
ℹ (01848) 331555. 🚌 🚆 Dumfries,
then bus. **Open** Easter–Aug:11am–
4pm daily. 🖥 ♿ ♿

Rising squarely from a grassy
platform, the massive fortress-
palace of **Drumlanrig Castle**
was built from pink sandstone
between 1679 and 1691 on the
site of a 15th-century Douglas

The Baroque front steps and doorway of
Drumlanrig Castle

stronghold. The castle's multi-turreted, formidable exterior conceals a priceless collection of art treasures as well as such Jacobite relics as Bonnie Prince Charlie's camp kettle, sash and money box. Hanging within oak-panelled rooms are paintings by Leonardo da Vinci (including *The Madonna of Yarnwinder*, stolen in 2003 but returned in 2007), Holbein and Rembrandt. The emblem of a crowned and winged heart recalls the famous Douglas ancestor "The Good Sir James". Legend has it he bore Robert the Bruce's heart on crusade against the Moors in Spain.

The exterior of Burns Cottage, birthplace of Robert Burns

⓯ Burns Heritage Trail

South Ayrshire, Dumfries & Galloway.
ℹ️ Dumfries (01387) 253862, Ayr (01292) 290300. 🆆 visitdumfriesand galloway.co.uk

Robert Burns (1759–96) left behind a remarkable body of work ranging from satirical poetry to tender love songs. His status as national bard is unchallenged and an official Burns Heritage Trail leads visitors around sights in southwest Scotland where he lived.

In Dumfries, the **Robert Burns Centre** focuses on his years in the town, while **Burns House**, where he lived from 1793 to 1796, contains memorabilia. His Greek-style mausoleum can be found in St Michael's Churchyard.

At **Ellisland Farm** there are further displays, with some of Burns' family possessions. Mauchline, some 18 km (11 miles) east of Ayr, has the **Burns House and Museum** in another former residence.

Alloway, just south of Ayr, is the real centre of the Burns Trail. The **Robert Burns Birthplace**

Museum is set in beautiful countryside. It incorporates **Burns Cottage**, the poet's birthplace, which houses memorabilia and a collection of manuscripts. The ruins of Alloway Kirk and the 13th-century Brig o' Doon have the best period atmosphere.

🏛️ **Robert Burns Centre**
Mill Rd, Dumfries. **Tel** (01387) 253374. **Open** Apr–Sep: 10am–5pm Mon–Sat, 2–5pm Sun; Oct–Mar: 10am–1pm, 2–5pm Tue–Sat. 🅿️

🏛️ **Burns House**
Burns St, Dumfries. **Tel** (01387) 255297. **Open** Apr–Sep: 10am–5pm Mon–Sat, 2–5pm Sun; Oct–Mar: 10am–1pm, 2–5pm Tue–Sat.

🏛️ **Ellisland Farm**
Holywood Rd, Auldgirth. **Tel** (01387) 740426. **Open** Apr–Sep: 10am–1pm, 2–5pm Mon–Sat, 2–5pm Sun; Oct–Mar: 2–5pm Tue–Sat. 🅿️ ♿ ⬜

🏛️ **Burns House and Museum**
Castle St, Mauchline. **Tel** (01563) 554902. **Open** 10am–4pm Tue–Sat. 🅿️ ♿ limited.

🏛️ **Robert Burns Birthplace Museum**
Alloway. **Tel** (0844) 493 2601. **Open** Apr–Sep: 10am–5:30pm daily; Oct–Mar: 10am–4pm daily. 🅿️ ♿
🆆 burnsmuseum.org.uk

The sturdy island fortress of Threave Castle on the Dee

⓮ Threave Castle

Castle Douglas, Dumfries & Galloway. **Tel** (01556) 502611. 🚋 Dumfries. **Open** Apr–Sep: 9:30am–4:30pm daily; Oct: 9:30am–3:30pm daily. 🅿️
🆆 historic-scotland.gov.uk

A menacing giant of a tower, this 14th-century Black Douglas stronghold on an island in the Dee commands the most complete medieval riverside harbour in Scotland. Douglas's struggles against the early Stuart kings resulted in his surrender here after a two-month siege in 1455 – but only after James II had brought the cannon Mons Meg to batter the castle. Threave was dismantled after Protestant Covenanters defeated its Catholic defenders in 1640. Only the shell of the kitchen, great hall and domestic levels remain.

Scottish Textiles

Weaving in the Scottish Borders goes back to the Middle Ages, when monks from Flanders established a thriving woollen trade with the Continent. Cotton became an important source of wealth in the Clyde Valley during the 19th century, when handloom weaving was overtaken by power-driven mills. The popular Paisley patterns were based on original Indian designs.

A colourful pattern from Paisley

Moated fairy-tale Caerlaverock Castle with its red stone walls

⑯ Caerlaverock Castle

Near Dumfries, Dumfries & Galloway. **ℹ** (01387) 770244. **Open** Apr–Sep: 9:30am–5:30pm daily; Oct–Mar: 9:30am–4:30pm daily. **W** historic-scotland.gov.uk

This impressive, three-sided, red stone structure, with its distinctive moat, is the finest example of a medieval castle in southwest Scotland. It stands 14 km (9 miles) south of Dumfries, and was built in around 1270.

Caerlaverock came to prominence in 1300, during the Wars of Independence, when it was besieged by Edward I, king of England, setting a precedent for more than three centuries of strife. Surviving chronicles of Edward's adventures describe the castle in much the same form as it stands today, despite being partially demolished and rebuilt many times, due to the clashes between the English and Scottish forces during the 14th and 16th centuries. Throughout these troubles it remained the stronghold of the Maxwell family, and the Maxwell crest and motto remain over the door. It was the struggle between Robert Maxwell, who was the first Earl of Nithsdale and a supporter of Charles I, and a Covenanter army that caused the castle's ruin in 1640.

⑰ Kirkcudbright

Dumfries & Galloway. 🚗 3,400. 🚌 **ℹ** Harbour Sq (01557) 330494. **Open** Apr–Oct: daily. **W** kirkcudbright.co.uk

By the mouth of the River Dee, at the head of Kirkcudbright Bay, this town has an artistic heritage. The Tolbooth, dating from the late 1500s, is now the **Tolbooth Art Centre**, which exhibits work by Kirkcudbright artists from 1880 to the present day. The most celebrated was Edward Hornel (1864–1933), one of the Glasgow Boys, who painted striking images of Japanese women. Some of his work is displayed in his former home, Broughton House, on the High Street.

MacLellan's Castle in the town centre was built in 1582 by the then Provost of Kirkcudbright, while outside, the ruins of Dundrennan Abbey date from the 12th century. Mary, Queen of Scots spent her last night there before fleeing to England in May 1568.

🏛 Tolbooth Art Centre
High St. **Tel** (01557) 331556. **Open** 11am–4pm Mon–Sat (to 5pm May–Sep), 2–5pm Sun. ♿

🏰 MacLellan's Castle
Tel (01557) 331856. **Open** Apr–Sep: 9:30am–5:30pm daily. 🚗

⑱ Whithorn

Dumfries & Galloway. 🚗 850. 🚌 Stranraer. 🚌 **ℹ** Dashwood Sq, Newton Stewart (01671) 402431. **W** dumfriesandgalloway.co.uk

The earliest site of continuous Christian worship in Scotland, Whithorn (meaning white house) takes its name from the white chapel built by St Ninian in 397. Though nothing remains of the chapel, a guided tour of the archaeological dig reveals evidence of Northumbrian, Viking and Scottish settlements ranging from the 5th to the 19th centuries. **The Whithorn Story** provides audio-visual information on the excavations, and contains a fine collection of ancient carved stones.

🏛 The Whithorn Story
45–47 George St. **Tel** (01988) 500508. **Open** Easter–Oct: 10:30am–5pm. 🚗 🎫 ♿ **W** whithorn.com

⑲ Galloway Forest Park

Dumfries & Galloway. 🚌 Stranraer. **ℹ** Clatteringshaws Visitor Centre (01644) 420285, Glen Trool Visitor Centre (01671) 402420, Kirroughtree Visitor Centre (01671) 402165. **W** forestry.gov.uk

This is the wildest stretch of country in Southern Scotland, with points of historical interest as well as great beauty. The park

Traditional stone buildings on the shore at Kirkcudbright

For hotels and restaurants see pp172–7 and pp181–9

Loch Trool, Galloway Forest Park, site of one of Robert the Bruce's victories

⑳ The Rhinns of Galloway

Dumfries & Galloway. 🚃 Stranraer. 🚌 Stranraer, Portpatrick. 🚢 Stranraer. 🅹 28 Harbour St, Stranraer (01776) 702595.

In the extreme southwest of Scotland, this peninsula is almost separated from the rest of the country by Loch Ryan and Luce Bay. It has a number of attractions, including the Logan Botanic Garden, near Port Logan. Established in 1900, subtropical species in the garden benefit from the area's mild climate.

Stranraer on Loch Ryan is the main centre and ferry port for Northern Ireland. The nearby Portpatrick is a prettier town, featuring a ruined church dating from 1629 and the remains of 16th-century Dunskey Castle.

🏠 **Logan Botanic Garden**
Near Port Logan, Stranraer. **Tel** (01776) 860231. **Open** mid-Mar–Oct: 10am–5pm daily. 🚲 ♿

extends to 670 sq km (260 sq miles) just north of Newton Stewart. The principal focal point is Loch Trool. By Caldons Wood, to the west end of the loch, the Martyrs' Monument marks the spot where six Covenanters were killed at prayer in 1685. Bruce's Stone, above the north shore, commemorates an occasion in 1307 when Robert the Bruce routed English forces. The hills to the north of Loch Trool are a considerable size, and worthy of note. Bennan stands at 562 m (1,844 ft), Benyellary at 719 m (2,359 ft), while Merrick, at 843 m (2,766 ft), is the tallest mountain in Southern Scotland. A round trip from Loch Trool to Merrick's summit and back, via the silver sands of Loch Enoch to the east, is a total of 15 km (9 miles) over rough but very rewarding ground.

Galloway Forest Park Walk

This walk gives a taste of wild hill-country and remote, high-level lochs. Adequate footwear, waterproof clothing and a map are recommended. From the car park, descend towards the house, cross a bridge, and take a path northeast through a field. Follow the valley of the Gairland Burn for about 1.5 km (1 mile) to find Loch Valley. A few minutes further north, the path reaches lonely Loch Neldricken, from where you can return by the same route. This area is a combination of glaciated hills and small hill lochs, set in hollows scraped out by the ice thousands of years ago. If time is short, or the weather poor, there are shorter walks around Loch Trool.

Key

– – Footpath

═ Access road

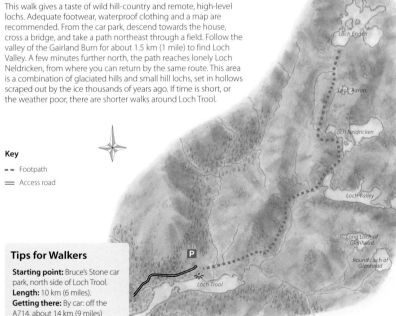

Tips for Walkers

Starting point: Bruce's Stone car park, north side of Loch Trool.
Length: 10 km (6 miles).
Getting there: By car: off the A714, about 14 km (9 miles) north of Newton Stewart, along an access road for 8 km (5 miles).

0 kilometres 2

0 miles 1

For additional map symbols *see back flap*

㉑ Culzean Castle

Standing on a cliff's edge in an extensive parkland estate, the late 16th century keep of Culzean (pronounced Cullayn), home of the Earls of Cassillis, was remodelled between 1777 and 1792 by the Neo-Classical architect Robert Adam. Restored in the 1970s, it is now a major showcase of Adam's later style of work. The grounds became Scotland's first public country park in 1969 and, with farming flourishing alongside ornamental gardens, they reflect both the leisure and everyday activities of life on a great country estate.

View of Culzean Castle (c.1815), by Nasmyth

KEY

① **The Clock Tower**, fronted by the circular carriageway, was originally the family coach house and stables. The clock was added in the 19th century, and today the buildings house a shop and an education room.

② **The State Bedroom and Dressing Rooms** contain typical mid-18th-century furnishings, including a gentleman's wardrobe of the 1740s.

③ **The Eisenhower Apartment**, on the top floor of Culzean and now a hotel, was where the General was granted lifetime tenancy in gratitude for his role in World War II.

④ **Carriageway**

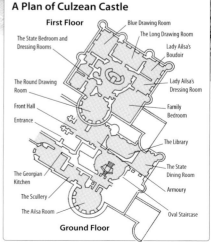

A Plan of Culzean Castle

First Floor

- Blue Drawing Room
- The Long Drawing Room
- The State Bedroom and Dressing Rooms
- Lady Ailsa's Boudoir
- The Round Drawing Room
- Lady Ailsa's Dressing Room
- Front Hall
- Family Bedroom
- Entrance
- The Library
- The Georgian Kitchen
- The State Dining Room
- The Scullery
- Armoury
- The Ailsa Room
- Oval Staircase

Ground Floor

For hotels and restaurants see pp172–7 and pp181–9

Armoury

On the walls are a collection of late 18th- and early 19th-century pistols, bayonets and swords installed by the 12th Earl of Cassillis who purchased them from the Tower of London.

Fountain Court
This sunken garden is a good place to begin a tour of the grounds to the east.

★ **Round Drawing Room**
With its restored 18th-century colour scheme, this elegant saloon perches on the cliff's edge 46 m (150 ft) above the Firth of Clyde. The carpet is a copy of one designed by Adam.

★ **Oval Staircase**
Illuminated by an overarching skylight, the staircase, with its Ionic and Corinthian pillars, is considered one of Adam's finest design achievements.

GLASGOW

Glasgow displays audacity in everything, from the profile of its contemporary buildings, such as the titanium-clad structures and tower of the Science Centre, to the presence of designer clothes shops and the wit of its people. As recently as the 1970s, this was a city with a fading industrial history and little sense of direction, but much has changed since then.

Glasgow's city centre, on the north bank of the River Clyde, has been occupied since ancient times. The Romans already had a presence in the area some 2,000 years ago, and there was a religious community here from the 6th century. Records show Glasgow's growing importance as a merchant town from the 12th century onwards.

Historic buildings such as Provand's Lordship, a 15th-century townhouse, remind visitors of its pre-industrial roots, but modern Glasgow grew from the riches of the British Empire and the Industrial Revolution. In the 18th century the city imported rum, sugar and tobacco from the colonies, while in the 19th century it reinvented itself as a cotton manufacturing centre. It then became a site for shipbuilding and for heavy engineering, attracting many incomers from poverty-stricken districts in the Scottish Highlands and islands, and in Ireland, in the process. Between the 1780s and the 1880s the population exploded from around 40,000 to over 500,000. The city boundaries expanded, and, despite an economic slump between the two World Wars, Glasgow clung to its status as an industrial giant until the 1970s, when its traditional skills were no longer needed. This was a bad time, but the city has since bounced back; it was named European Capital of Sport in 2003 and will host the 2014 Commonwealth Games. A £500 million project at Glasgow Harbour has reclaimed the city's old shipyards and dockland for commercial, residential and leisure usage.

Fashionable brasseries in the rejuvenated Merchant City area of Glasgow

◀ Gallery of Modern Art, Glasgow

Exploring Glasgow

Glasgow city centre is a neat grid of streets running east to west and north to south on the north bank of the River Clyde. This small area includes the main train stations, the principal shopping facilities and, at George Square, the tourist information office. Outside the centre, Byres Road to the west of Kelvingrove Park is the focus of the district known as "the West End", with its bars and restaurants near the University. Pollok Country Park, in the southwest, is home to the wonderful Burrell Collection.

Detail of St Mungo Museum's modern façade

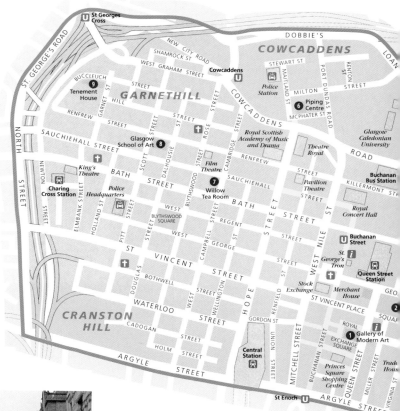

"SPT" sign outside St Enoch subway station

Getting Around

An extensive regional train service links Glasgow with its suburbs. In the city itself there is an underground system that operates daily in a simple loop around the centre, both north and south of the River Clyde. The M8 motorway (highway) cuts through central Glasgow, linking Inverclyde and the airport in the west with Edinburgh in the east. Buses and black cabs are other options.

Sights at a Glance

Historic Streets and Buildings
② George Square
⑤ Glasgow Cathedral and Necropolis
⑦ Willow Tea Room
⑱ Pollok House

Museums and Galleries
① Gallery of Modern Art
③ Provand's Lordship
④ St Mungo Museum of Religious Life and Art
⑨ Tenement House

⑩ Glasgow Science Centre
⑪ Riverside Museum
⑫ Kelvingrove Art Gallery and Museum
⑬ Scotland Street School Museum
⑭ Hunterian Art Gallery
⑯ People's Palace
⑲ Burrell Collection pp108–9

Parks and Gardens
⑮ Botanic Gardens

Arts Centres
⑥ Piping Centre
⑧ Glasgow School of Art
⑰ House for an Art Lover

Sauchiehall Street, the heart of the city's busy shopping district

Key
▫ Places of interest
▫ Other building
▫ Pedestrian street
═ Motorway

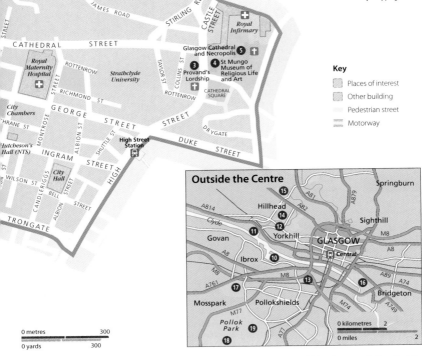

0 metres 300
0 yards 300

For additional map symbols see back flap

The imposing City Chambers in George Square, where a statue of Sir Walter Scott stands atop the central column

❶ Gallery of Modern Art

Royal Exchange Sq. **Tel** (0141) 287 3050. **Open** 10am–5pm Mon–Wed & Sat, 10am–8pm Thu, 11am–5pm Fri & Sun. 🚹 🖥 🔳 **glasgowlife.org.uk/ museums**

Once the home of Glasgow's Royal Exchange (the city's centre for trade), this building dates from 1829 and also incorporates a late 18th-century mansion that formerly occupied the site. The local authority took over the Exchange just after World War II, and for many years it served as a library. It finally opened its doors as the Gallery of Modern Art in 1996. One of the largest contemporary art galleries outside London, the GoMA is constantly building on its collection of work by Glasgow based artists. Accordingly, most of the gallery is home to a lively and thought-provoking programme of temporary exhibitions featuring work by Scottish and interna-tional artists. Many of these focus on contemporary and

Ornate tower of the Gallery of Modern Art

social issues, often featuring groups that are marginalized in today's society.

❷ George Square

City centre. City Chambers: **Tel** (0141) 287 4018. **Open** Mon–Fri, 10:30am & 2:30pm for guided tours. 🚹 🖋 Merchants House: **Tel** (0141) 221 8272. 🖋 by appt.

George Square was laid out in the late 18th century as a residental area, but re-development during Victorian times conferred its enduring status as the city's focal point. The only building not to be affected by the later 19th-century makeover is the Millennium Hotel (1807) on the north side of the Square.

The 1870s saw a building boom, with the construction of the former Post Office (1876) at the southeast corner, and the **Merchants House** (1877) to the west side. The latter is home to Glasgow's Chamber of Commerce. Founded in 1781, it is the oldest organization of its kind in the UK. The most dominant structure in George Square, however, is the **City Chambers on** the east side. Designed by William Young in an Italian Renaissance style, the imposing building

was opened in 1888 by Queen Victoria. With the elegant pro-portions of the interior decor-ated in marble and mosaic, the opulence of this building makes it the most impressive of its type in Scotland.

❸ Provand's Lordship

3 Castle St. 📞 (0141) 552 8819. **Open** 10am–5pm Tue–Thu & Sat, 11am–5pm Fri & Sun.

Provand's Lordship was orig-inally built as a canon's house in 1471, and is now Glasgow's oldest surviving house, as well as a museum. Its low ceilings and wooden furnishings create a vivid impression of life in a wealthy 15th-century house-hold. Mary, Queen of Scots (see p48) may have stayed here when she visited Glasgow in 1566 to see her cousin, and husband, Lord Darnley.

Provand's Lordship, Glasgow's only medieval house

④ St Mungo Museum of Religious Life and Art

2 Castle St. **Tel** (0141) 276 1625. **Open** 10am–5pm Tue–Thu & Sat, 11am–5pm Fri & Sun. ♿ 🅿 by appointment. 📷 🅿
w glasgowlife.org.uk/museums

Glasgow has strong religious roots, and the settlement that grew to become today's city started with a monastery founded in the 6th century AD by a priest called Mungo. He died in the early years of the 7th century, and his body lies buried underneath Glasgow Cathedral. The building itself dates from the 12th century, and stands on ground blessed by St Ninian as long ago as AD 397. The ever-growing numbers of visitors to the cathedral eventually prompted plans for an interpretive centre. Despite the efforts of the Society of Friends of Glasgow Cathedral, however, sufficient funds could not be raised. The local authority

Detail from the St Mungo Museum

decided to step in with money, and with the idea for a more extensive project – a museum of religious life and art. The site chosen was adjacent to the cathedral, where the 13th-century Castle of the Bishops of Glasgow once stood. The museum has the appearance of a centuries-old fortified house, despite the fact that it was completed in 1993. The top floor describes the story of the country's religion from a non-denominational perspective. Both Protestant and Catholic versions of Christianity are represented, as well as the other faiths of modern Scotland. The many, varied displays touch on the lives of communities as extensive as Glasgow's Muslims, who have had their own Mosque in the city since 1984, as well as local converts to the Baha'i faith. The other floors are given over to works of art – among them is Craigie Aitchison's *Crucifixion VII*, which sits alongside religious artifacts and artworks, such as burial discs from Neolithic China (2,000 BC), contemporary paintings by Aboriginal Australians, and some excellent Scottish stained glass from the early part of the 20th century. Further displays in the museum examine issues of fundamental concern to people of all religions – war, persecution, death and the afterlife – and from cultures as far afield as West Africa and Mexico. In the grounds surrounding the building, there is a permanent Zen Garden, created by Yasutaro Tanaka. Such gardens have been a traditional aid to contemplation in Japanese Buddhist temples since the beginning of the 16th century.

An impressive stained-glass window at the St Mungo Museum of Religious Life and Art

Glasgow's medieval cathedral viewed from the southwest

⑤ Glasgow Cathedral and Necropolis

Cathedral Square. Cathedral: **Tel** (0141) 552 6891. **Open** Apr–Sep: 9:30am–5:30pm Mon–Sat, 1–5:30pm Sun; Oct–Mar: 9:30am–4:30pm Mon–Sat, 1–4:30pm Sun. ♿ Necropolis: **Open** 24hrs daily.
w glasgowcathedral.org.uk

As one of the few churches to escape destruction during the Scottish Reformation *(see p48)* by adapting itself to Protestant worship, this cathedral is a rare example of an almost complete original 13th-century church.

It was built on the site of a chapel founded by the city's patron saint, St Mungo, a 6th-century bishop of Strathclyde. According to legend, Mungo placed the body of a holy man, named Fergus, on a cart yoked to two wild bulls, telling them to take it to the place ordained by God. In the "dear green place" at which the bulls stopped, he built his church.

Because of its sloping site, the cathedral is built on two levels. The crypt contains the tomb of St Mungo, surrounded by an intricate forest of columns springing up to end in delicately carved rib-vaulting. The Blacader Aisle is reputed to have been built over a cemetery blessed by St Ninian.

Behind the cathedral, a likeness of Protestant reformer John Knox *(see p48)* surveys the city from his Doric pillar, overlooking a Victorian cemetery. The necropolis is filled with crumbling monuments to the dead of Glasgow's wealthy merchant families.

❻ Piping Centre

30–34 McPhater St. **Tel** (0141) 353 0220. **Open** 9am–5pm daily. 🚻 ♿
♿ ♿ **W** thepipingcentre.co.uk

The Piping Centre, which opened its doors in a refurbished church in 1996, aims to promote the study and history of piping in Scotland. It offers tuition at all levels, and houses the **National Museum of Piping**, which traces the development of the instrument. Displays show that bagpipes were first introduced to Scotland as early as the 14th century, although the golden age of piping was the 17th and 18th

Traditional bagpipes with brass drones

centuries. This was the era of the MacCrimmons of Skye (hereditary pipers to the chiefs of Clan MacLeod), when complex, extended tunes (ceol mor, or "the big music") were written for clan gatherings, battles and in the form of laments.

❼ Willow Tea Room

217 Sauchiehall St. **Tel** (0141) 332 0521. **Open** 9am–5pm Mon–Sat, 11am–5pm Sun. 🖥
W willowtearooms.co.uk

This is the sole survivor of a series of delightfully frivolous tea rooms created by the designer Charles Rennie

The Mackintosh-designed interior of the Willow Tea Room

Mackintosh (see opposite page) at the turn of the century for the celebrated restaurateur Kate Cranston. Everything in the tearoom, from the high-backed chairs to the tables and cutlery, was of Mackintosh's own design. The 1904 **Room de Luxe** sparkles with eccentricity: striking mauve and silver furniture, coloured glass and a flamboyant leaded door create a remarkable venue.

The exterior of the Glasgow School of Art, Mackintosh's masterpiece

❽ Glasgow School of Art

167 Renfrew St. **Tel** (0141) 353 4500. 🚻 ♿ mid-May–mid-Jun: scheduled tours daily; mid-Jun–mid-May: Mon–Sat by appt. ♿ limited. **W** gsa.ac.uk

Widely considered to be the greatest architectural work in the illustrious career of Charles Rennie Mackintosh, the Glasgow School of Art was built between 1897 and 1909 to a design he submitted in a competition. Due to financial constraints, it was built in two stages. The earlier eastern half displays a severity of style, likened by a contemporary critic to a prison. The later western half is characterized by a softer architectural style.

An art student will guide you through the building to the Furniture Gallery, Board Room and the Library, the latter being a masterpiece of spatial composition. Each room is an exercise in contrasts between

height, light and shade, with innovative details echoing the architectural themes of the structure. How much of the school can be viewed depends on curricular requirements at the time of visiting, as it still functions as an active and highly successful art college.

❾ Tenement House

145 Buccleuch St. **Tel** (0844) 493 2197. **Open** Mar–Oct: 1–5pm daily. 🚻 🎥 by appointment. NTS

More a time capsule than a museum, the Tenement House is an almost undisturbed record of life as it was in a modest Glasgow flat on a tenement estate in the early 20th century. Glasgow owed much of its vitality and neighbourliness to tenement life, though in later years many of these Victorian and Edwardian apartments were to earn a bad name for poverty and overcrowding, and many of them have been pulled down.

The Tenement House was the home of Miss Agnes Toward, who lived here from 1911 until 1965. It remained largely unaltered during that time and, since Agnes threw very little away, the house has become a treasure-trove of social history. In the parlour, which would have been used only on formal occasions, afternoon tea is laid out on a white lace cloth. The kitchen, with its coal-fired range and box bed, is filled with the tools of a vanished era, such as a goffering-iron for ironing lace, a washboard and a stone hot-water bottle.

Agnes's lavender water and medicines are still arranged in the bathroom, and it feels almost as though she stepped out of the house 70 years ago and simply forgot to return.

The preserved Edwardian kitchen of the Tenement House

For hotels and restaurants see pp172–7 and pp181–9

Glasgow Artists

The late 19th century was a time of great artistic activity in Glasgow, with painters such as Sir James Guthrie, Robert McGregor and others rising to prominence. But snobbery on the part of the Edinburgh-based arts establishment often led these men to seek recognition outside Scotland. The term "Glasgow School" was coined after an 1890 London exhibition, but the artists generally called themselves "Glasgow Boys". Art Nouveau designer Charles Rennie Mackintosh contributed his genius to the creative life of the city as well as to a new Glasgow School of Art, completed in two stages – 1899 and 1909. More recently, the term Glasgow Boys has been used to describe the generation of artists who attended the School of Art in the 1970s and '80s. Contemporary Glasgow artists include Ken Currie and Peter Howson.

Stirling Station, by William Kennedy (1859–1918), depicts the crowded platform with people waiting for a train. The rich colours, and steam from the trains, contribute to the atmosphere of this bustling station.

A Star (1891) by Sir John Lavery is indicative of the artist's dashing, fluid, style as a portraitist. Born in Belfast, Lavery studied at Glasgow and was part of the Whistler- and Impressionist-influenced Glasgow School.

In The Wayfarer, by Edward Arthur Walton (1860–1922), the winding path leads the viewer into the distance, in the direction of the wayfarer's gaze.

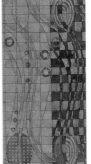

Mackintosh's stylized tulips on a checkered background provide a striking example of Art Nouveau decoration, juxtaposing the organic with the geometric.

Designed by Mackintosh in 1901, the House for an Art Lover *(see p107)* was finally built in 1996. The design of the building and all of the furniture remains true to the original plans.

Mackintosh's unique fluidity of form is seen in this detail from a stained-glass door in the House for an Art Lover.

Charles Rennie Mackintosh

Glasgow's most celebrated designer (1868–1928) entered Glasgow School of Art at the age of 16. After his success with the Willow Tea Room, he became a leading figure in the Art Nouveau movement. His characteristic straight lines and flowing detail are the hallmark of early 20th-century style.

⑩ Glasgow Science Centre

50 Pacific Quay. **Tel** (0141) 420 5000. **Open** 10am–5pm daily. 🚗 ♿
W glasgowsciencecentre.org

The impressive gleaming tower of this science park is an unmistakable landmark on the city's skyline.

A three-storey science mall introduces the world of popular, everyday science through a range of dynamic interactive exhibits, laboratories and multimedia. Scotland's only IMAX Theatre stands next door, projecting breathtaking images from the natural and scientific world onto its 24-m (80-ft) by 18-m (60-ft) screen. Other notable exhibits include a lab where you can examine your hair and skin. The 127-m (416-ft) rotating tower is Scotland's tallest freestanding structure.

⑪ Riverside Museum

100 Pointhouse Place. **Tel** (0141) 287 2729. **Open** 10am–5pm Mon–Thu & Sat, 11am–5pm Fri & Sun. ♿ 💻
W glasgowlife.org.uk/museums

This landmark attraction sits on the Clyde in a dramatic zinc-panelled building designed by architect Zaha Hadid. Focused on transport, it is crammed with locomotives, trams, cars and bikes of all styles and vintages. It also explores the social impact of transport on the city, with interactive and audio-visual features to bring the past to life.

George Henry's *Japanese Lady with a Fan* (1894), at Kelvingrove

⑫ Kelvingrove Art Gallery and Museum

Argyle St, Kelvingrove. **Tel** (0141) 276 9599. **Open** 10am–5pm Mon–Thu & Sat, 11am–5pm Fri & Sun. 🚗 💻
W glasgowlife.org.uk/museums

An imposing red sandstone building, Kelvingrove is Scotland's most popular gallery, housing a magnificent art collection. Exhibits are grouped to reflect different aspects of the main collection. Among these are 19th-century British artists including Turner and Constable and French Impressionist and Dutch Renaissance painters. Scottish art and design is well represented with rooms dedicated to the Scottish Colourists and the Glasgow Style *(see p105)*. Included here are two works by Charles Rennie Macintosh – a fine gesso panel and a 1904 writing cabinet.

LS Lowry's painting *VE Day* hangs here again after it was cut from its frame and stolen in 1992. You can also see Salvador Dalí's *Christ of St John of the Cross*. There is a vast natural history collection too, with displays on Scotland's wildlife.

⑬ Scotland Street School Museum

225 Scotland Street, Glasgow. **Tel** (0141) 287 0500. **Open** 10am–5pm Tue–Thu & Sat, 11am–5pm Fri & Sun. ♿ 🚗 💻 **W** glasgowlife.org.uk/museums

This museum is housed in a former school designed by Charles Rennie Mackintosh between 1903 and 1906. It uses displays, audio-visual exhibits and reconstructed and restored classrooms to tell the story of the developments in education in Scotland from the Victorian era to the 1960s. You can read and listen to recollections of former pupils, decade by decade, covering topics such as classroom discipline, evacuation and World War II, school attire and playground games.

⑭ Hunterian Art Gallery

82 Hillhead St. **Tel** (0141) 330 5431. **Open** 10am–5pm Tue–Sat. **Closed** 24 Dec– 4 Jan. **W** gla.ac.uk/hunterian/

Built to house a number of paintings bequeathed to Glasgow University by an ex-student and physician, Dr William Hunter (1718–83), the Hunterian Art Gallery contains Scotland's largest print collection. There are also works by many major European artists, dating from the 16th century. A collection of work by the designer Charles Rennie Mackintosh *(see p105)* is supplemented by a complete reconstruction of No. 6 Florentine Terrace, where he lived from 1906 to 1914. There is a major collection of 19th- and 20th-century Scottish art, but by far the most famous collection is of

Kelvingrove Art Gallery and the Glasgow University buildings, seen from the south

work by the Paris-trained American painter, James McNeill Whistler (1834–1903), who influenced so many of the Glasgow School painters.

Whistler's *Sketch for Annabel Lee* (c.1869), Hunterian Art Gallery

⑮ Botanic Gardens

Great Western Rd. **Tel** (0141) 276 1614. **Open** 7am–dusk. 🚻 🅿 by appt.

These gardens form a peaceful space in the heart of the city's West End, by the River Kelvin. Originally founded at another site in 1817, they were moved to the current location in 1839 and opened to the public three years later. Aside from the main range of greenhouses, with assorted displays including palm trees and an area of tropical crops, one of the most interesting features is the **Kibble**

One of the greenhouses in Glasgow's peaceful Botanic Gardens

Palace. Built at Loch Long in the Highlands by John Kibble, the glass palace was moved to its present site in the early 1870s. It houses a collection of carnivorous plants and tropical orchids and the national collection of tree ferns.

⑯ People's Palace

Glasgow Green. **Tel** (0141) 276 0788. **Open** 10am–5pm Tue–Thu & Sat, 11am–5pm Fri & Sun. 🚻 🖥

This Victorian sandstone structure was purpose-built in 1898 as a cultural museum for the people of Glasgow's East End. It houses everything from temperance tracts to trade-union banners, suffragette posters to the comedian Billy Connolly's banana-shaped boots, and thus provides a social history of the city from the 12th to the 20th century. A superb conservatory contains an exotic winter garden.

⑰ House for an Art Lover

Bellahouston Park, 10 Dumbreck Rd. **Tel** (0141) 353 4770. **Open** 10am–4pm Mon–Thu, 10am–12:30pm Fri, 10am–2pm Sat, 10am–1:30pm Sun. **Closed** regularly during functions. 📷 🚻 🅿 by appt. 🖥 Ⓦ **houseforanartlover.co.uk**

Plans for the House for an Art Lover were submitted by Charles Rennie Mackintosh and

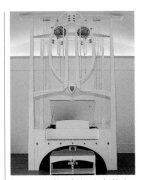

Distinctive Mackintosh piano in the Music Room, House for an Art Lover

his partner Margaret Macdonald in response to a competition in a German magazine in the summer of 1900. The competition brief was to create a country retreat for someone of elegance and taste who loved the arts. As it was a theoretical exercise, the couple were unrestrained by logistics or budget and won a special prize for their efforts. The plans lay unused for over 80 years until consulting engineer Graham Roxburgh, who had worked on the refurbishment of other Mackintosh interiors in Glasgow, decided to build the House for an Art Lover. Work began in 1989 and was completed in 1996. The House is host to a digital design studio and post-graduate study centre for students at the Glasgow School of Art. The rooms on the main floor give a real insight into the vision of Mackintosh and the artistic talent of Macdonald. The Oval Room is a beautifully proportioned space in a single light colour, meant as a tranquil retreat for ladies, while the Music Room and its centrepiece piano that is played to add to the atmosphere is also bright and inspiring. The Main Hall leads into the Dining Room, with its long table, sideboard and relief stone fireplace. The great attention to detail shown throughout the House, in the panelling, light fixtures and other elements, is enormously impressive. The exterior of the building is also an extraordinary achievement in art and design.

The Georgian Pollok House, viewed from the south

⑱ Pollok House

(NTS): 2060 Pollokshaws Rd. **Tel** (0844) 493 2202. **Open** 10am–5pm daily.

Pollok House is Glasgow's finest 18th-century domestic building and contains one of Britain's best collections of Spanish paintings. The NeoClassical central block was finished in 1750, the sobriety of its exterior contrasting with the exuberant plasterwork within. The Maxwells have lived at Pollok since the mid-13th century, but the male line ended with Sir John Maxwell, who added the grand entrance hall in the 1890s and designed most of the terraced gardens and parkland beyond. Hanging above the family silver, porcelain, hand-painted Chinese wallpaper and Jacobean glass, the Stirling Pollok paintings are strong on British and Dutch schools, including William Blake's Sir Geoffrey Chaucer and the Nine and Twenty Pilgrims (1745) as well as William Hogarth's portrait of James Thomson, who wrote the words to Rule Britannia. Spanish 16th- to 19th-century art predominates: El Greco's Lady in a Fur Wrap (1541) hangs in the library, while the drawing room contains works by Francisco de Goya and Esteban Murillo. In 1966 Anne Maxwell Macdonald gave the house and 146 ha (361 acres) of parkland to the City of Glasgow. The park provides the site for the city's fascinating Burrell Collection.

⑲ Burrell Collection

Given to the city in 1944 by Sir William Burrell (1861–1958), a wealthy shipping owner, this internationally acclaimed collection is the gem in Glasgow's crown, with objects of major importance in numerous fields of interest. The building housing these pieces was purposebuilt in 1983. When the sun shines in, the stained glass blazes with colour, while the shaded tapestries seem a part of the surrounding woodland.

Hutton Castle Drawing Room
This is a reconstruction of the Drawing Room at Burrell's own home – the 16th-century Hutton Castle, near Berwick-upon-Tweed. The Hall and Dining Room can also be seen nearby.

Bull's Head
Dating from the 7th century BC, this bronze head from Turkey was once part of a cauldron handle.

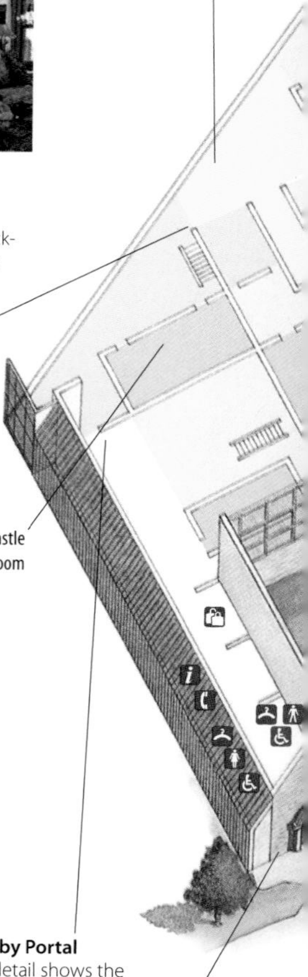

Hutton Castle Drawing Room

Hornby Portal
This detail shows the arch's heraldic display. The 14th-century portal comes from Hornby Castle in Yorkshire.

Figure of a Luohan
This sculpture of Buddha's disciple dates from the Ming Dynasty (1484).

Main entrance

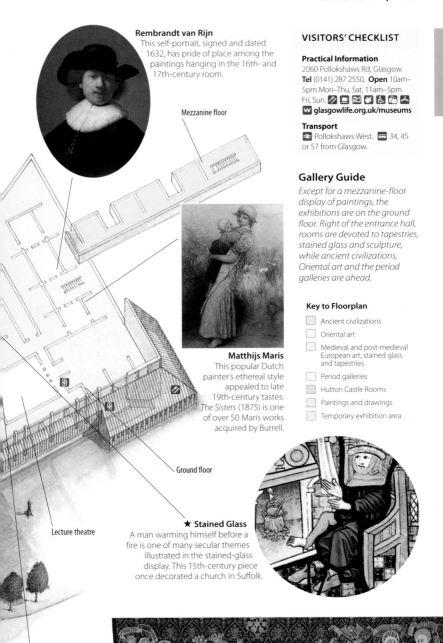

Rembrandt van Rijn
This self-portrait, signed and dated 1632, has pride of place among the paintings hanging in the 16th- and 17th-century room.

Mezzanine floor

VISITORS' CHECKLIST

Practical Information
2060 Pollokshaws Rd, Glasgow.
Tel (0141) 287 2550. **Open** 10am–5pm Mon–Thu, Sat, 11am–5pm Fri, Sun. 🖊️ 🏠 🖼️ 🎒 ♿ 🚻 📷
w glasgowlife.org.uk/museums

Transport
🚉 Pollokshaws West. 🚌 34, 45 or 57 from Glasgow.

Gallery Guide
Except for a mezzanine-floor display of paintings, the exhibitions are on the ground floor. Right of the entrance hall, rooms are devoted to tapestries, stained glass and sculpture, while ancient civilizations, Oriental art and the period galleries are ahead.

Matthijs Maris
This popular Dutch painter's ethereal style appealed to late 19th-century tastes. *The Sisters* (1875) is one of over 50 Maris works acquired by Burrell.

Key to Floorplan

☐ Ancient civilizations
☐ Oriental art
☐ Medieval and post-medieval European art, stained glass and tapestries
☐ Period galleries
☐ Hutton Castle Rooms
☐ Paintings and drawings
☐ Temporary exhibition area

Ground floor

Lecture theatre

★ Stained Glass
A man warming himself before a fire is one of many secular themes illustrated in the stained-glass display. This 15th-century piece once decorated a church in Suffolk.

★ Tapestries
Scenes from the Life of the Virgin (c.1450), a Swiss work in wool and linen, is one of many tapestries on show.

SHOPPING IN GLASGOW

While Glasgow itself is home to some 570,000 people, as the focal point of a great conurbation in west central Scotland it provides the main shopping centre for almost half of the country's population. The large number of potential customers is allied to Glasgow's reputation as Scotland's most fashion-conscious city: the best alternative fashion and design boutiques are in the West End, around Byres Road. A trip to the colourful Barras street market, which is held every weekend, offers a much more traditional, if somewhat anarchic, Glaswegian shopping experience.

St Enoch Centre, one of the city's malls

Department Stores and Malls

The impressive Buchanan Galleries has many well-known shops including a **John Lewis** department store. The **Italian Centre**, in the Merchant City area and **Princes Square**, houses designer boutiques. The St Enoch Centre houses a **Debenhams** department store. **House of Fraser** is one of the longest established department stores.

Markets

No visit to Glasgow is complete without a trip to **The Barras**, a weekend market in the east end of the city centre. The name is a dialect version of "The Barrows", and dates from a time when goods were sold from barrows.

The current site, between the Gallowgate and London Road, has been an official market since the 1920s. Every Saturday and Sunday, thousands of bargain hunters descend on stalls that sell virtually everything from old junk to cheap clothes and CDs.

Fashion

Many fashion stores are housed in the malls in the city centre. Outside the malls, **Cruise** sells well-known designer names for men and women, while streetwise **Diesel** has an outlet on Buchanan Street. Further along this street, **Karen Millen** is the store for the chic professional woman. **Schuh** sells a range of fashionable footwear for both men and women, as does **Dune**. For special occasions, **Ella Bulloch** is the best place to buy or hire a lady's hat. For a luxurious range of underwear, try **Pampas Lingerie**. Second-hand clothes stores abound. **Mr Ben** offers 1950s American chic, while **Starry Starry Night** is more classic and traditional in style. **Graham Tiso** is great for clothing and equipment for the outdoors. Tartan fans should seek out **Hector Russell**, a Highland outfitter that makes made-to-measure kilts. The West End is home to many small boutiques, such as **Pink Poodle**, which sells funky clothes and accessories.

Food and Drink

Glasgow's finest independent delicatessen is **Fratelli Sarti**, a traditional Italian food store also offering a good selection of wines. **Peckham's**, a chain of delis, has an excellent branch on Glassford Street, and its scope goes far beyond Italy. A man once described as the UK's top cheesemonger, **Iain Mellis** opened an outlet in Glasgow in 1995. It is the best place in the entire west of Scotland for artisan cheeses

Glenlivet whisky

Traditional, "barrow-style" fruit stall in Glasgow's Barras Market

made from unpasteurized milk. **Roots, Fruits and Flowers** is Glasgow's leading fruit and vegetable store. For divine handmade chocolates pay **Chocolatier of Glasgow** a visit. Aside from national chains selling beer, wine and spirits, such as **Oddbins**, there is **The Whisky Shop** in the city centre and the **Ubiquitous Chip Wine Shop** in the west end.

Book Stores

Glasgow is fairly well served by bookshops. **Waterstone's** on Sauchiehall Street is a multi-floor chain store complete with a coffee shop. In the West End, **Caledonia Books** and **Voltaire & Rousseau** sell a variety of second-hand and antiquarian books on a wide range of subjects and are well worth a visit.

Shopping on Argyle Street, with its profusion of high-street stores

Art and Design

There are a number of small galleries concentrated in the streets behind the Tron Theatre, such as the **Glasgow Print Studio** and **Art Exposure**. The **Redcoat Gallery** is another great place to pick up reasonably priced and exciting work. **Welcome Home**, in the foyer of the Centre for Contemporary Arts, sells interesting and affordable local handmade art and crafts. Fans of antiques should try **Lovatt Antiques**, close to the River Clyde. For furniture and interior design ideas, visit **Designworks** or **Dallas and Dallas**.

DIRECTORY

Department Stores and Malls

Debenhams
97 Argyle St, G2 8AR.
Tel (0141) 221 0088.

House of Fraser
45 Buchanan St, G1 3HR.
Tel (0141) 221 3880.

Italian Centre
7 John St, G1 1HP.
Tel (0141) 552 6368.

John Lewis
Buchanan Galleries, G1 2GF. **Tel** (0141) 353 6677.

Princes Square
48 Buchanan St, G1 3JN.
Tel (0141) 221 0324.

Fashion

Cruise
180 Ingram St, G1 1DN.
Tel (0141) 572 3232.

Diesel
116–120 Buchanan St, G1 2JW.
Tel (0141) 221 3200.

Dune
105–7 Buchanan St, G1 3HF. **Tel** (0141) 226 8873.

Ella Bulloch
461 Clarkston Rd, G44 3LW.
Tel (0141) 633 0078.

Graham Tiso
129 Buchanan St, G1 2JA.
Tel (0141) 248 4877.

Hector Russell
110 Buchanan St, G1 2JN.
Tel (0141) 221 0217.

Karen Millen
36 Buchanan St, G1 3JX.
Tel (0141) 243 2136.

Mr Ben
101 King St, G1 5RB.
Tel (0141) 553 1936.

Pampas Lingerie
74 Hyndland Rd, G12 9UT.
Tel (0141) 357 2383.

Pink Poodle
181 Byres Road, G12 8TS.
Tel (0141) 357 3344.

Schuh
112–114 Argyle St, G2 8BH.
Tel (0141) 248 7331.

Starry Starry Night
19–21 Dowanside Lane, G12 9BZ.
Tel (0141) 337 1837.

Food and Drink

Chocolatier of Glasgow
Princes Square, 38–42 Buchanan St, G1 3JX.
Tel (0141) 222 2224.

Fratelli Sarti
133 Wellington St, G2 2XD.
Tel (0141) 248 2228.

Iain Mellis
492 Great Western Rd, G12 8EW.
Tel (0141) 339 8998.

Oddbins
132 Woodlands Rd, G3 6LF.
Tel (0141) 332 1663.

Peckham's
61–65 Glassford St, G1 1UG.
Tel (0141) 553 0666.

Roots, Fruits and Flowers
1137 Argyle St, G3 8ND. **Tel** (0141) 229 0838.

Ubiquitous Chip Wine Shop
12 Ashton Lane, G12 8SJ.
Tel (0141) 334 5007.

The Whisky Shop
220 Buchanan St, G1 2GF.
Tel (0141) 331 0022.

Book Stores

Caledonia Books
483 Great Western Rd, G12 8HL.
Tel (0141) 334 9663.

Voltaire & Rousseau
12–14 Otago Lane, G12 8PB.
Tel (0141) 339 1811.

Waterstone's
153–7 Sauchiehall St, G2 3EW.
Tel (0843) 290 8345.

Art and Design

Art Exposure
19 Parnie St, G1 5RJ.
Tel (0141) 552 7779.

Dallas and Dallas
18 Montrose St, G1 1RE.
Tel (0141) 552 2939.

Designworks
38 Gibson St, G12 8NX.
Tel (0141) 339 9520.

Glasgow Print Studio
Trongate 103, G1 5HD. **Tel** (0141) 552 0704.

Lovatt Antiques
121 Lancefield St, G3 8HZ.
Tel (0141) 639 3000.

Redcoat Gallery
323 North Woodside Rd, G20 6RY.
Tel (0141) 341 0069.

Welcome Home
350 Sauchiehall St, G2 3JD.
Tel (0141) 352 4900.

ENTERTAINMENT IN GLASGOW

The dance music that emerged during the 1990s found a natural home in Glasgow, which has possibly the most exuberant nightlife in Scotland. With the Scottish Exhibition and Conference Centre housing two major rock venues, and Barrowlands still a fixture on the concert circuit, popular music is very prominent. There are a number of mainstream cinemas in the city, as well as the Glasgow Film Theatre, a centre for arthouse releases. The annual Celtic Connections Festival in January is an international folk music event and there is plenty of culture in the city as a whole. Some major orchestras, the Scottish Ballet and Scottish Opera are based here. The Citizens' is a highly acclaimed theatre and the Tramway and the Arches both stage large, innovative productions.

Scottish Opera performing *Eugene Onegin* on stage at the Theatre Royal

Sources of Information

The twice-monthly arts and entertainment magazine *The List* covers all events in Glasgow and Edinburgh, as does *The Skinny* (www.skinnymag.co.uk).

Classical Music and Opera

Scotland's national opera company, Scottish Opera, is based at the **Theatre Royal** and stages some eight productions each season.

Glasgow Royal Concert Hall is the main venue for the Royal Scottish National Orchestra; it also hosts visits from major international orchestras. The RSNO's annual concert series runs from October to April. Family classical concerts are performed all year.

For more intimate shows, the **Royal Scottish Academy of Music and Drama** has two smaller halls, while many venues across the city host recitals and concerts.

Rock, Jazz and World Music

Rock bands have a choice of venues. There is the main auditorium at the **Scottish Exhibition and Conference Centre**, and the **Armadillo** in the same centre. It is **Barrowlands**, however, that remains the city's principal rock venue. There is also **King Tut's Wah Wah Hut**, where Oasis were discovered, and the **O2 Academy**. Jazz sessions take place at **Cottier's** and the **O2 ABC**. The Royal Concert Hall holds a Celtic Connections Festival. It also hosts international music, as does the **Old Fruitmarket**.

Cinema

There are 18 screens at the **Cineworld**, while the **Odeon at the Quay** has 12. The **Glasgow Film Theatre**, or GFT, shows arthouse and foreign-language movies. Glasgow's new **IMAX Theatre** is also well worth a visit.

The stylish café-bar at the Tron Theatre in the city centre

Theatre and Dance

The Scottish ballet stages its Glasgow performances at the Theatre Royal *(see Classical Music and Opera)*. Visiting dance companies, from classical to contemporary, also perform here and it is a noted stop on the touring circuit for major theatre companies from the rest of the UK and overseas.

The **Citizens' Theatre** is the main venue for serious drama, from Greek tragedies to modern pieces, and it rightly claims to

Musicians outside City Chambers during a Festival of Jazz

be Scotland's best. Both the **Tramway** and the **Arches** are acclaimed for their experimental works. Smaller-scale productions can be seen at the **Tron** and Cottier's Theatre *(see Rock, Jazz and World Music)*. Commercial productions, such as musicals and pantomimes, are a staple at the popular **King's**.

Original road sign for the West End

Bars and Clubs

Visitors can choose from traditional pubs or fashionable bars with a contemporary atmosphere. Old-fashioned pubs such as the **Horseshoe**, the **Griffin** and the **Halt**, have long been popular in Glasgow. Modern venues include **Home**

and **Bar 91**, both in the Merchant City, and the first-floor bar at the **Radio** in the West End. **Bar Soba** is another popular cocktail bar while **Chinaskis** has a New York lounge feel but also a great beer garden. The city's club culture is one of the best in the UK. Each venue has different styles of music on different nights, including house, hip-hop, techno or drum-and-bass. The Arches *(see Theatre and Dance)*, **The Sub Club**, **The Tunnel**, **The Soundhaus** and **Artá** are among the best.

Sports

Glasgow is home to the country's most successful football (soccer) clubs, **Celtic** and **Glasgow**

Rangers (although the Rangers no longer play in the top division), and each has an impressive stadium. The football season runs from August to May, and there is a game most weeks. Scotland's **Hampden National Stadium** hosts the finals of domestic cup competitions in November and May each year, and major international games.

Celtic fans cheering on their football (soccer) team from the stands

DIRECTORY

Classical Music and Opera

Glasgow Royal Concert Hall
2 Sauchiehall St, G2 3NY.
Tel (0141) 353 8000.
w glasgowconcert
halls.com

Royal Scottish Academy of Music and Drama
100 Renfrew St, G2 3DB.
Tel (0141) 332 5057.

Theatre Royal
282 Hope St, G2 3QA.
Tel (0844) 871 7647.

Rock, Jazz and World Music

Barrowlands
244 Gallowgate, G4 0TT.
Tel (0141) 552 4601.

Cottier's
93 Hyndland St, G11 5PU.
Tel (0141) 357 5825.

King Tut's Wah Wah Hut
272a St Vincent St, G2
5RL. **Tel** (0141) 221 5279.

O2 ABC
300 Sauchiehall St, G2
3JA. **Tel** (0844) 477 2000.

O2 Academy
121 Eglington St, G5 9NT.
Tel (0141) 418 3000.

Old Fruitmarket
Albion St, G1 1NQ.
Tel (0141) 353 8000.

Scottish Exhibition and Conference Centre/Armadillo
Exhibition Way, G3 8YW.
Tel (0141) 248 3000.
w secc.co.uk

Cinema

Cineworld
7 Renfrew St, G2 3AB.
Tel (0871) 200 2000.

Glasgow Film Theatre
12 Rose St, G3 6RB.
Tel (0141) 332 6535.

IMAX Theatre
50 Pacific Quay, G51 1EA.
Tel (0141) 420 5000.

Odeon at the Quay
Paisley Road,
G5 8NP.
Tel (0871) 224 4007.

Theatre and Dance

Arches
253 Argyll St, G2 8DL.
Tel (0141) 565 1000.

Citizens' Theatre
119 Gorbals St, G5 9DS.
Tel (0141) 429 0022.

King's
297 Bath St, G2 4JN.
Tel (0844) 871 7627.

Tramway
25 Albert Drive, G41 2PE.
Tel (0845) 330 3501.

Tron
63 Trongate, G1 5HB.
Tel (0141) 552 4267.

Bars and Clubs

Artá
62 Albion St, G1 1PA.
Tel (0845) 166 6018.

Bar 91
91 Candleriggs, G1 1NP.
Tel (0141) 552 5211.

Bar Soba
11 Mitchell Lane, G1 3NU.
Tel (0141) 204 2404.

Chinaskis
239 North St, G3 7DL.
Tel (0141) 221 0061.

Griffin
266 Bath St, G2 4JP.
Tel (0141) 331 5171.

Halt
160 Woodlands Rd, G3
6LF. **Tel** (0141) 353 6450.

Home
80 Albion St, G1 1NY.
Tel (0141) 552 1734.

Horseshoe
17 Drury St, G2 5AE.
Tel (0141) 248 6368.

Radio
44–46 Ashton Lane, G12
8SJ. **Tel** (0845) 166 6011.

The Soundhaus
47 Hyde Park St, G3 8BW.
Tel (0141) 221 4659.

The Sub Club
22 Jamaica St, G1 4QD.
Tel (0141) 248 4600.

The Tunnel
84 Mitchell St, G1 3NA.
Tel (0141) 204 1000.

Sports

Celtic
Celtic Park, 95 Kerrydale
St, G40 3RE.
Tel (0871) 226 1888.

Glasgow Rangers
Ibrox Stadium, G51 2XD.
Tel (0871) 702 1972.

Hampden National Stadium
Hampden Park, Letherby
Drive, G42 9BA.
Tel (0141) 620 4000.

CENTRAL SCOTLAND

Central Scotland is a contrast of picturesque countryside and major urban centres, where a modern industrialized country meets an older and wilder landscape. Historically, it was here that the English-speaking Lowlands bordered the Gaelic Highlands, and there is still a strong sense of transition for anyone travelling north.

The Highland Boundary Fault is a geological feature running through Central Scotland from Arran in the southwest to Stonehaven on the northeast coast. The Fault divides the Highlands from the Lowlands, making Central Scotland an area of contrasts, with both mountainous areas and green farmland. For hundreds of years, this line was also a meeting place, or border, between two very different cultures. To the north and west was a Gaelic-speaking people, who felt loyalty to their local clan chiefs. This way of life began to be marginalized in the late 18th century, as the more Anglicized Lowlands established their dominance.

In the Lowlands, Scotland's industry developed, drawing on coal reserves in districts such as Lanarkshire and the Lothians, while the Highlands were depopulated and eventually set aside for sporting estates and sheep farming.

Because Central Scotland is so compact, the opposing characteristics of Highland and Lowland, industrial and pre-industrial, exist side by side. Stirling Castle, parts of which date from the 16th century, is sited close to the petro-chemical plants and power plants on the upper reaches of the Forth. The tranquillity of the Trossachs and the hills of Arran are easily accessible from Glasgow, Scotland's largest, and largely industrial, city. The country's first coal-run ironworks was built at Carron in 1759, very close to Falkirk, where Bonnie Prince Charlie had enjoyed one of his last military successes as claimant to the British throne 13 years earlier. Perth and Dundee are important centres of commerce just a short distance from the relative wildness of the southern Highlands. From gritty cities to the great outdoors, the region displays huge contrasts.

The view from Goatfell Ridge, near Brodick, across to the spectacular mountains of Arran

◄ Canal through the Argyll and Bute countryside

Exploring Central Scotland

Central Scotland has a huge variety of landscapes. The Goatfell ridge on the Isle of Arran, off the west coast, has one of the most inspiring island hill walks in the entire country while, just to the north, the Isle of Bute is a more placid tourist destination. On the mainland, the Trossachs, near Callander, is an area of outstanding mountain beauty, very different from the lowlands of the Forth Valley futher east. Stirling Castle stands at the head of the Forth under the shadow of the Ochil Hills, while Perth occupies a similar position on the Tay. The Firth of Tay, with its open views, is home to Dundee, Scotland's fourth city.

Loch Katrine in the Trossachs

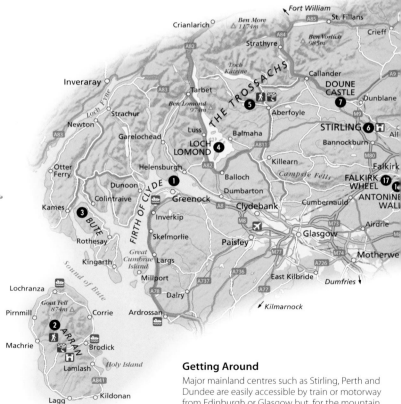

Getting Around

Major mainland centres such as Stirling, Perth and Dundee are easily accessible by train or motorway from Edinburgh or Glasgow but, for the mountain areas in Central Scotland (the Trossachs or minor ranges), a car is recommended. Reaching Arran or Bute is best done by car or train from Glasgow, then car ferry from ports on the Ayrshire coast (Ardrossan, Wemyss Bay). The islands are small enough to make bicycle touring possible.

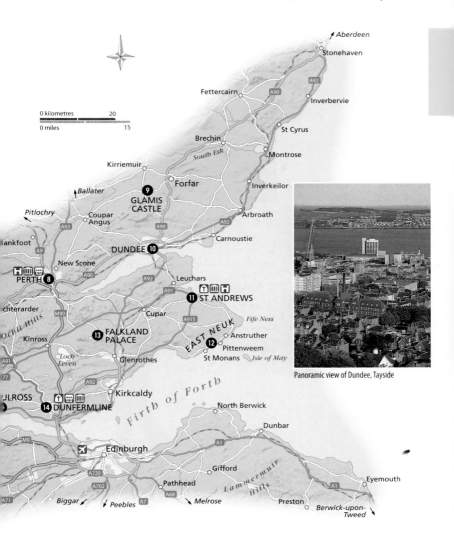

0 kilometres 20
0 miles 15

Aberdeen
Stonehaven
Fettercairn
Inverbervie
St Cyrus
Brechin
South Esk
Montrose
Kirriemuir
Forfar
Inverkeilor
Ballater
9
GLAMIS CASTLE
Pitlochry
Coupar Angus
Arbroath
ankfoot
Carnoustie
DUNDEE 10
New Scone
Leuchars
PERTH 8
St Andrews
11 ST ANDREWS
chterarder
Cupar
Fife Ness
Ochil Hills
13 FALKLAND PALACE
EAST NEUK
Kinross
12
Anstruther
Pittenweem
Loch Leven
Glenrothes
St Monans
Isle of May
Kirkcaldy
JLROSS
Firth of Forth
14 DUNFERMLINE
North Berwick
Dunbar
Edinburgh
Gifford
Biggar
Pathhead
Lammermuir Hills
Eyemouth
Peebles
Melrose
Preston
Berwick-upon-Tweed

Panoramic view of Dundee, Tayside

Key

▬▬ Motorway (highway)
▬▬ Major road
— Minor road
=== Other road
— Scenic route
⊸ Main line railway
— Minor railway
△ Summit

Sights at a Glance

1 Firth of Clyde
2 Arran
3 Bute
4 Loch Lomond
5 *The Trossachs pp120–21*
6 *Stirling pp124–5*
7 Doune Castle
8 Perth
9 Glamis Castle
10 Dundee

11 St Andrews
12 East Neuk
13 Falkland Palace
14 Dunfermline
15 Culross
16 Antonine Wall
17 Falkirk Wheel

For additional map symbols *see back flap*

❶ Firth of Clyde

Numerous counties west of Glasgow.
🚆 Helensburgh and Dumbarton in the north; Troon and Ayr in the south. 🚢 from Largs to Great Cumbrae; from Gourock to Dunoon. ℹ️ Largs (01475) 686212; Dumbarton (08452) 255121.

As might be expected of a waterway that leads from Glasgow, a former economic powerhouse of the British Empire *(see p50)*, to the Irish Sea and the Atlantic, the Firth of Clyde has many reminders of its industrial past. **Greenock**, some 40 km (25 miles) west of Glasgow, was once a ship-building centre. Few visit for the town's beauty, but the **McLean Museum and Art Gallery**, with its exhibits and information on the engineer James Watt *(see p28)*, a native of Greenock, is worth a visit. Princes Pier is a departure point for cruises along the Clyde. **Dumbarton**, 24 km (15 miles) from Glasgow on the northern bank, dates from the 5th century AD. Its ancient castle perches on a rock overlooking the rest of the town.

The Firth itself is L-shaped, heading northwest as it opens up beyond the Erskine Bridge. On reaching Gourock, just west of Greenock, the Firth branches south to more open water. Kip Marina at nearby **Inverkip** is a major yachting centre, while many towns on the Ayrshire coast have served as holiday resorts for Glasgow since Victorian times. **Largs**, site of the clash between Scots and Vikings in 1263, has a multimedia centre about the Vikings in Scotland, as well as a

The old harbour at Brodick, with Goatfell ridge in the distance

modern monument to the 1263 battle. A ferry service is offered to **Great Cumbrae Island**, which lies just off the coast. The main town on the island is Millport, which is built around a picturesque bay. The western side of the Firth of Clyde is much less developed, bordered by the Cowal Peninsula with its hills and lochs. The only town of note in this wild country is **Dunoon**. Again once a Victorian holiday resort, it still relies on tourism for its income. For many years there was a strong American influence in Dunoon due to the US nuclear submarine base at Holy Loch that is now closed.

🏛️ McLean Museum and Art Gallery
15 Kelly St, Greenock. **Tel** (01475) 715624. **Open** 10am–5pm Mon–Sat.

❷ Arran

North Ayrshire. 🚶 5000. 🚢 from Ardrossan to Brodick; from Claonaig (Isle of Mull) to Lochranza (Apr–Oct only). ℹ️ Ayr (01292) 290300. 🌐 ayrshire-arran.com

Arran is thought to have been populated as long ago as the end of the last Ice Age. The island's neolithic chambered burial tombs, such as the one at **Torrylinn** near Lagg in the south, indicate this. Bronze Age stone circles can also be seen around **Machrie** on the west coast. Vikings arrived from about AD 800 and exerted an influence for more than four centuries. After the Battle of Largs in 1263, when Alexander III defeated the Norsemen, Scotland bought Arran from the Vikings in 1266.

Today, visitors tend to come to Arran for outdoor pursuits. Golf is especially popular, with 18-hole courses at Brodick, Whiting Bay and Lamlash. Fishing is also popular.

Brodick is the island's only real town. The more mountainous parts offer some of the most spectacular hillwalking in Central Scotland. **The Goatfell ridge** to the east of Glen Rosa and **Beinn Tarsuinn** to the west have a particular rugged beauty.

Golfer on the island of Arran

Robert the Bruce stayed on Arran on his return to Scotland in 1307. His followers had already been harassing the garrison at **Brodick Castle**, then occupied by supporters of the King of England. Legend states that it was from Arran that Bruce saw a signal fire on the Ayrshire coast that told him it was safe to return to the mainland and launch the campaign against the English *(see p47)*. Parts of the Castle still date from the 13th century, though it has had many later additions.

🏰 Brodick Castle
Brodick. **Tel** (0844) 493 2152. **Open** May–Sep: 11am–4pm (to 3pm Apr & Oct); gardens all year. 🅿️ ♿ NTS

Largs seafront, the departure point for ferries to Great Cumbrae Island

The snowy peak of Ben Lomond rising majestically over Loch Lomond, part of the West Highland Way

❸ Bute

Argyll & Bute. 🚠 7,000. 🚢 from Wemyss Bay to Rothesay; from Colintraive to Rhubodach. 🚌 from Dunoon. 🛈 Rothesay (01700) 502151.

Bute is almost an extension of the Cowal Peninsula, and the small ferry from Colintraive takes only five minutes to cross the Kyles of Bute to Rhubodach on the island. This route is a long drive from Glasgow, however, and most people choose to travel via Wemyss Bay on the Firth of Clyde across to the island's main town, Rothesay.

Just 25 km (16 miles) long by 8 km (5 miles) at its widest point, Bute has been occupied since at least the Bronze Age. The remains of the chapel at St Ninian's Point on the west coast date from around the 6th century, while **Rothesay Castle**, now ruined, is mostly a 12th-century structure and was the site of struggles between islanders and Vikings in the 13th century. Over the last 120 years or so, Bute has played a more placid role as a popular holiday resort.

One of Bute's attractions is **Mount Stuart House**, 5 km (3 miles) south of Rothesay. This aristocratic house, built in 1877 by the third Marquess of Bute, is set in 18th-century gardens. The features of this Gothic edifice reflect the Marquess's interests in mythology, religion and astronomy.

🏰 Rothesay Castle
Castle Hill St, Rothesay. **Tel** (01700) 502 691. **Open** Apr–Sep: 9:30am–5:30pm daily; Oct: 9:30am–4:30pm daily; Mar: 9:30am–4:30pm Sat–Wed. 🅿
🆆 historic-scotland.gov.uk

🏰 Mount Stuart House
Mount St. **Tel** (01700) 503877. **Open** Apr–Oct: 11am–5pm daily. 🅿
🅿 ♿ 🖥 🆆 mountstuart.com

View of Bute with 14th-century Kames Castle, at the head of Kames Bay

❹ Loch Lomond

West Dunbartonshire, Argyll & Bute, Trossachs. 🚆 Balloch, Tarbet. 🚌 Balloch, Balmaha. 🛈 Balloch (01389) 753533.

Of Scotland's many lochs, Lomond is perhaps the most popular and best loved. Lying just 30 km (19 miles) northwest of Glasgow, its accessibility has helped its rise to prominence. The loch is the largest body of fresh water in the British Isles, 35 km (22 miles) long and 8 km (5 miles) at its widest point in the south, where there is a scattering of over 30 islands, some with ancient ruins. Duncryne, a small hill some 5 km (3 miles) northeast of **Balloch** on the southern shore, gives an excellent view of the Loch. Much of the area became Scotland's first national park in 2002, fronted by the **Loch Lomond Shores** visitor centre complex in Balloch.

In general, the western shore is the more developed, with villages such as **Luss** and **Tarbet** attracting large numbers of visitors. The contrast between the Loch and **Ben Lomond**, 974 m (3,196 ft), high above its eastern shore adds to the spectacle. Many walkers pass this way since Scotland's most popular long-distance footpath, the West Highland Way *(see p199)* from Glasgow to Fort William, skirts the eastern shore. Boat trips around the loch operate regularly from Balloch Pier. The area is also good for watersports enthusiasts – speed boats, kayaks and jet skis can all be rented.

5 The Trossachs

Combining the ruggedness of the Grampians with the pastoral tranquillity of the Borders, this beautiful region of craggy hills and sparkling lochs is the colourful meeting place of the Lowlands and Highlands. Home to a wide variety of wildlife, including the golden eagle, peregrine falcon, red deer and the wildcat, the Trossachs and their inhabitants have inspired numerous writers, including Sir Walter Scott *(see p90)* who made the area the setting for several of his novels. In 2002, a large part of the area was designated as Loch Lomond and The Trossachs National Park, the first national park in Scotland.

Loch Katrine
The setting of Sir Walter Scott's *Lady of the Lake* (1810), this freshwater loch can be explored on the Victorian steamer *Sir Walter Scott*, which cruises from the Trossachs Pier.

Loch Lomond
Britain's largest freshwater lake was immortalized in a ballad composed by a local Jacobite soldier, dying far from home. He laments that though he will return home before his companions who travel on "the high road", he will be doing so on "the low road" (of death).

Luss
With its exceptionally picturesque cottages, Luss is one of the prettiest villages in Central Scotland. Surrounded by grassy hills, it occupies one of the most scenic parts of Loch Lomond's western shore.

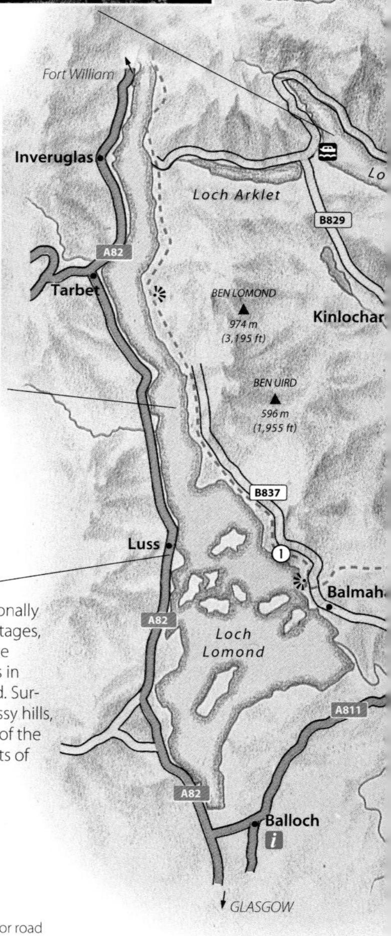

KEY

① **The West Highland Way** provides a good footpath through the area.

② **Rob Roy's grave**

③ **The Duke's Pass**, between Callander and Aberfoyle, affords some of the finest views in the area.

Key

▬ Major road

▬ Minor road

▬ Narrow lane

╍ Footpath

0 kilometres   5

0 miles   5

Map labels: Fort William, Inveruglas, Loch Arklet, B829, A82, Tarbet, BEN LOMOND 974 m (3,195 ft), Kinlochar, BEN UIRD 596 m (1,955 ft), B837, Luss, ① , Balmah, A82, Loch Lomond, A811, A82, Balloch ℹ, GLASGOW, Lo

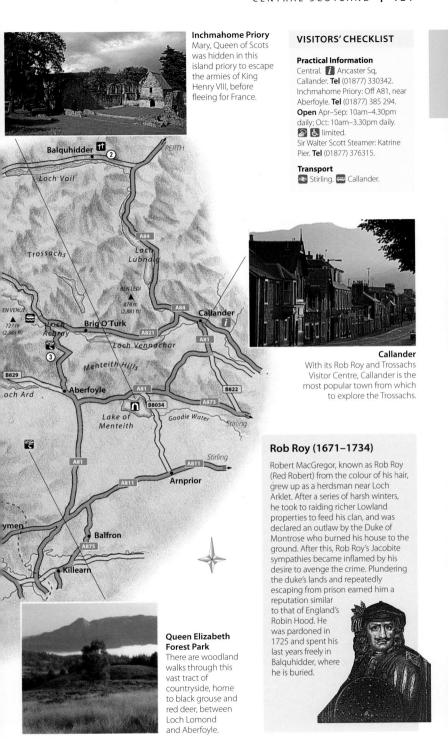

Inchmahome Priory

Mary, Queen of Scots was hidden in this island priory to escape the armies of King Henry VIII, before fleeing for France.

VISITORS' CHECKLIST

Practical Information
Central. 🛈 Ancaster Sq, Callander. **Tel** (01877) 330342. Inchmahome Priory: Off A81, near Aberfoyle. **Tel** (01877) 385 294. **Open** Apr–Sep: 10am–4.30pm daily; Oct: 10am–3.30pm daily. 🕗 🚻 limited. Sir Walter Scott Steamer: Katrine Pier. **Tel** (01877) 376315.

Transport
🚆 Stirling. 🚌 Callander.

Callander

With its Rob Roy and Trossachs Visitor Centre, Callander is the most popular town from which to explore the Trossachs.

Rob Roy (1671–1734)

Robert MacGregor, known as Rob Roy (Red Robert) from the colour of his hair, grew up as a herdsman near Loch Arklet. After a series of harsh winters, he took to raiding richer Lowland properties to feed his clan, and was declared an outlaw by the Duke of Montrose who burned his house to the ground. After this, Rob Roy's Jacobite sympathies became inflamed by his desire to avenge the crime. Plundering the duke's lands and repeatedly escaping from prison earned him a reputation similar to that of England's Robin Hood. He was pardoned in 1725 and spent his last years freely in Balquhidder, where he is buried.

Queen Elizabeth Forest Park

There are woodland walks through this vast tract of countryside, home to black grouse and red deer, between Loch Lomond and Aberfoyle.

For additional map symbols *see back flap*

The 17th-century town house of the Dukes of Argyll

❻ Stirling

Central. 🚉 34,000. 🚆 🚌 ℹ️ Old Town Jail, St John St. (01786) 475019. 🌐 visitstirling.org

Situated between the Ochil Hills and the Campsie Fells, the town of Stirling grew up around its castle, historically one of Scotland's most important fortresses. Below the castle the Old Town is still protected by the original walls, built in the 16th century to keep Mary, Queen of Scots safe from Henry VIII. The medieval **Church of the Holy Rude**, on Castle Wynd, where the infant James VI was crowned in 1567, has one of Scotland's few surviving hammerbeam oak roofs. In front of the church, the ornate façade of **Mar's Wark** is all that remains of a grand palace which, though never completed, was commissioned in 1570 by the first Earl of Mar. It was destroyed by the Jacobites in 1746.

Environs

Three kilometres (2 miles) south of Stirling, the **Bannockburn Heritage Centre** stands by the field where Robert the Bruce defeated the English in 1314 (see p47). After the battle, he dismantled the castle so it would not fall back into English hands. A bronze equestrian statue commemorates the man who became an icon of Scottish independence.

ℹ️ **Bannockburn Heritage Centre**
Glasgow Rd. **Tel** (0844) 493 2139.
Open Mar–Oct: 10am–5:30pm daily.
Closed Nov–Feb. 📷 ♿ 🏠 NTS

Stirling Castle

Rising high on a rocky crag, this magnificent castle, which dominated Scottish history for centuries, now remains one of the finest examples of Renaissance architecture in Scotland. Legend says that King Arthur wrested the original castle from the Saxons; however, the first written evidence of a castle is from 1100. The present building dates from the 15th and 16th centuries and was last defended, against the Jacobites, in 1746. From 1881 to 1964 it was used as a depot for recruits into the Argyll and Sutherland Highlanders, though it now serves no military function.

Robert the Bruce
In the esplanade, this modern statue shows Robert the Bruce sheathing his sword after the Battle of Bannockburn in 1314.

Entrance

Stirling Castle in the Time of the Stuarts, painted by Johannes Vorsterman (1643–99)

◀ The William Wallace Monument at Abbey Craig, Stirling

★ Palace
The sumptuous interiors of the royal apartments contain the carved, wooden Stirling Heads. The rooms have been restored to their mid-16th-century appearance.

VISITORS' CHECKLIST

Practical Information
Castle Esplanade, Stirling.
Tel (01786) 450000.
Open Apr–Sep: 9:30am– 6pm daily; Oct–Mar: 9:30am– 5pm daily. 🅿 🚻 museum. ♿ limited. 🚫 🖥 📷
Ⓦ stirlingcastle.gov.uk

★ Chapel Royal
Seventeenth-century frescoes by Valentine Jenkins adorn the chapel, built in 1594.

Grand Battery
Following the unrest after the deposition of the Stuarts (see p49), this parapet was built in 1708, to strengthen the castle's defences.

KEY

① Forework

② Prince's Tower

③ **The King's Old Building** houses the Regimental Museum of the Argyll and Sutherland Highlanders.

④ Nether Bailey

⑤ **The Great Hall**, built in 1500, has a roof similar to that of Edinburgh Castle (see pp64–5).

⑥ **The Elphinstone Tower** was originally home to the constable of the castle.

Stirling Battles

At the highest navigable point of the Forth and holding the pass to the Highlands, Stirling occupied a key position in Scotland's struggles for independence. Seven battlefields can be seen from the castle; the 67-m (220-ft) Wallace Monument at Abbey Craig recalls William Wallace's defeat of the English at Stirling Bridge in 1297, foreshadowing Bruce's victory in 1314.

The Victorian Wallace Monument

Perth seen from the east across the Tay

❼ Doune Castle

Doune, Central. **Tel** (01786) 841742.
🚆 🚌 Stirling then bus. **Open** Apr–
Sep: 9:30am–5:30pm daily; Oct: 9:30–
4:30 daily; Nov–Mar: 9:30am–4:30pm
Sat–Wed. 🅿️ 🅰️ limited. 🆆 historic-
scotland.gov.uk

Built as the residence of Robert,
Duke of Albany, in the late 1300s,
Doune Castle was a Stuart stronghold until it fell into ruin in the
18th century. Now fully restored, it
offers a unique view into the life
of the medieval royal household.
    The Gatehouse leads through
to the central courtyard, from
which the Great Hall can be
entered. Complete with its open-
timber roof, minstrels' gallery and
central fireplace, the Hall adjoins
the Lord's Hall and Private Room
with its original privy and well-
hatch. A number of private stairs
and narrow passages illustrate
the ingenious means by which
the royal family protected itself
during times of danger.

The film *Monty Python and the
Holy Grail* was shot here, making
the castle a popular destination
for Python fans.

❽ Perth

Perthshire. 🅰️ 45,000. 🚆 🚌 🔽
ℹ️ Lower City Mills, West Mills St. **Tel**
(01738) 450600. 🆆 perthshire.co.uk

Once the capital of medieval
Scotland, Perth has a rich
heritage that is reflected in many
of its buildings. It was in the
Church of St John, founded in
1126, that the preacher John
Knox delivered the fiery sermons
that led to the destruction of
many local monasteries. The
Victorianized **Fair Maid's House**
(c.1600), on North Port, is one of
the oldest houses in town and
was the fictional home of the
heroine of Sir Walter Scott's
The Fair Maid of Perth (1828).
    In **Balhousie Castle**, the
Museum of the Black Watch

commemorates the first ever
Highland regiment, while the
Museum and Art Gallery has
displays on local industry and
exhibitions of Scottish painting.

Environs
Three km (2 miles) north of
Perth, Gothic **Scone Palace**
stands on the site of an abbey
destroyed by John Knox's
followers in 1559. Between the
9th and 13th centuries, Scone
guarded the sacred Stone of
Destiny, now in Edinburgh
Castle (*see pp64–5*).

🏠 **Balhousie Castle**
RHQ Black Watch, Hay St.
Tel (01738) 638152. **Open** May–Sep:
10am–4:30pm Mon–Sat; Oct–Apr:
10am–3:30pm Mon–Fri.
Closed 23 Dec–18 Mar.

🏛️ **Museum and Art Gallery**
78 George St. **Tel** (01738) 632488.
Open 10am–5pm Mon–Sat. 🅰️

🏠 **Scone Palace**
A93 to Braemar. **Tel** (01738) 552300.
Open Apr–Oct daily. 🅿️ 🅰️

❾ Glamis Castle

Glamis, outside Forfar, Tayside.
Tel (01307) 840393.
🚆 🚌 Dundee then bus. **Open** Apr–
Oct: 10am–6pm. 🅿️ 🍴 🅰️ grounds.
🆆 glamis-castle.co.uk

With the pinnacled outline of
a Loire chateau, the imposing
medieval towerhouse of **Glamis
Castle** began as a royal hunting

Glamis Castle with statues of James VI (left) and Charles I (right)

lodge in the 11th century but underwent reconstruction in the 17th century. It was the childhood home of the late Queen Elizabeth the Queen Mother, and her former bedroom can be seen with a youthful portrait by Henri de Laszlo (1878–1956).

Many rooms are open to the public, including Duncan's Hall, the oldest in the castle and Shakespeare's setting for the king's murder in *Macbeth*. Together, the rooms present an array of china, paintings, tapestries and furniture spanning 500 years. In the grounds stand a pair of wrought-iron gates made for the Queen Mother on her 80th birthday in 1980.

⑩ Dundee

Tayside. 🏔 142,000. ✈ 🚉 🚌
ℹ Discovery Point (01382) 527527.
📅 daily. 🌐 **angusanddundee.co.uk**

Famous for its fruit cake and marmalade, the city of **Dundee** was also a major ship-building centre in the 18th and 19th centuries, a period which is recreated at the Victoria Docks.

HMS Unicorn, built in 1824, is the oldest British-built warship still afloat and is fitted as it was on its last voyage. Berthed at Riverside is the royal research ship **Discovery**. Built here in 1901 for the first of Captain Scott's voyages to the Antarctic, the *Discovery* was one of the last sailing ships to be made in Britain. Housed in a Victorian Gothic building, the **McManus**

The Birthplace of Golf

Scotland's national game *(see pp194–7)* was pioneered on the sandy links around St Andrews. The earliest record of the game being played dates from 1457, when golf was banned by James II because

it was interfering with his subjects' archery practice. Mary, Queen of Scots was berated in 1568 for playing immediately after her husband, Darnley, had been murdered.

Mary, Queen of Scots at St Andrews in 1563

View of St Andrews over the ruins of the cathedral

Galleries provide a glimpse of Dundee's industrial heritage, with exhibitions of archaeology and Victorian art.

Environs

Along the coast, **Arbroath** is famed for its red stonework, ancient Abbey and "Arbroath Smokies" (salted haddock smoked over a beech and oak fire). Arbroath Abbey displays a copy of *The Declaration of Arbroath*, attesting Scotland's independence.

🏛 **HMS Unicorn**
Victoria Docks, **Tel** (01382) 200900.
Open Easter–Oct: 10am–5pm; Nov–Mar: noon–4pm Wed–Fri (from 10am Sat & Sun). 🚻 🚹 limited.

🏛 **Discovery**
Discovery Point. **Tel** (01382) 309 060.
Open daily. 🚻 🚹 🚹 🚹 by appt.

🏛 **McManus Galleries**
Albert Institute, Albert Square.
Tel (01382) 307200. **Open** daily.

⑪ St Andrews

Fife. 🏔 17,000. 🚉 Leuchars. 🚌
ℹ 70 Market St (01334) 472021.
🌐 **standrews.co.uk**

Scotland's oldest university town and one-time ecclesiastical capital, **St Andrews** is now a shrine to golfers from all over the world. Its main streets and cobbled alleys, full of crooked housefronts, dignified university buildings and medieval churches, converge on the venerable ruins of the 12th-century **cathedral**. Once the largest cathedral in Scotland, it was later pillaged for its stones, which were used to build the town. **St Andrew's Castle** was built for the town's bishops in the year 1200 and the dungeon can still be seen. St Andrews' golf courses occupy the land to the west of the city, and each is open for a modest fee.

The **British Golf Museum**, which tells how the city's Royal and Ancient Golf Club became the ruling arbiter of the game, will delight golf enthusiasts.

One of the chief pleasures of a visit here is a walk along the sands, immortalized in the film, *Chariots of Fire*.

🏰 **St Andrew's Castle**
The Scores. **Tel** (01334) 477196.
Open daily. 🚻 🚹 🚹

🏛 **British Golf Museum**
Bruce Embankment. **Tel** (01334)
4600046. **Open** daily. 🚻 🚹

The central courtyard of Falkland Palace, bordered by rose bushes

⓬ East Neuk

Fife. 🚆 Leuchars. 🚌 Glenrothes & Leuchars. 𝒊 St Andrews (01334) 472021. 🅦 eastneukwide.co.uk

A string of pretty fishing villages peppers the shoreline of the **East Neuk** (the eastern "corner") of Fife, stretching from Earlsferry to Fife Ness. Much of Scotland's medieval trade with Europe passed through these ports, a connection reflected in the Flemish-inspired crow-stepped gables of many of the cottages. Although the herring industry has declined and the area is now a peaceful holiday centre, the sea still dominates village life. The harbour is the heart of St Monans, a charming town of narrow twisting streets, while Pittenweem is the base for the East Neuk fishing fleet.

The town is also known for **St Fillan's Cave**, the retreat of a 9th-century hermit whose relic was used to bless the army of Robert the Bruce before the Battle of Bannockburn (see p47). A church stands among the cobbled lanes and colourful cottages of Crail; legend goes that the stone by the church gate was hurled across to the mainland from the Isle of May by the Devil.

A number of 16th- to 19th-century buildings in the village of Anstruther contain the **Scottish Fisheries Museum,** which tells the area's history with the aid of cottage interiors, boats and displays on whaling. From the village you can go to the nature reserve on the **Isle of May**, which teems with seabirds and a colony of grey seals. The statue of Alexander Selkirk in Lower Largo recalls the local boy whose seafaring adventures inspired Daniel Defoe's novel *Robinson Crusoe* (1719). After disagreeing with his captain, he was put ashore on an uninhabited island where he survived for four years.

🏛 **Scottish Fisheries Museum**
St Ayles, Harbour Head, Anstruther. **Tel** (01333) 310628. **Open** daily.
🗺 🅿 ♿ ▭

The Palace Keeper

Due to the size of the royal household and the necessity for the king to be itinerant, the office of Keeper was created by the medieval kings who required custodians to maintain and replenish the resources of their many palaces while they were away. Now redundant, it was a hereditary title and gave the custodian permanent and often luxurious lodgings.

James VI's bed in the Keeper's Bedroom at Falkland Palace

⓭ Falkland Palace

Falkland, Fife. **Tel** (0844) 4932 186. 🚆 Ladybank, then bus. **Open** Mar–Oct: 11am–5pm Mon–Sat, 1–5pm Sun (until 4pm Nov–Feb). 🗺 ♿ 🅽🆃🆂 🅦 nts.org.uk

This stunning Renaissance palace was designed as a hunting lodge for the Stuart kings. Although its construction was begun by James IV in 1500, most of the work was carried out by his son, James V, in the 1530s. Under the influence of his two French wives, he employed French workmen to redecorate the façade of the East Range with dormers, buttresses and medallions, and to build the beautifully proportioned South Range. The palace fell into ruin during the years of the Commonwealth and was occupied briefly by Rob Roy (see p121) in 1715.

After buying the estates in 1887, the third Marquess of Bute became the Palace Keeper and subsequently restored the building. The richly panelled interiors are filled with superb furniture and contemporary portraits of the Stuart monarchs. The royal tennis court, built in 1539 for King James V, is the oldest in Britain.

⓮ Dunfermline

Fife. 🚾 48,000. 🚆 🚌 𝒊 1 High St (01383) 720999.

Scotland's capital until 1603, Dunfermline is dominated by the ruins of the 12th-century abbey and palace, which recall its royal past. The town first came to prominence in the 11th century as the seat of King Malcolm III, who founded a priory on the present site of the **Abbey Church**. With its Norman nave and 19th-century choir, the abbey church contains the tombs of 22 Scottish kings and queens, including that of the renowned Robert the Bruce.

The ruins of the **palace** soar over the beautiful gardens of Pittencrieff Park. Dunfermline's most famous son, the philanthropist Andrew Carnegie (1835–1919), had been forbidden entrance to the park as a boy. After making his fortune, he bought the entire Pittencrieff estate and gave it to the people of Dunfermline. Carnegie emigrated to Pennsylvania in his teens and through iron and steel, became one of the wealthiest men in the world. He donated some $350 million for the benefit of mankind. **Carnegie Birthplace Museum** tells his story.

🏛 Abbey Church
Tel (01383) 723005. **Open** Apr–Oct: daily (Sun pm only).

🏛 Carnegie Birthplace Museum
Moodie St. **Tel** (01383) 724302. **Open** Mar–Nov: daily (Sun pm only).

The 12th-century Norman nave of Dunfermline Abbey Church

⓯ Culross

Fife. 🚶 400. 🚍 Dunfermline. 🚆 Dunfermline. 🛈 (0844) 493 2189. **NTS** 🌐 nts.org.uk

An important religious centre in the 6th century, the town of Culross is reputed to have been the birthplace of St Mungo in 514. Now a beautifully preserved 16th- and 17th-century village,

Culross prospered in the 16th century due to the growth of its coal and salt industries, most notably under the genius of Sir George Bruce. Descended from the family of Robert the Bruce, Sir George took charge of the colliery in 1575 and created a drainage system called the "Egyptian Wheel" which cleared a mine 1.5 km (1 mile) long, running underneath the River Forth.

The National Trust for Scotland began restoring the town in 1932 and now provides a guided tour. This starts at the **Visitors' Centre,** housed in the one-time village prison.

Built in 1577, Bruce's **palace** has the crow-stepped gables, decorated windows and red pantiles typical of the period. The interior retains its original painted ceilings, which are among the finest in Scotland. Crossing the square past the **Oldest House**, dating from 1577, head for the **Town House** to the west. Behind it, a cobbled street known as the Back Causeway leads to the turreted **Study**, built in 1610 as a house for the Bishop of Dunblane. The main room is open to visitors and should be seen for its original Norwegian ceiling. Continuing northwards to the ruined abbey, fine church and Abbey House, don't miss the Dutch-gabled **House with the Evil Eyes**.

🏛 Palace, Town House and Study
Open late Mar–May & Sep: 12–5pm Thur–Mon; Jun–Aug 12–5pm daily; Oct 12–4pm Fri–Mon. 🚗 🚻 limited.

The 16th-century palace of industrialist George Bruce, at Culross

⓰ Antonine Wall

Falkirk. 🛈 Falkirk Wheel, Lime Rd, (01324) 620244. 🚍 Falkirk. **Open** Mon–Sat.

The Romans invaded Scotland for a second time around AD 140, in the reign of Emperor Antonius and built a 60 km (37 mile) earth rampart across Central Scotland from the Firth of Clyde to the Firth of Forth. The rampart was further defended by ditches and forts at strategic points. One of the best preserved sections of the fortifications can be seen at Rough Castle, west of Falkirk.

⓱ Falkirk Wheel

Lime Rd, Tamfourhill, Falkirk. **Tel** (08700) 500208. 🚍 Falkirk. **Open** 10am–5:30pm daily. 🚗 for boat trip. 🚻 🏠 🌐 thefalkirkwheel.co.uk

This impressive, elegant boat lift is the first ever to revolve and the centrepiece of Scotland's ambitious canal regeneration scheme. Once important for commercial transport, the Union and the Forth and Clyde canals were blocked by numerous roads during the 1960s. Now the Falkirk Wheel gently swings boats between the two waterways creating an uninterrupted link between Glasgow and Edinburgh. This huge, moving sculpture rotates continuously, lifting boats 35m, a height equivalent to 11 traditional locks, in just 15 minutes. Visitors can ride the wheel on one of the boats that leave the visitor centre every 40 minutes.

The rotating Falkirk Wheel boat lift

THE HIGHLANDS AND ISLANDS

Most of the stock images of Scottishness – clans and tartans, whisky and porridge, bagpipes and heather – originate in the Highlands, and enrich the popular picture of Scotland as a whole. But for many centuries the Gaelic-speaking, cattle-raising Highlanders had little in common with their southern neighbours.

Clues to the non-Celtic ancestors of the Highlanders lie scattered across the Highlands and islands in the form of stone circles, brochs and cairns spanning over 5,000 years. By the end of the 6th century, the Gaelic-speaking Celts had arrived from Ireland, as had St Columba, who taught Christianity to the monastic community he established on the island of Iona. The later fusion of Christianity with Viking culture in the 8th and 9th centuries produced the beautiful St Magnus Cathedral in the Orkney Islands.

For over 1,000 years, Celtic Highland society was founded on a clan system, built on family ties to create loyal groups dependent on a feudal chief. However, the clans were systematically broken up by England after 1746, following the defeat of the Jacobite attempt on the British crown led by Bonnie Prince Charlie *(see p157)*. A more romantic vision of the Highlands began to emerge in the early 19th century, largely due to Sir Walter Scott's novels and poetry depicting the majesty and grandeur of a country previously considered merely poverty-stricken and barbaric. Another great popularizer was Queen Victoria, whose passion for Balmoral Castle helped establish the trend for acquiring Highland sporting estates. But behind the sentimentality lay harsh economic realities that drove generations of Highland farmers to seek a new life overseas.

Today, over half the inhabitants of the Highlands and islands still live in communities of less than 1,000 people. But thriving oil and tourist industries now supplement fishing and whisky, and population figures are rising.

A group of puffins congregating on the rocks, a common sight on Scottish islands

◄ Rugged mountain slopes on the Isle of Skye

Exploring the Highlands and Islands

To the north and west of Stirling, the historic gateway to the Highlands, lie the magnificent mountains and glens, fretted coastlines and lonely isles that are the epitome of Scottish scenery. Inverness, the Highland capital, makes a good starting point for exploring Loch Ness and the Cairngorms, while Fort William holds the key to Ben Nevis. Inland from Aberdeen lie Royal Deeside and the Spey Valley whisky heartland. The romantic Hebridean Islands are a ferryride from Oban, Mallaig or Ullapool.

Highland cattle grazing on the Isle of Skye

Getting Around

There are no motorways in the region, though travel by car is made easy by a system of A roads (major roads). Single-track roads predominate on the isles, which are served by a substantial ferry network and a free bridge to Skye. The rail link ends to the west at Kyle of Lochalsh and to the north at Wick and Thurso. There are regular flights from London to Inverness, Aberdeen and Wick.

Sights at a Glance

Key

- Major road
- Minor road
- Other road
- Scenic route
- Main line railway
- Minor railway
- △ Summit

For additional map symbols *see back flap*

❶ Inveraray Castle

Inveraray, Argyll & Bute. 🚆 Dalmally, then bus. 🚌 from Glasgow. **Tel** (01499) 302203. **Open** Apr–Oct: 10am–5:45pm daily. 🅿 🖷 💻 ♿ **W** inveraray-castle.com

The pinnacled Gothic exterior of Inveraray Castle

This multi-turreted mock Gothic palace is the family home of the powerful Clan Campbell, who have been the Dukes of Argyll since 1701. It was built in 1745 by architects Roger Morris and William Adam on ruins of a 15th-century castle. The conical towers were added later, after a fire in 1877.

The magnificent interiors, designed by Robert Mylne in the 1770s, form a backdrop to such treasures as Regency furniture, a huge collection of Oriental and European porcelain and portraits by Ramsay, Gainsborough and Raeburn. The Armoury Hall contains early weaponry collected by the Campbells to fight the Jacobite rebels. The Combined Operations Museum commemorates the 250,000 allied troops who trained at Inveraray during World War II.

❷ Auchindrain Museum

Inveraray, Argyll & Bute. **Tel** (01499) 500235. 🚌 Inveraray, then bus. **Open** Apr–Oct: 10am–5pm daily. 🅿 ♿ limited. **W** auchindrain.org. uk

The first open-air museum in Scotland, Auchindrain illuminates the working lives of the kind of farming community typical of the Highlands until the late 19th century. Constituting a township of some 20 thatched cottages, the site was communally farmed by its tenants until the last one retired in 1962. Visitors can wander through the houses, most of which combine living space, kitchen and a cattle shed all under one roof. They are furnished with box beds and rush lamps, and edged by herb gardens. Auchindrain is a fascinating memorial to a time before the Highland farmers made the transition from subsistence to commercial farming.

A traditional crofter's plough at the Auchindrain Museum

❸ Crarae Gardens

Crarae, Argyll & Bute. **Tel** (0844) 493 2210. 🚌 Inveraray, then bus. **Open** Apr–Oct: 9:30am–sunset daily. 🅿 ♿ 🖷 by appointment. **W** nts.org.uk

Considered the most beguiling of the many gardens of the West Highlands, the Crarae Gardens (see also pp26–7) were created in the 1920s by Lady Grace Campbell. She was the aunt of explorer Reginald Farrer, whose specimens from Tibet were the beginnings of a collection of exotic plants.

The gardens now resemble a Himalayan ravine, nourished by the warmth of the Gulf Stream and the high rainfall of the region. Although unusual Himalayan rhododendrons flourish here, the gardens are also home to exotic plants from Tasmania, New Zealand and the US. Great plant collectors still contribute to the gardens, which thrive in late spring.

❹ Jura

Argyll & Bute. 🚶 190. 🚌 from Kennacraig to Islay, Islay to Jura. ℹ Bowmore (01496) 810254.

Barren, mountainous and overrun by red deer, the Isle of Jura has only one road, which connects the single village of Craighouse to the Islay ferry. Though hiking is restricted from July through October during the deer-stalking season (see p200), Jura offers superb hillwalking, especially on the slopes of the three main peaks known as the Paps of Jura. The tallest of these is Beinn An Oir at 784 m (2,572 ft). Beyond the northern tip of the isle are the notorious whirlpools of Corryvreckan. The author George Orwell, who came to the island to write his final novel, 1984, nearly lost his life here in 1946 when he fell into the water. A legend tells of

Lagavulin distillery, producer of one of Scotland's finest malts, on Islay

Mist crowning the Paps of Jura, seen at sunset across the Sound of Islay

Prince Breackan who was drowned in his attempt to win the hand of a princess. He tried to keep his boat anchored in the whirlpool for three days, held by ropes made of hemp, wool and maidens' hair, until one rope, containing the hair of an unfaithful girl, finally broke.

❺ Islay

Argyll & Bute. 🏔 3,500. 🚢 from Kennacraig. 🛈 Bowmore (01496) 810254. 🆆 islayinfo.com

The most southerly of the Western Isles, Islay (pronounced "Eyeluh") is the home of such respected Highland single malt whiskies (see p36) as Lagavulin and Laphroaig. Most of the island's distilleries produce heavily peated malts with a distinctive tang of the sea. The Georgian village of Bowmore has the island's oldest distillery and a circular church designed to minimize the Devil's possible lurking places. The **Museum of Islay Life** in Port Charlotte contains a wealth of fascinating information concerning the island's social and natural history. Eleven kilometres (7 miles) east of Port Ellen stands the Kildalton Cross. A block of local green stone adorned with Old Testament scenes, it is one of the most impressive 8th-century Celtic crosses in Britain. Worth a visit for its archaeological and historical interest is the

medieval stronghold of the Lords of the Isles, **Finlaggan**, which is under excavation. Islay's superb beaches support a variety of bird life, some of which can be seen at the Royal Society for the Protection of Birds (RSPB) reserve at Gruinart.

🏛 **Museum of Islay Life**
Port Charlotte. **Tel** (01496) 850358.
Open Apr–Sep: 10:30am–4:30pm
Mon–Fri. 🐾 ♿ ♿

❻ Kintyre

Argyll & Bute. 🏔 8,000. 🚢 Oban. 🚌 Campbeltown. 🛈 Campbeltown (01586) 552056.
🆆 visitscottishheartlands.com

A long, narrow peninsula stretching far south of Glasgow, Kintyre has superb views across to the islands of Gigha, Islay and Jura. The 14 km (9 mile) Crinan Canal, which opened in 1801 and has a total of 15 locks,

bustles with pleasure craft in the summer. The town of Tarbert (meaning "isthmus" in Gaelic) takes its name from the neck on which it stands, which is narrow enough to drag a boat across, between the waters of Loch Fyne and West Loch Tarbert. This feat was first achieved by the Viking King Magnus Barfud who, in 1198, was granted by treaty as much land as he could sail around.

Travelling further south past Campbeltown, the B842 road ends at the headland known as the Mull of Kintyre, which was made famous when former Beatle Paul McCartney commercialized a traditional pipe tune of the same name. Westward from Kintyre lies the isle of Rathlin. It is here that Robert the Bruce learned patience in his constant struggles against the English by observing a spider weaving an elaborate web in a cave.

Sailing boats moored at Tarbert harbour, Kintyre

❼ Loch Awe

Argyll. 🚋 🚌 Dalmally. ℹ️ Inveraray
(01499) 302063. 🌐 loch-awe.com

One of the longest freshwater
lochs in Scotland, Loch Awe
stretches 40 km (25 miles)
across a glen in the southwestern Highlands. A short
drive east from the town of
Lochawe are the remains of
Kilchurn Castle, abandoned
after being struck by lightning
in the 18th century. Dwarfing
the castle is Ben Cruachan. The
huge summit of 1,125 m (3,695
ft) can be reached by the
narrow Pass of Brander, where
Robert the Bruce fought the
Clan MacDougal in 1308. Near
the village of Taynuilt, the
preserved Lorn Furnace at
Bonawe is a reminder of the
iron-smelting industry that
destroyed much of the area's
woodland in the last centuries.

On the A816, to the south of
the loch, is **Kilmartin House**.
The museum here displays
artifacts from local prehistoric
sites, as well as reconstructions
of boats, utensils and jewellery,
providing a vivid glimpse of life
in prehistoric Scotland.

🏛 **Kilmartin House**
Kilmartin. **Tel** (01546) 510278. **Open**
daily. 🅿️ ♿ 💻 🌐 kilmartin.org

McCaig's Tower looming over the houses
and fishing boats of Oban

❽ Oban

Argyll. 🅰 8,000. 🚋 🚌 ⛴
ℹ️ North Pier, (01631) 563122.
🌐 oban.org.uk

Known as the "Gateway to the
Isles", this bustling port on the
Firth of Lorne commands fine
views of the Argyll coast. Shops
crowd the seafront around the
"little bay" which gives Oban its
name, and fresh fish is always
for sale on the busy pier. Regular
ferries leave for Mull, Coll, Tiree,
Barra, South Uist, Islay, Colonsay
and Lismore, making Oban one
of the most visited places on
the west coast. Built on a steep
hill, the town is dominated by
the immense **McCaig's Tower**,
an eccentric Colosseum-like

structure built in the 1800s.
Other major landmarks are the
pink granite cathedral and the
600-year-old ruined keep,
Dunollie Castle, once the
northern outpost of the
Dalriadic Scots. Among Oban's
other attractions are working
centres for glass and pottery,
and Oban Distillery, producers
of fine malt whisky. On rainy
days a good option is the old-
fashioned **Oban War and Peace
Museum** for its interesting
insight into local culture.

Early in August yachts con-
verge on the town for West
Highland Week, while at the
end of the month, Oban's
Highland Games take place.
Nearby Kilmore, Taynuilt and
Tobermory, on Mull, also host
summer Highland Games.

Environs
A few miles north of Oban, off
the A85, is the 13th-century
Dunstaffnage Castle where
Flora MacDonald was briefly
imprisoned for helping Bonnie
Prince Charlie escape in 1746.
Further north at Barcaldine is
the **Scottish Sealife Sanctuary**.
This centre combines looking
after injured and orphaned
seals, with displays of underwater life. The Isle of Seil is
reached via the 18th century
"Bridge over the Atlantic". The
Easdale Folk Museum, on the
tiny island of Easdale off Seil,
describes the history of slate
mining in the area. South of
Oban along the coast is
Arduaine Garden, noted for its
varieties of spring blooming
rhododendrons and azaleas.

🏛 **Oban War and Peace Museum**
Corran Esplanade. **Tel** (01631) 570007.
Open Mar–Nov daily.

🏰 **Dunstaffnage Castle**
Connel. **Tel** (01631) 562465. **Open** daily.
Closed Nov–Mar: Thu & Fri. 🅿️ 📷

🐟 **Scottish Sealife Sanctuary**
Barcaldine, near Connel. **Tel** (01631)
720386. **Open** daily. 🅿️ ♿

🏛 **Easdale Folk Museum**
Easdale. **Tel** (01852) 300173.
Open late Mar–mid-Oct daily.

🌷 **Arduaine Garden**
Arduaine. **Tel** (0844) 493 2216. **Open**
daily. 🅿️ ♿ 📷 by appointment. 🅽🆃🆂

The ruins of Kilchurn Castle on the shore of Loch Awe

The picturesque kaleidoscope of houses in Tobermory, one of Mull's most favoured tourist stops

❾ Mull

Argyll. 🚶 2,700. 🚢 from Oban, Lochaline and Kilchoan; from Fionnphort, on Mull, to Iona. ℹ️ Tobermory (01688) 302017; Craignure (01680) 812377.

The largest of the Inner Hebridean islands, Mull features rough moorlands, the rocky peak of Ben More and a splendid beach at Calgary. Most roads follow the coastline, affording wonderful seaviews.

On a promontory to the east of Craignure lies the 13th-century **Duart Castle**, home of the chief of Clan Maclean. You can visit the Banqueting Hall, State Rooms and the dungeons that once held prisoners from a Spanish Armada galleon, sunk in 1588 by one Donald Maclean.

At the northern end of Mull is the town of **Tobermory**, with its brightly coloured buildings along the seafront. Built as a fishing village in 1788, it is now a popular port for yachts. The harbourside **Marine Visitor Centre** provides an insight into the workings of the port and the local natural history. With its touch pools and cinema, it holds great appeal for kids.

Environs
The small and very beautiful island of **Iona** is one of the biggest attractions on Scotland's west coast. A restored abbey stands on the site where Irish missionary St Columba began his crusade in 563 and made Iona the home of Christianity in Europe. In the abbey graveyard, 48 Scottish kings are said to be buried. During the summer months the abbey has a large influx of visitors.

If the weather is fine, make a trip to **Fingal's Cave** on the Isle of Staffa *(see p21)*. One of Scotland's natural wonders, the cave is surrounded by "organ pipes" of basalt, the inspiration for Mendelssohn's *Hebrides Overture*. Boat trips run there from Fionnphort and Ulva, and to the seven **Treshnish Isles**. These uninhabited isles are a sanctuary for thousands of seabirds, including puffins, razorbills, kittiwakes and skuas. Lunga is the main stop for tour boats.

🏛 **Marine Visitor Centre**
Taigh Solais, Tobermory. **Tel** (01688) 302876. **Open** Easter–Oct daily. ♿ limited.

🏰 **Duart Castle**
Off A849, near Craignure. **Tel** (01680) 812309. **Open** May–mid-Oct: daily. 📷 🅿

🐦 **Fingal's Cave and Treshnish Isles**
🚢 Easter–Oct. **Tel** (01688) 400242. Timetable varies, call for details. 📷

❿ Coll and Tiree

Argyll. 🚶 950. 🚢 from Oban. ✈️ from Glasgow to Tiree only. ℹ️ Oban (01631) 563122. 🌐 guide.visitscotland.com

Despite frequent notices of winter gale warnings, these islands, the most westerly in the Inner Hebrides, record more hours of sunshine than the rest of Britain. They offer beautiful beaches and impressive surf. Tiree's soil is 60 per cent shell sand, so no trees can grow. As a result, it is perhaps the windiest place in Scotland. Wild flowers flourish here in spring.

Breacachadh Castle, the 15th-century home of Clan Maclean until 1750, overlooks a bay in south Coll but is not open to the public. Tiree has two free museums, the **Sandaig Thatched House Museum**, with items from the late 19th and early 20th centuries, and the **Skerryvore Lighthouse Museum** in Hynish – the lighthouse stands 20 km (12 miles) offshore.

A traditional croft building on the island of Coll

The Three Sisters, Glencoe, rising majestically in the late autumn sunshine

⓫ Glencoe

Lochaber. 🚆 Fort William. 🚌 Glencoe. 🛈 NTS Visitor Centre, Ballachulish (0844) 493 2222. **Open** Apr–Oct: 9:30am–5:30pm daily; Nov–Mar: 10am–4pm Thu–Sun. 🅿 💻 ♿
🌐 **glencoe-nts.org.uk**

Renowned for its awesome scenery and savage history, Glencoe was compared by Dickens to "a burial ground of a race of giants". The precipitous cliffs of Buachaille Etive Mor and the knife-edged ridge of Aonach Eagach present a formidable challenge even to experienced mountaineers. Against a backdrop of craggy peaks and the tumbling River Coe, the Glen offers superb hill-walking. Stout footwear, waterproofs and attention to safety warnings are essential. Details of routes, ranging from an easy walk in the vicinity of Signal Rock (from which the signal was given to commence the massacre) to a stiff 10-km (6-mile) haul up the Devil's Staircase can be had from the Visitor Centre. Guided walks are offered in summer by the NTS Ranger Service. East of Glencoe lies Rannoch Moor, one of the emptiest areas in Britain. A dramatic way to view it is from the chairlift at the **Glencoe Mountain Resort**.

To the southwest, a minor road leads down beautiful Glen Etive to the head of Loch Etive. This impressive sea loch eventually emerges on the coast at the Connel Bridge north of Oban.

At the Ballachulish Bridge a side road branches to Kinlochleven. This village, at the head of a long attractive loch, combines two contrasting images of dramatic mountains and an austere aluminium works.

🎿 **Glencoe Mountain Resort**
Kingshouse, Glencoe. **Tel** (01855) 851226. **Open** daily. 🅿 ♿ limited.

⓬ Fort William

Lochaber. 🅰 11,000. 🚆 🚌 🛈 (01397) 701801. 🌐 **visithighlands.com**

Fort William, one of the major towns on the west coast, is noted not for its looks but for its location at the foot of Ben Nevis. The **Jacobite Steam Train** runs the magical route from here to Mallaig (see p141), as do ordinary trains.

🚂 **Jacobite Steam Train**
🚆 Fort William. **Tel** (01524) 732100. Departs 10:20am & 2:30pm; May, Jun & Oct: Mon–Fri; late Jun–late Sep: daily.

The Massacre of Glencoe

In 1692, the chief of the Glencoe MacDonalds was five days late in registering an oath of submission to William III, giving the government an excuse to root out a nest of Jacobite supporters. For ten days 130 soldiers, captained by Robert Campbell, were hospitably entertained by the unsuspecting MacDonalds. At dawn on 13 February, in a terrible breach of trust, the soldiers fell on their hosts, killing some 38 MacDonalds. Many more died in their wintry mountain hideouts. The massacre, unsurprisingly, became a political scandal, though there were to be no official reprimands for three years.

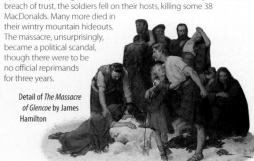

Detail of *The Massacre of Glencoe* by James Hamilton

⑲ Ben Nevis

Lochaber. 🚆 Fort William. 🚌 Glen Nevis. ℹ️ Glen Nevis Visitor Centre, Glen Nevis (01397) 705922. **Open** 9am–5pm daily (to 3pm Nov–Mar). ♿

With its summit in cloud for about nine days out of ten, and capable of developing blizzard conditions at any time of the year, Britain's highest mountain is a mishmash of metamorphic and volcanic rocks. The sheer northeastern face poses a technical challenge to experienced rock climbers. By contrast, thousands of visitors each year make their way to the peak via a relatively gentle, but long and stony, western path. Motorbikes, even cars, have ascended via this path, and runners pound up and down it during the annual Ben Nevis

Ben Nevis as seen from the northwest

Race. On one of the rare fine days, visitors who make their way to the summit will be rewarded with breathtaking views. On a cloudy day, a walk through the

lush landscape of **Glen Nevis** may be more rewarding than making an ascent, which will reveal little more at the summit than a ruined observatory and memorials testifying to the tragic deaths of walkers and climbers.

To the north of Ben Nevis, the **Nevis Range Gondola** provides access to a ski centre, restaurant and other tourist facilities, all situated at 650 m (2,130 ft).

🚠 **Nevis Range Gondola**
Off A82, Torlundy. **Tel** (01397) 705825. **Open** 10am–5pm daily (weather permitting).

Climbing Ben Nevis

The main path up Ben Nevis, called the Old Bridle Path, starts in Glen Nevis. Numerous visitors each year are lulled into a false sense of security by mild weather conditions in the Glen, occasionally with fatal results. You must wear stout footwear (not trainers) and take hat and gloves and enough layers of clothing to allow for sub-zero temperatures at the top, even on a summer day. Also take plenty of food and drink and an Ordnance Survey map and compass, even if you think you won't need them. It is very easy to lose the path in cloudy or snowy conditions, especially when starting the descent.

Tips for Walkers

Starting Point 1: Visitor Centre.
Starting Point 2: Achintee.
Starting Point 3: 400 m (440 yds) beyond campsite (very limited parking).
Length: 16 km (10 miles); 6–8 hours average for round trip.
Weather Information: (01397) 705922. 🌐 **mwis.org.uk**
Level: moderate difficulty on a dry day with broken cloud, but prone to rapid weather change; extremely difficult in snow.

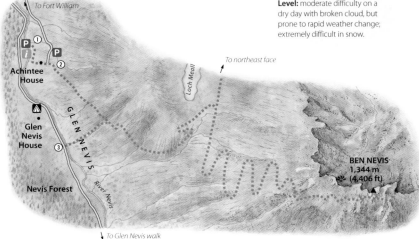

Key
▪️▪ Old Bridle Path
══ Minor road

0 metres / 1,000
0 yards / 1,000

For additional map symbols see back flap

⑭ Road to the Isles Tour

This scenic route goes past vast mountain corridors, breathtaking beaches of white sand and tiny villages to the town of Mallaig, one of the ferry ports for the isles of Skye, Rum, Eigg, Muck and Canna. In addition to stunning scenery, the area is steeped in Jacobite history *(see p151)*.

Tips for Drivers

Tour length: 72 km (45 miles).
Stopping-off points: Glenfinnan NTS Visitors' Centre (0844 493 2221) explains the Jacobite risings and serves refreshments; the Old Library Lodge in Arisaig serves excellent Scottish food.

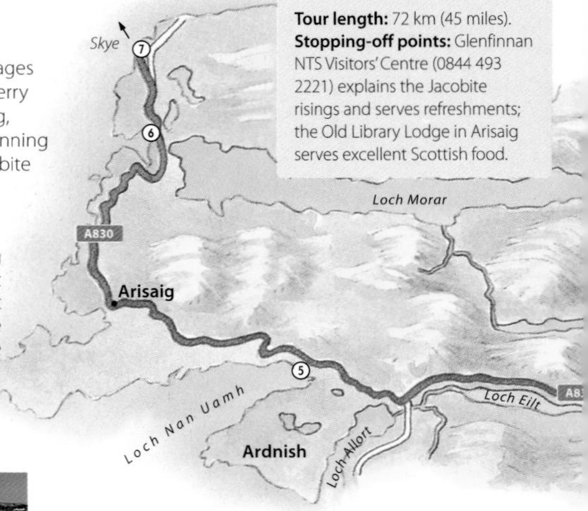

Skye ⑦

⑥

Loch Morar

A830

Arisaig

⑤

Loch Nan Uamh

Loch Eil A8

Ardnish

⑦ Mallaig
The Road to the Isles ends at Mallaig, an active little fishing port with a very good harbour and one of the ferry links to Skye *(see pp156–7)* and the Small Isles.

⑥ Morar
The road continues through Morar, renowned for its white sands, and Loch Morar, rumoured to be the home of a 12-m (40-ft) monster known as Morag.

⑤ Prince's Cairn
The road crosses the Ardnish Peninsula to Loch Nan Uamh, where a cairn marks the spot from which Bonnie Prince Charlie left for France in 1746.

⑮ Ardnamurchan Peninsula

Argyll. 🚢 Corran Ferry on A82 from Glencoe to Fort William, or Fishnish (Mull) to Kilchoan. 🛈 (01967) 402382.

This peninsula and the adjacent areas of Moidart and Morvern are some of the west coast's best-kept secrets. They are characterized by a sinuous coastline, rocky mountains and beaches. Some of the best beaches are found at the tip of the peninsula, the most westerly point of mainland Britain.

The **Ardnamurchan Point Visitor Centre** at Kilchoan explores the history of lighthouses and light-keeping. The 1846 lighthouse was designed by Alan Stevenson, uncle of author Robert Louis Stevenson. It is one of many built by the Stevenson family throughout Britain.

The award-winning **Nàdurra Centre** at Glenmore has encouraged wildlife to inhabit its "living

A view from Roshven, near Arisaig, across to the islands of Eigg and Rum

building", and wild red deer can even graze on its turf roof. An enchanting wooded road runs from Salen to Strontian, or you can go north to Acharacle.

🛈 Ardnamurchan Point Visitor Centre
Kilchoan. **Tel** (01972) 510210.
Open Apr–Oct: daily. 🅿 ♿

🏛 Nàdurra Centre
Glenmore. **Tel** (01972) 500209.
Open Feb, Mar & Nov: Tue–Fri & Sun; Easter–Oct: daily. 🅿 ♿

⑯ Rum, Eigg, Muck and Canna

Small Isles. 🔼 150. 🚢 from Mallaig or Arisaig. 🚢 Canna only. 🛈 Fort William, (01397) 701801.

Each of the four "Small Isles" has an individual character and atmosphere, but shares a sense of tranquillity. Canna is a narrow island surrounded by cliffs and has a scattering of unworked archaeological sites. Once

④ Glenfinnan Monument
This 20-m (66-ft) high monument commemorates those who rose in support of Bonnie Prince Charlie in the 1745 Jacobite rebellion. He first raised his standard in Glenfinnan.

③ Corpach
Looking east from the town of Corpach, across Loch Linnhe, there are fine views of Ben Nevis.

② Neptune's Staircase
A flight of eight locks, designed by Thomas Telford, forms the most spectacular part of the Caledonian Canal (see p153).

① Fort William
From here you can tackle Ben Nevis, Britain's highest peak at 1,344 m (4,410 ft).

Key
▬ Tour route
═ Other road

owned by Gaelic scholar John Lorne Campbell, it now belongs to the National Trust for Scotland. It has few inhabitants and little accommodation.

Eigg is the most varied of the four islands. Dominated by the distinctive sugarloaf hill, the Sgurr of Eigg, it has a glorious beach with "singing sands" that make odd noises when moved by feet or by the wind. Here the islanders symbolize the spirit of community land ownership, having successfully led a high-profile campaign to buy their island from their landlord.

Muck takes its name from the Gaelic for "pig", which it is said to resemble in shape. The smallest of the islands, but no less charming, it is owned by a family who live and farm on the island. Rum is the largest and most magnificent island,

with scabrous peaks that bear Norse names and are home to an unusual colony of Manx shearwater birds. The island's rough tracks make it best suited to the active visitor. Now owned by Scottish Natural Heritage and a centre for red deer research, it previously belonged to the wealthy Bullough family. They built the lavish **Kinloch Castle** whose design and furnishings were revolutionary at the time.

Colourful fishing boats in Mallaig harbour

Visitors to the castle can stay at the on-site hostel.

🏠 **Kinloch Castle, Rum**
Tel (01687) 462037. **Open** Apr–Oct: daily; Nov–Mar: call for details.

⑰ Mallaig

Lochaber. 🚶 800. 🚢 🚌 🚢 from Ardvasar (Skye). 🛈 Fort William, (01397) 701801.

The heart of Mallaig is its harbour, which has an active fishing fleet and ferries that serve the "small isles" and Skye. The atmosphere is rather more commercial than leisurely, but it is set in an area of outstanding beauty. The **Mallaig Heritage Centre** is a local history museum covering fishing, railways, steamers and ferries.

🏛 **Mallaig Heritage Centre**
Tel (01687) 462085. **Open** 11am–4pm Mon–Fri, 12–4pm Sat. 🏠 🎫 by appointment.

For additional map symbols see back flap

⑱ Killiecrankie Walk

In an area famous for its scenery and historical connections, this circular walk offers views that are typical of the Highlands. The route is fairly flat, though ringed by mountains, and meanders through a wooded gorge, passing the Soldier's Leap and a Victorian viaduct.

There are ideal picnic spots along the way, and the shores of man-made Loch Faskally are lined with beautiful trees. Returning along the River Tummel, the route crosses one of Queen Victoria's favourite Highland areas before it doubles back to complete the circuit.

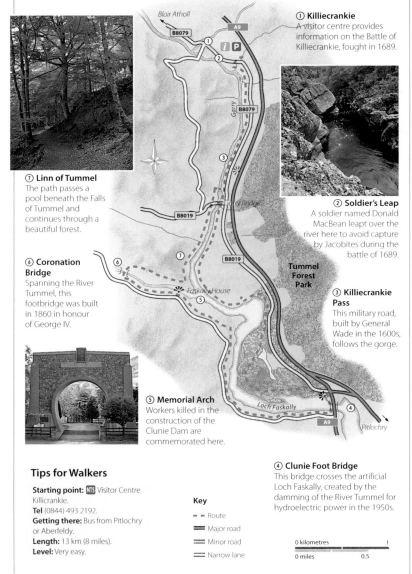

① Killiecrankie
A visitor centre provides information on the Battle of Killiecrankie, fought in 1689.

⑦ Linn of Tummel
The path passes a pool beneath the Falls of Tummel and continues through a beautiful forest.

② Soldier's Leap
A soldier named Donald MacBean leapt over the river here to avoid capture by Jacobites during the battle of 1689.

⑥ Coronation Bridge
Spanning the River Tummel, this footbridge was built in 1860 in honour of George IV.

③ Killiecrankie Pass
This military road, built by General Wade in the 1600s, follows the gorge.

⑤ Memorial Arch
Workers killed in the construction of the Clunie Dam are commemorated here.

Blair Atholl
B8079
A9
Garry
B8079
B8019
Garry Bridge
B8019
Faskally House
Tummel Forest Park
Loch Faskally
A9
Pitlochry

Tips for Walkers

Starting point: NTS Visitor Centre Killicrankie.
Tel (0844) 493 2192.
Getting there: Bus from Pitlochry or Aberfeldy.
Length: 13 km (8 miles).
Level: Very easy.

④ Clunie Foot Bridge
This bridge crosses the artificial Loch Faskally, created by the damming of the River Tummel for hydroelectric power in the 1950s.

Key
- - Route
▬▬ Major road
═══ Minor road
═══ Narrow lane

0 kilometres   1
0 miles   0.5

The distinctive white turrets and façade of the ducal Blair Castle

⑲ Blair Castle

Blair Atholl, Perthshire.
Tel (01796) 481207. 🚆 Blair Atholl.
Open late Mar–Oct: 9:30am–5:30pm daily. 🅿 🎫 💳 ♿ limited.
W blair-castle.co.uk

This rambling, turreted castle has been altered and extended so often in its 700-year history that it now provides a unique insight into the history and changing tastes of aristocratic life in the Highlands.

The elegant 18th-century wing, with its draughty passages hung with antlers, has a display that includes the gloves and pipe of Bonnie Prince Charlie (see p157), who spent two days here gathering support for a Jacobite uprising (see p151). Family portraits span 300 years and include paintings by such masters as Johann Zoffany and Sir Peter Lely. Sir Edwin Landseer's *Death of a Hart in Glen Tilt* (1850) hangs in the ballroom.

Queen Victoria visited the castle in 1844 and conferred on its owners, the Dukes of Atholl, the distinction of being allowed to maintain a private army. The Atholl Highlanders are still in existence today.

⑳ Pitlochry

Perthshire. 🚹 2,500. 🚆 🚌 🎫 22 Atholl Rd (01796) 472215.
W perthshire.co.uk

Surrounded by the pine-forested hills of the central Highlands, Pitlochry became a famous town after Queen Victoria described it as one of the finest resorts in Europe.

In early summer, wild salmon leap up the ladder built into the Power Station Dam on their way to spawning grounds up the river. The **Scottish Hydro Electric Visitor Centre** outlines the hydro-electric scheme, which harnesses the waters of the River Tummel.

Blair Athol Distillery, the home of Bell's whisky, offers guided tours in the art of whisky making (see pp36–7). One of Scotland's most famous stages,

the **Festival Theatre**, is located in Port-na-Craig. It operates a year-round programme with performances changing daily.

🏠 Blair Athol Distillery
Perth Rd. **Tel** (01796) 482003.
Open Easter–Oct: daily; Nov–Easter: Mon–Fri. 🅿 🎫 💳 limited.

🎭 Festival Theatre
Port-na-Craig. **Tel** (01796) 484626.
Open mid-May–Oct: daily. 🅿 for plays. 💳 🎫 🖥

🛈 Scottish Hydro Electric Visitor Centre
Port-na-Craig. **Tel** (01796) 473152.
Open Apr–Oct: Mon–Fri; Jul–Aug: daily. 🅿 🎫

The ruins of Dunkeld Cathedral

㉑ Dunkeld

Tayside. 🚹 1,200. 🚆 Birnam. 🚌
🛈 The Cross (01350) 727688.

Situated by the River Tay, this ancient and charming village was all but destroyed in the Battle of Dunkeld, a Jacobite defeat, in 1689. The **Little Houses** lining Cathedral Street were the first to be rebuilt, and remain fine examples of an imaginative restoration.

The partly ruined 14th-century **cathedral** enjoys an idyllic setting on shady lawns beside the Tay, against a backdrop of steep and wooded hills. The choir is used as the parish church, and its north wall contains a Leper's Squint (a little hole through which lepers could see the altar during mass). It was while on holiday in the countryside around Dunkeld that the children's author Beatrix Potter found the inspiration for her Peter Rabbit stories.

Salmon ladder at the Power Station Dam in Pitlochry

For hotels and restaurants see pp172–7 and pp181–9

㉒ The Cairngorms

Rising to a height of 1,309 m (4,296 ft), the Cairngorm mountains form the highest landmass in Britain. Cairn Gorm itself is the site of one of Britain's first ski centres. A weather station at the summit provides regular reports, essential in an area known for sudden changes of weather. Walkers should be sure to follow the mountain code without fail. During the summer a funicular railway climbs Cairn Gorm affording superb views over the Spey Valley. Many estates in the valley have centres which introduce the visitor to Highland land use.

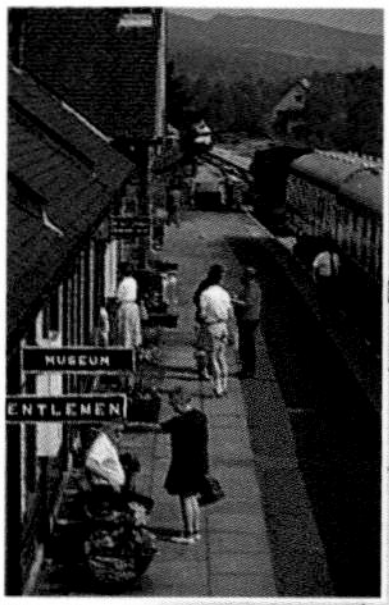

Strathspey Steam Railway
This track between Aviemore and Broomhill dates from1863.

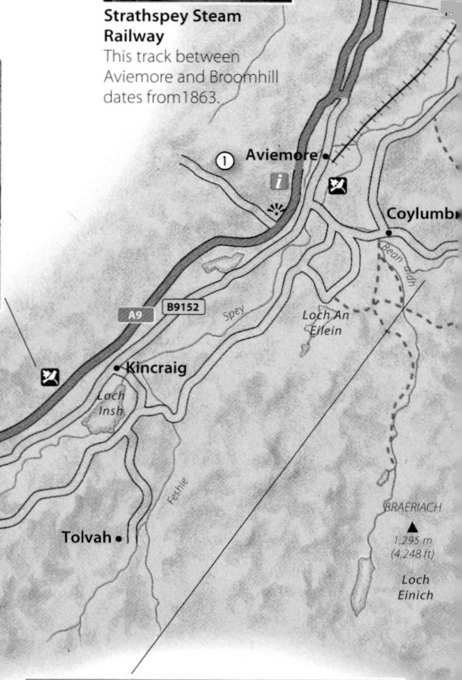

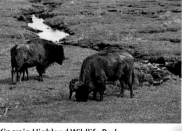

Kincraig Highland Wildlife Park
Driving through this park, the visitor can see bison alongside bears, wolves and wild boar. All of these animals were once common in the Highlands.

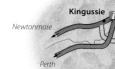

Key

- Major road
- Minor road
- Narrow lane
- Footpath

KEY

① **Aviemore**, the commercial centre of the Cairngorms, provides buses to the main ski area 13 km (8 miles) away.

② **The Cairngorm Reindeer Centre** provides walks in the hills among Britain's only herd of reindeer.

③ **Ben MacDhui** is Britain's second highest peak, after Ben Nevis.

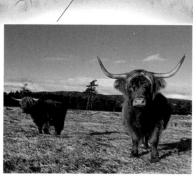

Rothiemurchus Estate
Highland cattle can be seen among many other creatures at Rothiemurchus. A visitor centre provides guided walks and illustrates life on a Highland estate.

For hotels and restaurants see pp172–7 and pp181–9

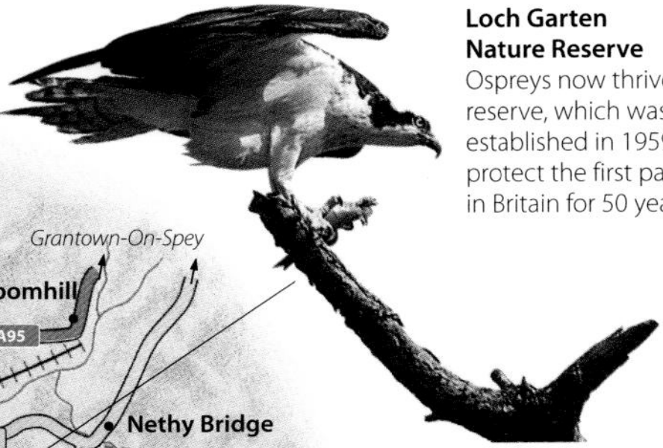

Loch Garten Nature Reserve
Ospreys now thrive in this reserve, which was established in 1959 to protect the first pair seen in Britain for 50 years.

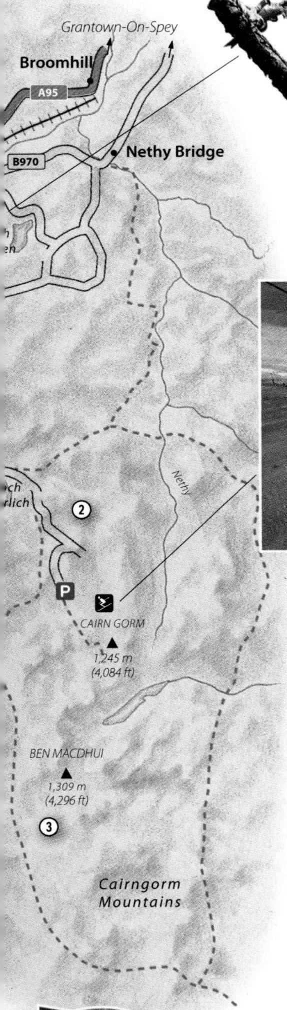

Grantown-On-Spey
Broomhill
A95
B970
Nethy Bridge
0 kilometres 5
0 miles 5
Nethy
2
P
CAIRN GORM
1,245 m
(4,084 ft)
BEN MACDHUI
1,309 m
(4,296 ft)
3
Cairngorm Mountains

VISITORS' CHECKLIST

Practical Information
The Highlands. Grampian Rd, Aviemore (01479) 810930.
Cairngorm Reindeer Centre:, Loch Morlich. **Tel** (01479) 861228.
Open daily.
Kincraig Highland Wildlife Park: **Tel** (01540) 651270.
Open daily (weather permitting).
Rothiemurchus Visitor Centre:, near Aviemore.
Tel (01479) 812345.
Open daily.
Loch Garten Nature Reserve:
Tel (01479) 831476.
Open daily.
Skiing & Funicular Railway:
Tel (01479) 861261.

Transport
Aviemore.

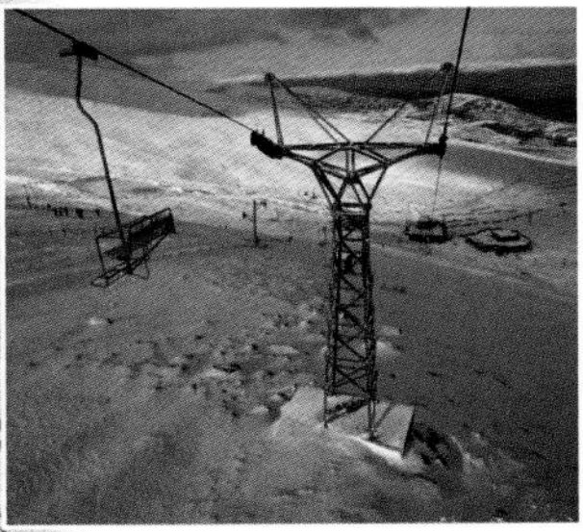

Skiing
During the winter, chairlifts and tows provide access to more than 28 ski runs on Cairn Gorm's northern flanks.

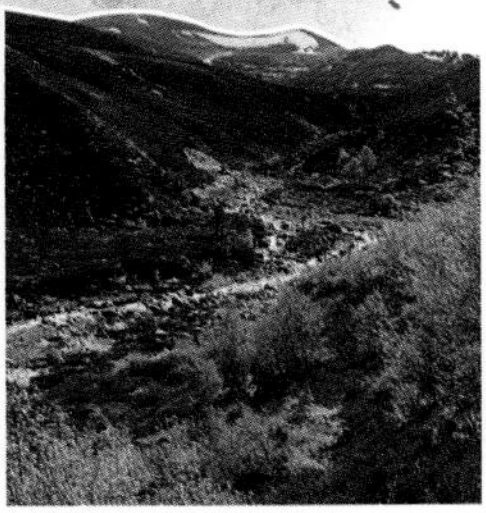

The Cairngorms by Aviemore

Flora of the Cairngorms

With mixed woodland at their base and the summits forming a sub-polar plateau, the Cairngorms present a huge variety of flora. Ancient Caledonian pines (once common in the area) survive in Abernethy Forest, while arctic flowers flourish in the heights.

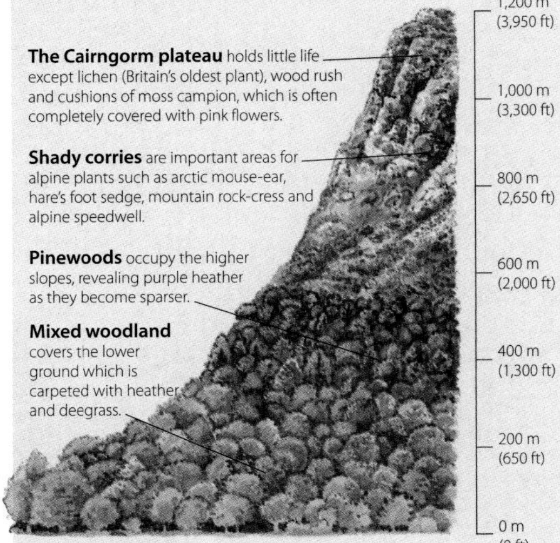

1,200 m (3,950 ft)
1,000 m (3,300 ft)
800 m (2,650 ft)
600 m (2,000 ft)
400 m (1,300 ft)
200 m (650 ft)
0 m (0 ft)

The Cairngorm plateau holds little life except lichen (Britain's oldest plant), wood rush and cushions of moss campion, which is often completely covered with pink flowers.

Shady corries are important areas for alpine plants such as arctic mouse-ear, hare's foot sedge, mountain rock-cress and alpine speedwell.

Pinewoods occupy the higher slopes, revealing purple heather as they become sparser.

Mixed woodland covers the lower ground which is carpeted with heather and deegrass.

An idealized section of the Cairngorm plateau

For additional map symbols *see back flap*

❶ Aberdeen

Scotland's third-largest city and Europe's offshore oil capital, Aberdeen has prospered since the discovery of oil in the North Sea in the early 1970s. The sea bed has now yielded 50 oilfields. Widely known as the Granite City, its forbidding and rugged outlines are softened by year-round floral displays in the public parks and gardens, the Duthie Park Winter Gardens being the largest indoor gardens in Europe. Aberdeen's busy harbour can be observed from the picturesque village of Footdee at the southern end of the city's 2 mile (3 km) sandy beach.

The spires of Aberdeen, rising behind the city harbour

Exploring Aberdeen
The city centre flanks the 1.5 km (1 mile) long Union Street, ending at the Mercat Cross. The cross stands by Castlegate, the one-time site of the city castle, and now only a marketplace. From here, the cobbled Shiprow meanders southwest and passes Provost Ross's House on its way to the harbour. A bus can be taken 1.5 km (1 mile) north of the centre to Old Aberdeen, which, with its medieval streets and wynds (narrow, winding lanes), has the peaceful character of a separate village. Driving is restricted in some streets.

🏛 King's College
College Bounds, Old Aberdeen.
Tel (01224) 272000.
Open daily. 🚶

Founded in 1495, King's College was the city's first university. The visitor centre gives background on its long history. The interdenominational chapel, consecutively Catholic and Protestant in the past, has a distinctive lantern tower, rebuilt in 1633. Douglas Strachan's stained-glass windows add a modern touch to the interior, which contains a 1540 pulpit, later carved with heads of Stuart monarchs.

🏛 St Andrew's Cathedral
King St. **Tel** (01224) 640119. **Open** May–Sep: 11am–4pm Tue–Fri; Oct–Apr: by appointment. 🚶 🎫 by arrangement.

The Mother Church of the Episcopal Church in

Lantern tower, King's College

the United States, St Andrew's has a memorial to Samuel Seabury, the first Episcopalian bishop in the US, who was consecrated in Aberdeen in 1784. A series of coats of arms contrast colourfully with the white walls and pillars. They represent the American states and the Jacobite families of Aberdeenshire.

🏛 Art Gallery
Schoolhill. **Tel** (01224) 523700. **Open** 10am–5pm Tue–Sat, 2–5pm Sun. 🚶 🖥 🌐 aagm.co.uk

Housed in a Neo-Classical building, the Art Gallery has a wide range of exhibitions, with an emphasis on modern works. A collection of Aberdonian silver is included among the decorative arts on the ground floor. A permanent collection of 18th- to 20th-century art features such names as Toulouse-Lautrec, Raeburn and Reynolds. Local granite merchant Alex Macdonald bequeathed a number of the works on display.

🏛 St Nicholas Kirk
Union St. **Tel** (01224) 643494. **Open** May–Sep: noon–4pm Mon–Fri, 9:30am–1pm Sun; Oct–Apr: Mon–Fri am only. 🚶 🌐 kirk-of-st-nicholas.org.uk

Founded in the 12th century, St Nicholas is Scotland's largest parish church. Though the present structure dates from 1752, many earlier relics can be seen inside. After damage during the Reformation, the interior was divided into two. A chapel in the East Church holds iron rings used to secure witches in the 17th century, while in the West Church there are embroidered panels attributed to Mary Jameson (1597–1644).

🏛 Maritime Museum
Shiprow. **Tel** (01224) 337700. **Open** 10am–5pm Tue–Sat, noon–3pm Sun. 🖥 🚶 🌐 aagm.co.uk

Overlooking the harbour is the Provost Ross's House, dating back to 1593. It now houses the Maritime Museum, which traces the history of Aberdeen's seafaring tradition. The exhibitions cover numerous topics from shipwrecks, rescues and shipbuilding to models that illustrate the workings of the many oil installations situated off the east coast of Scotland.

🏛 St Machar's Cathedral
The Chanonry. **Tel** (01224) 485988. **Open** Apr–Oct: 9am–4:30pm daily; Nov–Mar: 10am–4pm daily. 🚶 🌐 stmachar.com

This 15th-century cathedral is the city's oldest granite building. One of its arches dates back to the 14th century. The nave is a parish church and its ceiling is adorned with coats of arms of popes and emperors.

Provost Skene's House

Guestrow. **Tel** (01224) 641086. **Open** 10am–5pm Mon–Sat. 🏛 🚹 limited. Once the home of Sir George Skene, a 17th-century provost (mayor) of Aberdeen, the house was built in 1545 and remains one of the oldest houses in the city. Inside, period rooms span 200 years of design. The Duke of Cumberland stayed here during the weeks preceding the Battle of Culloden (*see p150*).

VISITORS' CHECKLIST

Practical Information
Grampian. 🚂 220,000.
ℹ️ Union St (01224) 269180.
📅 Fri, Sat.

Transport
✈ 13 km (8 miles) NW of
Aberdeen. 🚆 🚌 Guild St.

The 18th-century Parlour, with its walnut harpsichord and covered fire-side chairs, was the informal room in which the family would have tea.

The Regency Room typifies early 19th-century elegance. A harp dating from 1820 stands by a Grecian-style sofa and a French writing table.

The Painted Gallery has one of Scotland's most important cycles of religious art. The panels are early 17th century, though the artist is unknown.

The 17th-century Great Hall contains heavy oak dining furniture. Provost Skene's wood-carved coat of arms hangs above the fireplace.

The Georgian Dining Room, with its Classical design, was the main formal room in the 16th century and still has its original flagstone floor.

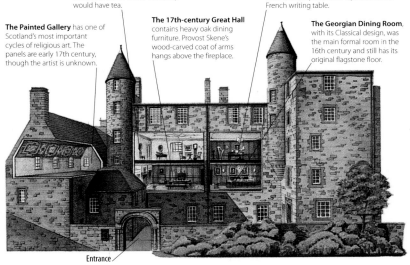

Entrance

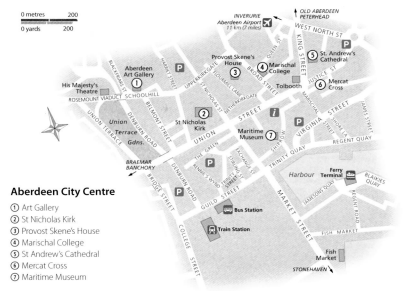

Aberdeen City Centre

1. Art Gallery
2. St Nicholas Kirk
3. Provost Skene's House
4. Marischal College
5. St Andrew's Cathedral
6. Mercat Cross
7. Maritime Museum

For map symbols *see back flap*

㉔ Royal Deeside Tour

Since Queen Victoria's purchase of the Balmoral Estate in 1852, Deeside has been best known as the summer home of the British Royal Family, though it has been associated with royalty since the time of Robert the Bruce in the 1300s. This route follows the Dee, one of the world's most prolific salmon rivers, through some magnificent Grampian scenery.

④ Muir of Dinnet Nature Reserve
An information centre on the A97 provides an excellent place from which to explore this beautiful mixed woodland area, formed by the retreating glaciers of the last Ice Age.

⑥ Balmoral
Bought by Queen Victoria for 30,000 guineas in 1852, after its owner choked to death on a fishbone, the castle was rebuilt in the Scottish Baronial style at Prince Albert's request.

⑤ Ballater
The old railway town of Ballater has royal warrants on many of its shop fronts. It grew as a 19th-century spa town, its waters reputedly providing a cure for tuberculosis.

㉕ Speyside Malt Whisky Trail

Moray. 🛈 Elgin (01343) 562608.
🆆 maltwhiskytrail.com

Such are the climate and geology of the Grampian mountains and glens bordering the River Spey that half of Scotland's whisky distilleries are found on Speyside. They span a large area so a car is required. The signposted "Malt Whisky Trail" takes you to seven distilleries and one cooperage (a place where barrels are made), all with excellent visitor centres and tours of their premises.

There is no secret to whisky distilling (see pp34–6): essentially barley is steeped in water and allowed to grow, a process called "malting"; the grains are then dried with peat smoke, milled, mixed with water and allowed to ferment; the frothy liquid goes through a double process of distillation. The final result is a raw, rough whisky that is then stored

Oak casks, in which the maturing whisky is stored at the distilleries

in old oak sherry casks for 3 to 16 years, during which time it mellows. Worldwide, an average of 30 bottles of Scotch whisky are sold every second.

The visitor centres at each Whisky Trail distillery provide similar, and equally good, guided tours of the workings and audio-visual displays of their individual histories. Their entry charges are usually redeemable against the purchase of a bottle of whisky. A different slant on the process is given at the **Speyside Cooperage**. Here the visitor can learn about the making of the wooden casks that are eventually used to store the whisky.

🏛 **Benromach Distillery**
Forres. **Tel** (01309) 675968. **Open** Oct–Apr: Mon–Fri; May & Sep: Mon–Sat; Jun–Aug: daily, Sun pm only. 🅿 ♿ 🛍

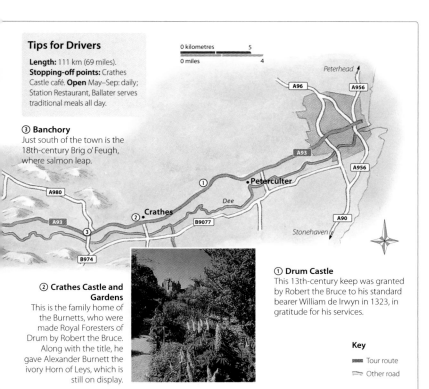

Tips for Drivers

Length: 111 km (69 miles).
Stopping-off points: Crathes
Castle café. **Open** May–Sep: daily;
Station Restaurant, Ballater serves
traditional meals all day.

0 kilometres 5

0 miles 4

③ **Banchory**
Just south of the town is the
18th-century Brig o' Feugh,
where salmon leap.

Peterhead

A96
A956
A93
A956
A980
Dee
A93
• *Petercultter*
B9077
A90
Stonehaven
B974

② **Crathes Castle and Gardens**
This is the family home of
the Burnetts, who were
made Royal Foresters of
Drum by Robert the Bruce.
Along with the title, he
gave Alexander Burnett the
ivory Horn of Leys, which is
still on display.

① **Drum Castle**
This 13th-century keep was granted
by Robert the Bruce to his standard
bearer William de Irwyn in 1323, in
gratitude for his services.

Key

⚑ Tour route

⚞ Other road

🏰 **Cardhu Distillery**
Knockando. **Tel** (01340) 872555.
Open Jan–Jun: Mon–Fri; Jul–Sep:
Mon–Sun; Oct–Dec: Mon–Fri. 🅿 &

🏰 **Dallas Dhu Distillery**
Forres. **Tel** (01309) 676548.
Open Apr–Sep: Mon–Sun; Oct–Mar:
Mon–Wed, Sat & Sun. 🅿 &

🏰 **Glenfiddich Distillery**
Dufftown. **Tel** (01340) 820373.
Open daily. & 🅿

🏰 **Glen Grant Distillery**
Rothes. **Tel** (01340) 832118.
Open daily. 🅿 🅿 & limited.

🏰 **The Glenlivet Distillery**
Glenlivet. **Tel** (01340) 821720.
Open Easter–Oct: daily. 🅿 🅿
& limited.

🏰 **Speyside Cooperage**
Craigellachie. **Tel** (01340) 871108.
Open 9am–4pm Mon–Fri. 🅿 🅿 &
limited. 🖵

🏰 **Strathisla Distillery**
Keith. **Tel** (01542) 783044.
Open Easter–Oct. 🅿
& limited.

㉖ **Elgin**

Moray. 🔼 26,000. 🚌 🚍 ℹ 17 High
St (01343) 562608. 🛒 Sat.

With its cobbled marketplace
and crooked lanes, Elgin retains
much of its medieval layout. The
13th-century **cathedral** ruins
are all that remain of one of
Scotland's architectural
triumphs. Once known as the
Lantern of the North, the
cathedral was severely
damaged in 1390 by the Wolf of
Badenoch (the son of Robert II)
in revenge for his
excommunication by the
Bishop of Moray. Further
damage came in 1576 when
the Regent Moray ordered the
lead roofing to be stripped.
Among the remains is a Pictish
cross-slab in the nave and a
basin where one of the town's
benefactors, Andrew Anderson,
was kept as a baby by his
homeless mother. The **Elgin
Museum** has anthropological
and geological displays, while

---

the **Moray Motor Museum** has
over 40 cars and motorbikes,
dating back to 1904.

🏛 **Elgin Museum**
1 High St. **Tel** (01343) 543675.
Open Apr–Oct: 10am–5pm Mon–Fri,
11am–4pm Sat. 🅿 & 🅿

🏛 **Moray Motor Museum**
Bridge St. **Tel** (01343) 544933. **Open**
Easter–Oct: 11am–5pm daily. 🅿 &

Details of the central tower of the
13th-century Elgin Cathedral

An aerial picture of Fort George, illustrating its imposing position

㉗ Fort George

Inverness. **Tel** (01667) 460232. 🚆 🚌 Inverness, Nairn. **Open** Apr–Sep: 9:30am–5:30pm daily; Oct–Mar: 9:30am–4:30pm daily. 🐾 🅿 ♿ 🖥 **W** historic-scotland.gov.uk

One of the finest examples of European military architecture, Fort George holds a commanding position on the Moray Firth, ideally located to suppress the Highlands. Completed in 1769, the fort was built after the Jacobite risings to discourage further rebellion, and has remained a military garrison ever since.

The **Regimental Museum** of the Highlanders Regiment is housed in the Fort. Some of the barrack rooms have been reconstructed to show the conditions of the common soldiers stationed here more than 200 years ago. The **Grand Magazine** contains an outstanding collection of arms and military equipment. Fort George's battlements also make an excellent place from which to watch dolphins playing in the waters of the Moray Firth.

㉘ Culloden

Inverness. 🚆 🚌 Inverness. [NTS]

The desolate battlefield of Culloden looks much as it did on 16 April 1746, the date of the last battle to be fought on British soil (*see p49*). Here the Jacobite cause, with the help of Bonnie Prince Charlie's leadership (*see*

p157), perished under the onslaught of nearly 9,000 troops, led by the Duke of Cumberland. Visitors can roam the battlefield, visit the clan graves and experience the audio-visual displays at the **NTS Visitor Centre**.

Environs
Roughly 1.5 km (1 mile) east of Culloden are the outstanding Neolithic burial sites at **Clava Cairns**.

ℹ NTS Visitor Centre
On the B9006 east of Inverness. **Tel** (0844) 493 2159. **Open** daily. 🐾 ♿ 🖥 **W** nts.org.uk

㉙ Cawdor Castle

On B9090 (off A96). **Tel** (01667) 404 401. 🚆 Nairn, then bus or taxi. 🚌 from Inverness. **Open** May–early Oct: 10am–5:30pm daily (last entry 5pm). 🐾 🅿 ♿ gardens and ground floor only. **W** cawdorcastle.com

With its turreted central tower, moat and drawbridge, Cawdor Castle is one of the most romantic stately homes in the Highlands. Though the castle is famed for being the 11th-century home of Shakespeare's tragic character Macbeth, and the scene of his murder of King Duncan, it is historically unproven that either figure came here.

An ancient holly tree preserved in the vaults is said to be the one under which, in 1372, Thane William's donkey stopped for a rest during its master's search for a place to build a fortress. According to legend, this was how the site for the castle was chosen. Now, after

600 years of continuous occupation (it is still the home of the Thanes of Cawdor) the house contains a number of rare tapestries and portraits by the 18th-century painters Joshua Reynolds (1723–92) and George Romney (1734–1802). Furniture in the Pink Bedroom and Woodcock Room includes work by the 18th-century designers Chippendale and Sheraton. In the Old Kitchen, the huge Victorian cooking range stands as a shrine to below-stairs drudgery. The castle's grounds provide beautiful nature trails, as well as a nine-hole golf course.

The drawbridge on the eastern side of Cawdor Castle

㉚ Inverness

Highland. 🅜 58,000. 🚆 🚌 ℹ Castle Wynd (01463) 252401. **W** visithighlands.com

In the Highlands, all roads lead to the region's "capital", Inverness, the centre of communication, commerce and administration for six million outlying acres and their scattered populations. Despite

A contemporary picture, *The Battle of Culloden* (1746), by D Campbell

The red sandstone exterior of Inverness Castle, high above the city centre, in the light of the setting sun

being the largest city in the north, it is more like a town in its atmosphere, with a compact and easily accessible centre. Although sadly defaced by modern architecture, Inverness earns a worthy reputation for its floral displays in summer, and for the River Ness, which flows through the centre and adds considerable charm. The river is frequented by salmon fishermen during the summer, even where it runs through the city centre. Holding the high ground above the city is **Inverness Castle**, a Victorian building of red sandstone, now used as the court house. Just below the castle, next to the tourist information office, is **Inverness Museum and Art Gallery**, which houses permanent and touring exhibitions and runs workshops for children. The main shopping area fans out in three directions from here and includes a lively pedestrian precinct where pipers and other musicians can be found busking.

Just across the river is the **Scottish Kiltmaker Visitor Centre**, part of the Highland House of Fraser Group. Here visitors will get an insight into the history, culture and tradition of the kilt, with audio-visual and workshop presentations of kiltmaking. On the banks of the Ness, stands **Eden Court Theatre**,

Kilt maker with Royal Stuart tartan

which has a varied programme of local and international performers. Following the tree-lined banks of the river further upstream leads to the **Island Walks**, accessed by a pedestrian suspension bridge. Beyond this, further upstream still, is **Inverness Sports Centre and Aquadome**, which offers swimming pools, spas and a variety of wild, spiralling flumes. Thomas Telford's Caledonian Canal (*see pp152–3*), constructed between 1804 and 1822, is still in constant use and can be viewed at Tomnahurich Bridge. From here, **Jacobite Cruises** runs summer cruises along the length of Loch Ness – an excellent way to spend a sunny afternoon. Inverness is an ideal base for touring the rest of the Highlands, as it lies within easy reach of most of the region's best-known attractions, including the battlesite of Culloden, 8 km (5 miles) to the east (*see opposite*).

Ⅲ Inverness Museum and Art Gallery
Castle Wynd. **Tel** (01463) 237114. **Open** 10am–5pm Mon–Sat. ♿
Ⓦ inverness.highland.museum

Ⅲ Scottish Kiltmaker Visitor Centre
4–9 Huntly St. **Tel** (01463) 222781. **Open** daily. ♿

Eden Court Theatre
Bishop's Rd. **Tel** (01463) 234234. ♿
Ⓦ eden-court.co.uk

Inverness Sports Centre and Aquadome
Bught Lane. **Tel** (01463) 667500. **Open** daily. ♿

Jacobite Cruises
Tomnahurich Bridge, Glenurquhart. **Tel** (01463) 233999. ♿

The Jacobite Movement

The first Jacobites (mainly Catholic Highlanders) were the supporters of James VII of Scotland (James II of England) who was deposed by his Parliament in the "Glorious Revolution" of 1688. With the Protestant William of Orange on the throne, the Jacobites' desire to restore the Stuart monarchy led to the uprisings of 1715 and 1745. The first, in support of James VIII, the "Old Pretender", ended at the Battle of Sheriffmuir

James II, by Samuel Cooper (1609–72)

(1715). The failure of the second uprising, with the defeat at Culloden, saw the end of Jacobite hopes and led to the demise of the clan system and the suppression of Highland culture for more than a century.

㉛ The Great Glen

Following the path of a geological fault, the Great Glen forms a scenic route from Inverness on the east coast to Fort William on the west. The glacial rift valley was created when the landmass split and moved 400 million years ago. A series of four lochs includes the famous Loch Ness, home of the elusive monster. The Caledonian Canal, built by Thomas Telford, provides a link between the lochs, and has been a shipping channel as well as a popular tourist route since 1822. Hiring a boat or taking a leisurely drive are ideal ways to view the Glen.

The Great Glen

Steall Waterfall
Located at the foot of the magnificent Ben Nevis, this impressive waterfall tumbles down into a valley of wild flowers. The walk takes 45 minutes and passes through a dramatic gorge. It's the perfect place to picnic.

KEY

① **Ben Nevis** (see p139) is Britain's highest mountain at 1,343 m (4,406 ft), but its broad, indefinable shape belies its immense size.

② **Loch Lochy**, Lochy is one of the four beautiful lochs of the Great Glen, formed by a fissure in the earth and erosion by glaciers. There are caves nearby where Bonnie Prince Charlie is said to have hidden after the Battle of Culloden.

③ **Spean Bridge** is home to a Woollen Mill selling traditional knitwear and tweeds. Close to the village is the impressive Memorial to all the Commandos who lost their lives in World War II. The surrounding rugged terrain was their training ground.

④ **Fort Augustus** is a pretty village situated at the southwestern end of Loch Ness. The base for boat cruises around the loch, it is also the site of a Benedictine Abbey.

⑤ **Falls of Foyers** nestle among the trees above Loch Ness; a winding path yields spectacular views.

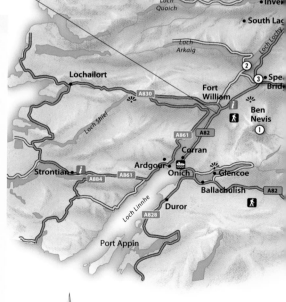

0 kilometres 10
0 miles 10

VISITORS' CHECKLIST

Practical Information
Highland. ℹ Castle Wynd,
Inverness (01463) 252401.
ⓦ visitscotland.com
The Loch Ness Centre and
Exhibition: **Tel** (01456) 450573.
Open daily. 🅿 ♿
Urquhart Castle: **Tel** (01456)
450551. **Open** daily. 🅿

★ **Loch Ness**
Scotland's most famous loch, the 37 km
(23 miles) of Loch Ness provide a beautiful
route through the Glen. Urquhart Castle rises
imposingly over the water.

The Loch Ness Monster

First sighted by St Columba in
the 6th century, "Nessie" has
attracted attention since
photographs – later revealed to
be faked – were taken in the
1930s. Though serious
investigation is often under-
mined by hoaxers, sonar
techniques continue to yield
enigmatic results: plesiosaurs,
giant eels and too much whisky
are the most popular
explanations. The Loch Ness
Centre, at Drumnadrochit,
presents the photographic
evidence and wide variety of
scientific explanations proffered
over the years.

Key

▬ Main route through
the Glen

▬ Major road

▬ Minor road

★ **Caledonian Canal**
This splendid canal
provides a base
from which to view
the Glen's beautiful
surroundings.
From Inverness, the
canal travels via Fort
Augustus to the eight
locks at Neptune's
Staircase – a feat of
engineering.

For additional map symbols *see back flap*

The shores of the Black Isle in the Moray Firth

🕮 Black Isle

Ross & Cromarty. ⚶ 9,500. 🚆 🚌
Inverness. 🛈 ⓦ visitscotland.com
(01463) 252401.

Though the drilling platforms in the Cromarty Firth recall how oil has changed the local economy, the broad peninsula of the Black Isle is still largely composed of farmland and fishing villages. The town of **Cromarty** was an important 18th-century port with rope and lace industries. Many of its merchant houses still stand. The award-winning museum in the **Cromarty Courthouse** provides heritage tours of the town. The thatched **Hugh Miller Museum** celebrates the life of theologian and geologist Hugh Miller (1802–56), who was born in Cromarty. **Fortrose** boasts a ruined 14th-century cathedral, while a stone on Chanonry Point commemorates the Brahan Seer, a 17th-century prophet. He was burnt alive in a barrel of tar by the Countess of Seaforth after he foresaw her husband's infidelity. For local archaeology, the **Groam House Museum** in the town of Rosemarkie is worth a visit.

🏛 Cromarty Courthouse
Church St, Cromarty. **Tel** (01381) 600418. **Open** May–Sep: 12–4pm Sun–Thu; Oct–Apr: by appointment. 🔊

🏛 Hugh Miller Museum
Church St, Cromarty. **Tel** (0844) 493 2158. **Open** late Mar–Sep: 12–5pm daily; Oct: 12–5pm Tue, Thu & Fri. 🔊 🔊 limited. 🅽🆃🆂

🏛 Groam House Museum
High St, Rosemarkie. **Tel** (01381) 620961. **Open** Apr–Oct 11am–4:30pm Mon–Fri, 2–4:30pm Sat; Nov–early Dec 2–4pm Sat. 🔊 🔊 ground floor only.

The Highland Clearances

During the heyday of the clan system *(see pp32–3)*, tenants paid their land-holding chieftains rent in the form of military service. However, with the destruction of the clan system after the Battle of Culloden *(see p150)*, landowners began to demand a financial rent, which their tenants were unable to afford, and the land was gradually bought up by Lowland and English farmers. In what became known as "the year of the sheep" (1792), thousands of tenants were evicted, sometimes forcibly, to make way for livestock. Many emigrated to Australia, America and Canada. The ruins of their crofts can still be seen, especially in Sutherland and the Wester Ross.

The Last of the Clan (1865) by
Thomas Faed

🕮 Strathpeffer

Ross & Cromarty. ⚶ 1,500.
🚆 Dingwall. 🚌 Inverness. 🛈 Real Sweets, The Pump Room, The Square, (07801) 759217. ⓦ visitscotland.com

Standing 8 km (5 miles) east of the Falls of Rogie, the holiday centre of Strathpeffer still retains the refined charm that made it well-known as a Victorian spa and health resort. The town's huge hotels and gracious layout recall the days when European royalty and lesser mortals flocked to the chalybeate- and sulphur-laden springs, believed to alleviate tuberculosis. It is still possible to sample the water at the unmanned **Water Tasting Pavilion** in the town centre.

🏛 Water Tasting Pavilion
The Square. **Open** Easter–Oct: daily.

🕮 Dornoch

Sutherland. ⚶ 1,200. 🚆 Golspie, Tain. 🚌 Inverness, Tain. 🛈 The Square (08452) 255121.
ⓦ visithighlands.com

With its first-class golf course and extensive sandy beaches, Dornoch is a popular holiday resort, but it has retained a peaceful atmosphere. The medieval cathedral (now the parish church) was all but destroyed in a clan dispute in 1570; it was finally restored in the 1920s for its 700th anniversary. More recently, the pop sstar Madonna chose the cathedral for the christening of her child.
A stone at the beach end of River Street marks the place where Janet Horne, the last woman to be tried for witchcraft in Scotland, was executed in 1722.

Environs
Nineteen kilometres (12 miles) northeast of the resort is the stately, Victorianized pile of **Dunrobin Castle**, magnificently situated in a great park with formal gardens overlooking the sea. Since the 13th century this has been the seat of the Earls of Sutherland. Many of its rooms are open to visitors.
The peaceful town of **Tain** to the south became an

administrative centre for the Highland Clearances, when the tolbooth was used as a jail. All is explained in the heritage centre, **Tain Through Time**.

🏠 **Dunrobin Castle**
Near Golspie. **Tel** (01408) 633177.
Open Apr–mid-Oct: daily. 🎟 🗹 🖥

🏛 **Tain Through Time**
Tower St. **Tel** (01862) 894089.
Open Apr–May & Sep–Oct: Mon–Fri; Jun–Aug: Mon–Sat. 🎟 ♿

The serene cathedral precinct in the town of Dornoch

35 Glen Shiel

Skye & Lochalsh. 🚂 Kyle of Lochalsh. 🚌 Glen Shiel. ℹ Bayfield House, Bayfield Road, Portree (01478) 614906.

Dominating one of Scotland's most haunting regions, the awesome summits of the Five Sisters of Kintail rear into view at the northern end of Loch Cluanie as the A87 enters Glen Shiel. The **visitor centre** at Morvich offers ranger-led excursions in the summer. Further west, the road passes the romantic **Eilean Donan Castle**, connected to the land by a causeway. After becoming a Jacobite (see p151) stronghold, it was destroyed in 1719 by English warships. In the 19th century it was restored, and it now contains a number of relics of the Jacobite cause.

🏠 **Eilean Donan Castle**
Off A87, near Dornie. **Tel** (01599) 555202. **Open** Feb–Dec: daily. 🎟 🖥

36 Isle of Skye

See pp156–7.

37 Wester Ross

Ross & Cromarty. 🚂 Achnasheen, Strathcarron. 🚌 Gairloch. ℹ Achtercairn, Gairloch, (01445) 712071. 🌐 visitscotland.com,

Leaving Loch Carron to the south, the A890 suddenly enters the northern Highlands and the great wilderness of Wester Ross. The Torridon Estate, sprawling on either side of Glen Torridon, includes some of the oldest mountains on earth (Torridonian rock is over 600 million years old), and is home to red deer, wild cats and wild goats. Peregrine falcons and golden eagles nest in the towering sandstone mass of Beinn Eighe, above the village of Torridon, with its breath-taking views over Applecross towards Skye. The **Torridon**

Typical Torridonian mountain scenery in the Wester Ross

Countryside Centre offers guided walks in season, and essential information on the natural history of the region.

Further north, the A832 cuts through the **Beinn Eighe National Nature Reserve**, Britain's oldest wildlife sanctuary. Remnants of the ancient Caledonian pine forest still stand on the banks and isles of Loch Maree, providing shelter for pine martens and wildcats. Buzzards and golden eagles nest on the alpine slopes. **Beinn Eighe Visitor Centre** has information on the reserve.

Along the coast, a series of exotic gardens thrive in the warming influence of the Gulf Stream. The most impressive is Inverewe Gardens (see p160).

🏛 **Torridon Countryside Centre**
Torridon. **Tel** (0844) 493 2229. **Open** Apr–Sep: Sun–Fri. 🎟 🗹 ♿ NTS

🦌 **Beinn Eighe Visitor Centre**
Near Kinlochewe, on A832. **Tel** (01445) 760258. **Open** Apr–Oct: daily. ♿

The western side of the Five Sisters of Kintail, seen from a viewpoint above Ratagan

㊱ Isle of Skye

The largest of the Inner Hebrides, Skye can be reached by the bridge linking Kyle of Lochalsh and Kyleakin. A turbulent geological history has given the island some of Britain's most varied and dramatic scenery. From the rugged volcanic plateau of northern Skye to the ice-sculpted peaks of the Cuillins, the island is divided by numerous sea lochs, leaving the traveller never more than 8 km (5 miles) from the sea. Limestone grasslands predominate in the south, where the hillsides, home of sheep and cattle, are scattered with the ruins of crofts abandoned during the Clearances *(see p154)*. Historically, Skye is best known for its association with Bonnie Prince Charlie.

Dunvegan Castle
For over seven centuries, Dunvegan Castle has been the seat of the chiefs of the Clan MacLeod. It contains the Fairy Flag, a piece of magical silk treasured for its protective powers.

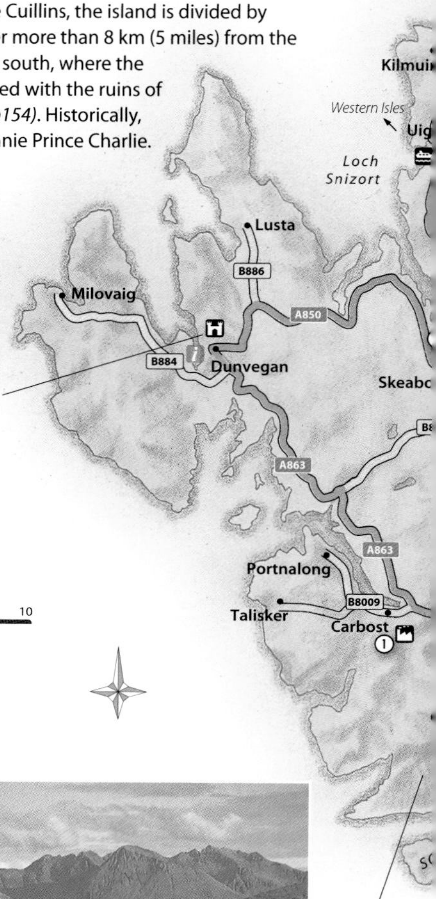

Key

▭ Major road
▭ Minor road
▭ Narrow lane

0 Kilometres   10
0 miles   5

Map labels: Kilmui, Western Isles, Uig, Loch Snizort, Lusta, B886, Milovaig, A850, Dunvegan, B884, Skeabo, A863, Portnalong, A863, Talisker, B8009, Carbost, Skeabos

KEY

① **The Talisker distillery** at Carbost, is famous for its Highland malts, often described as "the lava of the Cuillins".

② **Skeabost** has the ruins of a chapel which is associated with St Columba. Medieval tombstones can be found in the graveyard.

③ **Grave of Flora MacDonald**

④ **Kilt Rock**

⑤ **Loch Coruisk**

⑥ **Luib** has a beautiful thatched cottage, preserved as it was 100 years ago.

⑦ **Bridge to mainland**

⑧ **Otters** can be seen from the haven in Kylerhea.

⑨ **Armadale Castle Gardens and Museum of the Isles** houses the Clan Donald visitor centre.

Cuillins
Britain's finest mountain range is within walking distance of Sligachan, and in summer a boat sails from Elgol to the desolate inner sanctuary of Loch Coruisk. As he fled across the surrounding moorland, Bonnie Prince Charlie is said to have claimed: "even the Devil shall not follow me here!"

For hotels and restaurants see pp172–7 and pp181–9

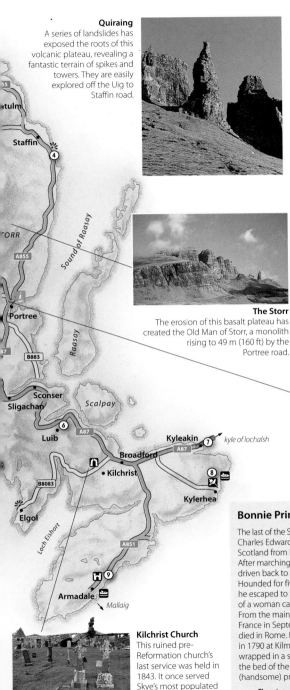

Quiraing

A series of landslides has exposed the roots of this volcanic plateau, revealing a fantastic terrain of spikes and towers. They are easily explored off the Uig to Staffin road.

The Storr

The erosion of this basalt plateau has created the Old Man of Storr, a monolith rising to 49 m (160 ft) by the Portree road.

VISITORS' CHECKLIST

Practical Information
The Highlands. 🖼 9,500.
🛈 Bayfield House, Portree (01478) 614906.
Dunvegan Castle: Dunvegan.
Tel (01470) 521206. **Open** Apr–mid-Oct: daily. 🅿 ♿ limited.
Armadale Castle: Armadale.
Tel (01471) 844305.
Open Apr–Oct: daily. 🅿 ♿
Talisker Distillery: Carbost.
Tel (01478) 614308.
Open Easter–Oct: daily; Nov–Easter: Mon–Fri. 🅿
♿ limited. 📷

Transport
🚈 Kyle of Lochalsh.
🚌 Portree.
⛴ From Mallaig or Glenelg.

Portree

With its colourful harbour, Portree (meaning "port of the king") is Skye's metropolis. It received its name after a visit by James V in 1540.

Bonnie Prince Charlie

The last of the Stuart claimants to the Crown, Charles Edward Stuart (1720–88), came to Scotland from France in 1745 to win the throne. After marching as far as Derby, his army was driven back to Culloden where it was defeated. Hounded for five months through the Highlands, he escaped to Skye, disguised as the maidservant of a woman called Flora MacDonald, from Uist. From the mainland, he sailed to France in September 1746, and died in Rome. Flora was buried in 1790 at Kilmuir, on Skye, wrapped in a sheet taken from the bed of the "bonnie" (handsome) prince.

The prince, disguised as a maidservant

Kilchrist Church

This ruined pre-Reformation church's last service was held in 1843. It once served Skye's most populated areas, though the surrounding moors are now deserted.

The castle of Eilean Donan, Loch Duich in Glen Shiel ▶

🅴 Inverewe Garden

On A832, near Poolewe, Ross-shire.
Tel (0844) 493 2225. **Open** daily. 🈂️
🈂️ 🈂️ 🈂️ 🈂️ **nts.org.uk**

Inverewe Garden attracts over 130,000 visitors a year and is considered a national treasure. The gardens contain an extraordinary variety of trees, shrubs and flowers from around the world, despite being at a latitude of 57.8° north.

Inverewe was started in 1862 by the 20-year-old Osgood Mackenzie after being given an estate of 4,860 ha (12,000 acres) of exposed, barren land next to his family's holding. At that time there was just one dwarf willow growing there. Mackenzie began by planting shelter trees and then went on to create a walled garden using imported soil. He found that the west coast's climate, warmed by the North Atlantic Drift from the Gulf Stream *(see p27)*, encouraged the growth of exotic species.

By 1922, the garden had achieved international recognition as one of the great plant collections. In 1952 it was donated to the National Trust for Scotland. At Inverewe today you can find Blue Nile lilies, the tallest Australian gum trees growing in Britain and fragrant rhododendrons from China.

Some of the many unusual plants cultivated at Inverewe Garden

Planting is designed to provide colour all year, but the gardens are at their best between spring and autumn.

🅵 Ullapool

Highland. 🅰️ 1,300. 🚆 Inverness. 🚍
🚍 ℹ️ Argyle St (01854) 612486.
🇼 **ullapool.com**

With its wide streets, whitewashed houses, palm trees and street signs in Gaelic, Ullapool is one of the prettiest villages on the west coast. Planned and built as a fishing station in 1788, it occupies a peninsula jutting into Loch Broom. Fishing is no longer important, except when East European

"klondyker" factory ships moor in the loch in the winter. The major activity is now the ferry to Stornoway on Lewis *(see table, p221)*. The **Ullapool Museum** offers an insight into local history.

🏛️ Ullapool Museum
7–8 West Argyle St. **Tel** (01854) 612 987.
Open Apr–Oct Mon–Sat. 🈂️ 🈂️ 🈂️

Environs
The natural wonders of this area include the rugged Assynt Mountains to the north, and, to the south, the deep and precipitous Corrieshalloch Gorge.

It is worth visiting **Achiltibuie Garden**, a "Garden of the Future", where flowers grow without soil. Achiltibuie also has a **Smokehouse** where the process of curing salmon can be viewed.

Achiltibuie is worth a visit for the scenic drive alone. Tour boats run from here, and from Ullapool, to the **Summer Isles** – a small, sparsely populated group, once the home of noted environmentalist, Frank Fraser Darling.

🍃 Achiltibuie Garden
Achiltibuie. **Tel** (01854) 622202. **Open** Mar–Sep: Mon–Fri. 🈂️ 🈂️ limited.

🈂️ Smokehouse
Achiltibuie. **Tel** (01854) 622353.
Open Easter–end Sep: Mon–Sat.

A tranquil, late-evening view of Ullapool and Loch Broom on the northwestern coast of Scotland

For hotels and restaurants see pp172–7 and pp181–9

Majestic cliffs on Handa Island, a welcome refuge for seabirds

⑩ Handa Island

Highland. 🚢 from Tarbet, near Scourie, Apr–Aug, (07780) 967800. 🛈 Scottish Wildlife Trust, (0131) 312 7765.

Located just offshore from Scourie on the west coast, this small island is an important breeding sanctuary for many species of seabirds.

In past centuries it was inhabited by a hardy people, who had their own queen and parliament. The last 60 inhabitants were evacuated in 1847 when their potato crop failed. The island was also used as a burial ground as it was safe from the wolves that inhabited the mainland.

The island is now managed by the Scottish Wildlife Trust. A walk takes visitors to the 100-m (328-ft) high northern cliffs. On the way you are liable to experience the intimidating antics of great and Arctic skuas (large migratory birds) swooping low over your head. Early in the year 11,000 pairs of razorbills can be found on Handa, and 66,000 pairs of guillemots.

Environs
The highest waterfall in Britain is **Eas Coul Aulin**, at 180 m (590 ft). It is best seen after rainfall, from a tour boat based at Kylesku, 24 km (15 miles) to the south of Handa.

⑪ Cape Wrath and the North Coast

Highland. 🚌 🚢 May–Sep (01971) 511246. 🛈 John O'Groats (01955) 611373.

The northern edge of mainland Scotland spans the full variety of Highland geography, from mountainous moorlands and dazzlingly white beaches to flat, green farmland.

Cape Wrath is alluring not only for its name but for its cliffs, constantly pounded by the Atlantic. There are many stacks rising out of the sea that swarm with seabirds. The lighthouse was among the last in Scotland to be automated in 1998. In summer, a mini-bus serves the 13-km (8-mile) road leading to Cape Wrath. In order to reach the bus, you must take the connecting **Cape Wrath Ferry** from the pier by the Cape Wrath Hotel, as the cape is cut off by the Kyle of Durness. At Durness is **Smoo Cave**, an awesome cavern hollowed out of limestone. **Smoo Innercave Tours** run trips there. Just outside Durness, a community of artists has established the **Balnakeil Craft Village**, displaying pottery, enamelwork, wood carving, print-making and paintings. Astonishingly white beaches follow one after the other along the coast, and the road then loops round Loch Eriboll – the deepest of the sea lochs and a

A nesting kittiwake

base for Atlantic and Russian convoys during World War II.

The **Strathnaver Museum** in Bettyhill explains the notorious Sutherland "Clearances", the forced evictions of 15,000 people to make way for sheep. At Rossal, 16 km (10 miles) south of Bettyhill, is an arch-aeological walk around an excavated village, which provides important information on life in pre-Clearance days.

A gigantic white dome at **Dounreay** marks the nuclear reprocessing plant, where you can tour the works and visit the free exhibition centre in summer. The main town on the coast here is Thurso, a village of solid stone buildings. Once famous for its locally quarried stone slabs, Thurso's industry died with the advent of cement. Each September, Thurso hosts "Northlands", the Scottish Nordic Music Festival.

John O'Groats is probably the most famous name on the map here, said to be the very northerly tip of the mainland, although this is in fact nearby **Dunnet Head**. Apart from a quaint harbour where day trips leave for Orkney, John O'Groats is a tourist trap. More rewarding are the cliffs at **Duncansby Head**, where you can enjoy the natural ferocity of the Pentland Firth.

🚢 **Smoo Innercave Tours**
Durness. **Tel** (01971) 511704.
Open Apr–Sep: daily. ♿

🏛 **Strathnaver Museum**
Clachan, Bettyhill. **Tel** (01641) 521418. **Open** Apr–Oct: Mon–Sat. ♿ 🛍 limited.

Duncansby Head, Caithness, at the far northeast corner of Scotland

ⓐ Orkney Islands

Beyond the Pentland Firth, less than 10 km (6 miles) off the Scottish mainland, the Orkney archipelago consists of some 70 islands and rocky skerries boasting the densest concentration of archaeological sites in Britain. Today, only about 16 of these islands are permanently inhabited. Orkney's way of life is predominantly agricultural – it's said that, whereas the Shetlanders are fishermen with crofts, the Orcadians are farmers with boats. The climate is tempered by the Gulf Stream, and the rich soils overlying old red sandstone produce lush green turf and summer crops of grain.

The delightfully frescoed Italian Chapel, in East Mainland

Kirkwall

The winding flagstoned streets of Orkney's capital are lined with period houses and craft shops. Opposite **St Magnus Cathedral**, an 870-year-old masterpiece of red and yellow stone, lie the ruins of the **Bishop's Palace**, dating mostly from the 16th century. Also nearby, in a former manse called Tankerness House, the excellent **Orkney Museum** illustrates the history of habitation on the islands. South of the town centre, the **Highland Park Distillery** dispenses a fine dram at the end of its guided tours.

Orcadian man on a bicycle

🏛 St Magnus Cathedral
Tel (01856) 874894. **Open** Mon–Fri (daily in summer). 🗎

🏛 Bishop's Palace
Tel (01856) 871918. **Open** Apr–Oct. 🗎

🏛 Orkney Museum
Tel (01856) 873535. **Open** Mon–Sat.

🏛 Highland Park Distillery
Tel (01856) 874619. **Open** Apr & Sep: Mon–Fri; May–Aug: daily; Oct–Mar: Mon–Fri pm only. 🗎 (includes tasting). 🗎 🗎

The rich-coloured exterior of St Magnus Cathedral

West Mainland

Many of the waterfront buildings in **Stromness**, the main town on Orkney's largest island, date from the 18th and 19th centuries. Among them, the **Pier Arts Centre** contains a fine collection of 20th-century works. The **Stromness Museum** traces Orkney's history as a trading port.

West Mainland is renowned for its prehistoric sites. Said to date from around 2750 BC, **Maeshowe** is a chambered tomb aligned with the winter solstice. Vikings plundered it around 1150, leaving a fascinating legacy of runic graffiti on the walls. Nearby are the huge **Standing Stones of Stenness** and the **Ring of Brodgar**, a megalithic henge of 36 stones. The Neolithic village of **Skara Brae** was discovered when a storm stripped dunes from the site in 1850. Beneath the sands lay wonderfully preserved evidence of everyday life in the Stone Age, such as beds, fireplaces and shelves.

The cliffs of **Marwick Head**, overlooking Birsay Bay, are one of several RSPB reserves on West Mainland, home to thousands of nesting seabirds in early summer. A memorial commemorates Lord Kitchener and the crew of HMS *Hampshire*, sunk off this headland by a German mine in 1916.

🏛 Pier Arts Centre
Tel (01856) 850209. **Open** 10:30am–5pm.

🏛 Stromness Museum
Tel (01856) 850025. **Open** Mon–Sat (daily Apr–Sep). 🗎 🗎

🏛 Maeshowe
Tel (01856) 761 606. **Open** daily. 🗎 🗎

🏛 Standing Stones of Stennes and Ring of Brodgar
Open daily. 🗎

🏛 Skara Brae
Tel (01856) 841001. **Open** daily. 🗎 🗎

East Mainland

East of Kirkwall, the road runs through quiet agricultural land over a series of causeways linking the southernmost islands to the mainland. The **Churchill Barriers** were built by Italian prisoners of war during the 1940s to protect the British fleet stationed in Scapa Flow. In their spare time, these POWs also constructed the remarkable **Italian Chapel**, whose beautiful frescoed interior is well worth seeing.

On South Ronaldsay, the 5,000-year-old **Tomb of the Eagles** was excavated by a local farmer. Some 340 burial sites were unearthed at this clifftop location, along with stone tools and the talons of many sea eagles.

🏛 Italian Chapel
Tel (01856) 781268. **Open** daily (Mass: 1st Sun of mth, Apr–Sep). 🗎

🏛 Tomb of the Eagles
Tel (01856) 831339. **Open** Mar–Oct; Nov–Feb by appt. 🗎 🗎 🗎 🗎

For hotels and restaurants see pp172–7 and pp181–9

Hoy

Orkney's second-largest island takes its name from the Norse word for "high island", which refers to its spectacular cliff-lined terrain. Hoy is very different from the rest of the archipelago, and its northern hills make excellent walking and birdwatching country. The **Old Man of Hoy**, a 137-m (450-ft) vertical stack off the western coast, is the island's best-known landmark, a popular challenge to keen rock-climbers. Near Rackwick, the 5,000-year-old **Dwarfie Stane** is a unique chambered cairn cut from a single block of stone.

At Lyness, on the eastern side of Hoy, the **Scapa Flow Visitor**

Centre contains a fascinating exhibition on this huge deep-water naval haven. It recounts the events of 16 June 1919, when the captured German fleet was scuttled on the orders of its commanding officer to prevent handover: 74 ships were sunk. Many of these have since been salvaged; others provide one of the world's great wreck-diving sites. Tours from Houton Pier, using a remote-controlled vehicle fitted with an underwater camera, give a glimpse of this eerie sub-aquatic graveyard.

ℹ️ Scapa Flow Visitor Centre
Tel (01856) 791300. **Open** Apr–Mon–Fri; May–Oct: Mon–Sat. ♿
ⓦ scapaflow.co.uk

The Northern Isles

Orkney's outlying islands are sparsely populated and mostly the preserve of seals and seabirds. They include **Rousay**, known as the "Egypt of the North" for its many archaeological sites, and **Egilsay**, the scene of St Magnus's grisly murder in 1115. The 12th-century round-

towered church dedicated to his memory is a rare example of Irish-Viking design. **Sanday** is the largest of the northern isles, its fertile farmland fringed by sandy beaches. **North Ronaldsay**, the northernmost of the Orkney Islands, is noted for its hardy, seaweed-eating sheep and rare migrant birds.

Day Trips to Remote Islands

There are flights from Kirkwall to a dozen outlying islands several times a week, as well as daily ferries. The two-minute hop between **Westray** and **Papa Westray** is the world's shortest scheduled air route. Inter-island transport is weather-dependent.

The Old Man of Hoy, a majestic stone column off the coast of Hoy

Key

━━ Major road
══ Minor road
▲ Summit

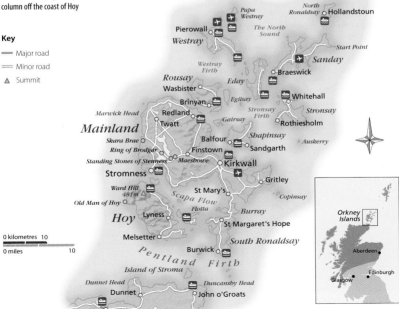

ⓐ Shetland Islands

More than 100 rugged, cliff-hemmed islands form Scotland's most northerly domain. Nowhere in Shetland is further than 5 km (3 miles) from the sea. Fishing and salmon-farming are mainstays of the economy, boosted in recent decades by revenue from the North Sea oil industry. In winter the islands suffer severe gales and storms, but in high summer, the sun may shine for as long as 19 hours, and a twilight known as the "simmer dim" persists throughout the night.

Lerwick

Shetland's chief town is a pretty place of grey stone buildings and narrow, flagstoned lanes. First established by Dutch fishermen in the 1600s, it grew to become wealthy from the whaling trade. The increase in North Sea oil traffic has made the harbour area very busy.

At the heart of the town is Commercial Street, its northern end guarded by **Fort Charlotte**, which affords fine views from its battlements. At the **Shetland Museum and Archive**, on Hay's Dock, you can admire a fine collection of historic boats, archaeological finds and Shetland textiles tracing the islands' history.

On Lerwick's outskirts lie the **Clickimin Broch**, a prehistoric fort dating from around 700 BC, and the 18th-century **Böd of Gremista**, birthplace of Arthur Anderson, co-founder of the P&O shipping company. The building now houses a maritime museum.

The fortified tower of Mousa Broch

🏛 **Shetland Museum and Archive**
Tel (01595) 695057. **Open** daily. ♿ 🖥

🏛 **Böd of Gremista**
Tel (01595) 696729. **Open** May–Sep: Tue–Sat. ♿

Central Mainland

Sheltering Lerwick from the winter gales is **Bressay**, an island with fine walks and views. Boats run from Lerwick to tiny **Noss**, off Bressay's east coast. This nature reserve is home to thousands of breeding seabirds, including gannets and great skuas (or bonxies).

West of Lerwick is the quiet fishing port of **Scalloway**, Shetland's second town and the islands' former capital. **Scalloway Castle** is a fortified tower dating from 1600, while the **Scalloway Museum** contains an exhibition on the "Shetland Bus", a wartime resistance operation that used fishing boats to bring refugees from German-occupied Norway. North of Scalloway, near Weisdale, the fertile region

The 17th-century Scalloway Castle, Central Mainland

of **Tingwall** is a well-known angling centre. Connected by bridges to Central Mainland's west coast are the islands of **Burra** and **Trondra**, with lovely beaches and good walks.

🏛 **Scalloway Museum**
Tel (01595) 880734. **Open** May–Sep: daily.

🦅 **Noss National Nature Reserve**
Tel (01595) 693345. **Open** May–Aug: Tue, Wed, Fri–Sun. 🚤

South Mainland

This area offers two important archaeological sights. The ornate **Mousa Broch**, on an easterly islet reached by a summer ferry, is the best example of this type of ancient fortified tower in Britain. The dry-stone walls make ideal nestboxes for a colony of storm petrels. **Jarlshof**, in the far south, spans over 3,000 years of occupation from Neolithic to Viking times.

The impressive cliffs and lighthouse (an RSPB centre) at **Sumburgh Head** are also worth visiting. The island of **St Ninian's** is linked to South Mainland by a causeway of dazzling silver sand.

🏛 **Mousa Broch**
Tel (01856) 841815. **Open** Apr–Sep. 🚤 included in boat fare.

🏛 **Jarlshof Prehistoric and Norse Settlement**
Tel (01950) 460112. **Open** daily. 🚤 ♿ limited. 🎧 by request.

🦅 **Sumburgh Head Lighthouse (RSPB)**
Tel (01595) 694688. **Open** daily.

Early evening lights over Lerwick Harbour

or the snowy owl. Unst has the most varied scenery and the richest flora and fauna, plus an excellent visitor centre at the **Hermaness National Nature Reserve**. Beyond the lighthouse of Muckle Flugga is **Out Stack**, Britain's most northerly point.

West of Mainland, **Foula** has dramatic sea cliffs, while **Fair Isle**, midway between Orkney and Shetland, is owned by the National Trust for Scotland.

🎿 **Hermaness National Nature Reserve**
Tel (01595) 693345. **Open** daily (visitors' centre: Apr–Sep).

Day Trips to Remote Islands
There are regular, inexpensive internal flights in Shetland to Fair Isle, Foula and Papa Stour, as well as lots of inter-island ferries. Most routes depart from Tingwall, on the Central Mainland.

An inquisitive otter, one of a large population on the island of Yell

Key

=== Minor road

△ Summit

North Mainland
North of Lerwick, Shetland rises to its highest point at **Ronas Hill** (454 m/1,475 ft) amid tracts of bleak, empty moorland. The sheltered sea loch of **Sullom Voe** is dominated by the jetties and support buildings of Europe's biggest oil and gas terminal. The west coast has

The red granite cliffs of Esha Ness, North Mainland

spectacular natural scenery, notably the red granite cliffs and blow-holes at **Esha Ness**, from where you can see the wave-gnawed stacks of **The Drongs** and a huge rock arch called **Dore Holm**. Offshore, the island of **Papa Stour** has further startling formations of volcanic rock.

Outlying Islands
The northern isles of **Yell**, **Fetlar** and **Unst** have regular, though weather-dependent, boat connections to the Mainland. Yell has a large otter population, and on Fetlar there's a chance of glimpsing rare migrant birds, like the red-necked phalarope

Birds on Orkney and Shetland

Millions of migrant and local birds can be admired on these islands. Over 20 species of seabirds regularly breed here, and over 340 different species have been recorded passing through Fair Isle, one of the world's great staging posts. Inaccessible cliffs provide security at vulnerable nesting times for huge colonies of gannets, guillemots, puffins, kittiwakes, fulmars and razorbills. Species found in few other UK locations include great skuas and storm petrels.

Puffin

For additional map symbols see back flap

❹ Western Isles

Western Scotland ends with this remote chain of islands, made of some of the oldest rock on earth. Barren landscapes are divided by countless waterways, while the western, windward coasts are edged by white sandy beaches. For centuries, the eastern shores, composed largely of peat bogs, have provided islanders with fuel. Man has been here for 6,000 years, living off the sea and the thin turf, though abandoned monuments, including a Norwegian whaling station on Harris, attest to the difficulties faced in commercializing traditional local skills. Gaelic, part of an enduring culture, is widely spoken, and most signs are in both English and Gaelic.

The interior of a croft house at The Blackhouse

The monumental Standing Stones of Callanish in northern Lewis

Lewis and Harris

Forming the largest landmass of the Western Isles, Lewis and Harris are a single island, though Gaelic dialects differ between the two areas. From the administrative centre of **Stornoway**, with its bustling harbour and colourful house fronts, the ancient **Standing Stones of Callanish** are only 26 km (16 miles) to the west. Just off the road on the way to Callanish are the cone-shaped ruins of **Carloway Broch**, a Pictish (see p45) tower over 2,000 years old. The more recent past can be explored at Arnol's **Blackhouse** – a showcase of crofting life as it was until 50 years ago.

South of the rolling peat moors of Lewis, a range of mountains marks the border with Harris, which is entered by passing Aline Lodge at the head of Loch Seaforth. The mountains of Harris are a paradise for hill-walkers. From their summits on a clear day, the distant isle of St Kilda can be seen 80 km (50 miles) to the west.

The ferry port of Tarbert stands on a slim isthmus sepa-rating North and South Harris.

The tourist office provides addresses for local weavers of the tough Harris Tweed. Some weavers still use indigenous plants to create the various dyes. From Leverburgh, on Harris' southern tip, a ferry sails to North Uist, linked by a causeway to Berneray.

🏛 **The Blackhouse**
Arnol. **Tel** (01851) 710395.
Open Mon–Sat. 📷 📷

The Uists and Benbecula

After the dramatic scenery of Harris, the lower-lying, largely waterlogged southern isles may seem an anticlimax, though they nurture secrets well worth discovering. Long, white, sandy beaches fringe the Atlantic coast, edged with one of Scotland's natural treasures: the lime-rich soil known as *machair*. During the summer months, the soil is covered with wild flowers, the unique fragrance of which can be detected far out to sea.

From **Lochmaddy**, North Uist's main village, the A867 crosses 5 km (3 miles) of causeway to **Benbecula**, the isle from which the brave Flora MacDonald smuggled Bonnie Prince Charlie to Skye (see p157). Benbecula is a flat island covered by a mosaic of small lochs. Like its neighbours, it is known for good trout fishing. Here, and to the north, the Protestant religion holds sway, while Catholicism prevails in the southern islands. Benbecula's chief source of employment is the Army Rocket Range, which

The harbour at Stornoway, the principal town on Lewis and Harris

has its headquarters in the main village of Bailivanich. Another causeway leads to South Uist, with its golden beaches, which are renowned as a National Scenic Area.

Eriskay

One of the smallest and most enchanting of the Western Isles, Eriskay epitomizes their peace and beauty. The island is best known for the wrecking of the *SS Politician* in 1941, which inspired the book and film *Whisky Galore*. A bottle from its cargo and other relics can be seen in Eriskay's only bar. It was at the beautiful beach of Coilleag A'Phrionnsa (Prince's beach) that Bonnie Prince Charlie first set foot on Scotland at the start of his 1745 campaign. As a result, a rare convolvulus flower that grows here has become associated with him.

Blue waters off the coast of Barra, looking east to the Isle of Rum

Barra

The dramatic way to arrive on Barra is by plane – the airstrip is a beach and the timetable depends on the tide. Barra is a pretty island, with its central core of hills and circular road. The western side is almost all beaches. Over 1,000 species of flowers have been recorded.

The view over Castlebay from the Madonna and Child statue, on the top of Heaval hill, is particularly fine. The romantic **Kisimul Castle**, set on an island, is the 15th seat of the Clan MacNeil. It is currently being restored. Other attractions are the **Barra Heritage Centre** and also a golf course.

Kisimul Castle
Tel (01871) 810313. Open Apr–Sep: daily. includes boat trip.

Barra Heritage Centre
Tel (01871) 810413. Open May–Sep: Mon–Sat.

St Kildan men with their catch of seabirds

St Kilda

These "Islands on the Edge of the World" were the most isolated habitation in Scotland until the ageing population requested to be evacuated in 1930. The St Kildans developed a unique lifestyle based on harvesting seabirds. The largest gannetry in the world (40,000 pairs) is now to be found here. There are three islands and three stacks of awesome beauty, each with soaring cliffs rising sheer to 425 m (1,400 ft) at their highest. Such is their isolation that separate subspecies of mouse and wren have evolved. Tours are run by **Westernedge Charters** and **Island Cruising**. Volunteers can also pay to join summer work parties on the island, run by the National Trust for Scotland, owners of the **St Kilda World Heritage Site**.

Island Cruising
1 Erista, Uig, Isle of Lewis.
Tel (01851) 672381.

Westernedge Charters
Linlithgow. Tel (01506) 824227.

St Kilda World Heritage Site
Tel (0844) 493 2241. NTS
W nts.org.uk/volunteering/

Crofting

Crofts are small parcels of agricultural land, worked in conjunction with another source of income as they are too small to provide total subsistence. They originated in the early 1800s when landlords made available units of poor land on the coast, clearing the people from the more fertile areas, and making them dependent on wages from either fishing or collecting kelp (seaweed used to make commercial alkali). When these sources of income diminished, crofters endured over 50 years of extreme hardship through famine, high rents, eviction and lack of security. Not until 1886 was an Act passed which gave crofters security and allowed families the right of inheritance (but not ownership). Today there are 17,000 registered crofts, almost all in the Highlands and islands. Governed by special regulations prohibiting the creation of new crofts, the crofters are eligible for special grants. Most crofters raise sheep, but recent trends are tree planting and providing habitats for rare birds. Crofting remains a vital part of Highland communities.

A traditional, thatched crofter's house on the island of North Uist

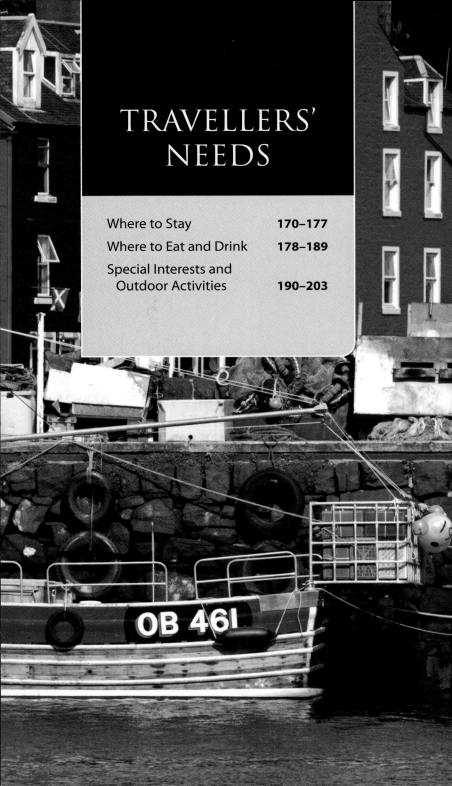

TRAVELLERS'
NEEDS

WHERE TO STAY

The range of hotels and other accommodation available in Scotland is extensive, and it is easy to find something to suit every budget. Different types of accommodation are described below, and the hotel listings on pages 172–7 include some of the best places to stay, from luxurious country house hotels and castles to cosy bed and breakfasts (B&Bs). This selection represents both excellence and good value. Self-catering holidays are also growing in popularity in Scotland. This type of accommodation is particularly well suited to those on a tight budget or families with young children. Campsites, from basic tent pitches to yurts and other more comfortable "glamping" options, provide a reasonably priced alternative to hotels and guesthouses. Booking online is usually the way to get the cheapest price. Alternatively, phone and ask if there are any special rates available.

A room in the Monachyle MHOR Hotel *(see p175)*

Hotel Classifications

The Quality Assurance Scheme run by **VisitScotland** is a useful guide when choosing holiday accommodation and covers hotels, B&Bs and self-catering options. A grade from "acceptable" to "exceptional" is awarded along with a classification of stars from one to five, indicating the facilities available.

Prices and Hidden Extras

Hotel rates are normally quoted per room and include VAT and service charge. Top of the range hotels can cost over £200 per night and an average hotel in Edinburgh or Glasgow, about £75–150 per night. Outside the main cities, expect to pay £60–100 for a similar standard, or £30–60 for a B&B. High rates are charged for telephone calls made from the room, so buy a phonecard, use the lobby telephone or check the cost of using your mobile.

Booking

Booking online has become the best way to snag a deal across most types of accommodation.

Booking ahead is always recommended, especially during the summer months and around Christmas and New Year. Some hotels require a non-refundable deposit. For a small fee, staff at VisitScotland Information Centres will book a room in your following destinations as part of the "Book A Bed Ahead" service. If you've arrived in town without a booking, staff at tourist offices can help find rooms at short notice.

Country House Hotels

A genuine country house hotel is situated in extensive grounds and filled with antiques and fine furnishing. However, the term "country house hotel" has been adopted liberally by hoteliers, some of whom consider gas log-fires and reproduction furniture sufficient to warrant the title.

Castles

Converted castles offer visitors the chance to live and dine like a lord. The atmosphere is intimate yet refined, with fine dining restaurants and well-stocked wine cellars. Room tariffs are high, but the level of comfort and luxury is unparalleled.

Hunting Lodges

In rural Scotland, shooting lodges, usually part of a large country estate, also provide accommodation. They are comfortably furnished without being luxurious. Guests may have the opportunity to join a hunting party and can expect fresh game to be served at meals.

Coaching Inns

Coaching inns can be found throughout Scotland. These former staging points for people journeying by horse and carriage allowed horses to rest and travellers to find lodging. Generally attractive historic buildings, inns are often the town's focal point. They nearly always have traditional decor, and often a reliable restaurant serving regional, home-cooked food in an informal atmosphere. Many offer excellent cuisine.

A majestic hotel on the quayside in Leith, near Edinburgh

Bed and Breakfast and Guesthouses

For inexpensive accommodation and a chance to meet the local people, B&Bs are ideal. Often family-owned, they are basic, no-frills establishments with a generous cooked breakfast included in the price.

◀ Brightly painted houses at Tobermory's harbour on the Isle of Mull

B&Bs dominate the lower price range, and in the remote areas of Scotland can be the only form of accommodation. The buildings are often cosy farmhouses with homely decor, and guests are likely to receive a more personal welcome than they would at the larger hotels.

Guesthouses also offer reasonably priced, basic accommodation. They usually contain a number of bedrooms, as well as a communal dining area.

In more remote areas, B&Bs and guesthouses may offer evening meals that can be prebooked. VisitScotland publishes the *Scotland: Bed-and-Breakfast* guide, which lists over 1,500 B&Bs and guesthouses.

Self-catering

The freedom of self-catering accommodation may appeal to those who are planning an extended stay or who require maximum flexibility, such as families travelling with young children. This is also often a more cost-effective accommodation option. There are many self-catering places over Scotland, from luxury apartments in the centre of cities to cottages with views of the coast.

Camping and Caravanning

A choice of campsites and caravan parks, normally open from Easter to October, can be found throughout the country. Two organizations, the **Caravan Club** and the **Camping and Caravanning Club**, publish guides listing their parks, and it may be useful for those with motor homes to become members. A typical camping or caravan site costs £8–15 per night. "Glamping", camping with a few home comforts, has taken off in the UK. Many campsites have yurts or pods that will accommodate a family for about £40 per night – a great way to camp without needing all of the equipment. Parks fill up quickly during the summer so it is advisable to book ahead.

A traditional croft cottage, one of many self-catering properties in Scotland

Youth Hostels

There are around 80 hostels in Scotland, owned by the **Scottish Youth Hostels Association (SYHA)**. Most have single-sex dormitories, but occasionally there are separate rooms for families. You must be a member of the SYHA to stay, but anyone can join upon arrival.

Recommended Hotels

The accommodation choices in this guide cover a range of options from gypsy caravans to relaxed B&Bs; from sleek boutique hotels to grand five-star resorts. The hotels are included based on two main criteria – quality and value for money, irrespective of the price bracket.

Hotels that come highly recommended are highlighted as DK Choice. They may be set in a historic landmark building, offer splendid views in a memorable location, or have excellent facilities and service.

DIRECTORY

Tourist Information Centre

Visit Scotland
Ocean Point One, 94 Ocean Drive, Edinburgh EH6 6JH.
Tel 0845 859 1006
W visitscotland.com

Camping and Caravanning

Camping and Caravanning Club
Tel 0845 130 7631
W campingandcaravanning club.co.uk

Caravan Club
Tel 01342 326 944
W caravanclub.co.uk

Youth Hostels

Scottish Youth Hostels Association (SYHA)
Tel 01786 891 400
W syha.org.uk

Invercoe campsite in Glencoe offering wonderful views

Where to Stay

Edinburgh

NEW TOWN: Gerald's Place £
B&B **Map** D4
21B Abercromby Place, EH3 6QE
Tel 0131 558 7017
W geraldsplace.com
Centrally located B&B with just
two rooms and a warm, friendly
owner.

**NEW TOWN: St. Bernards
House** £
Guesthouse **Map** D4
22 St Bernard's Crescent, EH4 1NS
Tel 0131 332 2339
W stbernardshouse.co.uk
Two-star guesthouse with some
en suite rooms, set in a charming
Victorian town house.

NEW TOWN: Tune Hotel £
Budget **Map** D4
7 Clifton Terrace, EH12 5DR
Tel 0131 347 9700
W tunehotels.com/our-hotels/
haymarket-edinburgh
This stylish budget option in the
West End offers excellent value
accomodation, but charges for
some extras such as toiletries.

NEW TOWN: The Bonham ££
Boutique **Map** D4
35 Drumsheugh Gardens, EH3 7RN
Tel 0131 226 6050
W townhousecompany.com/
thebonham
The Bonham offers individually
designed rooms in contemporary,
bold colours. Excellent restaurant
with a superb wine list.

NEW TOWN: Channings Hotel ££
Character **Map** D4
12–16 South Learmonth
Gardens, EH4 1EZ
Tel 0131 315 2226
W theedinburghcollection.com/
channings
Set in converted Edwardian town
houses on a cobbled street, this
smart hotel features individually
decorated rooms with elegant
furnishings and views over
private gardens.

A breakfast tray at The Knight Residence, Edinburgh

**NEW TOWN: The Chester
Residence** ££
Self-catering **Map** D4
9 Rothesay Place, EH3 7SL
Tel 0131 226 2075
W chester-residence.com
Plush, spacious apartments with
designer kitchens in a grand old
Georgian town house.

NEW TOWN: The George ££
Luxury **Map** D4
19-21 George Street, EH2 2PB
Tel 0131 225 1251
W edinburghgeorgehotel.co.uk
Delightful, long-established hotel
with high standards. Popular venue
for conferences.

NEW TOWN: Hotel Indigo ££
Boutique **Map** D4
51–59 York Place, EH1 3JD
Tel 0131 556 5577
W hotelindigoedinburgh.co.uk
Chic hotel with well-furnished,
fashionable rooms and superb
luxury suites.

NEW TOWN: Nira Caledonia ££
Boutique **Map** D4
10 Gloucester Place, EH3 6EF
Tel 0131 225 2720
W niracaledonia.com
Housed in a row of town houses,
Nira Caledonia offers modern
comforts such as iPod docks.

NEW TOWN: The Roxburghe ££
Historic **Map** D4
38 Charlotte Square, EH2 4HQ
Tel 0871 423 4896
W theroxburghe.com
Georgian hotel with facilities such
as a spa and indoor swimming
pool. Acclaimed restaurant on site.

**NEW TOWN: The Royal Terrace
Hotel** ££
Historic **Map** D4
18 Royal Terrace, EH7 5AQ
Tel 0131 557 3222
W primahotels.co.uk/royal
Classy hotel behind Calton Hill,
with comfortable guest rooms and
terraced private gardens.

NEW TOWN: Tigerlily ££
Boutique
Map D4
125 George Street,
EH2 4JN
Tel 0131 225 5005
W tigerlilyedinburgh.
co.uk
Award-winning
boutique hotel in
George Street with
individually styled
rooms. Fantastic on-
site restaurant.

NEW TOWN: The Balmoral £££
Luxury **Map** D4
1 Princes Street, EH2 2EQ
Tel 0131 556 2414
W thebalmoralhotel.com
International five-star retreat with
graceful façade and palatial
interiors. Champagne bar on site.

DK Choice

**NEW TOWN:
The Caledonian** £££
Luxury **Map** D4
Princes Street, EH1 2AB
Tel 0131 222 8888
W thecaledonianedinburgh.com
A city landmark, the Caledonian
was spectacularly reinvented in
2012. The hotel boasts stylish
rooms, a first-class brasserie and
a fine dining restaurant. Try the
Guerlain Spa for a sublime
experience.

OLD TOWN: The Bank Hotel £
Character **Map** D4
1 South Bridge, EH1 1LL
Tel 0131 556 9940
W bankhoteledinburgh.co.uk
This comfortable hotel located
on the Royal Mile was originally
built as a bank in 1923. No lift.

**OLD TOWN: Classic
Guest House** £
Guesthouse **Map** D4
50 Mayfield Road, EH9 2NH
Tel 0131 667 5847
W classichouse.demon.co.uk
Elegant Victorian house with
comfortably furnished rooms.

**OLD TOWN: The Knight
Residence** ££
Self-catering **Map** D4
12 Lauriston Street, EH3 9DJ
Tel 0131 622 8120
W theknightresidence.co.uk
Excellent, award-winning
serviced apartments. Superb
central location.

**OLD TOWN: The Macdonald
Holyrood Hotel** ££
Luxury **Map** D4
81 Holyrood Road, EH8 8AU
Tel 0844 879 9028
W macdonaldhotels.co.uk
Elegant rooms and a luxury spa
at this conveniently located hotel.

OLD TOWN: The Scotsman ££
Luxury Map D4
20 North Bridge, EH1 1TR, UK
Tel *0131 556 5565*
w thescotsmanhotel.co.uk
Housed in the historic *Scotsman* newspaper building with original Italian marble interiors.

OLD TOWN: Ten Hill Place ££
Historic Map D4
10 Hill Place, EH8 9DS
Tel *0131 662 2080*
w tenhillplace.com
Stylish hotel with sweeping views of Arthur's Seat from its top floor.

OLD TOWN: Hotel Missoni £££
Luxury Map D4
1 George IV Bridge, EH1 1AD
Tel *0131 220 6666*
w hotelmissoni.com
A favourite with both locals and celebrities. The rooms feature mod cons such as Nespresso machines and iPod docks.

OLD TOWN: The Sheraton Grand Hotel & Spa £££
Luxury Map D4
1 Festival Square, EH3 9SR
Tel *0131 229 9131*
w sheratonedinburgh.co.uk
Superb guest rooms, good business facilities. Relax at the world-class One Spa.

FURTHER AFIELD: Airlie £
Guesthouse Map D4
29 Minto Street, EH9 1SB
Tel *0131 667 3562*
w airlieguesthouse.co.uk
Small, welcoming place with en suite rooms and private parking.

FURTHER AFIELD: Blinkbonny House £
B&B Map D4
23 Blinkbonny Gardens, EH4 3HG
Tel *0131 467 1232*
w blinkbonnyhouse.co.uk
Charming bungalow with cosy but stylish furnishings and wooden flooring.

FURTHER AFIELD: Duck's at Kilspindie House £
Inn Map E4
Aberlady, East Lothian, EH32 0RE
Tel *01875 870682*
w ducks.co.uk
Simple hotel with comfortable rooms and an excellent restaurant.

FURTHER AFIELD: Forth Reflections £
Self-catering Map D4
5 Stoneycroft Rd, South Queensferry, EH30 9HX
Tel *0131 319 1118*
w forthreflections.com
Two-bedroom stone retreat with magnificent sea views.

Four-poster bed in Dalhousie Castle Hotel, just outside of Edinburgh

FURTHER AFIELD: Ivy Guest House £
Guesthouse Map D4
7 Mayfield Gardens, EH9 2AX
Tel *0131 667 3411*
w ivyguesthouse.com
Comfortable town house with private parking. Self-catering apartments also available.

FURTHER AFIELD: Kew House £
Guesthouse Map D4
1 Kew Terrace, EH12 5JE
Tel *0131 313 0700*
w kewhouse.com
Historic villa converted to a stylish and contemporary guesthouse.

FURTHER AFIELD: Orocco Pier £
Boutique Map D4
17 High Street, South Queensferry, EH30 9PP
Tel *0870 118 1664*
w oroccopier.co.uk
Stylish small hotel housed in a characterful old inn.

FURTHER AFIELD: Redcraig Bed & Breakfast £
B&B Map D4
Morton, Mid Calder, EH53 0JT
Tel *01506 884 249*
w bedandbreakfastnear edinburgh.co.uk
Friendly B&B with tastefully furnished rooms. Scottish and vegetarian breakfasts available.

FURTHER AFIELD: The Sun Inn £
Inn Map D4
Lothianbridge, Dalkeith, EH22 4TR
Tel *0131 663 2456*
w thesuninnedinburgh.co.uk
Cosy inn with an award-winning pub on the fringes of the city.

FURTHER AFIELD: Dakota ££
Boutique Map D4
Ferrymuir Retail Park, South Queensferry, EH30 9QZ
Tel *0131 319 3690*
w dakotahotels.co.uk
Sleek, ultramodern hotel near the Forth Bridge. Acclaimed bar and restaurant on site.

FURTHER AFIELD: Macdonald Marine Hotel & Spa ££
Luxury Map E4
Cromwell Rd, North Berwick, EH39 4LZ
Tel *0844 879 9130*
w macdonaldhotels.co.uk/our-hotels/marine
Refurbished 19th-century hotel with rooms offering great vistas.

FURTHER AFIELD: Dalhousie Castle Hotel £££
Country house Map D4
Bonnyrigg, EH19 3JB
Tel *01875 820 153*
w dalhousiecastle.co.uk
Indulge in highland luxury at this lovely castle retreat.

Southern Scotland

ABINGTON: Abington Hotel £
Family-friendly Map D5
78 Carlisle Rd, By Biggar, ML12 6SD
Tel *01864 502 467*
w ab-hotel.com
Characterful, welcoming hotel set in a former coaching inn with an attractive rural setting.

AYR: 26 The Crescent £
B&B Map C5
26 Bellevue Crescent, KA7 2DR
Tel *01292 287 329*
w 26crescent.co.uk
Five-star B&B featuring flat-screen TVs, posh toiletries and bathrobes.

GRETNA: Gretna Chase Hotel ££
Historic Map D5
Sark Bridge, Dumfriesshire, DG16 5JB
Tel *01461 337 517*
w gretnachase.co.uk
Housed in a 19th-century building, this hotel has spacious rooms.

KELSO: Edenwater House £
B&B Map E5
Ednam, Scottish Borders, TD5 7QL
Tel *01573 224 070*
w edenwaterhouse.co.uk
This restaurant with rooms offers wonderful food and great views.

For more information on types of hotels *see page 171*

KELSO: Roxburghe Hotel £££
Country house **Map** E5
Roxburghshire, TD5 8JZ
Tel *01573 450 331*
W roxburghe-hotel.com
Stately country house with first-rate facilities. There is a spa, a golf course and a trout loch.

MELROSE: Burts Hotel £
Budget **Map** E5
Market Square, TD6 9PN
Tel *01896 822 285*
W burtshotel.co.uk
Traditional, family-run hotel in a listed building. Popular bar and restaurant on site.

MELROSE: Roulotte Retreat £
Character **Map** E5
Bowden Mill House, TD6 OSU
Tel *0845 094 9729*
W roulotteretreat.com
Beautiful gypsy caravans in an idyllic lochside setting. Limited accommodation for children.

PEEBLES: Macdonald Cardrona Hotel,Golf & Spa £
Luxury **Map** D5
Cardrona, EH45 8NE
Tel *0844 879 9024*
W macdonaldhotels.co.uk
Perfect country retreat – spacious rooms, an 18-hole golf course, spa and first-class restaurant.

DK Choice

PEEBLES: Cringletie House ££
Country house **Map** D5
Edinburgh Road, EH45 8PL
Tel *01721 725 750*
W cringletie.com
Set in beautiful private grounds, Cringletie House boasts trad-itional and deluxe rooms with modern amenities such as flat-screen TVs and free Wi-Fi. The award-winning restaurant offers a fabulous eight-course tasting menu with fine wines to match.

PEEBLES: Horseshoe Inn ££
Inn **Map** D5
Eddleston, Peebles, EH45 8QP
Tel *01721 722 640*
W horseshoeinn.co.uk
This restaurant with rooms, on the road between Edinburgh and Peebles, features fluffy robes and designer toiletries.

PORTPATRICK: Knockinaam Lodge £££
Country house **Map** C6
Dumfries and Galloway, DG9 9AD
Tel *01776 810 471*
W knockinaamlodge.com
Enjoy the idyllic seaside location and savour first-rate cuisine at this luxurious hotel.

Beautiful garden setting of the Cringletie House, Peebles

SANQUHAR: The Station Master's House £
Self-catering **Map** D5
Station Road, DG4 6BT
Tel *0797 398 9831*
W sanquharstation.co.uk
Spacious place with a large family kitchen and cosy living room.

STRANRAER: Balyett B&B £
B&B **Map** C6
Cairnryan Road, DG9 8QL
Tel *01776 703 395*
W balyettbb.co.uk
Victorian B&B offering tastefully decorated rooms with sea views and a picturesque garden.

TURNBERRY: Turnberry Resort £££
Luxury **Map** C5
Ayrshire, KA26 9LT
Tel *01655 331 000*
W turnberryresort.co.uk
Luxurious resort hotel with plush rooms and self-catering lodges.

YARROW: Tibbie Shiels Inn £
Inn **Map** D5
St Marys Loch, Selkirk, TD7 5LH
Tel *01750 42231*
W tibbieshiels.com
This charming inn on the shores of St Marys Loch is popular with walkers and cyclists.

Glasgow

CITY CENTRE: Alison Guesthouse £
Guesthouse **Map** D4
26 Circus Drive, G31 2JH
Tel *0141 556 1431*
W alisonguesthouse.co.uk
Lovely Victorian house that retains many of its original features. Good Scottish breakfast menu.

CITY CENTRE: The Brunswick £
Guesthouse **Map** D4
106–108 Brunswick St, G1 1TF
Tel *0141 552 0001*
W brunswickhotel.co.uk
This contemporary hotel offers compact but comfortable rooms.

CITY CENTRE: Grasshoppers £
Inn **Map** D4
87 Union Street, G1 3TA
Tel *0141 222 2666*
W grasshoppersglasgow.com
Decent modern rooms with flat-screen TVs and power showers.

CITY CENTRE: Blythswood Square ££
Luxury **Map** D4
11 Blythswood Square, G2 4AD
Tel *0141 248 8888*
W townhousecompany.com/blythswoodsquare
Housed in a spectacular old building, this hotel and spa boasts designer interiors.

CITY CENTRE: Grand Central Hotel ££
Historic **Map** D4
99 Gordon Street, G1 3SF
Tel *0141 240 3700*
W thegrandcentralhotel.co.uk
Much-loved city icon impressively refurbished into a superb four-star hotel.

CITY CENTRE: Hotel Indigo ££
Boutique **Map** D4
75 Waterloo Street, G2 7DA
Tel *0141 226 7700*
W hotelindigoglasgow.com
Boutique hotel offering stylish and modern rooms as well as a trendy bar and grill on site.

CITY CENTRE: Malmaison ££
Character **Map** D4
278 W George St, G2 4LL
Tel *08446 930 653*
W malmaison.com/locations/glasgow
Boutique hotel set in an old church, with bright interiors.

CITY CENTRE: Radisson Blu Hotel Glasgow ££
Luxury **Map** D4
301 Argyle Street, G2 8DL
Tel *141 204 3333*
W radissonblu.co.uk/hotel-glasgow
Ultra-modern design hotel with stylish rooms. Swimming pool and gym in the basement.

CITY CENTRE: The Art House £££
Luxury **Map** D4
129 Bath Street, G2 2SZ
Tel *0141 221 6789*
W abodehotels.co.uk/glasgow
Grand historic hotel with modern, well-appointed rooms and a remarkable old-fashioned lift.

WEST END: Kirklee Hotel £
Character **Map** D4
11 Kensington Gate, G12 9LG
Tel *0141 334 5555*
W kirkleehotel.co.uk
Red sandstone Edwardian town house with antique furnishings.

Key to Price Guide *see page 172*

DK Choice

WEST END: Hotel du Vin £££
Luxury   **Map** D4
1 Devonshire Gardens, G12 0UX
Tel 08447 364 256
Ⓦ hotelduvin.com/locations/
glasgow/
Housed in a quintet of Victorian
town houses, the stunning Hotel
du Vin is Glasgow's most famous
hotel. The emphasis throughout
is on opulent luxury, from the
spacious and unique rooms to
the fantastic whisky bar and
restaurant. Impeccable service.

FURTHER AFIELD: Dakota Hotel £
Luxury   **Map** D4
*1–3 Parklands Avenue, Eurocentral
Business Park, Motherwell, ML1 4WQ*
Tel 01698 835 444
Ⓦ dakotahotels.co.uk
A chic hotel with stylish rooms.
legant bar and grill serves
delicious food.

Central Scotland

DK Choice

ARRAN: Auchrannie Resort ££
Resort   **Map** C5
Auchrannie Rd, Brodick, KA27 8BZ
Tel 01770 302 234
Ⓦ auchrannie.co.uk
Whether families, groups or
couples on their honeymoon,
Auchrannie Resort has something for everyone. Set in a
dramatic location overlooking
the Arran Hills, the place is
equipped with leisure facilities
such as a spa and indoor
swimming pools as well as a
play barn for children.

AUCHTERARDER: The Gleneagles Hotel £££
Luxury   **Map** D4
Perthshire, PH3 1NF
Tel 01764 662 231
Ⓦ gleneagles.com
Palatial retreat with an excellent
spa, a championship golf course
and two Michelin-starred
restaurants.

BALQUIHIDDER: Monachyle MHOR Hotel £££
Luxury   **Map** C4
Lochearnhead, Perthshire, FK19 8PQ
Tel 01877 384 622
Ⓦ mhor.net
Family-run restaurant with cosy
rooms. Most produce is sourced
from the farm and kitchen
garden. Reached via a testing
single-track road.

BUTE: Munro's £
B&B   **Map** C4
17 Ardmory Road, Rothesay, PA20 0PG
Tel 01700 502 346
Ⓦ visitmunros.co.uk
Cosy B&B run by a lovely couple
who give useful advice about the
area. Delicious breakfasts.

CALLANDER: Roman Camp Country House & Restaurant ££
Country house   **Map** D4
Off Main Street, FK17 8BG
Tel 01877 330 003
Ⓦ romancamphotel.co.uk
Luxury manor house located in
the Trossachs National Park.

CUPAR: The Peat Inn £££
Country house   **Map** D4
Fife, near St Andrews, KY15 5LH
Tel 01334 840 206
Ⓦ thepeatinn.co.uk
Cosy country inn with elegantly
decorated luxury suites and a
fine Michelin-starred restaurant.

DUNBLANE: DoubleTree by Hilton Dunblane Hydro ££
Luxury   **Map** D4
Perth Road, FK15 0HG
Tel 01786 822 551
Ⓦ doubletreedunblane.com
Historic spa hotel with stunning
interiors and impressive grounds.

DUNDEE: Apex Dundee City Quay Hotel & Spa ££
Luxury   **Map** D4
1 West Victoria Dock Road, DD1 3JP
Tel 0845 365 0000
Ⓦ apexhotels.co.uk
Elegant waterfront hotel with all
modern facilities. Boasts amazing
views of the River Tay.

KILFINAN: Kilfinan House £££
Self-catering   **Map** C4
Argyll, PA21 2BE
Tel 01381 610 496
Ⓦ kilfinanhouse.co.uk
Designed as a holiday home, this
retreat offers tastefully furnished,
individually styled rooms.

LOCH LOMOND: Cameron House £££
Country house   **Map** C4
Alexandria, G83 8QZ
Tel 0871 222 4681
Ⓦ devere-hotels.co.uk/hotel-
lodges/locations/cameron-house
This sumptuous hotel boasts a
spa, a private 18-hole golf course,
a Michelin-starred restaurant and
splendid loch views. Arrive in
style by seaplane.

METHVEN: Cloag Farm £
Self-catering   **Map** D4
Cloag Farm, PH1 3RR
Tel 01738 840 239
Ⓦ cloagfarm.co.uk
Excellent value farm with three
cosy cottages. A great base for
exploring Perth and the area.

PERTH: Parklands ££
Character   **Map** D4
2 St Leonard's Bank, PH2 8EB
Tel 01738 622 451
Ⓦ theparklandshotel.com
Comfortable rooms and park
views. Fine dining restaurant, as
well as a more informal bistro.

PORTAVADIE: Portavadie Marina £££
Luxury   **Map** C4
Loch Fyne, Argyll, PA21 2DA
Tel 01700 811 075
Ⓦ portavadiemarina.com
Glitzy waterfront hotel offering
apartments with their own
saunas, cosy cottages, hotel
rooms and rather plush
dormitories.

ST ANDREWS: Old Course Hotel £££
Luxury   **Map** E4
Kingdom of Fife, KY16 9SP
Tel 01334 474 371
Ⓦ oldcoursehotel.kohler.com
One of the world's great resort
hotels overlooking the world's
most famous golf course. Book an
Old Course room for a view of the
range and the Scottish coastline.

Elegant executive room in Auchrannie Resort, Arran

For more information on types of hotels *see page 171*

STANLEY: Ballathie House ££
Country house **Map** D4
Kinclaven, Perthshire, PH1 4QN
Tel *01250 883 268*
ⓦ ballathiehousehotel.com
Grand country hotel on the River
Tay with its own private estate.
Excellent restaurant and bar.

**STIRLING: The Stirling Highland
Hotel** ££
Historic **Map** D4
Spittal Street, Stirlingshire, FK8 1DU
Tel *01786 272 727*
ⓦ pumahotels.co.uk/hotels/
stirling-highland-hotel
Historic hotel with its own
working observatory. Short walk
from the landmark castle.

STRACHUR: The Creggans Inn ££
Inn **Map** C4
Argyll, PA27 8BX
Tel *01369 860 279*
ⓦ creggans-inn.co.uk
Whitewashed inn with lovely
views over Loch Fyne. Popular
bar for fine dining.

The Highlands and
Islands

**ABERDEEN: Arden Guest
House** £
Guesthouse **Map** E3
61 Dee Street, AB11 6EE
Tel *01224 580 700*
ⓦ ardenguesthouse.co.uk
Welcoming guesthouse set in a
traditional granite building.

**ABERDEEN: Malmaison
Aberdeen** ££
Character **Map** E3
49–53 Queens Road, AB15 4YP
Tel *0844 693 0649*
ⓦ malmaison.com/locations/
aberdeen
Spacious en suite rooms with
well-stocked mini bars on offer.
Cosy grill restaurant and bar.

**ACHILTIBUIE: Summer Isles
Hotel** ££
Luxury **Map** C2
Ross-shire, IV26 2YG
Tel *01854 622 282*
ⓦ summerisleshotel.co.uk
Romantic hideaway with elegant
rooms. Stunning views over the
Summer Isles and the Hebrides.

APPLECROSS: Applecross Inn £
Inn **Map** C2
Wester Ross, IV54 8LR
Tel *01520 744 262*
ⓦ applecross.uk.com/inn
Whitewashed inn with a
restaurant known for its quality
seafood and generous portions.
Idyllic location.

**ARDEONAIG: Ardeonaig Hotel &
Restaurant** ££
Luxury **Map** D3
*South Loch Tay Side, near Killin,
FK21 8SU*
Tel *01567 820 400*
ⓦ ardeonaighotel.co.uk
Historic inn with comfortable
rooms, African safari style shiels
and sumptuous cottage suites.

ARDUAINE: Loch Melfort Hotel £
Country house **Map** C4
by Oban, Argyll, PA34 4XG
Tel *01852 200 233*
ⓦ lochmelfort.co.uk
A three-star hotel with fine views
of Scotland's majestic west coast.

**ARISAIG: The Old Library Lodge
& Restaurant** £
B&B **Map** B3
Road to the Isles, PH39 4NH
Tel *01687 450 651*
ⓦ oldlibrary.co.uk
Modest waterfront restaurant
with rooms, housed in 200-year-
old stables. Excellent food.

AULDEARN: Boath House £££
Luxury **Map** D2
Nairn, IV12 5TE
Tel *01667 454 896*
ⓦ boath-house.com
Nestled amid beautiful grounds,
Boath House offers elegant rooms
furnished with antiques.

**AVIEMORE: Macdonald
Aviemore Resort** ££
Resort **Map** D3
Inverness-shire, PH22 1PN
Tel *0844 879 9152*
ⓦ macdonaldhotels.co.uk/our-
hotels/macdonald-aviemore-resort
With four hotels and 18 luxurious
wooden lodges, this resort offers
something for all budgets. 3D
cinema and adventure playground.

BALLATER: Morvada House ££
B&B **Map** D3
Braemar Road, AB35 5RL
Tel *01339 756 334*
ⓦ morvada.com
Friendly B&B set in a traditional
Victorian villa. Great breakfasts.

Luxurious room with period decor in Boath
House, Auldearn

BARRA: Castlebay Hotel ££
Character **Map** A3
Castlebay, Isle of Barra, HS9 5XD
Tel *01871 810 223*
ⓦ castlebay-hotel.co.uk
Charming hotel with pleasant en
suite rooms. Fantastic views of
Kisimul Castle and Vatersay island.

COLL: The Coll Hotel ££
Guesthouse **Map** B3
Ariangour, Isle of Coll, PA78 6SZ
Tel *01879 230 334*
ⓦ collhotel.com
Family-run hotel with splendid
views of Staffa, Iona and Jura.
Superb seafood restaurant.

CRINAN: Crinan Hotel ££
Luxury **Map** C4
Lochgilphead, Argyll, PA31 8SR
Tel *01546 830 261*
ⓦ crinanhotel.com
Tasteful rooms, some with
balconies. Panoramic views.

DINNET: Loch Kinord Hotel £
Self-catering **Map** E3
Ballater Road, Royal Deeside, AB34 5JY
Tel *01339 885 229*
ⓦ lochkinord.com/self-catering-
lodges-in-royal-deeside
Two- and three-bedroom lodges
with fully equipped kitchens and
spacious living areas.

**DUNKELD: Birnam Guest
House** £
Guesthouse **Map** D3
4 Murthly Terrace, Birnam, PH8 0BG
Tel *01350 727 201*
ⓦ birnamguesthouse.co.uk
Friendly, family-run guesthouse
with comfortable en suite rooms.
Offers good Scottish breakfasts.

**DUNKELD: Royal Dunkeld
Hotel** £
Historic **Map** D3
Atholl Street, PH8 0AR
Tel *01350 727 322*
ⓦ royaldunkeld.co.uk
Cosy hotel with traditional decor
and simply furnished rooms in an
old coaching inn.

ERISKA: Isle of Eriska Hotel £££
Country house **Map** C3
Benderloch, Argyll, PA37 1SD
Tel *01631 720 371*
ⓦ eriska-hotel.co.uk
Enchanting country house hotel
with grand rooms. Self-catering
accommodation also available.

FORT AUGUSTUS: The Lovat £
Historic **Map** C3
Inverness-shire, PH32 4DU
Tel *01456 490 000*
ⓦ thelovat.com
At the southern tip of Loch Ness,
this eco-friendly hotel offers
good dining options.

The magnificent living room of The Torridon hotel, Torridon

FORT WILLIAM: The Grange ££
B&B **Map** C3
Grange Road, PH33 6JF
Tel *01397 705 516*
W grangefortwilliam.com
Historic B&B with individually styled, luxury rooms. Spectacular views across Loch Linnhe.

FORT WILLIAM: Inverlochy Castle £££
Country house **Map** C3
Torlundy, PH33 6SN
Tel *01397 702 177*
W inverlochycastlehotel.com
Fine luxury hotel with antique furnishings and period decor.

FRASERBURGH: Cortes House £££
Self-catering **Map** E2
Lonmay, AB43 8UU
Tel *0845 057 4211*
W perfect-manors.com/cortes
Stunning Regency mansion with individually styled rooms. Large living area and spacious kitchen.

HARRIS: Blue Reef Cottages £££
Self-catering **Map** B2
Scarista, Isle of Harris, HS3 3HX
Tel *01859 550 370*
W stay-hebrides.com
Cosy luxury retreat, made of two uniquely designed cottages built into the hillside. Amazing views.

INVERNESS: No. 41 Serviced Townhouse £££
Self-catering **Map** D2
41 Huntly Street, IV3 5HR
Tel *01463 712 255*
W no41townhouse.co.uk
Contemporary house overlooking the River Ness. Well-equipped kitchen and lovely living room.

ISLE OF SKYE: The Stein Inn £
Inn **Map** B2
Waternish, IV55 8GA
Tel *01470 592 362*
W steininn.co.uk
An 18th-century inn on the remote Waternish peninsula with cosy rooms. Lively bar.

ISLE OF SKYE: The Three Chimneys £££
Luxury **Map** B2
Colbost, Dunvegan, IV55 8ZT
Tel *01470 511 258*
W threechimneys.co.uk
Famous restaurant with rooms, offering lavish sea-view suites and exquisite fine dining.

KILCHRENAN: Ardanaiseig £££
Country house **Map** C4
By Taynuilt, Argyll, PA35 1HE
Tel *01866 988 273*
W ardanaiseig.com
Plush hotel on the banks of Loch Awe. Book the private waterfront boat shed for a romantic stay.

MONESS: Moness Resort £
Historic **Map** D3
Crieff Road, Aberfeldy, PH15 2DY
Tel *0188 782 2108*
W moness.com
Moness Resort offers hotel rooms as well as self-catering cottages, with all modern amenities.

MULL: Pennygate Lodge £
Guesthouse **Map** B4
Craignure, Isle of Mull, PA65 6AY
Tel *01680 812 333*
W isleofmullguesthouse.co.uk
This Georgian manse overlooking Craignure Bay is sorrounded by beautiful grounds.

MULL: Highland Cottage ££
Character **Map** B3
24 Breadalbane Street, Tobermory, Isle of Mull, PA75 6PD
Tel *01688 302 030*
W highlandcottage.co.uk
Individually styled, luxuriously furnished rooms. Innovative modern Scottish cuisine.

ORKNEY ISLANDS: The Foveran £
Guesthouse **Map** F3
Kirkwall, St Ola, KW15 1SF
Tel *01856 872 389*
W foveranhotel.co.uk
Family-run hotel with en suite rooms and a superb restaurant. Wonderful views over Scapa Flow.

PITLOCHRY: East Haugh House £
Guesthouse **Map** D3
East Haugh, Perthshire, PH16 5TE
Tel *01796 473 121*
W easthaugh.co.uk
Small, family-run hotel. The rooms are furnished with lush fabrics and period decor.

PLOCKTON: Plockton Hotel ££
Character **Map** C2
41 Harbour St, Ross-Shire IV52 8TN
Tel *01599 544 274*
W plocktonhotel.co.uk
Waterfront hotel with comfortable rooms. Breathtaking views over the bay and surrounding hills.

SHETLAND ISLANDS: The Queen's Hotel £
Historic **Map** G2
Commercial St, Lerwick, ZE1 0AB
Tel *01595 692 826*
W kgqhotels.co.uk
Welcoming hotel overlooking Lerwick Harbour. Lively public bar.

SHETLAND ISLANDS: Skeoverick £
B&B **Map** G2
Brunatwatt, Walls, ZE2 9PJ,
Tel *01595 809 349*
W visitscotland.com/info/accommodation/skeoverick-p191921
Welcoming and spacious B&B in a picturesque lochside location.

SPEYSIDE: Craigelachie Hotel ££
Historic **Map** D2
Victoria St, Banffshire, AB38 9SR
Tel *0843 178 7114*
W bespokehotels.com/craigellachiehotel
Delightful country house hotel located on the River Spey. Famous Quaich whisky bar on site.

TARBERT: Stonefield Castle ££
Historic **Map** C4
Loch Fyne, Argyll, PA29 6YJ
Tel *0844 414 6582*
W stonefieldcastlehotel.com
Stunning baronial castle with well-furnished rooms.

DK Choice

TORRIDON: The Torridon ££
Country house **Map** C2
Achnasheen, Wester Ross, IV22 2EY
Tel *01445 700 300*
W thetorridon.com
Located on the shores of Loch Torridon, this luxury hotel offers fine views of the surrounding mountains and countryside. The Torridon features elegant rooms, opulent self-catering accommodation as well as a budget inn. Excellent fine dining restaurant and outdoor activity centre.

For more information on types of hotels *see page 171*

WHERE TO EAT AND DRINK

Scotland's restaurant scene has come far from its once-dismal reputation, partly due to an influx of foreign chefs and cooking styles, as well as a greater knowledge about food among increasingly discerning local diners. Visitors can now sample a wide range of international cuisine across Scotland, with the greatest choice in Glasgow and Edinburgh. Home-grown restaurateurs have also woken up to the world-class seafood, red meat and game that Scotland's rich natural larder offers in such abundance. In major towns and cities, it is possible to enjoy good meals at any budget. The more rural establishments are, however, less flexible. Affordable, well-prepared but less elaborate food is making a mark in all types of cafés, brasseries and restaurants throughout the country. The listings on pages 181–9 feature some of the best places to eat. Note that it is illegal to smoke in any Scottish restaurant, bar or café.

A selection of beer and whisky on display in a typical Scottish pub

Prices and Booking

All restaurants are required by law to display their current prices outside the door. These amounts include VAT at 20 per cent. Any service or cover charge should also be specified.

Wine can be pricey when dining out in Scotland, and extras such as coffee and bottled water may be disproportionately expensive compared to the cost of the food. Service charges (usually between 10 and 15 per cent) are sometimes added automatically to the bill. If service has not been included, you are expected to leave a tip. The majority of restaurants accept credit cards. Pubs often prefer cash to cards.

City restaurants are very busy, and some of the more renowned establishments can be fully booked up to a month in advance. It is advisable to book ahead; if you cannot keep a reservation, cancel it by phone.

Breakfast, Lunch and Dinner

Traditionally, breakfast in Scotland begins with cereal and milk, sometimes followed by bacon, eggs and tomato, and usually black pudding (blood sausage), haggis or white (oatmeal) pudding. It may also be accompanied by toast and marmalade, and tea.

The most popular lunchtime foods are sandwiches, salads, baked potatoes and ploughman's lunches (a roll, hunk of cheese or ham and relishes), found mainly in pubs. A traditional Sunday lunch of roast meat and vegetables is served in some pubs and restaurants.

Generally there are three courses to a meal, although grand hotels may have six-course feasts and contemporary restaurants often offer multi-course tasting menus. Dessert may be followed by a range of superb specialist cheeses. Outside the larger towns and cities, dinner is usually eaten between 6pm and 9pm, and no later. In Scotland lunch is sometimes called "dinner" and the evening meal may be called "tea".

Afternoon Tea

No visitor should miss the experience of a proper Scottish afternoon tea. There are many tearooms all over Scotland, offering a choice of delicious sandwiches and cakes, or Scotch pancakes swimming in butter.

Afternoon tea in Scotland, an elegant and enjoyable pastime

Children

Many places welcome junior diners and some actively encourage families, at least during the day and early evening. They may have a separate children's menu, or simply offer half portions. Many will also provide highchairs. Even pubs, which are all non-smoking, are generally relaxing their rules and some

A fish and chip shop on the Portobello promenade in Edinburgh

provide special play areas for kids. In city centre bars, don't be surprised or offended to see signs stating the pub is for over-18s only.

Vegetarian Food

Britain is ahead of many of its European counterparts in providing vegetarian alternatives to meat dishes, and Scotland is no exception. Edinburgh and Glasgow have the widest choice, but restaurants in smaller towns and villages are also increasingly likely to offer meat-free dishes.

Vegetarians wishing to find a wider choice than is offered by Scottish and English food should try Indian, Chinese, Middle Eastern, or other ethnic restaurants with a tradition of vegetarian cuisine.

Seafood

With more than 16,000 km (10,000 miles) of coastline, fish and shellfish play an important part in the Scottish diet and economy. North Sea cod, haddock (often smoked as kippers or Arbroath Smokies),

herring and mackerel can all be found in shops and restaurants, while farms on the west coast rear much of Scotland's Atlantic salmon and rainbow trout. Lobsters, crabs and prawns are also common in Scottish waters. Recently more emphasis has been placed on the cultivation and conservation of sustainable natural shellfish stocks, including mussels, oysters and scallops.

Fast Food

Scotland is rightly famed for its "fish suppers" and there are many seaside fish bars selling wonderfully fresh fish and chips. Away from the coast, the fish may not be as amazingly fresh, but there are plenty of good places to choose from. Most also offer other options including fried chicken.

Visitors will find the usual fast food chains as well as sandwich bars and "greasy spoon" cafés, which mainly serve fried food, including large traditional breakfasts.

Pubs and Bars

Scottish licensing laws are different from the rest of Britain, mostly in the closing times of pubs and bars. In Scotland, particularly in urban centres, many pubs stay open until midnight or even 1 or 2am. During the Edinburgh Festival in August (see pp82–3), bars often do not close until 3am, and some are open 24 hours.

The large selection of beer and whisky available in a typical Scottish pub is impressive and

sampling a few "drams" with the locals is an essential undertaking on any tour of the country. Lately, the old-fashioned, boozer has had considerable competition from cosmopolitan bars and posh gastro pubs. Found in towns and cities, bars can be noisy and tend to attract a younger clientele with lively happy hours and interesting cocktails. Gastro pubs place an emphasis on food, serving high quality traditional pub meals that may be prepared with organic or sustainably sourced ingredients. They will also have a number of craft beers to choose from.

Recommended Restaurants

The restaurants, cafés and bistros outlined in this guide have been chosen because they offer quality and reasonable value for money. They range from inexpensive and cheerful cafés to fine dining temples and Michelin-starred restaurants. A Scottish restaurant will serve traditional dishes such as haggis, whereas somewhere offering more flavours and contemporary twists on the old is considered modern Scottish.

Entries highlighted as DK Choice have been chosen for their exceptional features, which may include gourmet dishes or a spectacular location. All DK Choice entries offer a memorable dining experience.

Secret Garden dining room in the Witchery by the Castle (see p182), Edinburgh

The elegant Douglas Bistro at the Douglas Hotel (see p186), on the Isle of Arran

The Flavours of Scotland

At its best, Scottish food is full of the natural flavour of the countryside. Served with few sauces or spices, its meat is lean and tasty. Beef doesn't get better than Aberdeen Angus, the lamb is full flavoured, and the venison superb. Scottish salmon and trout are renowned, but there are also excellent mussels, lobster and crabs. Wheat does not grow here, so oatcakes and bannocks (flat, round loaves) replace bread. The Scots have a sweet tooth, not just for cakes and shortbread but also for toffee and butterscotch.

Smoked salmon

Purebred Highland cattle grazing the Scottish moors

porridge to oatcakes. Pearl barley is also a staple, used in Scotch broth (made with mutton and vegetables) or in a milk pudding. Oats are also used in the making of haggis, a round sausage of sheep or venison offal – the "chieftain o' the puddin' race", as the poet Robert Burns described it. It is often served with "neeps and tatties" (mashed swede (rutabaga) and potato).

The Highlands

From the Highlands comes wonderful game, including grouse, partridge, capercaillie (a large type of grouse) and deer. Fish are smoked around the coast, the west coast producing kippers, the east coast Finnan haddock, notably Arbroath Smokies. Smoked white fish is the main ingredient of Cullen Skink, a soup served on Burns' Night.

The Lowlands

The pasturelands of southern Scotland nourish dairy cattle and sheep, producing cheeses such as Bonnet, Bonchester and Galloway Cheddar. To accompany them are summer fruits such as loganberries, tayberries and strawberries that ripen in the Carse of Gowrie beside the River Tay. Oats, the principal cereal, appears in much Scottish cookery, from

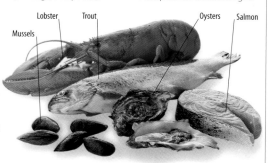

Lobster Trout Oysters Salmon Mussels

Selection of fresh Scottish fish and seafood

Traditional Scottish Food

Kippers (oak-smoked herrings) are one way to start the day in Scotland, and porridge – traditionally served with salt rather than sugar – is another, although oatcakes or some other kind of griddled scone are usually present. A bowl of porridge would once last all week, just as one-pot Scotch broths bubbled in iron cauldrons over peat fires for days. Sometimes broths were made with kale or lentils, or they might contain an old boiling fowl and leeks, in which case they were known as cock-a-leekie. Any leftover meat went into making stovies, a potato and onion hash. The evening meal in Scotland is traditionally "high tea" taken in the early evening which might start with smoked fish, cold meats and pies, followed by shortbread, fruit cake or drop scones, all washed down with cups of tea.

Oats

Haggis with neeps and tatties
This is the definitive Scottish dish, traditionally served on Burns' Night (25 January).

Where to Eat and Drink

Edinburgh

NEW TOWN: The Abbotsford £
Pub   **Map** D4
3–5 Rose Street, EH2 2PR
Tel *0131 225 5276*
Lively bar with traditional wood-panelled decor. Serves the usual pub food such as fish and chips with more options in the restaurant "Above". Good beer.

NEW TOWN: The Cambridge Bar £
Pub   **Map** D4
20 Young Street, EH2 4JB
Tel *0131 226 2120*
Mismatched furniture, stone floors and subdued natural lighting give this bar a cellar-like feel. Good food including hearty burgers and vegetarian dishes.

NEW TOWN: Coffee Angel £
Café   **Map** D4
24–27 Brandon Terrace, EH3 5DZ
Tel *0131 622 6235*
Bright and welcoming café offering takeaway sandwiches, salads, cakes and creative dine-in options such as spicy meatball soup and Mexican beef wraps.

NEW TOWN: The Dome £
Modern Scottish   **Map** D4
14 George Street, EH2 2PF
Tel *0131 624 8624*
Housed in a magnificent 18th-century building, the Dome has a bar, two restaurants and a café. The Grill Room features a modern Scottish menu and the Club Room serves coffee and cocktails.

NEW TOWN: Urban Angel £
International   **Map** D4
121 Hanover Street, EH2 1DJ
Tel *0131 225 6215*
Urban Angel features an eclectic menu of dishes such as pan fried fillet of salmon with glass noodles in Asian-style broth, Mediterranean inspired salads and New York vanilla baked cheesecake.

NEW TOWN: Vincaffè £
Café   **Map** D4
11 Multrees Walk, EH1 3DQ
Tel *0131 557 0088*
Run by an Italian family, Vincaffè offers dishes such as pasta with spicy Italian sausages. Superb coffee and wines.

NEW TOWN: Café St Honoré ££
French   **Map** D4
34 North West Thistle Street Lane, EH2 1EA
Tel *0131 226 2211*
Neil Forbes, one of Edinburgh's finest chefs, is at the helm of this buzzing bistro, serving skilfully and imaginatively cooked food made from locally sourced produce.

NEW TOWN: Centotre ££
Italian   **Map** D4
103 George Street, EH2 3ES
Tel *0131 225 1550*
Edinburgh's grandest Italian restaurant, Centotre serves authentic pasta dishes. A great place for lunch, dinner or just a quick snack.

NEW TOWN: Chao Phraya ££
Thai   **Map** D4
4th Floor, 33 Castle Street, EH2 3DN
Tel *0131 226 7614*
This stylish restaurant enjoys unparalleled views over Edinburgh Castle. They dare to veer from the usual mainstays of Thai cuisine, but still rustle up a decent red curry or pad Thai.

NEW TOWN: Galvin Brasserie de Luxe ££
Brasserie   **Map** D4
Princes Street, EH1 2AB
Tel *0131 222 8988*
This swish brasserie in the hotel Caledonian is a real treat for lovers

Price Guide
Prices are based on a three course meal for one, with half a bottle of house wine inclusive of tax and service charges.

£	up to £35
££	£35–£50
£££	over £50

of French cuisine. Features a crustacean bar and superb wine list. Great value set menus.

NEW TOWN: Kyloe Restaurant & Grill ££
International   **Map** D4
1–3 Rutland Street, EH1 2AE
Tel *0131 229 3402*
Guests choose from a variety of steak cuts at this carnivore heaven. Located in the Rutland Hotel, with fine castle views.

NEW TOWN: A Room in the West End ££
Scottish   **Map** D4
26 William Street, EH3 7NH
Tel *0131 226 1036*
Located below the busy Teuchters bar, this cosy restaurant is full of little nooks and crannies. Modern Scottish fare of steaks, white fish and haggis on offer.

NEW TOWN: Stac Polly ££
Modern Scottish   **Map** D4
29–33 Dublin Street, EH3 6NL
Tel *0131 556 2231*
Stac Polly serves dependable and interesting Scottish cooking – delicacies include excellent steak with black pudding and fantastic white fish dishes.

NEW TOWN: 21212 £££
Modern Scottish   **Map** D4
3 Royal Terrace, EH7 5AB
Tel *0131 523 1030* **Closed** *Sun & Mon*
Enjoy innovative, eye-catching cuisine by chef Paul Kitching at this Michelin-starred restaurant.

NEW TOWN: Number One £££
Modern Scottish   **Map** D4
1 Princes Street, EH2 2EQ
Tel *0131 557 6727*
Michelin-starred restaurant in the five-star Balmoral Hotel. Try the sublime seven-course tasting menu with matching wines.

NEW TOWN: The Pompadour by Galvins £££
French   **Map** D4
Princes Street, EH1 2AB
Tel *0131 222 8777* **Closed** *Sun*
This city icon has been spectacularly reinvented by the Galvin Brothers. It is a world class restaurant in The Caledonian offering exemplary cuisine.

Parisian-style interior in the romantic Café St Honoré, Edinburgh

For more information on types of restaurants *see page 179*

OLD TOWN: David Bann £
Vegetarian   Map D4
56–58 St Mary's Street, EH1 1SX
Tel *0131 556 5888*
Stylish fine dining restaurant with dishes such as leek, tarragon and butternut squash risotto, or tartlet made with Ardrahan smoked cheese and slow dried tomatoes.

OLD TOWN: Mother India's Café £
Indian   Map D4
3–5 Infirmary Street, EH1 1LT
Tel *0131 524 9801*
Superb Indian cooking to suit all tastes from the mild and creamy chicken *tikka makhni* to spicy chilli fishcakes. Dine on a selection of small tapas-style dishes.

OLD TOWN: MUMS Great Comfort Food £
Scottish   Map D4
14a Forrest Road, EH1 2QN
Tel *0131 260 9806*
Diner-style comfort food, including sausage and mash, and steak and ale pie. Remarkable prices given the quality.

OLD TOWN: Outsider £
Bar   Map D4
15 George IV Bridge, EH1 1EE
Tel *0131 226 3131*
This perennially popular, lively bar-restaurant features a varied menu that includes lentil and goat cheese salad, venison ravioli and grilled monkfish. Great value dish of the day.

OLD TOWN: Spoon £
Café   Map D4
6a Nicolson Street, EH8 9DH
Tel *0131 623 1752*   **Closed** *Sun*
This modern, arty café serves the finest vegetarian breakfast in the city as well as a good carnivore's version. Good choice for lunch.

OLD TOWN: Amber ££
Scottish   Map D4
354 Castlehill, The Royal Mile, EH1 2NE
Tel *0131 477 8477*
Located within the Scotch Whisky Experience on the Royal Mile.

Well-lit dining room at Wedgwood the Restaurant, Edinburgh

Extensive whisky list and well-executed whisky-infused dishes, popular with visitors and locals.

OLD TOWN: Kanpai ££
Japanese   Map D4
8–10 Grindlay Street, EH3 9AS
Tel *0131 228 1602*   **Closed** *Mon*
An award-winning eatery with stylish decor, Kanpai serves the finest sushi and sashimi in the city. Good dry Japanese beers.

OLD TOWN: Michael Neave Kitchen and Whisky Bar ££
Modern Scottish   Map D4
21 Old Fishmarket Close, EH1 1RW
Tel *0131 226 4747*
Bright and fun eponymous eatery from one of Scotland's most exciting young chefs. Tasty fare, made from locally sourced produce. Superb whisky bar.

OLD TOWN: Wedgwood the Restaurant ££
Modern Scottish   Map D4
267 Canongate, EH8 8BQ
Tel *0131 558 8737*
At this fine restaurant on the Royal Mile, chef Paul Wedgwood creates delicious, beautifully presented cuisine, using seasonal, local produce. Superb wine list.

OLD TOWN: Ondine £££
Seafood   Map D4
2 George IV Bridge, EH1 1AD
Tel *0131 226 1888*
Ondine serves inspirational cooking based on sustainable sourcing. Try the heavenly shellfish platter warmed with garlic butter or served French style, over ice.

OLD TOWN: The Witchery by the Castle £££
Modern Scottish   Map D4
Castlehill, Royal Mile, EH1 2NF
Tel *0131 225 5613*
Good steak and lobster dishes. Excellent value pre- and post-theatre set menus. The Secret Garden dining room is Edinburgh's most romantic setting.

FURTHER AFIELD: Al Dente £
Italian   Map D4
139 Easter Road, EH7 5QA
Tel *0131 652 1932*   **Closed** *Sun*
This no-frills restaurant popular with locals serves superb regional Italian cooking at great prices. Excellent wine list.

FURTHER AFIELD: Chop Chop £
Chinese   Map D4
76 Commercial Street, EH6 6LX
Tel *0131 553 1818*
This Chinese restaurant serves excellent dishes including savoury steamed and fried dumplings. Try one of their great value all-you-can-eat banquets for a real treat.

FURTHER AFIELD: La Favorita £
Italian   Map D4
321 Leith Walk, EH6 8SA
Tel *0131 555 5564*
A strong contender for the city's best pizzeria, the bustling La Favorita serves pizzas with an exhaustive variety of toppings. Save space for an ice-cream treat.

FURTHER AFIELD: The King's Wark £
Pub   Map D4
36 The Shore, EH6 6QU
Tel *0131 554 9260*
Edinburgh's best gastro pub offers hearty dishes. Dine by candlelight in the main pub or the cosier dining room. Good range of beers.

FURTHER AFIELD: Loopy Lorna's Tea House £
Café   Map D4
Church Hill Theatre, 33a Morningside Road, EH10 4DR
Tel *0131 447 3042*
Relish a quintessential afternoon tea of delicate sandwiches accompanied by a selection of miniature cakes.

Relaxed, modern decor at La Favorita in Leith, Edinburgh

Key to Price Guide *see page 181*

Bright and comfortable interiors of The Kitchin in Leith, Edinburgh

FURTHER AFIELD: Orocco Pier £
International **Map** D4
17 High Street, South Queensferry, EH30 9PP
Tel *0870 118 1664*
Choose from the pub fare of Antico Café Bar or seafood in the Samphire Bar and Grill. Sweeping views of the Forth estuary.

FURTHER AFIELD: The Lobster Shack £
Seafood **Map** E4
The Harbour, North Berwick, EH39 4JL
Tel *07910 620 480* **Closed** *Nov–Mar*
This seasonal restaurant – more a beach hut with outdoor chairs – is the best choice for affordable, fresh and delicious shellfish. Great harbour-side location.

FURTHER AFIELD: The Sun Inn £
Pub **Map** D4
Lothianbridge, Dalkeith, EH22 4TR
Tel *0131 663 2456*
This award-winning gastro pub has an eclectic menu with food to suit all occasions, from a business lunch or a romantic meal to a less formal get-together.

FURTHER AFIELD: The Waterside Bistro £
Modern Scottish **Map** E4
1–5 Waterside, Haddington, EH41 4AT
Tel *01620 825 674*
Set on the banks of the River Tyne, this welcoming, family-run bistro serves well-sourced local produce in cosy surroundings. They have a big box of toys for kids to enjoy.

FURTHER AFIELD: Ducks At Kilspindie House ££
Modern Scottish **Map** E4
Main Street, Aberlady, EH32 0RE
Tel *01875 870 682*
Legendary restaurateur Malcolm Duck is the man behind this intimate dining venue. Fine-dining restaurant as well as a relaxed bistro.

FURTHER AFIELD: John Paul at the Marine ££
Scottish **Map** E4
Cromwell Road, N Berwick, EH39 4LZ
Tel *0844 879 9130*
Located in the seaside Macdonald Marine Hotel & Spa, this elegant restaurant offers delicious food including the 28-day aged Scottish steak. Refined service.

FURTHER AFIELD: La Potinière ££
International **Map** E4
Main St, Gullane, EH31 2AA
Tel *01620 843 214* **Closed** *Mon & Tue*
A local favourite, this high-class eatery offers a fine dining menu that makes the most of seasonal local produce.

FURTHER AFIELD: The Boat House ££
Seafood **Map** D4
22 High Street, South Queensferry, EH30 9PP
Tel *0131 331 5429*
Charming seafood restaurant with an informal bistro. Do not miss the signature truffled scallops by Chef Paul Steward.

FURTHER AFIELD: Champany Inn £££
Modern Scottish **Map** D4
Linlithgow, West Lothian, EH49 7LU
Tel *01506 834 532*
This restaurant with rooms serves superb steaks and has a lobster tank on site. Good selection of wines. Food also served at the Inn's Chop & Ale House.

FURTHER AFIELD: Chez Roux £££
French **Map** E4
Muirfield, Gullane, EH31 2EG
Tel *01620 842 144*
Located in the historic Greywalls Hotel, this fine restaurant offers a unique culinary experience. The classic French menu makes the best of Scottish ingredients.

FURTHER AFIELD: Livingston's £££
Scottish **Map** D4
52 High Street, Linlithgow, EH49 7AE
Tel *01506 846565* **Closed** *Sun & Mon*
Creative cooking using fresh Scottish produce. The menu includes perfectly seared scallops, tender beef and cod infused with spices. Save room for dessert.

FURTHER AFIELD: Restaurant Martin Wishart £££
French **Map** D4
54 The Shore, Leith, EH6 6RA
Tel *0131 553 3557* **Closed** *Sun & Mon*
Chef Martin Wishart offers a truly memorable experience for lovers of French food. Classic cooking with sublime use of Scottish ingredients. Excellent service.

FURTHER AFIELD: The Dungeon Restaurant £££
French **Map** D4
Bonnyrigg, EH19 3JB
Tel *01875 820 153*
Set in the barrel-vault dungeons of Dalhousie Castle Hotel, this romantic, candle-lit restaurant offers classic French dishes.

DK Choice

**FURTHER AFIELD:
The Kitchin** £££
Modern Scottish **Map** D4
78 Commercial Quay, EH6 6LX
Tel *0131 555 1755*
Closed *Sun & Mon*
A famous face on TV screens, the inspirational Scottish chef Tom Kitchin runs the kitchen at this eponymous Michelin-starred restaurant. The well-balanced menus at The Kitchin feature superb seasonal offerings such as sea urchin bisque and whole grouse. Great wines.

Southern Scotland

EYEMOUTH: Mackays of Eyemouth £
Fish and Chips **Map** E4
20–24 High St, Berwickshire TD14 5EU
Tel *01890 751 142*
Tuck into a fish supper or binge on lobster and chips for a real treat. Diners can watch local fishing boats heading out to sea.

KELSO: The Terrace Café £
Café **Map** E5
Floors Castle, Roxburghe Estates Office, Roxburghshire, TD5 7SF
Tel *01573 225 714*
This popular and charming café offers wholesome soups, sandwiches and tasty home-style baking. More substantial main dishes, such as venison casserole, are on the menu as well.

DK Choice

KELSO: The Roxburghe Hotel & Golf Course £££
Modern Scottish **Map** E5
Roxburghshire, TD5 8JZ
Tel *01573 450 331*
Enjoy fine dining at this grand country-style hotel on the Roxburghe Estate. Head Chef Neville Merrin works wonders in the kitchen using the best of Scottish red meat, game and fish. He also forages ingredients such as wild garlic from the grounds. Superb wine list and a broad selection of whisky.

For more information on types of restaurants *see page 179*

Rustic wall decor at the atmospheric City Merchant in Glasgow

LAUDER: Black Bull Hotel £
Pub **Map** E5
Market Place, Berwickshire, TD2 6SR
Tel *01578 722 208*
Traditional pub serving quality food in a Georgian dining room or a cosy bar-lounge. Dishes include fish and chips and chunky burgers. Good kids' menu.

MELROSE: Burts Hotel ££
Inn **Map** E5
Market Square, TD6 9PN
Tel *01896 822 285*
The restaurant at Burts Hotel is a Melrose institution with its high standards of service and cooking. Excellent food using meat from the local butcher and seafood from Eyemouth.

PEEBLES: Coltman's Delicatessen & Kitchen
Café **Map** D5
71–73 High Street, EH45 8AN
Tel *01721 720 405*
Charming deli and restaurant with views over the River Tweed. Offers sandwiches, platters and dishes with an international flavour. Good three-course set menu.

PEEBLES: The Sunflower £
Scottish **Map** D5
4 Bridgegate, EH45 8RZ
Tel *01721 722 420*
This welcoming café serves fresh, wholesome dishes such as wraps and home-made soup during the day. The evening menu features steaks and burgers. Coffee and cake served only before noon.

PEEBLES: Horseshoe Inn £££
Modern Scottish **Map** D5
Eddleston, EH45 8QP
Tel *01721 722 640*
Creative cooking by Head Chef Alistair Craig features Orkney scallops served with air-dried ham, apricot and orange purée, braised chicory and salted grapes. Bar meals on offer as well.

PORTPATRICK: Knockinaam Lodge £££
International **Map** C6
Dumfries and Galloway, DG9 9AD
Tel *01776 810 471*
Scotland's premier dining destination, Knockinaam Lodge boasts a Michelin star and lovely seaside location. Superb multi-course tasting menu by Chef Tony Pierce.

SANQUHAR: Blackaddie Country House Hotel £££
Modern Scottish **Map** D5
Dumfries & Galloway, DG4 6JJ
Tel *01659 50270*
Quality local produce expertly cooked makes this intimate restaurant a must-visit. Sample the tender beef and venison. Great wine list.

TROON: MacCallum's of Troon Oyster Bar ££
Seafood **Map** C5
Harbourside, Ayrshire, KA10 6DH
Tel *01292 319 339* **Closed** Mon
Known for its oysters. Other delicacies include lemon sole with capers, prawn tempura and *cullen skink* (thick fish soup).

TURNBERRY: 1906 £££
French **Map** C5
Ayrshire, KA26 9LT
Tel *0165 533 1000*
Located in the Turnberry Resort, 1906 excels on every level: elegant decor, stunning sea views, smooth service and fine-dining cuisine.

Glasgow

CITY CENTRE: Café Gandolfi £
Café **Map** D4
64 Albion Street, G1 1NY
Tel *0141 552 6813*
A city institution and part of the local Gandolfi mini empire. Come here for the great breakfasts, light lunches or substantial dinners.

CITY CENTRE: The Chippy Doon the Lane £
Fish and Chips **Map** D4
84 Buchanan Street, McCormick Lane, G1 3AJ
Tel *0141 225 6650*
This relaxed restaurant serves up superb food including monkfish tails, hake and lemon sole, cod and haddock. The kids'"sweetie tray" is a nice touch.

CITY CENTRE: Red Onion £
International **Map** D4
257 West Campbell Street, G2 4TT
Tel *0141 221 6000*
Red Onion offers a good value varied menu featuring dishes such as sirloin steak and Finnan haddie fishcake. Reserve ahead.

CITY CENTRE: Stereo Café Bar £
Vegetarian **Map** D4
20–28 Renfield Lane, G2 5AR
Tel *0141 222 2254*
This popular vegan restaurant is housed in a striking building by Charles Rennie Mackintosh. Offers fritters, mezze platters and pizzas. Good cakes with plenty of gluten-free options.

CITY CENTRE: City Merchant ££
Scottish **Map** D4
97–99 Candleriggs, G1 1NP
Tel *0141 553 1577*
Bustling family-run eatery known for its quality seafood and friendly service. Choose from fresh creamy oysters, perfectly cooked crab, langoustines and lobster. Plenty of options for non-fish eaters too.

CITY CENTRE: Gamba ££
Seafood **Map** D4
225a West George Street, G2 2ND
Tel *0141 572 0899*
Gamba offers an innovative menu with mains such as king scallops and organic salmon steamed in paper with ginger, spring onions and sesame. Good service.

Sophisticated dining room in the Blackaddie Country House Hotel, Sanquhar

CITY CENTRE: Gandolfi Fish   ££
Seafood   Map D4
84 Albion Street, G1 1NY
Tel *0141 552 9475*
Fine seafood restaurant with a
wealth of options, including an
oyster platter and perfectly
cooked king scallops and lobster.

CITY CENTRE: Jamie's Italian   ££
Italian   Map D4
7 George Square, G2 1DY
Tel *0141 404 2690*
British TV chef Jamie Oliver is
behind this superb Italian restaurant chain. Everything from
simple rocket and parmesan
salads to truffle infused risottos,
and a good range of Italian wines.

**CITY CENTRE: Malmaison
Glasgow Brasserie**   ££
Brasserie   Map D4
278 W George Street, G2 4LL
Tel *08446 930 653*
The perfectly cooked steaks are
the main attraction in this
subterranean retreat. Fish of the
day is also a good option. Choose
from a list of well-priced wines.

CITY CENTRE: Rogano   ££
Scottish   Map D4
11 Exchange Place, G1 3AN
Tel *0141 248 4055*
Established in 1935, this popular
restaurant features multiple
dining choices including a simple
bar and an elaborate dining room.
Try the shellfish here.

**CITY CENTRE: Two Fat Ladies at
the Buttery**   ££
Modern Scottish   Map D4
652–654 Argyle Street, G3 8UF
Tel *0141 221 8188*
Set in an old Victorian coaching
inn with wood panels and tartan
carpets, this Glasgow favourite
offers dishes like whole grilled
plaice with banana, white wine
and chive butter.

**CITY CENTRE: Brian Maule at
Chardon d'Or**   £££
French   Map D4
176 West Regent Street, G2 4RL
Tel *0141 248 3801*   **Closed** *Sun*
Acclaimed chef Brian Maule uses
locally sourced ingredients such
as poultry, game and fresh fish to
create superb French cuisine.

**CITY CENTRE: Restaurant at
Blythswood Square**   £££
International   Map D4
11 Blythswood Square, G2 4AD
Tel *0141 248 8888*
Refined hotel-restaurant with a
grand dining room. Offers first-
rate cooking and attentive service
in a sophisticated ambience. Great
value fixed-price lunch.

Bottles on display in the Oyster Bar at the Rogano, Glasgow

WEST END: The Ashoka   £
Indian   Map D4
19 Ashton Lane, G12 8SJ
Tel *0141 337 1115*
Welcoming Indian restaurant
with a varied menu offering
unusual dishes such as haggis
pakora (fried dumpling). Good-
value supper menu. Book ahead.

WEST END: Distill   £
Pub   Map D4
1102–1106 Argyle Street, G3 8TD
Tel *0141 337 3006*
This cosy bar offers more than
100 varieties of rum, cocktails
and real ales. The menu features
the usual pub fare such as fish
and chips, but they also serve
Moroccan-inspired mains such as
lamb tagine and mezze platter.

WEST END: Mother India   £
Indian   Map D4
*28 Westminster Terrace, Sauchiehall
Street, G3 7RU*
Tel *0141 221 1663*
Very popular Indian restaurant
set in a grand old Glasgow town
house. Tuck into a wide range of
fresh and wholesome curry
dishes, naans and rice dishes.
Friendly staff.

WEST END: Òran Mór   £
Brasserie   Map D4
Byres Road, G12 8QX
Tel *0141 357 6200*
A multi-space venue featuring a
bar, brasserie, theatre, club and
popular whisky bar. The Scottish
menu includes haggis with
neeps and tatties, and burgers.
Reservations recommended.

WEST END: The Two Figs   £
Pub   Map D4
5 and 9 Byres Road, G11 5RD
Tel *0141 334 7277*
Lively bar with an extensive
drinks list including potent
cocktails and boozy hot
chocolate. A varied, reasonably
priced menu with everything
from breakfast and burgers to
seared fillet of sea bass.

WEST END: The University Café £
Café   Map D4
87 Byres Road, G11 5HN
Tel *0141 339 5217*
Café with a pleasant retro feel.
Serves old favourites such as
mince and tatties along with
sandwiches, soups and bacon
rolls. Delicious ice creams.

DK Choice

WEST END: Crabshakk   ££
Seafood   Map D4
1114 Argyle Street, G3 8TD
Tel *0141 334 6127*   **Closed** *Mon*
Lively restaurant with wooden
tables and chairs and a shiny
champagne bar. The busy staff
at Crabshakk is always moving
between tables with heaving
plates of mussels, oysters and
scallops infused with creative
spices and culinary twists. Good
value wine list. Excellent service.

WEST END: La Parmigiana   ££
Italian   Map D4
447 Great Western Road, G12 8HH
Tel *0141 334 0686*
Small, welcoming and incredibly
popular eatery. The menu features
first-rate Italian dishes including
squid gnocchi, lobster ravioli and
a fish and shellfish *bouillabaisse*.

WEST END: Stravaigin   ££
International   Map D4
28 Gibson Street, G12 8NX
Tel *0141 334 2665*
Bustling café-bar with a varied
menu. Serves award-winning
food that draws on global
influences – curried duck, *nasi
goreng* and Shetland mussels.

WEST END: Bistro du Vin   £££
Modern Scottish   Map D4
One Devonshire Gardens, G12 0UX
Tel *08447 364 216*
Fine dining restaurant housed in
the stately Hotel du Vin. Offers a
menu featuring Scotland's finest
red meat and fish. Treat yourself
to the seven-course tasting menu.

For more information on types of restaurants *see page 179*

WEST END: Ubiquitous Chip £££
Modern Scottish   **Map** D4
12 Ashton Lane, G12 8SJ
Tel *0141 334 5007*
A Glasgow pioneer, Ubiquitous
Chip serves creative and well-
sourced Scottish cuisine. The post-
modern dining space is a delight.
They also have a relaxed bar.

FURTHER AFIELD: Art Lover's
Café   £
Café   **Map** D4
Bellahouston Park, 10 Dumbreck
Road, G41 5BW
Tel *0141 353 4779*
This artistic café, in the House for
an Art Lover designed by Charles
Rennie Mackintosh, features
dishes such as smoked venison
loin with honey-roasted pears.

Central Scotland

ABERDOUR: Room with
a View   ££
Seafood   **Map** D4
Hawkcraig Point, Fife, KY3 0TZ
Tel *01383 860 402* **Closed** *Mon & Tue*
The ingenious chef Tim Robson
creates culinary masterpieces in
this small restaurant in the Forth
View Hotel. Delicacies include
giant black tiger prawns in filo
pastry. Wonderful location
looking across the Firth of Forth
to Edinburgh.

ANSTRUTHER: Anstruther Fish
Bar   £
Fish and Chips   **Map** E4
42–44 Shore Street, Fife, KY10 3AQ
Tel *01333 310 518*
Legendary fish and chip shop
that takes being a chippy very
seriously – they even have their
own fishing boat. Look out for
the more exotic offerings such as
prawns, mackerel and lobster.

ARRAN: Auchrannie Resort £££
Scottish   **Map** C5
Auchrannie Rd, Brodick, KA27 8BZ
Tel *01770 302 234*
The Auchrannie resort offers a
choice of three restaurants. The
Cruize Bar Brasserie and Brambles
Seafood and Grill have a light
informal menu while the superb
eighteen69 (open Easter to Oct)
offers fine dining.

ARRAN: The Douglas Bistro ££
Brasserie   **Map** C5
Isle of Arran, KA27 8AW
Tel *01770 302 968*
The bistro at the Douglas Hotel
offers mouthwatering grilled
steaks and perfectly cooked local
seafood. The island views are as
epic as the food.

AUCHTERARDER: Andrew
Fairlie at Gleneagles   £££
Modern Scottish   **Map** D4
Perthshire, PH3 1NF
Tel *01764 694 267*   **Closed** *Sun*
The grand Gleneagles Hotel is
the setting for Scotland's only
two Michelin-starred restaurant.
The chef works his magic with
an international twist on locally
sourced produce. Try the smoked
lobster and roast Anjou squab.

BALQUIDDER: Monachyle
Mhor   £££
Modern Scottish   **Map** C4
Lochearnhead, Perthshire, FK19 8PQ
Tel *01877 384 622*
Chef Tom Lewis grows his own
vegetables and rears his own
livestock. Try the sublime five-
course *table d'hôte* menu.

BRIDGE OF EARN: The Roost
Restaurant   ££
Scottish   **Map** D4
Forgandenny Road, Kintillo, PH2 9AZ
Tel *01738 812 111*
This cosy restaurant is just south
of Perth. Enjoy simple, well-cooked
seasonal dishes that showcase
the best of Perthshire produce.

BUTE: No. 29   £
Modern Scottish   **Map** C4
29 Gallowgate, Rothesay, PA20 0HR
Tel *01700 500 685*   **Closed** *Mon*
Contemporary eatery serving
creative modern cooking. The
crispy battered local haddock
and chips is particularly delicious.

CALLANDER: Roman Camp
Country House & Restaurant ££
International   **Map** D4
Off Main Street, FK17 8BG
Tel *01877 330 003*
Dine in the shadow of the Romans
at this plush hotel-restaurant. Try
the six-course tasting menu.
Extensive wine list.

The luxurious restaurant at Gleneagles, run
by Andrew Fairlie

COMRIE: Deil's Cauldron
Restaurant and Wine Bar   £
Scottish   **Map** D4
27 Dundas Street, PH6 2LN
Tel *01764 670 352*
Friendly and informal eatery
known for its consistently good
food and wine. Lighter lunch
options include baked seafood
pancakes. Tapas available at night.

CUPAR: The Peat Inn   £££
Modern Scottish   **Map** D4
Fife, near St Andrews, KY15 5LH
Tel *01334 840 206* **Closed** *Sun & Mon*
Michelin-starred rural retreat run
by Chef Geoffrey Smeddle. The
menu uses local produce such as
salmon, langoustine and beef.
Come here to savour the multi-
course tasting menu.

DUNDEE: Jute Café Bar   £
Café   **Map** D4
152 Nethergate, DD1 4DY
Tel *01382 909 246*
This café at the Dundee
Contemporary Arts Centre serves
both light lunches as well as a
three-course evening meal. Solid
cooking that includes dishes such
as steak and chocolate torte.

ELIE: Sangster's   ££
Seafood   **Map** E4
51 High Street, Fife, KY9 1BZ
Tel *01333 331 001*   **Closed** *Mon*
Michelin-starred restaurant by
Bruce and Jackie Sangster's culin-
ary team. Try the twice-baked
cheese soufflé.

FALKLAND: Pillars of Hercules £
Vegetarian   **Map** D4
Strathmiglo Road, Fife, KY15 7AD
Tel *01337 857 749*
Tasty vegetarian food from spicy
soups and hearty sandwiches to
delicious home-baking and salads.
An outdoor deck with chunky
furniture and a rustic children's
sandpit are added attractions.

LAKE OF MENTEITH: The Lake of
Menteith Hotel & Waterfront
Restaurant   ££
Scottish   **Map** D4
Port of Menteith, Perthshire, FK8 3RA
Tel *01877 385 258*
Splendid restaurant in an
impressive location overlooking
the lake. Serves fresh seafood
and expertly cooked meat dishes.

LOCH LOMOND: Martin Wishart
at Loch Lomond   £££
French   **Map** C4
Alexandria, Dunbartonshire, G83 8QZ
Tel *01389 722 504* **Closed** *Mon & Tue*
One of Scotland's finest chefs runs
this Michelin-starred restaurant
located in the Cameron House
Hotel. Sublime tasting menus.

Charmingly decorated dining room in the Boath House, Auldearn

NORTH QUEENSFERRY: The Wee Restaurant ££
Modern Scottish   Map D4
17 Main Street, Fife, KY11 1JG
Tel *01383 616 263*   **Closed** *Mon*
Savour delicacies such as the roast sirloin to share or the Shetland mussels at this small restaurant. An intimate and highly recommended dining experience.

PERTH: 63 Tay Street ££
Modern Scottish   Map D4
63 Tay Street, PH2 8NN
Tel *01738 441 451*   **Closed** *Sun & Mon*
Contemporary eatery serving first-rate modern Scottish food in elegant surroundings. The menu's highlights include monkfish tail, Perthshire venison and Aberdeen Angus beef steak.

PERTH: Deans @ Let's Eat ££
Modern Scottish   Map D4
77–79 Kinnoull Street, PH1 5EZ
Tel *01738 643 377*   **Closed** *Sun & Mon*
This fine-dining restaurant has a well-deserved reputation for serving up consistently good Scottish food with a modern twist. Good wine list.

PORTAVADIE: Marina Restaurant and Bar ££
Scottish   Map C4
Loch Fyne, Argyll, PA21 2DA
Tel *01700 811 075*
Spectacular waterfront dining room in the Portavadie Marina. Serves fresh seafood and oysters from Loch Fyne. Splendid views of the Kintyre and the distant Arran Hills. Good for drinks.

SHERIFFMUIR: Sheriffmuir Inn ££
Pub   Map D4
Dunblane, FK15 0LN
Tel *01786 823 285*   **Closed** *Mon.*
Seventeenth-century inn set by one of Scotland's most famous battlefields. Savour dishes such as Shetland mussels and venison by a cosy fire.

ST ANDREWS: The Seafood Restaurant £££
Seafood   Map E4
Bruce Embankment, Fife, KY16 9AB
Tel *01334 479 475*
Stylish restaurant with floor-to-ceiling glass windows offering stunning views of the coastline. Great value lunch menu.

ST MONANS: Craig Millar @ 16 West End ££
Modern Scottish   Map E4
16 West End, Fife, KY10 2BX
Tel *0133 730 327*   **Closed** *Mon & Tue*
Waterfront eatery with lovely sea views. Predominantly seafood, the menu includes simple dishes as well as more creative flavour combinations.

STANLEY: Ballathie House ££
Modern Scottish   Map D4
Kinclaven, Perth, PH1 4QN
Tel *01250 883 268*
The chef here makes the best of Scottish produce such as Pittenweem langoustines and Perthshire venison by giving them a modern twist in this elegant restaurant. Wonderful desserts.

The Highlands and Islands

ABERDEEN: The Silver Darling £££
Seafood   Map E3
Pocra Quay, North Pier, AB11 5DQ
Tel *01224 576 229*   **Closed** *Sun*
The Silver Darling offers fresh seafood expertly cooked and given a French twist by. Good French wine list. Magnificent sea views.

ABOYNE: At the Sign of the Black Faced Sheep £
Café   Map E3
Ballater Road, AB34 5HN
Tel *01339 887 311*
Lovely coffee shop and emporium with impressive crockery display.

This upmarket café serves interesting sandwiches, sun-dried tomato scones and seafood platters.

ACHILTIBUIE: Summer Isles Hotel £££
Seafood   Map C2
Ross-shire, IV26 2YG
Tel *01854 622 282*
The award-winning restaurant at the Summer Isles Hotel delivers exceptional seafood by Chef Alan White in elegant surroundings.

APPLECROSS: Applecross Inn £
Pub   Map C2
Wester Ross, IV54 8LR
Tel *01520 744 262*
Remarkable local seafood such as huge prawns and plump lobster served in generous portions.

ARDEONAIG: Ardeonaig Hotel & Restaurant ££
Modern Scottish   Map D3
South Loch Tay Side, near Killin, FK21 8SU
Tel *01567 820 400*   **Closed** *Mon & Tue*
Pleasantly appointed dining room overlooking Loch Tay. The inventive menu includes dishes such as venison loin and hay smoked salmon.

ARDUAINE: Asknish Bay Restaurant ££
Modern Scottish   Map C4
by Oban, Argyll, PA34 4XG
Tel *01852 200 233*
The dining room at Loch Melfort Hotel has fine views of the Atlantic and its isles. Try the evening tasting menu with perfectly matched wines from around the world.

AULDEARN: Boath House £££
Modern Scottish   Map D2
Nairn, IV12 5TE
Tel *01667 454 896*
Award-wining food and wonderful views at the luxurious Boath House hotel. The menu includes scallops and deer. Try the six-course tasting menu.

Splendid views from the waterfront Seafood Restaurant, St Andrews

For more information on types of restaurants *see page 179*

Elegantly laid-out table in the Three Chimneys, Isle of Skye

AVIEMORE: Mountain Café £
Café   Map D3
111 Grampian Road, PH22 1RH
Tel *01479 812 473*
Friendly and informal café selling
everything from wholesome soups
and hearty burgers to delicious
home baking. Children's books and
toys keep the little ones occupied.

BADACHRO: Badachro Inn £
Pub   Map C2
Gairloch, Ross-shire, IV21 2AA
Tel *01445 741 255*
Friendly local pub serving bar
lunches and evening meals.
Jacket potatoes, panini and
sandwiches feature alongside
fresh shellfish, seafood, Scottish
beef and lamb.

**CAIRNDOW: Loch Fyne Oyster
Bar**   ££
Seafood   Map C4
Clachan, PA26 8BL
Tel *01499 600 236*
Savour the freshest of oysters and
mussels grown in clear, fertile
waters of the eponymous loch
outside the restaurant.

COLL: Gannet Restaurant ££
Seafood   Map B3
Ariangour, PA78 6SZ
Tel *01879 230 334*
Waterfront restaurant in the Coll
Hotel boasting fresh seafood
from around the island. Try the
lobster spaghetti with cream,
which uses home-made pasta.

FINDHORN: The Bakehouse £
Café   Map D2
91–92 Forres, IV36 3YG
Tel *01309 691 826*
The Bakehouse is known for its
locally sourced organic produce
and mainly vegetarian menu.
There are also some meat
options available. Mouth-
watering home baking.

FORT WILLIAM: Crannog ££
Seafood   Map C3
Town Pier, PH33 6DB
Tel *01397 705 589*
Splendid seafood restaurant over-
looking Loch Linnhe. Offers dishes
with interesting culinary twists.
Uses white fish, molluscs and
crustaceans sourced from the
local loch.

FORT WILLIAM: Lime Tree ££
Modern Scottish   Map C3
*The Old Manse, Achintore Road,
PH33 6RQ*
Tel *01397 701 806*
Highly praised hotel-restaurant
known for its warm welcome and
excellent food. Specialities include
pan seared Glenfinnan venison,
mackerel, west coast crab and
smoked haddock.

**FORT WILLIAM: Inverlochy
Castle**   £££
Modern Scottish   Map C3
Torlundy, PH33 6SN
Tel *01397 702 177*
The three regal dining rooms at
Inverlochy Castle make for a truly
memorable experience. Sample
Scottish dishes with a French
twist. Do not miss the hot
cranachan soufflé.

GLENCOE: Clachaig Inn £
Pub   Map C3
Argyll, PH49 4HX
Tel *01855 811 252*
Characterful old inn set in the
heart of Glencoe. Hearty pub
fare, fine ales and a range of malt
whiskies to choose from.

INVERIE: The Old Forge £
Pub   Map C3
Knoydart, Mallaig, PH41 4PL
Tel *01687 462 267*
The most remote pub in the UK.
A good place to try white fish
and shellfish culled from around
the Knoydart Peninsula.

**INVERNESS: Rocpool
Restaurant**   ££
Brasserie   Map D2
1 Ness Walk, IV3 5NE
Tel *01463 717 274*
Contemporary eatery serving
modern food. Relish dishes such
as Parma ham salad served with
balsamic roasted purple figs and
baked parmesan brûlée. Good
wine list.

**ISLE OF SKYE: The Three
Chimneys**   £££
Modern Scottish   Map B2
Colbost, Dunvegan, IV55 8ZT
Tel *01470 511 258*
Enjoy a superb dining experience
at a spectacular location. Charac-
terful converted stone croft with
self-taught, visionary chef, Shirley
Spear. Reserve ahead.

KILBERRY: The Kilberry Inn ££
Inn   Map C4
Argyll and Bute, PA29 6YD
Tel *01880 770 223*   **Closed** *Mon*
This award-winning inn serves
flawless dishes created with local
ingredients such as surf clam with
spaghetti, white wine and cream.
Warm and cosy atmosphere.

DK Choice

**KINLOCHLEVEN: Lochleven
Seafood Café**   £££
Seafood   Map C3
*Onich, Fort William, Inverness-
shire PH33 6SA*
Tel *01855 821 048*
A heaven for seafood lovers,
Lochleven Seafood Café offers
tennis-ball sized scallops,
delicious oysters and an
impressively fresh shellfish
platter with refreshing white
wines to ease it all down.
Outside tables in summer offer
splendid views of Loch Leven
and Pap of Glencoe.

Outdoor terrace with stunning views at Lochleven Seafood Café, Kinlochleven

KILCHRENAN: Ardanaiseig £££
Modern Scottish Map C4
by Taynuilt, Argyll, PA35 1HE
Tel *01866 833 333*
Renowned forager and local
produce advocate Gary Goldie
creates excellent gourmet meals
in this grand country house hotel.
Five-course dinner served at 7pm.

KISHORN: Kishorn Seafood Bar £
Seafood Map C2
Strathcarron, Ross-shire, IV54 8XA
Tel *01520 733 240*
Deceptively simple wooden cabin
offering world-class food. Try the
great-value seafood platter laden
with crab, oysters, scallops and
squat lobsters.

KYLESKU: Kylesku Hotel £
Scottish Map C1
by Lairg, Sutherland, IV27 4HW
Tel *01971 502 231*
Spacious bar-lounge in a former
coaching inn. Serves quality meals
including creel-caught lobster,
langoustine and crab. Scottish
meats and fish on offer as well.

MULL: Highland Cottage ££
Scottish Map B3
24 Breadalbane Street, Tobermory,
Argyll, PA75 6PD
Tel *01688 302 030*
Talented Chef Jo Currie delivers
a menu brimming with quality
local produce in this intimate
dining room. Good wine list.

OBAN: Waterfront Fishouse
Restaurant ££
Seafood Map C4
1 Railway Pier, PA34 4LW
Tel *01631 563 110*
Plump langoustines, large king
scallops and local lobster are on
offer at this waterfront restaurant.
Spectacular views over the
beautiful bay.

Bright and cheerful Frankie's Fish and Chips
in Brae, Shetland Islands

The graceful façade of Stonefield Castle in Tarbert, location of Loch Fyne Restaurant

PLOCKTON: Plockton Hotel ££
Seafood Map C2
41 Harbour St, Ross-shire, IV52 8TN
Tel *01599 544 274*
A varied menu featuring fresh
fish and shellfish including scampi
tails and langoustines. Mains such
as venison casserole, burgers and
fish and chips as well. Outdoor
tables with wonderful sea views.

PLOCKTON: Plockton Inn &
Seafood Restaurant ££
Seafood Map C2
Innes Street, Ross-shire, IV52 8TW
Tel *01599 544 222*
Award-winning, traditional inn
in picturesque Plockton village.
Sumptuous seafood platters, local
beef, lamb and game on offer.
Vegetarian options available.

PORT APPIN: The Airds Hotel &
Restaurant £££
French Map C3
Argyll and Bute, PA38 4DF
Tel *01631 730 236*
The fine-dining menu at this
hotel-restaurant has a modern
French style but uses local
Scottish produce. Savour hand-
dived scallops, Mallaig halibut
and slow-poached chicken.

SCRABSTER: The Captain's
Galley £££
Seafood Map D1
The Harbour, KW14 7UJ
Tel *01847 894 999* **Closed** *Sun & Mon*
Set in a former ice house with
exposed brickwork, The Captain's
Galley offers a dozen different
kinds of fish fresh from the
morning's catch on its menu.

SHETLAND ISLANDS: Frankie's
Fish and Chips £
Fish and Chips Map C1
Brae, Shetland, ZE2 9QJ
Tel *01806 522 700*
Award-winning fish and chips
restaurant on Shetland's Mainland.
Fresh sustainable fish with some

unusual treats such as scallops
and blue mussels. Full breakfasts
also available.

TARBERT: Loch Fyne
Restaurant ££
Scottish Map C4
Loch Fyne, Argyll, PA29 6YJ
Tel *08444 146 582*
Pleasantly situated restaurant in
the Stonefield Castle hotel. Tasty
food backed-up by good service.
Menu highlights include fish and
shellfish from the eponymous
loch. Decent wine list.

TORRIDON: The Torridon
Restaurant £££
Modern Scottish Map C2
Achnasheen, Wester Ross, IV22 2EY
Tel *01445 700 300*
Stately dining room at the grand
Torridon hotel. Perfect setting for
the fine-dining dishes expertly
cooked by Chef Bruno Birckbeck.
Savour the sumptuous five-
course tasting menu.

TYNDRUM: The Real Food Café £
Café Map C4
Perthshire, FK20 8RY
Tel *01838 400 235*
Arguably the best fish and chips
to be had in Scotland. Enjoy a
large or small fish supper and
sample excellent coffee and
cakes. Children's menu available.

A table with magnificent mountain views
at The Torridon, Torridon

For more information on types of restaurants *see page 179*

SPECIAL INTERESTS AND OUTDOOR ACTIVITIES

Scotland may not be able to guarantee sunshine or offer beach culture, but its popularity as a holiday destination is due in no small part to its opportunities for outdoor activities, as well as cultural pursuits. Over the years, the tourist industry has matured to occupy an important role in the Scottish economy, and local businesses have become adept at providing visitors with what they are looking for. That could be playing golf by the sea, fishing on the Tweed, cruising to see whales off the west coast during the summer, skiing in the Cairngorms in winter, eating fresh oysters at a lochside restaurant or searching for information on ancestors who left the country 200 years ago. Facilities for all kinds of activities have never been better, and this section outlines some of the best.

Searching for records of ancestors, Edinburgh

Tracing Genealogy

From the time of the infamous Clearances of the 18th century onwards (see p154), Scots have emigrated to Australia, Canada, New Zealand, South Africa, the US and elsewhere in search of an easier life. There are now millions of foreign nationals who can trace their heritage back to Scotland, and uncovering family history is a popular reason for visiting the country.

Professional genealogists can be commissioned, but those interested in conducting investigations themselves should try the **General Register Office for Scotland** (which has records of births, deaths and marriages dating from the 1500s), the **Scottish Genealogy Society** or the **National Archives of Scotland**, all in Edinburgh.

Gaelic Studies

The northwest of Scotland is the heartland for the Gaelic language. Historically, this was a Celtic language that spread from mainland Europe to Ireland in the 4th century BC, and later into Scotland where it became the national language. By the 18th century, however, under English rule, Gaelic had become identified with a rebellious clan system that was persecuted after the Jacobite rising of 1745 (see p49). It was marginalized and suffered a decline.

A renaissance aims to revive this once-dominant culture with Gaelic broadcasts and by teaching it to children. **An Comunn Gaidhealach**, Scotland's official Gaelic society, organizes the annual Royal National Mod (see p42), a performing arts competition. Other Gaelic societies are **Comunn An Luchd Ionnsachaidh** and **Comunn na Gàidhlig**. **Sabhal Mor Ostaig**, a college on the Isle of Skye, runs short Gaelic courses for visitors.

Food and Drink Tours

Scotland has a justified reputation for fine produce, and there has been an upsurge in the number of noteworthy restaurants in Edinburgh and Glasgow. Indeed, Edinburgh has established itself as the number two city for eating out in the British Isles, after London.

One way of sampling Scottish cuisine is to book a holiday through **Connoisseurs Scotland**, which arranges stays at country house hotels with a reputation for top-class cooking, such as the Crinan Hotel in Argyll, or Gleneagles.

The **Scotch Malt Whisky Society** has information for lovers of this spirit. Distilleries are a popular attraction (see pp36–7 and p148), with names such as **Glenfiddich**

Learning about whisky, the "water of life", at a Speyside distillery

Distillery operating tours. The production of cask-conditioned beers is explained at Edinburgh's **Caledonian Brewery**. An exhibition at **Inverawe Smokehouses**, near Taynuilt in the Highlands, shows the techniques used in smoking fish such as salmon.

Viewing Wildlife

In comparison with much of the rest of the British Isles, Scotland still has large areas of moor and mountain wilderness and a long, relatively undeveloped coastline that supports a range of animals (see pp22–3). In the

Sighting a porpoise as it breaks the calm surface of a sea loch

Walkers on the lookout for red deer and birds of prey at Glen Coe

mountains near Aviemore, rangers from the **Cairngorm Reindeer Centre** take parties of people on to the mountain to walk among a herd of reindeer.

A convenient way to see the abundant sealife is on a boat trip run by **Maid of the Forth Cruises**, which operates from South Queensferry on the Forth near Edinburgh – dolphins and common seals are resident in these waters. More adventurous are the trips in search of whales offered by **Sea Life Surveys** from the Isle of Mull, but even a casual tourist in the Highlands can spot birds of prey, otters in the lochs and herds of red deer

on the mountainsides. With a large share of Britain's resident and visiting birds, Scotland is also home to a number of important bird sanctuaries, the most celebrated being Handa Island off Scourie on the far northwest coast (see p161). St Abb's Head (see p88) east of Edinburgh and Baron's Haugh near Motherwell (on the outskirts of Glasgow) are nearer the cities.

Many wildlife tours are small-scale private businesses that operate according to seasonal and daily demand, so always check the details with the local tourist information offices.

DIRECTORY

Outdoor Activities at a Glance

Only a handful of inland lochs and coastal waters have been exploited by commercial boating and watersports companies, though it is possible to use private vessels on many minor lochs in wilderness areas. Likewise, organized skiing is confined to just five centres. Of the country's several hundred golf courses, most are concentrated in central and southern Scotland. This map plots the main centres for various popular activities. For further information about particular sports across Scotland, *see pages 194–203.*

Handa Island, off the far northwest coast, is one of a number of seabird reserves.

Stornoway

Ullapool

Rock climbers and mountaineers *(see p200)* usually head for Glencoe, the Cairngorms and the Cuillin Hills on Skye. The Torridon range and other formations further north are also popular choices.

Kyle of Lochalsh

Mallaig

Fort William

Oban

The five skiing centres *(see p201)* are Glencoe, the Nevis Range, Cairngorm, Glenshee and the Lecht. The skiing season usually gets under way in December and lasts until April.

The West Highland Way is the most famous long-distance walk in Scotland, encompassing a wonderful variety of terrain.

Campbeltown

Key

- 🪂 Watersports
- ⛵ Sailing
- ⛳ Major golf course
- 🔭 Birdwatching
- ⛷ Skiing
- 🎣 Fishing
- 🐴 Pony trekking
- 🚶 Major walking area
- — Long-distance walk route

Stranraer

Sailing *(see p203)* is popular off the west coast and the islands. The calm waters of sheltered bays are suitable for beginners, while the open sea can be both exhilarating and treacherous. Inland, Loch Ness offers sailing opportunities.

Bird-watching *(see p191)* is in itself a reason to visit Scotland. The best sanctuaries are in remote coastal areas where such delightful species as puffins make their home on the sheer, wave-lashed cliffs.

Watersports *(see p203)* include canoeing, surfing, windsurfing and diving. Visitors can book equipment and courses through activities centres scattered around the country.

Golf *(see pp194–7)* attracts thousands of visitors every year, especially to the most famous courses in Central Scotland, such as St Andrews and Carnoustie.

Walking *(see pp198–9)* is tremendously popular in Scotland, and vast swathes of the countryside are open to the public.

Pony trekking opportunities *(see p202)* are within easy reach of the cities, in the gentle countryside of southern and central Scotland, and in the great moor and mountain wilderness of the Highlands.

Fishing *(see p202)* is well catered for on the River Tweed in southern Scotland, and on Loch Ness in the Highlands.

Golf in Scotland

The ancient game of golf is synonymous with Scotland and has been played here for hundreds of years. Wherever you choose to stay, there will be a golf course not far away. Few countries can rival Scotland for the number, quality and variety of courses – over 550 at the last count, with new ones opening every year. Similarly, few golfing destinations can lay claim to such magnificent, unspoilt scenery. Golf is played by people of all ages and capabilities in Scotland – it's a game for everyone to enjoy. Whether your game is suited to one of the legendary championship courses or to a less daunting challenge, you will find a hearty welcome here.

Early History

Variations on the game of golf as we know it today were being played across Europe as long ago as the 14th century, and possibly even in Roman times. However, it is the Scottish who must be credited with establishing the official game and encouraging its development across the world. It was in Scotland that the passion for golf was born. By the middle of the 16th century, the game had become a popular pastime at the highest levels of society – James VI himself was a keen player, as was his mother, Mary, Queen of Scots.

In the late 1800s, wealthy middle-class Englishmen began to follow the example of the Royal Family by taking their holidays in Scotland. The expansion of the railway system at this time allowed people to get to the seaside courses, and the English became so infatuated with the game of golf that they took it home with them. In 1744 the Gentlemen Golfers of Leith, led by Duncan Forbes, drew up the first *Articles & Laws in Playing at Golf*. Although later revised and updated, these original rules, set down by the Scottish professionals of the time, formed the framework for the modern game of golf.

Tools of the Trade

The Scottish influence on golf was not to end there. Many of the professionals playing at the time were also skilled carpenters, instrumental in developing the clubs and balls used in the game. Willie Park Senior was a master clubmaker, and winner of the first Scottish Open in 1860, while Old Tom Morris became a legend in the game for both his playing and craftsmanship. In the days before machinery, the wooden clubs were made entirely by hand. The earliest irons were also fashioned by hand, followed by aluminium-headed clubs that differ very little from clubs today. The "guttie" ball was invented in 1848, replacing the expensive and easily damaged "feathery", thus making the game more affordable. The modern, rubber-core ball in use today appeared at the beginning of the 20th century.

A scenic view of Gleneagles, one of Scotland's championship courses

Arranging a Game

Nearly all Scottish golf clubs welcome visitors, although there may be restrictions on non-members at popular times. Check booking arrangements carefully. Almost all clubs have websites and many have online booking capabilities; others require a formal written application. To be certain of a round on the more famous courses, book well in advance, or take a golfing package that includes guaranteed tee times at your chosen venues.

For a comprehensive list of all Scotland's golf courses, including prices and amenities and other useful golfing information, order a free copy of the annual *Official Guide to Golf in Scotland* brochure, produced by VisitScotland.

Etiquette

Scotland isn't a snobbish place to play golf, but some clubs are more conservative than others. Some frown on jeans or trainers (running shoes), and a few insist on jackets and ties in the clubhouse lounge. Remember to bring your handicap certificate along each time you visit.

Old railway poster advertising the lure of St Andrews

When to Play

It's easier (and cheaper) to get a game during the week rather than at a weekend, and outside busy holiday periods. The main golfing season runs from about April to mid-October, but most clubs stay open all year round, especially the links (coastal) courses, where the climate is milder. May and September are ideal times to play: temperatures are moderate and the scenery is at its most beautiful. The further north you go, the more variable the hours of daylight are. At midsummer, you can tee off at midnight on Orkney and Shetland.

Golfing Events

Many keen golfers combine a visit to Scotland with a well-known golfing event. Besides the famous Open Championship, held at least every other year, professional fixtures attracting visitors to Scotland are the Barclays Scottish Open, staged at Loch Lomond in late summer; the Dunhill Links Championship (Oct); and two women's championships: the Women's British Open and the Ladies' Scottish Open. Popular amateur events include the St Andrews Links Trophy (Jun) and the Scottish Amateur Championship (Jul–Aug). "Golf Weeks" are held at St Andrews (Apr), Royal Deeside and Machrihanish (both in May), and Pitlochry (Jun). The Fife, Ayrshire and Highland Classics are held at multiple venues.

Teeing off as the sun sets at Royal Troon Golf Club, Ayrshire

Facilities

A scheme called "Visiting Golfers Welcome", operated by VisitScotland, indicates which clubs provide facilities for non-members. Smarter clubs offer on-site accommodation; this can be extremely luxurious, with many leisure amenities, as at world-renowned **Gleneagles** or the **Ballater Golf Club** in Royal Deeside. Others can suggest hotels or bed and breakfasts nearby, many of which offer special rates or discounted green fees for golfers, along with storage facilities, drying rooms and early or late mealtimes. Look out for the "Golfers Welcome" logo, which indicates accommodation specially geared to golf lovers.

Clubs and hand trolleys can be hired at most courses, but

book ahead if you need a caddy. Buggies (ride-on golf carts) may be available if pre-booked at the larger courses, but the norm in Scotland is to walk the course unless you have a medical condition or physical disability.

Long Traditions

Many of Scotland's courses are steeped in history and tradition. Without a doubt, **St Andrews** in Fife is the true home of golf, where the game originated in the 15th century (records date back to 1457). The St Andrews Links Trust now operates seven superb courses on this hallowed stretch of seaside, the most venerable of which is the Old Course. Every golfer dreams of playing here. If you are lucky, your dream may come true – this legendary course is accessible to visitors at short notice via a democratic ballot system. Simply contact the Trust the day before you want to play, and your name will be included in the daily draw (successful applicants are posted on the club's website).

The Claret Jug trophy

St Andrews's resident Royal and Ancient Golf Club (R&A), founded in 1754, is the official ruling body of world golf. The R&A organizes the famous British Open Championship, traditionally hosted by St Andrews every five years. The winner of this prestigious contest is awarded the coveted Claret Jug trophy, crafted and hallmarked in 1873. The British Golf Museum, opposite the R&A clubhouse, is a must-visit attraction for any keen player.

Not far from St Andrews is the **Crail Golfing Society**, which began life in 1786. Its Balcomie links course is a tough seaside test. The **Royal Burgess**, instituted in 1735, is the oldest golfing society in the world. Upholding time-honoured golfing rules, it features a picturesque tree-lined course on the north side of Edinburgh. Visitor tee times are available.

The Scottish Open at Loch Lomond Golf Club

Aerial view of Machrihanish, a golf course overlooking the Atlantic Ocean

holiday course with superb vistas of Scapa Flow.

However, it is perhaps the classic links, or coastal courses, that are most typical of the Scottish game. Links courses present infinitely varied challenges: a dramatic opening drive across the Atlantic at **Machrihanish** in Argyll, or the lunar landscape at **Cruden Bay**, near Aberdeen. **Kingsbarns**, near St Andrews, is another top-flight coastal course. Up in the Highlands, **Royal Dornoch** is an all-time great links course designed by Tom Morris.

Championship Courses

Other famous courses on the Open circuit include **Carnoustie**, **Royal Troon** and the private course **Muirfield**, which hosted the Open Championship in 2013. **Prestwick** and **Royal Musselburgh** are splendid but no longer used because of the difficulty of accommodating large crowds. Other stunning courses used as Open qualifying venues are **North Berwick**, **Glasgow Gailes** and **Gullane** – course No. 1 is as close as you're likely to get to playing at Muirfield. Located on the Moray Firth and opened in 2009, **Castle Stuart Golf Links** hosted the Scottish Open for three years. Most famous is **Gleneagles**, a luxurious resort home to four courses. The Johnnie Walker Championship is held here annually in late summer.

Designer Golf

Carnoustie, Royal Musselburgh and the King's and Queen's courses at Gleneagles were designed by the great 1920s player James Braid, five-time winner of the Open. Visit Scotland's James Braid Trail explores some of the 250 or so courses he created or modified throughout the country, introducing features such as doglegs and pot bunkers. Famous Braid courses include **Nairn**, **Boat of Garten**, **Crieff**, **Haggs Castle**, **Brora** and **Dalmahoy**. Braid cut his golfing teeth on the links at **Elie**, where he was born, though he had little influence on the present course.

More recently, Dave Thomas has achieved great success as a course designer. Among his creations are **Deer Park** in Livingston, **Roxburghe** in the Borders and the **Spey Valley** championship course near Aviemore, dramatically set against the backdrop of the Cairngorm mountains.

The tranquil landscape at Cruden Bay golf course, near Aberdeen

Arresting Scenery

It's a rare Scottish golf course that doesn't boast a glorious setting. **Elgin** is one of the finest inland courses, in lush parkland surroundings, while **Kingussie** takes advantage of an amazing Cairngorm backdrop. **Pitlochry** is an ideal holiday course, and nine-hole **Traigh**, on the Road to the Isles, features a magnificent panorama towards the Inner Hebrides. **Shiskine** on the Isle of Arran is an unusual and little-known gem with 12 holes in a wonderful setting. The **Isle of Skye** is another small but beautiful course with sea and island views, while Orkney's **Stromness** is a demanding

Cutting Costs

Golf can be an expensive hobby, but it is possible to enjoy a round for under £20 – for example, at **Braid Hills** in Edinburgh, a superb public course with amazing views of the castle and city, or at **Merchants of Edinburgh**. If you don't want to spend too much at Fife's **Leven Links**, try the adjoining James Braid-designed nine-hole **Lundin Ladies** course, which costs a third of the price and welcomes visitors of either gender. **Colvend**, overlooking the Solway Firth, is also good value and even **Ballater** has reasonably priced mid-week day passes.

Another way to keep costs down is to take up one of the many deals and passes available through specialist operators, or listed in the *Official Guide to Golf* (*see p194*). These include the Freedom of the Fairways, which allows discounted play at 21 courses in the Borders, and the Aviemore & Cairngorms Golf Pass, which offers seven days' golf at eight different courses in the central Highlands.

Loch views from the green at the Isle of Skye Golf Club

DIRECTORY

Useful Websites
w scotlands-golf-courses.com
w scottishgolf.com
w golf.visitscotland.com

Golfing Organizations

Scottish Golf Union
Tel (01334) 466477.
w scottishgolf.org

Scottish Ladies Golfing Association
Tel (01738) 442357.
w slga.co.uk

Specialist Operators

Adventures in Golf
Tel 001 (877) 424 7320.
w adventures-in-golf.com

Golf International
Tel (800) 833 1389.
w golfinternational.com

Links Golf St Andrews
Tel (01334) 478639.
w linksgolfstandrews.com

Premier Golf
Tel 001 (866) 260 4409.
w premiergolf.com

Scottish Golf Tours
Tel (0131) 657 1984.
w scottish-golf tours.com

Edinburgh and Southern Scotland

Braid Hills
15 Braid Hills Approach, Edinburgh. Tel (0131) 447 6666. w edinburgh leisuregolf.co.uk

Colvend
Sandyhills, Colvend. Tel (01556) 630398. w colvendgolfclub.co.uk

Dalmahoy
Marriott Hotel & CC, Kirknewton, Edinburgh. Tel (0131) 333 1845.

Deer Park
Golf Course Rd, Livingston, West Lothian. Tel (01506) 446699.

Gullane
West Links Road, Gullane, East Lothian. Tel (01620) 842255. w gullanegolfclub.com

Merchants of Edinburgh
10 Craighill Gardens, Edinburgh. Tel (0131) 447 1219. w merchants golf.com

Muirfield
Duncur Rd, Gullane, East Lothian. Tel (01620) 842 123. w muirfield.org.uk

North Berwick
New Clubhouse, Beach Rd, North Berwick. Tel (01620) 895040. w north berwickgolfclub.com

Prestwick
2 Links Road, Prestwick, Ayrshire. Tel (01292) 477404. w prestwickgc.co.uk

Roxburghe
Village of Heiton, Kelso, Borders. Tel (01573) 450 333. w roxburghe golfclub.co.uk

Royal Burgess
181 Whitehouse Road, Barnton, Edinburgh. Tel (0131) 339 9440. w royalburgess.co.uk

Royal Musselburgh
Prestongrange House, Prestonpans, East Lothian. Tel (01875) 810276. w royalmusselburgh.co.uk

Royal Troon
Craigend Road, Troon, Ayrshire. Tel (01292) 311 555. w royaltroon.com

Glasgow and Central Scotland

Carnoustie
Links Parade, Carnoustie, Angus. Tel (01241) 802 270. w carnoustie golflinks.co.uk

Crail
Balcomie Clubhouse, Fifeness, Crail, Fife. Tel (01333) 450686. w crailgolfingsociety.co.uk

Crieff
Perth Road, Crieff, Perthshire. Tel (01764) 652909. w crieffgolf.co.uk

Elie
Golf Course Lane, Elie, Fife. Tel (01333) 333301. w golfhouseclub.org

Glasgow Gailes
Gailes, Irvine. Tel (0141) 942 2011. w glasgowgolfclub.com

Gleneagles
Gleneagles, Auchterarder, Perthshire. Tel (01764) 662 231. w gleneagles.com/golf

Haggs Castle
70 Dumbreck Road, Dumbreck, Glasgow. Tel (0141) 427 1157. w haggscastle golfclub.com

Kingsbarns
Kingsbarns, St Andrews, Fife. Tel (01334) 460860. w kingsbarns.com

Leven Links
The Promenade, Leven, Fife. Tel (01333) 428859. w leven-links.com

Lundin Ladies
Woodielea Road, Lundin Links, Fife. Tel (01333) 320832. w lundin ladiesgolfclub.co.uk

St Andrews Links
St Andrews Links Trust, Fife. Tel (01334) 466666. w standrews.org.uk

Shiskine
Blackwaterfoot, Shiskine, Isle of Arran. Tel (01770) 860226. w shiskinegolf.com

The Highlands and Islands

Ballater Golf Club
Victoria Rd, Ballater, Aberdeenshire. Tel (01339) 755567. w ballatergolfclub.co.uk

Boat of Garten
Boat of Garten, Invernesshire. Tel (01479) 831282. w boatgolf.com

Brora
Golf Road, Brora, Sutherland. Tel (01408) 621417. w broragolf.co.uk

Castle Stuart Golf Links
Inverness. Tel (01463) 796111. w castlestuartgolf.com

Cruden Bay
Aulton Road, Cruden Bay, Peterhead. Tel (01779) 812285. w cruden baygolf club.co.uk

Elgin
Birnie Road, Elgin, Moray. Tel (01343) 542338. w elgingolfclub.com

Isle of Skye
Sconser, Isle of Skye. Tel (01478) 650465. w isleofskyegolfclub.co.uk

Kingussie
Gynack Road, Kingussie. Tel (01540) 661600. w kingussie-golf.co.uk

Machrihanish
Campbeltown, Argyll. Tel (01586) 810213. w machgolf.com

Nairn
Seabank Road, Nairn. Tel (01667) 453208. w nairngolfclub.co.uk

Pitlochry
Golf Course Road, Pitlochry. Tel (01796) 472792. w pitlochrygolf.co.uk

Royal Dornoch
Golf Road, Dornoch, Sutherland. Tel (01862) 810219. w royaldornoch.com

Spey Valley
Dalfaber Golf & Country Club, Aviemore. Tel (0845) 601 1734. w resorts.macdonaldhotels.co.uk/spey-valley/

Stromness
Ness, Stromness, Orkney. Tel (01856) 850772. w stromnessgc.co.uk

Traigh
Traigh Golf Club, Arisaig. Tel (01687) 450337. w traighgolf.co.uk

Walking in Scotland

It can truly be said that Scotland is a paradise for ramblers. Many trails have been waymarked for the public making Scotland a fantastic place to walk, whether you wish to stroll for an afternoon or spend weeks on the trail. Superb scenery is reasonably accessible, and the variety of terrain encompasses everything from craggy mountains to gentle river valleys. Scotland also possesses a magnificent dramatic coastline, as well as numerous islands to explore. The local tourist information centre is always a good first port of call if you are looking for advice or suggested routes.

Long-distance trail signpost for walkers in the Spey river valley

Right of Access

In Scotland there is a statutory right of access to most land for recreational purposes. Access laws implemented in 2005 are balanced by a Scottish Outdoor Access Code giving guidance on responsible conduct for users and managers of such land.

Scotland's long tradition of open access has resulted in few routes being shown on Ordnance Survey or other maps, although historic rights of way are usually marked. **Scotways** hold the definitive maps showing these routes.

Guidebooks available at large bookshops such as **WHSmith** or **Waterstone's** describe the easily walkable routes, many of which are signposted. Outdoor chain **Tiso** also sells maps and hiking guides. There may be access

restrictions in mountain areas during the stag stalking season (July to late October), but not on any areas owned by the **National Trust for Scotland** (see p208).

Clothing and Equipment

The weather in Scotland is fickle. It can snow in June or be balmy in February, and conditions are liable to change rapidly. This makes selecting the right clothing and equipment tricky. Even in summer, you should take a waterproof jacket if venturing far from shelter. When going on a day walk, take waterproof trousers and a fleece or warm sweater.

The art of being comfortable is to make your clothing adaptable; several thin layers are better than one thick one. Head covering is worth considering – a cap for sunny days or a warmer hat for cold days.

For any walk of more than a couple of hours' duration, take a drink and snack. If you are going to be out all day, take energy foods and liquids.

Good footwear is essential. Countryside walks generally demand strong shoes or boots. Sturdy trainers can be worn on roads or firm tracks, but not on rough ground where you may need ankle support. Lightweight walking boots are suitable for most seasons.

Walking Opportunities

This section deals with low-level walking; mountain activities are covered on pages 200–1, and you can also obtain information from the **Mountaineering Council of Scotland**. Over the years, greatly improved path networks have been developed, some through the national **Paths for All Partnership**. The networks provide excellent, safe walking opportunities for visitors. Some of the best networks are in the Borders and around Galloway, in Perthshire (around Dunkeld and Pitlochry), in Aberdeenshire (around Huntly), at Braemar and on the island of Bute.

Walking boots

Local authorities and other agencies have created paths and published walking guides for remote areas, such as Wester Ross, the Western Isles, Orkney and Shetland. Some of these walks tie in with ferry services. Most have a cultural or natural history theme, or incorporate a castle, waterfall or other place of interest. The walks are generally from 6 to 12 km (4 to 7 miles) in length. Tourist information centres are good starting places for more details, or you can contact

Looking out over Rannoch Moor

Above the clouds in Knoydart, looking to the Cuillin Hills on Skye

VisitScotland to obtain their *New Walking Scotland* brochure, which describes walks in all parts of Scotland. Their brochure also lists walking festivals.

Compass of the type commonly used by walkers

These events, that last up to a week, offer a wide range of guided walks along with a programme of evening entertainment. The first such festival, held in the Borders, started in 1995. Others are now held in the Highlands, Deeside and Perthshire, with more starting up each year.

For information on organized walks, contact **Ramblers' Scotland**. There are also hundreds of miles of forest trails and walks across the country. The **Forestry Commission** can provide you with general information.

Longer low-level routes being developed include the Fife Coastal Path, the Clyde Walkway and the Speyside Way extension to Aviemore. All of these can easily be sampled as day walks.

Spring and autumn are especially lovely times of the year for walking in Scotland. The colouring is superb, and there is often a wider choice of accommodation available.

Long-distance Walks

Scotland has relatively few formal long-distance routes, though the potential for making up your own is limitless. The three "official" routes are the 152-km (95-mile) West Highland Way from Glasgow to Fort William, the 340-km (211-mile) Southern Upland Way from Portpatrick to Cockburnspath, and the 84-km (52-mile) Speyside Way from Spey Bay to Tomintoul.

Other routes developed by local authorities include the 100-km (62-mile) St Cuthbert's Way from Melrose to Lindisfarne, and the Fife Coastal Path from North Queensferry to Tayport near the bridge over the Tay to Dundee.

The three principal routes are shown on the activities map *(see pp192–3)*. For information about them, and others being developed, contact **Scottish Natural Heritage** and local tourist information centres.

Surveying the scenery on a wintry day in the Cairngorms

DIRECTORY

Forestry Commission
231 Corstorphine Rd, Edinburgh EH12 7AT.
Tel (0845) 367 3787.
[w] **forestry.gov.uk**

Mountaineering Council of Scotland
The Old Granary, West Mill St, Perth PH1 5QP.
Tel (01738) 493942.
[w] **mcofs.org.uk**

National Trust for Scotland
Hermiston Quay, 5 Cultins Rd, Edinburgh EH11 4DF.
Tel (0844) 493 2100.
[w] **nts.org.uk**

Paths for All Partnership
Inglewood House, Tullibody Rd, Alloa FK10 2HU.
Tel (01259) 218888.
[w] **pathsforall.org.uk**

Ramblers' Scotland
Kingfisher House, Auld Mart Business Park, Milnathort KY13 9DA.
Tel (01577) 861222.
[w] **ramblers.org.uk**

Scottish Natural Heritage
Great Glen House,
1 Leachkin Rd, Inverness IV3 8NW.
Tel (01463) 725000.
[w] **snh.gov.uk**

Scotways
24 Annandale St, Edinburgh EH7 4AN. **Tel** (0131) 558 1222.
[w] **scotways.com**

Tiso
123–125 Rose Street Precinct, Edinburgh EH2 3DT.
Tel (0131) 225 9486.

VisitScotland
Ocean Point One, 94 Ocean Drive, Edinburgh EH6 6JH.
Tel (0845) 859 1006.
[w] **visitscotland.com**

Waterstone's
83 George Street, Edinburgh EH2 3ES.
Tel (0843) 290 8309.
153–157 Sauchiehall Street, Glasgow G2 3EW.
Tel (0843) 290 8345.

WHSmith
10B Queensferry St, Edinburgh EH2 4PG.
Tel (0131) 225 9672.

Activities in the Mountains

Although Scotland's highest mountains rise to little over 1,200 m (4,000 ft), they offer a true challenge to the hill walker and rock climber alike. Noted worldwide for their beauty of form and variety of character, the mountains of Scotland command respect among all mountaineers, not least because the climate is so variable. During the winter, conditions can be arctic. Long days in the hills offer a sense of satisfaction and refreshment that is highly valued as a contrast to the hectic pace of modern life.

Hard hats and safety ropes – vital equipment for rock climbing

Safety in the Mountains

The mountains of Scotland demand respect at any time of the year, and this means being properly prepared. You should always take with you full waterproofs, warm clothes (including hat and gloves), and food and drink. Take a map and compass and know how to use them. Good boots are essential. Winter mountaineering demands knowledge of ice-axe and crampon techniques. **Glenmore Lodge** in Aviemore is a good centre offering courses in skiing, hill craft and mountaineering.

Mountaineering in Scotland

Recreation in the mountains takes several forms. Many people aim for the higher hills, known as "Munros" and "Corbetts". These vary in character from the rounded heathery domes of the Monadhliath or the Southern Uplands to the steep, craggy eminences of the west, many of which command superb sea views. Narrow ridges such as the Aonach Eagach above Glencoe, and the peerless Cuillins of Skye, offer exhilarating sport and a special challenge. Given the right conditions, most hills can be climbed in a day, but more remote peaks may demand an overnight camp, or a stay in one of the simple huts known as a "bothy". Winter mountaineering needs extra skills but it also reaps the fantastic reward of the most breathtaking scenery.

Rock and ice climbing in Scotland has a long and distinguished history stretching back over a century. The main climbing areas, including Glencoe, the Cairngorms and Skye, have provided tough training grounds for many climbers who later gained world renown. All year the huge northern faces of Ben Nevis *(see p139)* offer a multitude of climbs at all levels. New areas, including the far northwest and the islands, have been developed more recently, as have particular disciplines such as sea-stack climbing. Techniques are being continually extended and skills refined, so that ever tougher routes can be completed. The mountains of Scotland may be small, but the maritime climate and frequently wild winter weather produce ice climbs that are among the most serious and demanding in the world. The only "closed season" on Scotland's mountains is the period from July until late October, when restrictions apply in certain areas during the stag shooting season. The **Scottish Outdoor Access Code** website provides an interactive map and telephone numbers to call for local advice. **The Mountaineering Council of Scotland** website is another useful resource.

A rucksack for carrying provisions

Munros and Corbetts

Scottish mountains rising just above 914 m (3,000 ft) are often called "Munros" after Sir Hugh Munro, first president of the **Scottish Mountaineering Club** (SMC). In 1891 Munro published the first comprehensive list of mountains fulfilling this criterion. The list has been maintained by the SMC ever since, and the hills are now officially classed as Munros. Normally, the principal summits on a hill are Munros; the lesser summits are called "Tops". Revised several times, the list now totals 284 Munros.

The first known Munroist was the Rev AE Robertson in 1901. He finished his tour of the Munros on Meall Dearg, above Glencoe, and it is recorded that he kissed the cairn before kissing his wife, such was his

Rock climbers ascending Polldubh, Glen Nevis

Enjoying a superb mountain panorama in the northern Highlands

enthusiasm as the first of many dedicated Munroists.

In the 1920s, J Rooke Corbett published a list of the summits that measured 760–915 m (2,500–3,000 ft). These 221 "Corbetts", as they became known, have a clearer definition than the Munros – they must be single summits. A third list is available, of summits of 610– 760 m (2,000– 2,500 ft) called "Grahams". All summits in Scotland over 610 m have now been categorized and published. The hills are described, with ascent routes, in the SMC guides *The Munros* and *The Corbetts, and other Scottish Hills*, and in *The Munros Almanac* and *The Corbetts Almanac*. The third set is listed in a publication called *The Grahams*.

Skiing in Scotland

There are five ski centres in Scotland: **Glencoe** *(see p138)*, **Nevis Range** *(see p139)*, **The Lecht**, **Cairngorm** *(see pp144–5)* and **Glenshee**. The Lecht tends to have the gentlest runs, while White Corries has the steepest. These two centres are more informal than the others. Nevis Range, Glenshee and Cairngorm offer good facilities and runs for skiers of all abilities, including nursery slopes.

Ski centres are usually open from December to April, depending on the amount of snow cover. Unfortunately, snow is not wholly reliable in Scotland but when it does snow, the skiing is exhilarating. Hotels and guesthouses in the ski areas offer weekend and midweek packages, and there are ski schools in all the areas. The best advice is to keep an eye on the weather and take your chance as it arises.

Cross-country or Nordic skiing is a popular, informal sport in Scotland. Given good snow cover, there are many suitable areas, ranging from the Southern Uplands to the hills of the north and west, as well as hundreds of miles of forest trails all over Scotland.

DIRECTORY

Safety in the Mountains

Scotland has a well organized network of voluntary mountain rescue teams. Calls for rescue should be made to the police on 999.

Weather Forecasts
(the Highlands)
Tel 0870 900 0100.
W metoffice.gov.uk

Glenmore Lodge
Aviemore, Inverness-shire
PH22 1QU.
Tel (01479) 861256.
W glenmorelodge.org.uk

Mountaineering in Scotland

The Mountaineering Council of Scotland
The Old Granary, West Mill St, Perth PH1 5QP.
Tel (01738) 493942.
W mcofs.org.uk

Scottish Mountaineering Club
W smc.org.uk

Scottish Outdoor Access Code
W outdooraccess-scotland. com/hftsh

Skiing in Scotland

Ski Scotland
W ski.visitscotland.com

Cairngorm
Aviemore, Inverness-shire.
Tel (01479) 861261.
W cairngormmountain.co.uk

Glencoe
King's House, Glencoe, Argyll.
Tel (01855) 851226.
W glencoemountain.com

Glenshee
Cairnwell, Aberdeenshire.
Tel (01339) 741320.
W ski-glenshee.co.uk

The Lecht
Strathden, Aberdeenshire.
Tel (01975) 651440.
W lecht.co.uk

Nevis Range
Torlundy, Inverness-shire.
Tel (01397) 705825.
W snowsports.nevisrange. co.uk

Snowboarding on the Scottish slopes

Other Outdoor Activities

Scotland has a few surprises up its sleeve for people who still associate the country with old-fashioned tourist images. While traditional pursuits such as deerstalking or salmon fishing still thrive, they are now complemented by a wide range of more contemporary sports including mountain biking and even surfing. Flanked by the North Sea and the Atlantic, Scotland has ample water for sailing, windsurfing and fishing, while horse riding and cycling present excellent ways to explore the country's varied and dramatic landscapes.

Splendid catch of the day from the River Tweed, southern Scotland

Cycling through a stream, Glen Callater

Cycling and Mountain Biking

Cycling around Scotland is one of the best ways to view the country. The trails of the Highlands are near perfect mountain bike territory and the **Forestry Commission** has opened a lot of the forest road network to mountain bikers. There is also an expanding national cycle path network to explore. Edinburgh has a system of cycle paths on old train tracks. **BikeTrax** is just one of many hire shops in the city. **Scottish Cycling** has information on cycling events and races in and around the capital.

A *Cycling in Scotland* booklet is available from tourist offices. For details of cycling trips in Scotland, contact the **C.T.C. National Cyclists Organisation** and **Scottish Cycling Holidays**.

Fishing

Although Scotland is most associated with salmon fishing, there are opportunities for sea angling, coarse fishing, and game fishing for trout too. The **Salmon and Trout Association** has information on game

fishing – the season runs from mid-February to the end of October. For coarse fishing and sea angling a landowner's permission is required before casting off. The **Scottish Federation for Coarse Angling** and **Scottish Federation of Sea Anglers** provide all the necessary information. Contact the **Scottish Anglers National Association** for general advice.

Hunting

The tradition of recreational hunting can be traced back to the mid-1800s, when Queen Victoria and Prince Albert set up residence in Balmoral on Deeside. It became fashionable for British aristocrats to spend the autumn shooting in Scotland. Large parts of the Highlands became sporting estates. Scotland is recognized as providing Europe's best game

shooting and deerstalking. Red deer and grouse are plentiful, while many estuaries and firths are wintering grounds for birds.

Over the last 30 years or so, hunting in Scotland has also attracted overseas visitors. For information on gun licensing and where to shoot, contact the **British Association for Shooting and Conservation**.

Pony Trekking and Horse Riding

There are more than 60 trekking and riding centres across Scotland, catering to a wide range of abilities, including trips deep into the Highlands for experienced riders. Some offer accommodation, tuition and trail riding, others provide trekking by the hour. **VisitScotland** has a complete list of all the centres.

For rides in the Cairngorms head to **Newtonmore Riding Centre**. On Deeside is the **Glen Tanar Equestrian Centre**, and visitors to Skye should try **Skye Riding Centre**. For a full-blown trekking holiday contact **Highlands Unbridled**.

Visitors taking in the Scottish scenery on horseback

Sailing

Scotland is a country of firths, islands and sea lochs, and the best way to explore them is by boat. You do not necessarily have to be a skilled sailor to do this, as some companies now offer supervised yachting holidays for novices. Visitors also have the option of chartering a yacht. Centres such as **Port Edgar Marina** near Edinburgh or the **Scottish National Watersports Centre** on Cumbrae in the Firth of Clyde offer tuition for beginners, while experienced sailors will find serviced moorings for their own craft in beauty spots up and down the west coast and among the islands.

Kayaking on Loch Eil in the shadow of magnificent Ben Nevis

Wooden sailboat in the Sound of Sleat, just off the Isle of Skye

Watersports

Surfing is not an activity normally associated with Scotland, but a good wetsuit and a sense of determination are all that is needed. Pease Bay in East Lothian is a popular spot, as are some north coast locations such as Dunnet Bay by Thurso and the northwest tip of Lewis. September to October is the best time for the waves. Windsurfing is also a favourite activity. The **Royal Yacht Association** has information on sites across the country. The top venue is the remote island of Tiree, which hosts a major windsurfing event in October every year.

Canoes and kayaks can be rented on lochs and in sheltered bays. The **Scottish Water Ski Centre** has details on the best places to water ski.

DIRECTORY

Cycling and Mountain Biking

BikeTrax
13 Lochrin Place,
Edinburgh EH3 9QX.
Tel (0131) 228 6633.

C.T.C. National Cyclists Organisation
Parklands, Railton Rd,
Guildford, Surrey GU2 9JX.
Tel (0844) 736 8450.
Ⓦ ctc.org.uk

Forestry Commission
Silvan House, 231
Corstorphine Rd,
EdinburghEH12 7AT.
Tel (0845) 367 3787.
Ⓦ forestry.gov.uk

Scottish Cycling
Sir Chris Hoy Velodrome,
Emirates Arena,
1000 London Road,
Glasgow G40 3HY
Tel (0141) 554 6021
Ⓦ britishcycling.org.
uk/scotland

Scottish Cycling Holidays
87 Perth St, Blairgowrie,
Perthshire PH10 6DT.
Tel (01250) 876100.
Ⓦ scotcycle.co.uk

Fishing

Salmon and Trout Association
Siskin, Bonar Bridge,
Sutherland IV24 3AW.
Tel (01863) 766767.
Ⓦ salmon-troutscotland.org

Scottish Anglers National Association
National Game Angling
Centre, The Pier, Loch
Leven, Kinross KY13 8UF.
Tel (01577) 861116.
Ⓦ sana.org.uk

Scottish Federation for Coarse Angling
Tel (07812) 241816.
Ⓦ sfca.co.uk

Scottish Federation of Sea Anglers
Stitchill House, Kelso,
TD5 7TB.
Tel (01573) 470612.
Ⓦ fishpal.com

Hunting

British Association for Shooting & Conservation (Scotland)
Trochry, Dunkeld, Perth-
shire PH8 0DY. **Tel** (01350)
723226. Ⓦ basc.org.uk

Pony Trekking and Horse Riding

Glen Tanar Equestrian Centre
Glen Tanar, Aboyne,
Royal Deeside AB34 5EU.
Tel (01339) 886448.
Ⓦ glentanar.co.uk

Highlands Unbridled
Keepers Cottage,
The Doll, Brora,
Sutherland KW9 6NL.
Tel (01408) 622789.
Ⓦ highlands
unbridled.co.uk

Newtonmore Riding Centre
Biallid Farm, Fort William
Rd, Newtonmore,
Inverness-shire PH20 1BP.
Tel (01540) 670000.

Skye Riding Centre
Suladale, Portree,
Isle of Skye
IV51 9PA.
Tel (01470) 582419.
Ⓦ theisleofskye
trekkingcentre.co.uk

VisitScotland
Tel (0845) 859 1006.
Ⓦ visitscotland.com

Sailing

Port Edgar Marina
South Queensferry
EH30 9SQ.
Tel (0131) 331 3330.
Ⓦ portedgar.co.uk

Scottish National Watersports Centre
Isle of Cumbrae,
Ayrshire
KA28 0HQ.
Tel (01475) 530757.
Ⓦ nationalcentre
cumbrae.org.uk

Watersports

Royal Yacht Association
Caledonia House,
South Gyle,
Edinburgh
EH12 9DQ.
Tel (0131) 317 7388.
Ⓦ ryascotland.org.uk

Scottish Water Ski Centre
Townhill Country Park,
Townhill,
Dunfermline
KY12 0HT.
Tel (01383) 620123
Ⓦ waterskiscotland.
co.uk

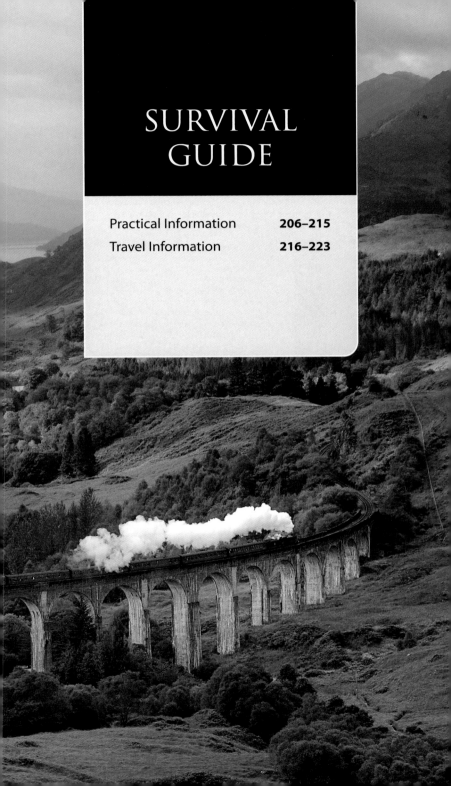

SURVIVAL
GUIDE

PRACTICAL INFORMATION

To enjoy Scotland fully, it is best to know something about the workings of everyday life. The range of facilities for tourists in Scotland has never been better – indeed tourism has become a major part of the country's economy – and VisitScotland is continually promoting better services around the country. This chapter gives advice about when best to visit Scotland; customs and immigration requirements; where to find tourist information; what to do or whom to turn to if things go wrong; banking and communications; and how to get around the country by public and private transport, including ferries to the islands.

Whether or not you find Scotland an expensive country will depend on the exchange rate between the pound and your own currency. Visitors travelling from London will find that costs are generally lower in Scotland's capital. Glasgow offers even better value for money.

Visitors' Centre in Callander, at the heart of the Trossachs

When to Visit

Scotland's climate is very changeable (see pp40–43). May and June are usually drier than July and August, although the latter are usually the warmest months. The west coast tends to be mild and wet, while the east coast is cool and drier.

Scotland's towns and cities are all year destinations, but many attractions open only between Easter and October. The main family holiday months, July and August, and public holidays (see p42) are always busy. Hotels are crammed at Christmas and New Year, particularly in Edinburgh for the Hogmanay street party (see p43). Spring and autumn offer a moderate climate and a lack of crowds. Whatever the time of year, it is wise to get an up-to-date weather forecast

Sign for the Mountain Rescue

before you set off on foot to remote hills or mountainous locations. Walkers and climbers can be surprised by the weather, and the Mountain Rescue services are frequently called out due to unexpectedly severe conditions. Weather reports are given on television and radio, in newspapers and by a weather phone service (see p201).

Insurance

It is sensible to take out travel insurance before travelling, to cover cancellation or curtailment of your holiday, theft or loss of money and possessions, and the cost of any medical treatment (see p210). If your country has a reciprocal medical arrangement with the UK you can obtain free treatment under the National Health Service. Australia, New Zealand and everywhere in the European Union (EU) has this arrangement. North American health plans, and student identity cards may give some protection against incurred costs, but always check the small print. If you want to drive a car in Scotland, it is advisable to take out fully comprehensive insurance. You must carry a valid driver's licence. If you are not an EU citizen, you must have an international driver's licence, available through the AAA for those in the US.

Advance Booking

Out of season, you should have few problems booking accommodation or transport at short notice, but in high season always try to book ahead if possible. Before you travel, contact **VisitScotland**, www.visitscotland.com, or a travel agent, for advice and information.

Customs and Immigration

A valid passport is needed to enter the United Kingdom. Visitors from the European Union (EU), the United States, Canada, Australia and New Zealand do not require visas to enter the UK, nor any inoculations or vaccinations. Once within the UK, visitors are free to travel to and from Scotland, England, Wales and Northern Ireland without passing any other frontier formalities.

When you arrive at any international air or sea port in the UK, you will find separate queues at immigration control: one for EU nationals and several others for everyone else. Scotland is a member of the EU, which means that anyone arriving from an EU member country can pass through a blue channel. Random checks are still made, however, for illegal goods, especially drugs. Travellers entering from outside the EU have to pass through the

Standard tourist information sign

◀ The Jacobite Steam Train, crossing the Glenfinnan Viaduct near the shores of Loch Shiel usual customs channels. Go through the green channel if you have nothing to declare over the customs allowances for overseas visitors, and the red channel if you have goods to declare. If you are unsure of importation restrictions, go through the red channel. Full details of these restrictions are available from HM Customs and Excise in London. Beware – never carry luggage or parcels through customs for someone else.

Tourist Information

Tourist bookings in Scotland are handled by **VisitScotland** via its call centre and website. The organization also has a base in central London. In addition to these, every region of Scotland has its own tourist board, providing information about local accommodation, entertainment and places of interest. Smaller, subsidiary tourist information offices can be found in many towns and public places, and at some of the principal locations of historical interest. Look out for the tourist information symbol, indicating an office. Often the best source of information for events in the area, these offices will also book accommodation for visitors. Pick up one of their brochures that give comprehensive listings of Tourist Board-accredited places to stay. The British Tourist Authority operates offices overseas.

Disabled Travellers

The facilities on offer in Scotland for disabled visitors are steadily improving. An increasing number of hotels and guesthouses now offer wheelchair access. This information is given in the headings for each entry throughout the guide. Given advance notice, FirstScotRail (see p219), ferry or coach (long-distance bus) staff will help any disabled passengers. Ask a travel agent about the Disabled Persons Railcard, which entitles the holder to discounted rail fares on services across the country. **Hertz Rent A Car** offers hand-controlled vehicles without any extra cost (see p223). For permission to use any disabled parking space, you need to display a special sign in your car.

Tourism for All is a UK charity dedicated to improving accessibility. It runs an excellent website offering information on accessibility throughout Britain: www.openbritain.net.

Visitors from the US can telephone the **Society for the Advancement of Travel for the Handicapped (SATH)** on (212) 447 7284 or visit www.sath.org before leaving. SATH publishes *ACCESS to Travel*, a magazine full of information.

DIRECTORY
Tourist Boards

VisitScotland
For brochures to any area in Scotland, or to book accommodation contact:
Tel (0845) 859 1006.
w visitscotland.com

Aberdeen & Grampian
Tel (01224) 269180.
w aberdeen-grampian.com

Angus & Dundee
Tel (01382) 527527.
w angusanddundee.co.uk

Argyll, The Isles, Loch Lomond, Stirling & The Trossachs
Tel (01786) 432003.
w visitscottishheartlands.com

Ayrshire & Arran
Tel (08452) 255121.
w ayrshire-arran.com

Dumfries & Galloway
Tel (0845) 859 1006.
w visitdumfriesandgalloway.co.uk

Edinburgh & Lothians
Tel (0845) 859 1006.
w edinburgh.org

Greater Glasgow & Clyde Valley
Tel (0141) 204 4400.
w seeglasgow.com

Highlands of Scotland
Tel (01463) 252401.
w visithighlands.com

Kingdom of Fife
Tel (01334) 472021.
w standrews.co.uk

Orkney Islands
Tel (01856) 872856.
w visitorkney.com

Perthshire
Tel (01738) 450600.
w perthshire.co.uk

Scottish Borders
Tel (01721) 723159.
w scot-borders.co.uk

Shetland Islands
Tel (01595) 693434.
w visitshetland.com

Western Isles
Tel (01851) 703088.
w visithebrides.com

Tobermory harbour on the Isle of Mull, popular with tourists

Glamis Castle, one of the sights that charges admission to visitors

Travelling with Children

Public holidays and school holidays (July–mid-August) have most to offer in the way of children's entertainment. Many places have activities suitable for children over the Christmas period, particularly pantomimes. Discounts for children and family tickets are available for travel, theatre and other entertainments. ScotRail allows two children aged between 5 and 15 to travel for free with an adult.

Accommodation that provides family rooms *(see pp172– 7)* is generally child friendly, or opt for self-catering (efficiency apartments). Many hotels provide baby-sitting or baby-listening services, and offer reductions or free accommodation for the very young.

Many restaurants welcome children, providing highchairs and special menus *(see pp181– 9)*. Pubs often admit children, if

Playing with interactive exhibits at Edinburgh's Museum of Childhood

accompanied by an adult. The legal drinking age is 18.

Admission Charges

These vary widely, from a nominal fee to a more substantial charge for popular attractions. Reductions are often available for groups, senior citizens, children or students. The majority of local churches, museums and art galleries are free, unless a special exhibition is showing, but donations are frequently expected. Some attractions in Scotland are run privately, either as commercial ventures or on a charitable basis.

Opening Hours

Many shops in Scotland open on Sundays, particularly in the city centres. In the Western Isles, however, Sunday is still very much regarded as a day of rest, and shops, cafés and restaurants are likely to be closed. Monday to Friday hours are around 9am to 6pm, but shop hours do vary, opening late one evening a week – usually Thursday. Museums and art galleries generally open for fewer hours on Sundays. Many attractions open on public and bank holidays, but almost all are closed on Christmas Day and New Year's Day.

VAT and Refunds

Value added tax (VAT) is charged at 20 per cent on most goods and services. When leaving the

UK, non-residents can redeem VAT on goods purchased from shops in the Retail Export Scheme. Refunds will be given if goods are faulty and are returned with the receipt as proof of purchase.

Student Travellers

Full-time students who have an International Student Identity Card (ISIC) are often entitled to discounts on travel, sports facilities and entrance fees. North American

Student ISIC card

students can also get medical cover but it may be very basic *(see p210)*. ISIC cards are available from **STA Travel**, or the **National Union of Students**. Inexpensive accommodation is also available (out of term time) at the university halls of residence in the main cities. This is a good way of staying in central locations when on a tight budget.

An **International Youth Hostel Federation** card enables you to stay in one of Scotland's many youth hostels. Contact the **Scottish Youth Hostels Association** directly *(see Directory)* for more detailed information.

National Trust for Scotland

Many of Scotland's historic buildings, parks, gardens, and vast tracts of countryside and coastline are cared for by the **National Trust for Scotland**. Entrance fees can often be relatively high compared to fees at other sights, so if you plan on visiting several NTS properties, it may be worth taking out annual membership, which allows free access thereafter to all NTS properties, as well as free admission to National Trust properties in England, Wales and Northern Ireland. Membership also includes a sticker for free parking at all NTS sites, along with a Trust magazine three times a year. Be aware, however, that many NTS

Charlotte Square, Edinburgh, home of the National Trust for Scotland

properties close during the winter months, so check ahead before visiting.

Historic Scotland

An agency within the Scottish Government, **Historic Scotland**, manages some 400 key heritage sites around the country. Admission prices, though generally very reasonable, soon add up if you have an interest in Scottish history, making their annual pass well worth considering. Both Edinburgh Castle (see pp64–5) and Stirling Castle (see pp124–5) are included in the pass, while a membership pack, a quarterly magazine, members only tours and lectures, and discounts at Historic Scotland shops and cafés also help justify the cost. Members also receive half-price admission at over 500 other historic attractions in England and Wales.

Electricity

The voltage in Scotland is 220/240 AC, 50 Hz. The electrical plugs have three square pins and take fuses of 3, 5 and 13 amps. In order to use your foreign appliances, such as hair dryers, you will need an adaptor. Most hotel bathrooms have two-pronged sockets for electric shavers.

Smoking and Alcohol

It is illegal to smoke in all public places in Scotland, including public transport systems, taxis, train stations, theatres and cinemas, bars, restaurants and shops.

There is a general ban on drinking in public in Greater Glasgow and the Clyde Valley area, although public drinking is discouraged throughout Scotland. This ban is usually lifted for the New Year street party at Hogmanay (31 December).

Conversion Chart

Britain is officially metricated in line with the rest of Europe. However imperial measures are still very much in common usage, including road distances and speed limits (measured in miles and miles per hour). Imperial pints and gallons are 20 per cent larger than US measures.

Imperial to metric
1 inch = 2.5 centimetres
1 foot = 30 centimetres
1 mile = 1.6 kilometres
1 ounce = 28 grams
1 pint = 0.6 litres
1 gallon = 4.5 litres

Metric to imperial
1 millimetre = 0.04 inch
1 centimetre = 0.4 inch
1 metre = 3 feet 3 inches
1 kilometre = 0.6 mile
1 gram = 0.04 ounce
1 kilogram = 2.2 pounds

Time

Scotland is on Greenwich Mean Time (GMT) during the winter months – that is, five hours ahead of Eastern Standard Time and ten hours behind Sydney. From the middle of March to the end of October, the clocks go forward one hour to British Summer Time (which is one hour ahead of GMT). To check the correct time, you can dial 123 to contact the Speaking Clock service.

DIRECTORY

Historic Scotland
Tel (0131) 668 8999.
w historic-scotland.gov.uk

National Trust for Scotland (NTS)
Tel (0844) 493 2100.
w nts.org.uk

Student Travellers

International Youth Hostel Federation
Tel (01707) 324170.
w hihostels.com

National Union of Students
Tel (0131) 556 6598.
w nus.org.uk/en/nus-scotland/

Scottish Youth Hostels Association
Tel (08452) 93 73 73.
w syha.org.uk

STA Travel
Tel (0333) 321 0099.
w statravel.co.uk

Embassies and Consulates

Australian High Commission
Australia House, Strand, London WC2B 4LA.
Tel (0207) 379 4334.
w uk.embassy.gov.au

Canadian High Commission
Macdonald House, 1 Grosvenor Square, London W1K 4AB.
Tel (020) 7258 6600.

New Zealand High Commission
New Zealand House, 80 Haymarket, London SW1Y 4TQ.
Tel (0207) 930 8422.

United States Consulate
3 Regent Terrace, Edinburgh EH7 5BW.
Tel (0131) 556 8315.
w edinburgh.usconsulate.gov

Bars lining historic street in the town centre of Perth

Personal Security and Health

Like any other country, Scotland has its share of social problems, but it is very unlikely that you will come across any violence. If you do encounter difficulties, do not hesitate to contact the police for help. The UK's National Health Service (NHS) can be relied upon for an emergency or routine treatment. However, you may have to pay for treatment if your country has no reciprocal arrangement with the UK. Below is some guidance for enjoying a trouble-free visit.

Hospitals and Medical Treatment

All visitors to Scotland, especially those from outside the European Union (EU), are strongly advised to take out medical insurance against the cost of emergency hospital care, repatriation and specialists' fees. Emergency medical treatment in an NHS Accident and Emergency department is free, but additional medical care could prove expensive. US visitors should check with their insurance companies to be sure they are covered.

EU residents and nationals of some other Commonwealth and European countries are entitled to free medical treatment under the NHS, though the process is bureaucratic. Before travelling, obtain a European Health Insurance Card (EHIC) from a post office; show this to anyone treating you. Be aware, however, that some treatments are not covered, and repatriation is not included, so medical insurance is preferable. For advice, or if you're unsure whether to call an ambulance, call the NHS 24 helpline (see Directory).

If you need to see a dentist, you will have to pay. The cost will vary depending on your entitlement to NHS treatment. Emergency dental treatment is available in some hospitals.

Pharmacists

You can buy a wide range of medicines without prescription from pharmacies in Scotland. Boots is the best known and largest supplier, with branches in most towns. Many medicines

A traditional, privately owned pharmacy in Leith, Edinburgh

are available only with a doctor's prescription, which you must take to a dispensing chemist (pharmacist). Either bring your own supply or ask your doctor to write out the generic name of the drug (as opposed to the brand name). If you are entitled to an NHS prescription, you will be charged a standard rate; without this, you will be charged the full cost. Ask for a receipt for any insurance claim. Some pharmacies stay open until midnight. Doctors' surgeries (offices) are usually open mornings and early evenings. Hospital Accident and Emergency departments are always open.

The Midge

Being bitten by midges is one of the most common hazards for visitors to Scotland. The chance of encountering these tiny biting flies is particularly heightened around lochs and on the coast, as they love damp conditions. They breed between April and October, and are at their worst at the start and end of the day. There is no way of escaping them altogether, but to ensure that you suffer only the minimum of bites, apply insect repellent (such as Autan) and avoid sitting near bright lights after dark. If they really are a nuisance you may want to invest in a midge net.

Crime and Suitable Precautions

Scotland is not a dangerous place for visitors, and it is most unlikely that your stay will be blighted by crime. There are, however, practical steps that can be taken to help you avoid loss of property or personal injury. Take good care of your belongings at all times. Make sure your possessions are adequately insured before you arrive. Never leave them unattended in public places. Keep your valuables well concealed, especially in crowds. In cinemas or theatres, keep handbags on your lap, not on the floor. And in pubs, do not put your bag over the back of

Woman police constable

Police constable

Traffic police officer

your chair; use the bag clips on the underside of tables where available.

It is advisable not to carry too much cash or jewellery with you; leave it in the safe in the hotel instead. Or keep most of your cash in a money belt worn under your clothing, with smaller amounts more easily accessible in a shoulder bag or pocket. Pickpockets tend to frequent crowded places like markets, busy shops and public transport.

If you are travelling alone at night try to avoid deserted and poorly lit buildings and places such as back streets and car parks. When driving, try to park in well-lit areas where it will be difficult for someone to tamper with your car without being noticed. A steering wheel lock is a good visual deterrent. If you are the victim of crime, contact your local police station. It is often necessary to report a crime in order to claim on insurance.

Women Travelling Alone

It is not unusual in Scotland for women to travel unaccompanied, or to visit a bar or restaurant with a group of female friends. Nor is it especially dangerous. But caution is advisable in deserted places, especially after dark. Try to avoid using public transport when there is just one other passenger or a group of young men. It is best to summon a licensed taxi (see p223) rather than to walk through a lonely area of a city at night, especially if you do not know the area well. It is illegal to carry any offensive weapons, including knives, guns, mace or tear-gas, even for self-defence. Personal alarms are permitted, however.

Police car

Ambulance

Fire engine

Police

The sight of a traditional British bobby patrolling the streets in a tall hat is now less common than the police patrol car, usually with wailing sirens and flashing lights. But the old-fashioned police constable does still exist in Scotland, particularly in rural areas and crowded city centres, and continues to be courteous, approachable and helpful. Unlike in many other countries, the police in Scotland do not carry guns. If you are lost, the traditional advice to ask a policeman or woman still applies. Traffic wardens may also be able to help with directions. If you have lost property it is worth contacting the local police station as someone may have handed it in.

In a crisis, dial 999 to reach police, fire and ambulance services who are on call 24 hours a day. Calls are free from any public or private phone, but they should only be made in real emergencies. In Scotland's coastal areas this number will also put you in touch with Britain's voluntary coastguard rescue service, the RNLI (Royal National Lifeboat Institution).

Logo of the Royal National Lifeboat Institution

Lost Property

If you are unlucky enough to lose anything or have anything stolen, go straight to the nearest police station to report your loss. If you want to claim on insurance for any theft, you will need a written report from the local police. All of the main bus and train stations have lost property centres. Most hotels disclaim all responsibility for valuables not kept in their safe.

It is advisable to make photo-copies of your vital documents such as passports and travel papers. If you lose your passport, contact your embassy or consulate in either Edinburgh or London (see p209).

DIRECTORY

Police, Fire and Ambulance Services

Tel 999. Calls are free (24-hour phoneline).

Hospital Accident and Emergency Departments

Aberdeen Royal Infirmary
Tel (0845) 456 6000.

Edinburgh Royal Infirmary
Tel (0131) 536 1000.

Glasgow Royal Infirmary
Tel (0141) 211 4000.

Inverness Raigmore
Tel (01463) 704000.

NHS 24 Helpline
Tel (0845) 424 2424.

Perth Royal Infirmary
Tel (01738) 623311.

Emergency Dental Care

Edinburgh Dental Hospital
Tel (0131) 536 4800.

Disabled Helpline

The Disability Helpline
Tel (0808) 800 3333.
w scope.org.uk

Banking and Currency

Visitors to most Scottish cities and large towns will find a number of options for exchanging currency and cashing travellers' cheques. High-street banks, travel agencies and bureaux de change all offer this service at different exchange and commission rates. Cashpoints (ATMs) can be found at many locations and can be used to dispense cash via your debit card. Credit cards and traveller's cheques are the safest methods of bringing currency with you to Scotland.

One of many banks to offer bureau de change facilities

Bureaux De Change

Although bureaux de change are often more conveniently located than banks and have longer opening hours, the exchange rates can vary considerably and commission charges can be high.

The reputable firms such as **International Currency Exchange** and **American Express** offer good exchange facilities. International Currency Exchange has just one branch at Edinburgh Airport; both **Thomas Cook** and American Express have branches throughout Scotland.

Scottish Banks

Branches of the three main Scottish banks (Royal Bank of Scotland, Bank of Scotland and Clydesdale), will be found in all cities and many towns. English banks such as NatWest and Barclays are rare outside the main cities. Most banks offer exchange facilities, but proof of identity may be required and the commission charges will vary.

Clydesdale Bank logo

Banks

Every large town and city in Scotland should have a branch of at least one of the following banks – Bank of Scotland, Royal Bank of Scotland, Lloyds TSB Scotland, Girobank and Clydesdale.

Most banks have a cashpoint (ATM), as do many building societies, shops and garages, from which you can obtain money with a bank or credit card and your personal identification number (PIN). Some of the most modern machines have easy-to-read computerized instructions in several languages. Cardholders from principal English banks, such as NatWest, HSBC, Lloyds TSB and Barclays, can withdraw money from most banks in Scotland. Check that your bank card is compatible with the cashpoint you are using or you may be charged a fee or have your card rejected.

You can also obtain money by contacting your own bank and asking them to wire cash to the nearest Scottish bank. Branches of American Express will do this for you. Visitors from the US can have cash dispatched through **Western Union** to a bank or post office. Take your passport as proof of identity. Banking hours vary from bank to bank, but the minimum opening times are 9:30am to 3:30pm Monday to Friday.

Credit Cards

Credit and store cards are widely accepted throughout Scotland, but some smaller shops, guesthouses and cafés may not take them. VISA is the most widely used card, but MasterCard, Diners Club and American Express are also accepted. You may be able to obtain a cash advance against your credit card at an ATM, although the interest rate may be quite high.

Traveller's Cheques

Traveller's cheques can be purchased at American Express and exchanged at their offices. Very few businesses accept traveller's cheques any more, and exchanging them can be inconvenient.

Bank of Scotland logo

The Royal Bank of Scotland
Royal Bank of Scotland logo

NatWest logo

DIRECTORY

Exchange Facilities

American Express
Tel (0870) 850 7814.

International Currency Exchange
Tel (0844) 800 3974.

Thomas Cook
Tel (0844) 335 7260.

Western Union
Tel (0808) 234 3943.

Currency

Britain's currency is the pound sterling (£), which is divided into 100 pence (p). There are no exchange controls in Britain, so you may bring in and take out as much cash as you like.

Scotland's own currency, the pound Scots, was replaced by the pound sterling in 1707. Today, Scotland has its own pound sterling notes, which are printed by the Bank of Scotland, the Royal Bank of Scotland and the

Clydesdale Bank. The notes represent the same value as an English note and can be accepted elsewhere in Britain, although it is usually with reluctance. Note: the Scottish £1 note will not be accepted outside Scotland. Bank of England and Northern Ireland notes can be used throughout Scotland; you will receive change in Scottish notes. All three countries use Bank of England coins.

Bank Notes

Scottish notes are produced in denominations of £1, £5, £10, £20, £50 and £100. Always get small denominations, as some shops may refuse the larger notes. Although Scotland has a £1 note, the English £1 coin, and all Bank of England currency, is legal tender.

£100 note

£10 note

£20 note

£1 note

£5 note

Coinage

Coins currently in use are £2, £1, 50p, 20p, 10p, 5p, 2p and 1p. The same coins are produced and accepted throughout the UK.

2 pounds (£2)

1 pound (£1)

50 pence (50p)

20 pence (20p)

10 pence (10p)

5 pence (5p)

2 pence (2p)

1 penny (1p)

Communications and Media

With continuously improving telecommunication systems staying in contact and making plans while travelling has never been easier. The telephone system in Scotland is efficient and inexpensive. Charges depend on when, where and for how long you talk. Mobile phone networks offer excellent coverage of most of the country, and Wi-Fi is available in most place, often free of charge. Mail services are generally considered reliable, even to more remote areas.

Traditional phone boxes outside the walls of Edinburgh Castle

Public Telephones

You can pay for a payphone using coins or a card. Payphones accept 10p, 20p, 50p and £1 pieces, while newer phones also accept £2 coins. The minimum cost of a call is 60p. If you expect a call to be short, use 10p or 20p pieces, as payphones only return unused coins. Some payphones accept credit and debit cards. The minimum fee for local and national calls is £1.20 and £1.50 for international calls, calls to premium rate numbers, mobile phones and calls made through the operator.

Directories, such as *Yellow Pages* and *Thomson Local*, list local businesses and services. They can be found at local Post Offices, libraries and often at your hotel. A number of operators now offer telephone directory enquiry services at different levels of cost to the caller.

Mobile Phones

Mobile phone use is all but universal among Scots who have four major cellular networks to choose from: **EE** (formerly Orange and T-Mobile) is the most popular network, followed by **O2**, **Vodafone** and then **3**. O2 usually has the best coverage in the remoter parts of Scotland, where all network services can be patchy.

Visitors with a phone that works on European frequencies should be able to use their home number automatically via a local network. Do check the roaming charges with your provider before leaving home – they can be prohibitive. It may be worth purchasing a SIM card from a mobile phone shop; prices are very low and usually include some credit. You may find that your handset is not compatible or hasn't been unlocked, in which case the best option may be to buy the most basic phone available, along with a prepaid plan (also called "pay-as-you-go").

Calls in Scotland are charged according to outgoing calls; incoming calls are free no matter where they originate.

Expect a call on the most basic prepaid plan to cost around 15p per minute.

Internet

All cities and most small towns across Scotland now have some form of public access to computers and the Internet. Free Internet access is often available at main library branches. Access is very cheap and is most reasonable during off-peak times.

Almost all hotels and many B&Bs and hostels provide Wi-Fi, sometimes free, as do many cafés and restaurants throughout the country. Wi-Fi hotspots can be found in the main cities in some public areas such as railway stations and airports – look out for the black-and-white symbol.

Collecting the mail via Postbus in rural Scotland

Postal Services

Besides main Post Offices that offer all the mail services available, there are many sub-Post Offices in newsagents, grocery stores and general information centres, particularly in more isolated areas and smaller towns. In many villages

24-hour Internet access at the easyInternetcafé

1st-class airmail letter

1st-class stamp

2nd-class stamp

Greetings stamps featuring characters from children's fiction

Airmail provides a speedy and cost-effective method of communication. Aerogrammes go first class anywhere in the world and cost the same regardless of destination. They take about three to four days to reach European cities, and between four and seven days for destinations elsewhere. All mail sent within Europe goes via airmail, while overseas mail rates are classed by weight. Sending post overseas by surface mail may be more economical, but it can take anywhere up to 12 weeks for it to reach its final destination. The Post Office offers an express delivery service called **Parcelforce Worldwide**. Available from most main Post Offices, Parcelforce is comparable in price to many private courier companies.

the Post Office is also the only shop. Post Offices are usually open from 9am to 5:30pm Monday to Friday, and until 12:30pm on Saturday. Mailboxes – in all shapes and sizes but always red – are found throughout cities, towns and villages. These may be either free-standing "pillar boxes" or wall safes, both painted bright red. Some pillar boxes have separate slots, one for overseas and first-class mail, another for second-class mail. Initials on older mail boxes indicate who was monarch at that time. Mailboxes are often embedded in Post Office walls. Collections are usually made several times a day during weekdays (less often on Saturdays and rarely on Sundays and public holidays); times are marked on the box.

Stamps can be bought at many outlets, including supermarkets and petrol stations. Hotels often have mailboxes at their reception. When writing to an address anywhere in the UK always include the postcode. Letters and postcards can be sent either first or second class within the UK. First-class service is more expensive but quicker, with most letters reaching their destination the following day (except Sunday); second-class mail takes a day or two longer.

Pillar box

Newspapers and Magazines

National newspapers in Scotland fall into two categories: serious publications, such as Edinburgh's *The Scotsman* or Glasgow's *The Herald*; and those that are heavy on gossip, such as *The Sun* or *The Daily Record*. Weekend newspapers, such as *Scotland on Sunday* and the *Sunday Herald*, are more expensive than dailies, with many supplements including sections on arts, restaurants, entertainment, travel and reviews.

Buying a tabloid newspaper from a stand in Glasgow

Television and Radio

The BBC (British Broadcasting Corporation) operates eight TV channels, most of which are also available in HD (high definition). BBC Alba is a part-time Scottish Gaelic digital-only channel. The BBC's main rivals are ITV, Channel 4 and Channel 5, but the BBC is the only one that does not show commericials. The BBC operates a number of radio stations including BBC Radio Scotland, and services for Shetland and Orkney, and in Gaelic. There are BBC digital-only stations as well as numerous competitors and local stations.

DIRECTORY

Mobile Phones

3
Tel (0800) 358 8460.
🅆 three.co.uk

EE
Tel (0800) 956 6000. 🅆 ee.co.uk

02
Tel (08448) 090222. 🅆 02.co.uk

Vodafone
Tel (08700) 700191.
🅆 vodafone.co.uk

Useful Numbers

Emergency Calls
Tel 999. Police, Fire, Ambulance, Coastguard, Mountain and Cave Rescue.

Directory Enquiries
Tel 118500 (BT).
International Tel 118505 (BT).
Directory Heaven Tel 118247.

Operator Assistance
Tel 100. International Tel 155.

International Dialling Codes
Tel 00 followed by country code: Australia (61), Canada (1), Ireland (353), New Zealand (64), South Africa (27), United States (1).

Postal Services

Parcelforce Worldwide
Tel (08448) 004466.
🅆 parcelforce.com

Royal Mail
Tel (08457) 740740.
🅆 royalmail.com

TRAVEL INFORMATION

As the UK is an international gateway for air and sea traffic, travelling to Scotland poses few problems. There are direct flights from North America and continental Europe. Coach travel from Europe via the ferries is a cheap, albeit slow, form of transport. Travelling by train using the Channel Tunnel is an efficient way of crossing to the UK. Travelling within Scotland itself is fairly easy. Internal flights are available between cities on the mainland, and also to the island groups. Another way to island-hop is to take the ferries. There is an extensive network of roads in urban areas and renting a car can be the best way of travelling. The inter-city rail network is limited in Scotland, but a small network of trains serves the country, some with scenic routes. Coach travel is the cheapest option; services run between most cities.

Check-in desks at Glasgow International Airport

Arriving by Air

Edinburgh and Glasgow are the principal airports in Scotland. The four other international airports are Prestwick, Aberdeen, Inverness and Sumburgh on Shetland.

Air France, **bmi regional**, **KLM** and **Lufthansa** offer direct flights from continental Europe. Glasgow and Edinburgh have the most frequent services, with direct and indirect flights to many major European destinations including Paris, Dublin and Brussels.

A number of transatlantic airlines offer direct services to Glasgow International Airport, including **British Airways**, **American Airlines**, **United Airlines** and **Air Canada**. Flights to Edinburgh and Glasgow are available from long-haul destinations such as North Africa, South Africa, Australia and the Far East. These are routed via a European capital, often Brussels or Amsterdam.

Flights direct to Glasgow can be expensive and it may be a more economical option to fly to London and then take a domestic flight north. These flights can cost as little as £29 one way. Alternatively, take the train north; it's only four hours to Edinburgh and just over five to Glasgow. It is advisable to book in advance for the best deals *(see p219)*.

The airports at Glasgow, Edinburgh and Aberdeen offer good facilities, including banking, shops, cafés, hotels and restaurants, as well as parking. Each of these airports is connected to the nearest city centres by regular and reliable shuttle bus services.

Travelling Within the UK from Scotland

Flights from Scotland to other British destinations operate from all the mainland international airports. British Airways offers express services to London's Heathrow and Gatwick airports. bmi also flies direct to Heathrow. **easyJet** and **Ryanair** operate between Scotland and the English airports of Luton, Stansted and London City.

There are also direct flights to other major cities in the UK, including Manchester, Newcastle upon Tyne, Leeds, Birmingham, Belfast and Cardiff, and to some of the smaller ones such as Bristol and Southampton. These flights can

Passengers from abroad passing through International Arrivals

Airport	ℹ Information	Distance to City Centre	Taxi Fare to City Centre	Public Transport to City Centre
Aberdeen	(0844) 571 7410	7 miles (11 km)	£13	Bus: 30 min Taxi: 20 min
Edinburgh	(0844) 481 8989	8 miles (13 km)	£18	Bus: 25 min Taxi: 20 min
Glasgow	(0844) 481 5555	8 miles (13 km)	£17	Bus: 25 min Taxi: 20 min
Prestwick	(0871) 223 0700	29 miles (47 km)	£42	Train: 45 min Taxi: 40 min

The terminal at Glasgow International Airport

be relatively expensive, so unless saving time is a priority, the cost may be prohibitive.

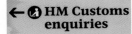

Sign directing passengers to locations within an airport

← 🅗 HM Customs enquiries

Directions to the department for information on customs

Internal Flights

Scotland's size means that internal air travel is quick, but it can prove an expensive mode of travel compared to rail, coach or car. There are good air connections between the Highlands and central Scotland. When travelling to the islands off the coast of Scotland, flying becomes a particularly viable option. **Flybe** and **Loganair**, both subsidiaries of British Airways, provide regular flights from all the major cities on the mainland to the Western Isles, Orkney Islands and Shetland Islands.

Transport from the Airports

Scotland's main international airports lie on the outskirts of Glasgow, Edinburgh and Aberdeen, where there are efficient transportation links. Taxis are the most convenient form of door-to-door travel, but they are also fairly expensive.

Coaches or buses provide cheaper transport to the town centres, though during rush hour or heavy traffic, coaches, buses and taxis may be slow. **National Express** as well as **Scottish Citylink** (see p219) provide direct coach services from the major airports to various destinations.

Prestwick International is served by its own train station; a service runs to Glasgow city centre every half an hour.

Air Fares

Air fares to Scotland are usually at their highest from June to September. The best deals are available from November to April, excluding the Christmas period – if you want to travel then, you should book well in advance.

Apex (Advance Purchase Excursion) fares are often the best value, though they must be booked a month ahead and are subject to restrictions, such as minimum and maximum stays and no refunds. Charter flights offer even cheaper seats, but with less flexibility.

Promotional fares are often available, and it is worth checking direct with the airlines for special offers. Cheap deals are sometimes offered by package operators and are advertised in newspapers and travel magazines. Students, those under 26 years old and senior citizens may be eligible for a discount. Children and babies travel for less.

If you choose a discount fare, always buy from a reputable operator, and check with the airline to ensure your seat has been confirmed. Packages may also be worth considering for cost-savings, even if you enjoy independent travel. Airlines and tour operators can put together a great range of flexible deals to suit your needs, sometimes with car rental or rail travel included. This can often be cheaper than arranging transport once you have arrived. A small airport tax is imposed on all those departing from British airports.

DIRECTORY

Arriving by Air

Air Canada
Tel (0871) 220 1111.
🅦 aircanada.com

Air France
Tel (0871) 663 3777.
🅦 airfrance.co.uk

American Airlines
Tel (0844) 499 7300.
🅦 americanairlines.co.uk

British Airways
Tel (0844) 493 0787.
🅦 britishairways.com

bmi regional
Tel (0844) 417 2600.
🅦 bmiregional.com

easyJet
Tel (0871) 989 1366.
🅦 easyjet.com

Flybe and Loganair
Tel (0871) 700 2000.
🅦 flybe.com

KLM
Tel (0871) 231 0000.
🅦 klm.com

Lufthansa
Tel (0781) 945 9747.
🅦 lufthansa.com

Ryanair
Tel (0871) 246 0000.
🅦 ryanair.com

United Airlines
Tel (0845) 607 6760.
🅦 united.com

Rental car collection point at Glasgow International Airport

Travelling by Rail and Road

Scotland has a privatized rail network, FirstScotRail, that covers most of the country and is generally efficient and reliable. A quarter-hourly service operates between Edinburgh and Glasgow, and lines radiate from both cities, with frequent services to many Scottish destinations and to most parts of England. Journey times to London are just over four hours from Edinburgh and just over five from Glasgow. Scotland also has a good coach (long-distance bus) service that is generally cheaper than the trains, although journeys can be slow. Weekend rail and coach services are popular, so book ahead.

The Flying Scotsman, one of the many swift inter-city train services

The Virgin Superfast train at Edinburgh's Waverley station

Train Tickets

Allow plenty of time to buy your ticket, and always ask about any special offers or reduced fares. Try to buy your tickets for intercity routes at least 14 days in advance. You'll find the best offers online. For shorter trips, reasonable fares are available from station ticket booths and machines on the day of travel. First-class tickets cost about one-third more than standard fares although sometimes first-class can be good value as prices depend on availability. It's usually cheaper to buy two singles on long-distance routes. ScotRail has some discounted fares; up to two children aged between 5 and 15 can travel free with each adult who purchases a "kids go free" ticket. Groups of more than three should enquire about discount fares.

Rail Passes

If you plan to travel a lot by train, it is a good idea to buy a rail pass. These can be purchased from agents such as **Rail Europe**, which operates in Europe, the US and Canada.

There are different passes available to suit every need. The

Freedom of Scotland pass allows unlimited rail travel around the country for a set period. The Highland Rover permits travel on the West Highland lines and the Inverness-to-Kyle line. The Central Scotland Rover is for use between Glasgow's Queen Street and Edinburgh's Waverley station on any three out of seven consecutive days. The passes are also valid on some coach and ferry services and on the Glasgow Underground (see p100).

One-third price discounts are available for 16- to 25-year-olds using a Young Person's Rail Card. The Senior Railcard and Disabled Railcard entitle the holder to a one-third discount on most fares. There are also railcards for 16- to 18-year-olds and families.

A leaflet about the steam train

General Tips

Britain's fastest and most comfortable trains are those on the inter-city routes. These popular services book up quickly. It is always advisable to reserve your seat in advance, especially if you want to travel at peak times such as Friday evenings and Sunday afternoons. Inter-city trains are fast, with a limited number of stops. The trip from Edinburgh to Glasgow, for example, takes around 50 minutes. A reduced service is usually in operation on Sundays and public holidays. Porters are often scarce at British stations, although trolleys are usually available for passengers to help themselves. If you are disabled and need assistance, contact the relevant train company before the day you travel.

Rail Map of Scotland

Key

— Principal routes
— Other routes
● Rail junction
○ Train station

Scenic Train Rides

When motor transportation made many rural railways redundant in the mid-20th century, picturesque sections of track, and many of the old steam engines, were rescued and restored to working order. Tourist offices or train ticket offices can provide you with information on where the lines are, and how much it will cost to take a ride on the trains.

Ride the Jacobite steam train from Fort William to Mallaig, passing over a spectacular viaduct at Glenfinnan; or take the Strathspey Steam Railway from Aviemore to Boat of Garten.

The Jacobite steam train on its picturesque journey to Mallaig

International Coach Travel

Although travelling by coach (long-distance bus) is cheap compared with other methods of transport, it is not the most comfortable way of crossing Europe. If you have a lot of spare time, however, and want to stop off en route at other destinations, it can be a convenient mode of transport. The ticket usually covers all parts of the journey, including the ferry or Channel Tunnel.

National Coach Network

The largest coach operators in Scotland are **Scottish Citylink**, **Stagecoach** and **National Express**, which runs services only between the main cities and to destinations in the rest of Great Britain. Buy a reserved ticket to guarantee a seat.

Discounts are available for full-time students or anyone under 25 with a coach pass. Over-50s and children aged between 5 and 15 years also qualify for reductions. Under-5s travel free on Scotland's national coaches. Brit Xplorer passes offered by National Express are ideal for those planning to cover many destinations over a limited period. They allow unlimited travel on all National Express services in Scotland and the rest of Britain. You can buy the pass in the UK at major international airports, at Glasgow's Buchanan Bus Station and at Edinburgh's Tourist Information Centre. The Explorer Pass, available from Scottish Citylink agents and from Glasgow Airport, allows travel only within Scotland and only on Scottish Citylink services.

Coach and Bus Tours

Dozens of coach tours are available in Scotland, catering for all interests, age groups and a host of different destinations. They may last anything from a couple of hours for a city tour to several days for a national tour.

Scottish Tours offers scheduled sightseeing tours of Edinburgh, Glasgow and Inverness and offers many multi-day tours. The Edinburgh-based **Scotline Tours** offers half- and full-day tours, while **Rabbie's Trail Burners** offers tours of three days or more.

Ask at your hotel or tourist office for details of local bus and coach tours. Most major towns and cities offer open-top bus tours.

Local buses are generally a cheap way to get about. In the more remote rural areas not served by public transport, **Royal Mail** operates the Postbus. Fare-paying passengers travel in the postal delivery van – an interesting if rather slow way to travel around. Details of routes are available from the Royal Mail and via its website.

The Postbus provides transport in remote parts of the Highlands

Open-top bus tour on the Royal Mile in Edinburgh

DIRECTORY

UK and Overseas Rail Numbers and Websites

National Rail Enquiries
Tel (08457) 484950.
w nationalrail.co.uk

Lost Property
Tel (0131) 550 2333 (Edinburgh).

Rail Europe
Tel (08448) 484 078 (UK).
Tel (1800) 622 8600 (US).
Tel (1800) 361 7245 (Canada).
w raileurope.co.uk

ScotRail
Tel (0845) 601 5929 (bookings).
w scotrail.co.uk

Coach and Bus Information

National Express
Tel (08717) 818178.
w nationalexpress.com

Rabbie's Trail Burners
Tel (0131) 226 3133.
w rabbies.com

Royal Mail
Tel (08457) 740 740.
w royalmail.com

Scotline Tours
Tel (0845) 774 2029.
w scotlinetours.co.uk

Scottish Citylink
Tel (0871) 266 3333.
w citylink.co.uk

Scottish Tours
Tel (0141) 237 4294.
w scottishtours.co.uk

Travelling by Sea

If you are travelling to Scotland from continental Europe by foot, car, coach or train, you will need to cross the English Channel or North Sea by ferry or Channel Tunnel. Ferry services operate between several ports on the Continent and Scotland and England, while the Channel Tunnel provides a nonstop rail link from France and Belgium. Fares between ferries and the Channel Tunnel are fiercely competitive. Island-hopping by ferry is an enjoyable and economical way to visit the beautiful islands situated off the coast of Scotland.

Logo of a Scottish ferry company

A car ferry travelling from Oban to Lochboisdale on South Uist

Travelling to Scotland by Ferry

There is no direct link between Scotland and the European continent. The closest service is to Newcastle in England from Amsterdam (see below), a journey of about 17 hours. From Newcastle there are frequent trains to Edinburgh or Glasgow.

From Northern Ireland, there is a frequent service operated by **Stena Line**, which runs between Belfast and Stranraer. **P&O Ferries** also offers daily crossings between Larne and Cairnryan, just north of Stranraer. Check the company's website for details.

Services to England from the Continent

A network of ferry services regularly crosses the North Sea and the English Channel from northern Europe to ports in the UK. Of those travelling to the north of England, **P&O Ferries** runs a daily crossing from Rotterdam or Zeebrugge to Hull, and **DFDS Seaways** runs from Kristiansand, Gothenburg and Amsterdam to Newcastle.

An alternative way to travel to Scotland from the Continent via England is the Channel Tunnel, which links the UK with France.

Passengers travelling by coach or car board the **Eurotunnel** train, and remain in their vehicle throughout the 35-minute journey from Calais to Folkstone. For those travelling on foot, the **Eurostar** train runs frequent services between Paris, Brussels and London.

Any visitors from outside the European Union should allow plenty of time for immigration control and customs clearance at British ports (see pp206–7).

Island-hopping in Scotland

Scotland has just under 800 islands scattered off its coastline, and travelling by ferry is a wonderful way to experience their rugged beauty. The islands can be roughly divided into two main groups: the Hebrides, situated off the west coast, and Orkney and Shetland, lying to the northeast of the mainland.

Caledonian MacBrayne has 30 ships, linking 23 of the westerly isles to the mainland and to each other. Destinations include Arran, Islay, Mull, Barra, Lewis, Harris, Skye, Raasay, Coll, Tiree and Eigg. The summer timetable runs from Easter to mid-October with a reduced service for the rest of the year. Most of the routes have two or three trips a day, but some have only one, so be sure to call ahead and check. Single, return and five-day tickets are available.

In addition, there are two special travel tickets. Island Hopscotch tickets are valid on a choice of fifteen routes for one month from the date of the first journey. The Island Rover gives you the freedom to choose your own route between the islands for 8 or 15 consecutive days from the date of the first journey. Although the Island Rover ticket is valid on all of Caledonian's services, it does not ensure a place on any particular sailing, and it is advisable to make vehicle reservations.

Northlink Ferries, a venture between Caledonian MacBrayne and The Royal Bank of Scotland has ferry routes from the Scottish mainland to Orkney and Shetland. All routes have large capacity purpose-built roll-on roll-off ferries with modern facilities including restaurants, cabins, shop and children's play area.

Passengers on the deck of a ferry leaving Tobermory on the Isle of Mull

A Caledonian MacBrayne ferry leaving the port of Mallaig

NorthLink sails from Scrabster, north of Thurso, to Stromness on Orkney Mainland and direct from Aberdeen to Orkney or to Shetland. Another service links Orkney and Shetland.

Pentland Ferries also offers a car service to Orkney. This runs between Gill's Bay west of John o'Groats and St Margaret's Hope on South Ronaldsay. This island is linked to Orkney Mainland via the Churchill Barrier causeways. The vehicle capacity of this older ferry is limited to 46 and booking in advance is recommended.

During the summer, **John o' Groats Ferries** runs a 40-minute passenger-only crossing to Burwick on South Ronaldsay with a coach link to Kirkwall on Orkney Mainland. Small passenger and car ferries link Orkney's nine large outer islands with Orkney Mainland.

Cruises

A cruise is a leisurely way to see the many different Scottish islands. Caledonian MacBrayne offers various non-landing, evening cruises departing from a number of locations on the west coast.

John o'Groats Ferries offers day cruises to Orkney Mainland from John o'Groats and Inverness. These can be extended to include accommodation in Kirkwall and a tour of the island's historic sites by bus.

It is also possible to take a cruise on some of Scotland's lochs and rivers. **Caledonian Discovery** offers six-day cruises along the Caledonian Canal from Fort William to Inverness.

DIRECTORY

Caledonian Discovery
Tel (01397) 772167.
w fingal-cruising.co.uk

Caledonian MacBrayne
Tel (0800) 066 5000.
w calmac.co.uk

DFDS Seaways
Tel (0871) 522 9955.
w dfdsseaways.co.uk

Eurostar
Tel (08432) 186 186.
w eurostar.com

Eurotunnel
Tel (08443) 353535.
w eurotunnel.com

John o' Groats Ferries
Tel (01955) 611353.
w jogferry.co.uk

NorthLink Ferries
Tel (0845) 600 0449.
w northlinkferries.co.uk

P&O Ferries
Tel (08716) 642121.
w poferries.com

Pentland Ferries
Tel (01856) 831226.
w pentlandferries.co.uk

Stena Line
Tel (08447) 707070.
w stenaline.co.uk

Cruising on Loch Ness with Caledonian Discovery's *Fingal of Caledonia*

Car Ferry Route	Information	Days	Last Check-in	Journey Time
Aberdeen–Kirkwall (Orkney)	(0845) 600 0449	alternate days	30 mins	6 hrs, 30 mins
Aberdeen–Lerwick (Shetland)	(0845) 600 0449	daily	30 mins	13 hrs
Ardrossan–Brodick (Arran)	(0800) 066 5000	daily	30 mins	55 mins
Gill's Bay–St Marg's Hope (Ork.)	(01856) 831226	daily	30 mins	1 hr
Kennacraig–Port Ellen (Islay)	(01880) 730253	daily	45 mins	2 hrs, 10 mins
Kilchoan–Tobermory (Mull)	(0800) 066 5000	Mon–Sun	30 mins	35 mins
Lerwick (Shet.)–Kirkwall (Ork.)	(0845) 600 0449	alternate days	30 mins	5 hrs 30 mins
Mallaig–Armadale (Skye)	(0800) 066 5000	daily	30 mins	30 mins
Oban–Castlebay (Barra)	(0800) 066 5000	daily ex. Wed	45 mins	5 hrs, 15 mins
Oban–Craignure (Mull)	(0800) 066 5000	daily	30 mins	45 mins
Scrabster–Stromness (Orkney)	(0845) 600 0449	daily	30 mins	1 hr, 30 mins
Uig (Skye)–Tarbert (Harris)	(0800) 066 5000	Mon–Sat	30 mins	1 hr, 35 mins
Ullapool–Stornoway (Lewis)	(0800) 066 5000	Mon–Sat	45 mins	2 hrs, 40 mins

Travelling Around by Car

In Scotland, and the rest of the UK, driving is on the left-hand side of the road, and distances are measured and signposted in miles. A network of toll-free motorways exists in the south and between Edinburgh and Glasgow; using these can reduce travelling time. In the larger towns traffic density can cause delays, and during public holiday weekends heading north to the Highlands is often slow work. Rural Scotland, with its striking scenery, is an enjoyable place to drive, and the roads to even the remote parts are generally good.

No stopping

Speed limit (mph)

No entry

No right-turn allowed

Railway level crossing

Yield to all vehicles

One-way traffic Gradient of a road

The A68 from Northern England to Scotland

What You Need

To drive in Scotland you need a current driving licence, with an international driving permit if required. In any vehicle you drive, you must carry proof of ownership or a rental agreement, plus insurance documents.

A motorway sign

Roads in Scotland

Peak rush-hour traffic can last from 8–9:30am and 5–6:30pm on weekdays in the cities. Radio Scotland and local radio stations broadcast regular reports of road conditions throughout the day. You can also contact **Keep Moving** for information on road conditions. You can save vital travel time by knowing which routes should be avoided. Outside the cities, a good

touring map is essential; the AA or RAC motoring atlases are straightforward to use. For exploration of more remote areas, the Ordnance Survey series is the best. Such areas often have only single-track roads with passing places and blind bends, that demand cautious driving.

On all road maps, motorways are indicated by an M followed by a number, such as the M8. Major roads, which are often dual (2-lane) carriageways, are labelled A roads. Secondary roads, often less congested than A roads, are called B roads. There are fewer roads in the Highlands.

Disabled drivers can contact the **AA Disability Helpline** for general motoring information.

Road Signs

Signs are now generally standardized in line with the rest of Europe. Directional signs are colour-coded: blue for motorways, green for major (A) roads and white for minor (B) roads. In the Highlands and islands, road signs display both English and Gaelic names. Brown signs with a blue thistle give visitor information on attractions and tourist centres. Warning signs are usually triangles in red and white, with easy to understand pictograms. Watch for electronic notices on motorways that warn of road works, accidents or dangerous driving conditions.

Level crossings at train tracks often have automatic barriers. If the lights are flashing red, it means a train is approaching; you are required to stop.

Rules of the Road

Speed limits are 50–65 km/h (30–40 mph) in built-up areas and 110 km/h (70 mph) on motorways or dual carriageways – look out for speed signs on other roads. Wearing seatbelts is compulsory in Scotland and it is illegal to drive and use a hand-held mobile phone. Severe penalties are imposed for drinking and driving.

Parking

In Scotland's towns and cities, on-street parking is often paid for by purchasing a ticket from a roadside machine. The ticket is then left on display inside the car. Some cities have "park and ride" schemes, where you take a bus from an out-of-city car park into the centre. Other towns have a "disc" parking scheme; ask the tourist office or a local newsagent for a disc to mark your arrival time. Many car parks operate on a pay-and-display system. Avoid double yellow lines at all times; you can park on single lines at evenings and weekends, but check roadside signs for variations to the rule. Traffic wardens will not hesitate to ticket, clamp or tow away your car if in breach of the rules. If in doubt, find a car park. Outside urban and popular visitor areas, parking is not such a problem. Look out for the letter P, which indicates legal parking spaces.

It is best to avoid driving in Edinburgh, as cars have limited access to the centre and the vast majority of sights can be reached on foot. Taxis, which you can hail on the street or find waiting at a taxi rank, are another option. Licensed cabs must display a "For Hire" sign. Mini-cabs must display a card proving the identity of the licensed driver. If there is no meter, ask the fare in advance.

One of Glasgow's black cabs

Fuel

North American visitors to Scotland may find petrol (gasoline) very expensive, particularly at motorway service stations. It is the large supermarkets that often have the lowest prices. Petrol is sold in four grades: diesel, 4-star (regular) super unleaded and premium unleaded. Most modern cars use unleaded petrol. Diesel and unleaded fuel are cheaper than 4-star. Most petrol stations are self-service but instructions at the pumps are easy to follow. Green hoses denote unleaded fuel pumps and deliveries are in litres.

Breakdown Services

Britain's major motoring organizations, the **AA** (Automobile Association) and the **RAC** (Royal Automobile Club), provide a comprehensive 24-hour breakdown and recovery service.

The busy M8 motorway on the outskirts of Glasgow

Both motoring organizations offer reciprocal assistance for members of overseas motoring organizations – before arrival check with your own group to see if you are covered. You can contact the AA or RAC from roadside SOS phones on all motorways. Most car rental agencies have their own cover, which includes membership of either the AA or the RAC while you are driving. Even if you are not a member of an organization, you can still call out a rescue service, although it will be expensive.

Always take the advice given on the insurance policy or rental agreement. If you have an accident that injures you or damages a vehicle, contact the police straight away.

Car Rental

Renting a car can be costly, but one of the more competitive companies is **Autosabroad**. Others include **Arnold Clark**, **Budget**, **Hertz**, **Europcar** and **National Car Rental**.

Many companies require a credit card number or a substantial cash deposit as well as your driving licence and passport. The normal age requirements are over 21 and under 70. Major airports, train stations and city centres have car rental outlets. Value for money car hire can also be found in some smaller towns.

RAC logo

General Index

Acknowledgments

Dorling Kindersley would like to thank the following people whose contributions and assistance have made the preparation of this book possible.

Design and Editorial Assistance
Namrata Adhwaryu, Jasneet Arora, Claire Baranowski, Hilary Bird, Emer FitzGerald, Claire Folkard, Camilla Gersh, Alrica Green, Kathleen Greig, Swati Gupta, Lydia Halliday, Carolyn Hewitson, Jessica Hughes, Donnie Hutton, Marie Ingledew, Laura Jones, Elly King, Kathryn Lane, Nicola Malone, Sue Megginson, Sonal Modha, Claire Naylor, Rakesh Kumar Pal, Catherine Palmi, Susie Peachey, Clare Pierotti, Tom Prentice, Rada Radojicic, Alice Reese, Ellen Root, the Scottish Tourist Board (especially Vineet Lal), Pamela Shiels, Helena Smith, Susana Smith, Vinita Venugopal, Stewart Wild, Christian Williams, Alice Wright, Sophie Wright.

Cartography
Uma Bhattacharya, Mohammad Hassan, Jasneet Kaur

DTP
Vinod Harish, Azeem Siddiqui, Vincent Kurien

Additional Photography
Sarah Ashun, Joe Cornish, Andy Crawford, Philip Dowell, Chris Dyer, Andreas Einsiedel, Peter Gathercole, Steve Gorton, Paul Harris, Dave King, Cyril Laubscher, Brian D. Morgan, Ian O'Leary, Stephen Oliver, Tim Ridley, Kim Sayer, Karl Shore, Clive Streeter, Kim Taylor, Mathew Ward, Stephen Whitehorne.

Additional Picture Research
Rachel Barber

Photographic and Artwork Reference
Aerographica: Patricia & Angus Macdonald; London Aerial Photo Library.

Photography Permissions
City of Edinburgh Council Heritage and Arts Marketing/ People's Story Museum; Royal Botanic Garden, Edinburgh; House for an Art Lover, Glasgow; Glasgow School of Art; Glasgow Botanic Gardens.

Picture Credits
a = above; b = below/bottom; c = centre; f = far; l = left; r = right; t = top.
The publisher would like to thank the following individuals, companies and picture libraries for their kind permission to reproduce their photographs:

3x1 Public Relations/Highland Spring: 79clb. **Aberdeen Tourist Board:** 55cra; **Aberdeen University Library:** George Washington Wilson Collection 167tc; **Aerographica:** Patricia & Angus Macdonald 20tl/bc, 21tl, 22cra; **Alamy Images:** Arch White 18tl; archphotography 211ca; Serda_ikrumoki 211tc; Bertrand Collet 180cla; BL images Ltd 52-3; Bill Coster 165br; Robert Estall photo agency 84; Tim Gainey 162tr; Doug Houghton 164tr; Iain Masterton 103bl; Skyscan Photolibrary 196tl; David Tipling 165cr; Travel Pictures 122-3; Worldwide Picture Library/ Iain Sarjent 165bl; **Allsport:** Craig Prentis 40br; T & R Annan & Son (D): 105br; **Andrew Fairlie at Gleneagles:** 186bc; **Auchrannie Resort:** 175br. **Bank of Scotland:** 212cb; **Blackaddie Country House Hotel:** 184br; **Boath House:** 176bc, 187tl; **Bridgeman Art Library, London/New York:** 31tr, 150bl, 151br (c); City of Edinburgh Museums & Galleries 32bl: Fine Art Society, London 105cl; Robert Fleming Holdings Limited, London 47crb; National Gallery of Scotland, Edinburgh 44; National Museet Copenhagen 46c; Collection of Andrew McIntosh Patrick, UK 105cla; Smith Art Gallery and Museum, Stirling 124br; South African National Gallery, Cape Town 105cra; Trinity College Library, Dublin 46tr; **Britainonview.com:** 195tc; **Burt Greener Communications:** 80crb. **Cafe St. Honore/Mitchell Macgregor PR:** 181bl; **Laurie Campbell:** 22clb/ bl, 131bc, 161tl/cl; Peter Evans 144tl; Gordon Langsbury 145tl; **City Merchant:** 184tl; **Corbis:** Christophe Boisvieux 204-5; Olimpio Fantuz/ SOPA 2-3; Will Gray/JAI 168-9; WildCountry 145c; **Doug Corrance:** 27br, 33br, 34c, 34bc, 35br, 42cla, 94tl, 112cl/b, 114, 137br, 143tl, 148crb, 150tl, 151t, 192cJ 193cra/crb/cb, 200cla, 202tr/br, 206cla, 220bl; **Eric Crichton Photos:** 27cb/cr; **Cringletie House:** 174tc; **Crown Copyright:** Historic Scotland 64tr/cl, 65bl, 125cra. **Dalhousie Castle Hotel & Spa:** 173tr; **Dreamstime.com:** Steve Alien 130; Astar321 114; Valeria Cantone 17bc; Claireshearer 98; Creativehearts 56; Lian Deng 9br; Diggerman 198br; Julietphotography 12bc; Orion9nl 13tr; Magspace 156-7; Michalakis Ppalis 8cla; David Purves 9tl; Elena Rostunova 11bc; Shutter1970 13bl; Vitaly Titov & Maria Sidelnikova

214cla; Yjacobzone 12tc; **The Douglas Hotel:** 179br. **Empics:** 113cra; **Mary Evans Picture Library:** 30tr/c/br, 48c, 49crb, 90bl, 92clb, 127bl, 157br, 169. **Falkirk wheel:** 129bl; **La Favorita:** 182bl; **Louis Flood:** 32br; **Frankie's Fish and Chips:** 189bl. **Gallery of Modern Art, Glasgow:** 10br; **Garden Picture Library:** John Glover 26tr; **Getty Images:** 201bl; Stanley Chou 195c; Richard Heathcote 195bl; Anna Henly 202cla; Three Lions/Stringer 6-7; VisitBritain/Britain on View 16; **Glasgow Museums:** Art Gallery & Museum, Kelvingrove 106tc, 138bl, 154b; Burrell Collection 108–109 except 108tl; Museum of Transport 29bl; **Ronald Grant Archive:** 31cl; **V. K. Guy Ltd:** Mike Guy 22cla, 38cl, 137t. **Robert Harding Picture Library:** 134tr; Van der Hars 146cla; Michael Jenner 166cla; Julia K. Thorne 24bl; Adina Tovy 24crb; Adam Woolfitt 144tr; **Dennis Hardley:** 38c, 39tl/crb, 86tr, 88cr/bc, 94bl, 95tl, 117cr, 118tc/ bl, 119bl, 140b, 141bc, 160b, 167br, 207bl; **Gordon Henderson:** 23cra, 39cra/b, 161br, 163cl, 166br, 221tl; **House of Lords Record Office:** Reproduced by permission of the Clerk of the Records 49tr; **Hulton Getty Collection:** 29cra, 50tl, 121br, 153crb; (c) **Hunterian Art Gallery, University of Glasgow:** 107tl; Mackintosh Collection 105crb; **Hutchison Library:** Bernard Gerard 19tl. **ISIC:** 208cra. **The Kitchin:** 183tl; **The Knight Residence:** 172bl. **Andrew Lawson:** 26bl, 27tl/tr, 160tc; **Lochleven Seafood Cafe:** 188br. **Monachyle Mhor:** 170cla; **Museum of Childhood, Edinburgh:** 62bl. **National Galleries of Scotland:** Scottish National Gallery of Modern Art Study For Les Constructeurs: The Team At Rest by Fernand Leger 1950 (c) Adagp, Paris And Dacs, London, 2011 73tl; **Natural History Photographic Agency:** Bryan & Cherry Alexander 41cra; Laurie Campbell 23clb, 40cl; Manfred Danegger 23br/crb; **Scottish National Portrait Gallery:** 67br; **National Museums of Scotland:** 66br, 67c; **National Portrait Gallery, London:** 68bc; **National Trust for Scotland:** 54br, 60bl, 96tl, 97tl/tr/br, 128bc, 209tl; Lindsey Robertson 97bl; Glyn Satterley 104br; **Network Photographers:** Laurie Sparham 18bl.
Ortak Jewellery, Edinburgh: 78cla.
Pa News: 35tl/bl; Chris Bacon 43c; Roslin Institute 29br; (c) 1996 **Polygram Filmed Entertainment:** 31br; **The Post Office:** 214cr, 215tl, 215cla; Glyn Satterley 219bc; **Powerstock/zefa:** 24cra; **RBS Group:** 212bc, 212crb; **Rex Features:** J. Sutton Hibbert 51crb; **Rogano:** 185tr; **Royal Automobile Club (Rac):** 223b; **Royal Botanic Garden, Edinburgh:** 27bl; **Royal Collection (c) 1999, Her Majesty Queen Elizabeth II:** 33tc; **Royal Photographic Society:** 29tl. **Science & Society Picture Library:** Science Museum 29crb; **Alastair Scott:** 21br, 23cla, 35cb, 199bc, 203cla; **Scottish Highland Photo Library:** 23tc, 139tc; **Scottish Viewpoint:** 162c; Iain McLean 11tr; Ken Patterson 10tl; Paul Tomkins 162c; VisitScotland 162bl; 196c; VisitScotland/ P Tomkins 196br; **The Seafood Restaurant:** 187br; **Phil Sheldon Golf Picture Library:** 194tr; **James Shuttleworth:** 219cla; **Still Moving Picture Company:** Gordon Allison 34br; Marcus Brooke 21tr; Wade Cooper 51tc; Doug Corrance 34tr, 85b, 134b, 190cl, 198cl; Peter Davenport 22br; Distant Images 93tr; Robert Lees 43b, 192ca, 199tl; Paisley Museum 93br; Ken Paterson 69tc; David Robertson 26cl, 153bl; Glyn Satterley 193tr; Colin Scott 35cl; Scottish Tourist Board 34bl, 144br, 190cla, 191tr; Paul Tomkins/STB 166tr, 190br, 192b; Stephen J. Whitehorne 121tl; Harvey Wood 143bl. Strathclyde Passenger Transport (Spt): Richard McPherson 100bl; **Stonefield Castle Hotel:** Street & Co PR 189tr. **The Three Chimneys:** 188tl; **The Torridon Hotel:** 177tl, 189br; **Tron Theatre:** Keith Hunter 112cr. **Charlie Waite:** 135t; **David Ward:** 138t; **Wedgwood the Restaurant/ Crimson Edge PR Ltd.:** Paul Wedgwood 182tc; **Stephen J. Whitehorne:** 23tl, 35cra, 38b, 41cl, 66tl, 67tr, 70bl, 87crb, 115b, 119t, 136tc, 152b, 167cl, 200br, 201tl, 203tr, 213cla, 215cl, 221clb; **The Witchery by the Castle:** 179bl.
Front Endpaper: **Alamy Images:** Robert Estall Photo Agency Lbl; **Dreamstime.com:** Steve Allen Ltl; Astar321 Lcl; Claireshearer Rcr; Creativehearts Rbr; Vitaly Titov & Maria Sidelnikova 214cla.
Jacket Front and Spine: **Alamy Images:** eli pascall-willis

All other images © Dorling Kindersley.
For further information see www.dk.com

Special Editions of DK Travel Guides

Travel Guides can be purchased in bulk quantities at discounted prices for use in promotions or as premiums. We are also able to offer special editions and personalized jackets, corporate imprints, and excerpts from all of our books, tailored specifically to meet your own needs.

To find out more, please contact:
(in the United States) **SpecialSales@dk.com**
(in the UK) **TravelSpecialSales@uk.dk.com**
(in Canada) DK Special Sales at **general@ tourmaline.ca**
(in Australia) **business.development@pearson. com.au**

Scottish Vocabulary

Gaelic is a Celtic language that is still spoken as a second language in the Highlands and Western Isles of Scotland. Estimates put the figure of Gaelic speakers throughout the country at around 80,000. The last decade has seen something of a revival of the language, due to the encouragement of both education and broadcasting authorities. However the majority of people are most likely to come across Gaelic today in the form of place names. Words such as glen, loch, eilean and kyle are all still very much in use. English remains the principal language of Scotland. However the country's very distinct education, religious,

political and judicial systems have given rise to a rich vocabulary that reflects Scottish culture. Many additional terms in current usage are colloquial. English as spoken by the Scots is commonly divided into four dialects. Central Scots can be heard across the Central Belt and the southwest of the country. As around a quarter of the population lives within 32 km (20 miles) of Glasgow, West Central Scots is one of the most frequently heard subdivisions of this dialect. Southern Scots is spoken in the east of Dumfries and Galloway and the Borders; Northern Scots in the northeast; and Island Scots in the Orkney and Shetland Islands.

Pronunciation of Gaelic Words

Letters	Example	Pronunciation
ao	craobh	this is pronounced similar to **oo**, as in cool
bh	dubh	"h" is silent unless at the beginning of a word in which case it is pronounced **v**, as in vet
ch	deich	this is pronounced as in the German composer Bach
cn	cnoc	this is pronounced **cr**, as in creek
ea	leabhar	this is pronounced e, as in get or **a**, as in cat
eu	sgeul	this is pronounced **ay**, as in say or **ea**, as in ear
gh	taigh-òsda	this is silent unless at the beginning of a word, in which case it is pronounced as in get
ia	fiadh	this is pronounced **ea**, as in ear
io	tiocaid	this is pronounced **ee**, as in deep or **oo**, as in took
rt	ceart	this is pronounced **sht**
th	theab	this is silent unless at the beginning of a word in which case it is pronounced **h**, as in house
ua	uaine	this is pronounced **oo**, as in poor

Words in Place Names

ben	mountain
bothy	farm cottage
brae	hill
brig	bridge
burn	brook
cairn	mound of stones marking a place
close	block of flats (apartments) sharing a common entry and stairway
craig	steep peak
croft	small plot of farmland with dwellings in the Highlands
dubh	black
eilean	island
firth	estuary
gate/gait	street (in proper names)
glen	valley
howff	a regular meeting place, usually a pub
kirk	a Presbyterian church
kyle	a narrow strait of river
links	golf course by the sea
loaning	field
loch	lake
moss	moor
Munro	mountain over 914 m (3,000 ft) high
strath	valley/plain beside river
wynd	lane
yett	gate

Food and Drink

Arbroath smokie	small haddock that has been salted and then smoked
breid	bread
clapshot	mashed turnips and potatoes
clootie dumpling	rich fruit pudding
Cullen skink	fish soup made from smoked haddock
dram	a drink of whisky
haggis	sheep's offal, suet, oatmeal and seasonings, usually boiled in the animal's intestine
Irn-Bru	popular soft drink
neeps	turnips
oatcake	a savoury oatmeal biscuit
porridge	a hot breakfast dish made with oats, milk and water
shortie	shortbread
tattie	potato
tattie scone	type of savoury pancake made with potato

Cultural Terms

Burns Night	25 January is the anniversary of the birth of the poet Robert Burns, celebrated with a meal of haggis
Caledonia	Scotland
ceilidh	an informal evening of traditional Scottish song and dance
clan	an extended family bearing the same surname (last name)
first foot	the first person to enter a house after midnight on New Year's Eve
Highland dress	Highland men's formal wear including the kilt
Hogmanay	New Year's Eve
kilt	knee-length pleated tartan skirt worn as traditional Highland dress
Ne'erday	New Year's Day
pibroch	type of bagpipe music
sgian-dubh	a small blade tucked into the outside of the sock on the right foot worn as part of the traditional Highland dress
sporran	pouch made of fur worn to the front of the kilt
tartan	chequered wool cloth, different colours being worn by each clan

Colloquial Expressions

auld	old
auld lang syne	days of long ago
Auld Reekie	Edinburgh
aye	yes
bairn	child
barrie	excellent
blether	chat
bonnie	pretty
braw	excellent
dreich	wet (weather)
fae	from
fitba	football
hen	informal name used to address a woman or girl
ken	to know; to have knowledge
lassie	a young woman/girl
lumber	boyfriend/girlfriend
Nessie	legendary monster of Loch Ness
Old Firm	Celtic and Glasgow Rangers, Glasgow's main football teams
wean	child
wee	small